THE FOOTBALLER'S

EYRE & SPOTTISWOODE (Publishers) LTD

COMPANION

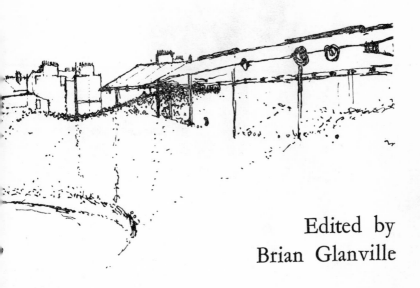

Edited by
Brian Glanville

"All that I know most surely
about morality and the obligations of man,
I owe to football." ALBERT CAMUS

22 HENRIETTA STREET · LONDON WC2

First published 1962
© 1962 *Brian Glanville*
Printed in Great Britain
by Billing & Sons Ltd
Guildford, Surrey
Cat No 6/2459/1

Contents

6 CONTENTS

PART IV: HALF TIME
GOALKEEPERS ARE CRAZY

PART V: FOOTBALL POETRY

PART VI: CLUBS

PART VII: THEY WERE TOUGH IN THOSE DAYS!

A*

Note on the Illustrations

SATURDAY AFTERNOON, an etching (7″ by 5″)
by Arthur Goodwin. *front endpaper*

STAMFORD BRIDGE STADIUM – two pen drawings (17½″ by 7″ and 13½″ by 8″ respectively)
by Susan Benson. *Courtesy John St John.*
Title page and rear endpaper

"Goalkeeper" drawing, from *Campioni del Mondo*
(by Vittorio Pozzo). *Courtesy Cen Roma.*
pages 321, 371

The drawings by Arthur Goodwin and Susan
Benson were first shown at the exhibition
Football and the Fine Arts (1953), sponsored by
the Football Association. The other drawings
are taken from *Printing Types* (1931, Stephenson,
Blake) and from Specimens of Polytype Orna-
ments cast by J. and R. M. Wood.

Introduction

We have been told, *ad nauseam*, that football is a game without a literature. What has astonished me, over the year spent in making this collection, is just how rich the material is. If there are limitations, they are surely linguistic and my own; I have contrived to translate the French and Italian pieces in this book, but how much more must there be in Spanish, German, Portuguese, Hungarian, Russian, Swedish! If I were prepared to take on trust what I cannot read for myself, the book might have been twice its length.

For the phenomenon of soccer is the way it has conquered the world, so that today there will be 180,000 spectators in the Maracana Stadium in Rio, tomorrow 90,000 in Moscow, then, successively, 120,000 at the Bernabeu, Madrid, 135,000 at Hampden Park, 100,000 at Wembley, and another 100,000 in Rome. The United States, it is true, has remained stubborn, but China and the "under-developed" countries of Africa and Asia are responding to the game in such a way as to make nonsense of the belief that it is purely the rank flower of an industrial civilization. One thinks of the high wire safety netting round those little Tuscan village pitches!

But quantity is one thing, quality another, and I confess I have had to adopt a double criterion. Certain pieces – notably those by Camus, Arnold Bennett, Robert Lynd, de Montherlant, Sillitoe, Ross, Giraudoux, Gatto, George Scott – are there for their intrinsic literary value. Others are included primarily because their theme or their author is important in the development of the game. Thus, the late Charlie Buchan's reminiscence of football before the first world war (which gives its title to the final section of the book) possesses a wonderfully authentic flavour which transcends questions of literary style. And who would sacrifice Mr Leslie Knighton's marvellous anecdote of how he "doped Arsenal for a Cup tie"?

In class-ridden Britain, football has, till very recently, been the preserve of the working and lower-middle – that is to say, the broadly non-literary – classes, even though it began in the public schools. This was never so on the Continent, where a great game was appreciated for what it was, and a revulsion from professionalism did not lead to embracing of the second best. (One must be polite as possible to Rugby football.) Besides, that strange, ultimately public school, dichotomy between hearties and aesthetes has never existed on the Continent. Many an English litterateur, study-bound, to whom the sports pages are anathema, will be astonished by the nostalgia of Camus, Giraudoux and Montherlant for the game which all three of them played. Montherlant – the austere, cerebral Montherlant – actually wrote a poem to a pair of football boots! (See page 379.)

And yet, just as cricket, for all its literary associations, has sadly failed to produce any fiction rooted in the professional game, so there is a bewildering lack of any good soccer fiction from Europe. The French Football Federation, with commendable enterprise, have for some thirty years been giving an annual prize for a short story about football, but the results have been negligible; always froth, schoolboy anecdote, rather than authenticity.

I have divided the book in a fairly obvious and straightforward way; fiction, poetry (again, there is a surprising amount, some of it very good), great matches, great players, clubs, reminiscence. The one maverick, perhaps, is provided by the section "Goalkeepers are Crazy" (the title of a story of my own), in which I have included fiction and player-portraits which should rightly appear in other sections. But I feel that this is justified; as a wise old German once said, "There are eleven players in every team; ten men and a goalkeeper". The goalkeeper will always remain blessedly the odd man out, the supreme individualist by function as well as by temperament. He alone is permitted to use his hands; his capacity for spectacle, for heroism, for fatal error, will always be greater than that of any other player on the field.

Though I hope that the final effect of this book will be to give a panorama of the game, in depth and development, there is no attempt to make the sections on great players and matches comprehensive. Ideally, one would like a match report on the Brazil v. Uruguay World Cup decider of 1950, in Rio, and portraits of Di Stefano, Puskas, and Pelé. But there has been surprisingly little good writing on players; Delaney and Edelston's *Masters of Soccer* is an oasis, and I do not apologize for representing it so well. In Britain, the fault is partly one of habit and custom. There have never been so many good writers on the game as there are today, but the exigencies of journalism seldom make it possible for them to attempt a full-length study of a player. Ideally, one would have liked to include such writers as Bob Ferrier, Tony Pawson, and Bernard Joy – but an anthologist must cull what he can; he cannot set his writers a subject.

The beauty of football is its plasticity; each country that embraces it has something new to give; British efficiency and endurance, Latin flair and fire, South American virtuosity and acrobatics, Central European perfectionism. And in each country, the game means something different. Even in Britain its significance is changing, for what began in the public schools, then grew into a consolation for an exploited proletariat, shivering for a shilling under soaked newspapers on windy terraces, has become an entertainment, rather than a compulsive ritual. At the very moment when the "posh" papers and the clever young men have discovered football, the working classes who played it and made it are drifting away. Fifteen years ago, a million people a week watched League football; today, more than a quarter of a million of them have defected.

Television, the "new deal" in players' wages, the World and European Cups, all these are changing the shape and substance of football. It will not die; its mythic and symbolic value for our age remains too great, though still obscure. After all, the hold of cricket is as strong as ever, and its legion of armchair followers undiminished, although the county grounds in mid-week are as bare as snow-slopes.

In the next ten years I expect the standard of football writing steadily to rise. Perhaps someone will even bring off that *ignis fatuus* the Football Novel – as David Storey has brought off the Rugby League novel – but it can be done only by a writer deeply involved with that strange, closed world, whose social background is the footballer's own. And he has yet to appear.

My thanks are particularly due to the Football Association, who so kindly gave me the run of their Library.

BRIAN GLANVILLE

London
November, 1961

PART I

Football Fiction

"Life itself is but a game of football."

SIR WALTER SCOTT

Callear's Goal

ARNOLD BENNETT

"I'll tell you," said Denry, "I wanted to be the youngest mayor that Bursley's ever had. It was only a kind of notion I had a long time ago. I'd given it up, because I knew there was no chance unless I came before Bloor, which of course I couldn't do. Now he's dead. If I could upset old Barlow's apple-cart I should just be the youngest mayor by the skin of my teeth. Huskinson, the mayor in 1884, was aged thirty-four and six months. I've looked it all up this afternoon."

"How lovely if you *could* be the youngest mayor!"

"Yes. I'll tell you how I feel. I feel as though I didn't want to be mayor at all if I can't be the youngest mayor . . . you know."

She knew.

"Oh!" she cried, "do upset Mr Barlow's apple-cart. He's a horrid old thing. Should I be the youngest mayoress?"

"Not by chalks," said he. "Huskinson's sister was only sixteen."

"But that's only playing at being mayoress!" Nellie protested. "Anyhow, I do think you might be youngest mayor. Who settles it?"

"The Council, of course."

"Nobody likes Councillor Barlow."

"He'll be still less liked when he's wound up the Bursley Football Club."

"Well, urge him on to wind it up, then. But I don't see what football has got to do with being mayor."

She endeavoured to look like a serious politician.

"You are nothing but a cuckoo," Denry pleasantly informed her. "Football has got to do with everything. And it's been a disastrous mistake in my career that I've never taken any interest in football. Old Barlow wants no urging on to wind up the Football Club. He's absolutely set on it. He's lost too much over it. If I could stop him from winding it up, I might. . . . "

"What?"

"I dunno."

She perceived that his idea was yet vague.

II

Not very many days afterwards the walls of Bursley called attention, by small blue and red posters (blue and red being the historic colours of the Bursley Football Club), to a public meeting, which was to be held in the Town Hall, under the presidency of the Mayor, to consider what steps could be taken to secure the future of the Bursley Football Club.

There were two "great" football clubs in the Five Towns – Knype, one of the oldest clubs in England, and Bursley. Both were in the League, though Knype was in the first division while Bursley was only in the second. Both were, in fact, limited companies, engaged as much in the pursuit of dividends as in the practice of the one ancient and glorious sport which appeals to the reason and the heart of England. (Neither ever paid a dividend.) Both employed professionals who, by a strange chance, were nearly all born in Scotland; and both also employed trainers who, before an important match, took the teams off to a hydropathic establishment far, far distant from any public house. (This was called "training".) Now, whereas the Knype club was struggling along fairly well, the Bursley club had come to the end of its resources. The great football public had practically deserted it. The explanation, of course, was that Bursley had been losing too many matches. The great football public simply sulked. It did not kick a man that was down; it merely ignored him, well knowing that the man could not get up without help. It cared nothing whatever for fidelity, municipal patriotism, fair play, the chances of war, or dividends on capital. If it could see victories it would pay sixpence, but it would not pay sixpence to assist at defeats.

Still, when at a special general meeting of the Bursley

Football Club, Limited, held at the registered office, the Coffee House, Bursley, Councillor Barlow, J.P., Chairman of the Company since the creation of the League, announced that the Directors had reluctantly come to the conclusion that they could not conscientiously embark on the dangerous risks of the approaching season, and that it was the intention of the Directors to wind up the club, in default of adequate public interest – when Bursley read this in the *Signal*, the town was certainly shocked. Was the famous club, then, to disappear for ever, and the football ground to be sold in plots, and the grand stand for firewood? The shock was so severe that the death of Alderman Bloor (none the less a mighty figure in Bursley) had passed as a minor event.

Hence the advertisement of the meeting in the Town Hall caused joy and hope, and people said to themselves: "Something's bound to be done; the old club can't go out like that." And everybody grew quite sentimental. And although nothing is supposed to be capable of filling Bursley Town Hall except a political meeting and an old folk's treat, Bursley Town Hall was as near full as made no matter for the football question. Many men had cheerfully sacrificed a game of billiards and a glass of beer in order to attend it.

The Mayor, in the chair, was a mild old gentleman who knew nothing whatever about football and had probably never seen a football match; but it was essential that the meeting should have august patronage, and so the Mayor had been trapped and tamed. On the mere fact that he paid an annual subscription to the golf club, certain parties built up the legend that he was a true sportsman, with the true interests of sport in his soul.

He uttered a few phrases, such as "the manly game", "old associations", "bound up with the history of England", "splendid fellows", "indomitable pluck", "dogged by misfortune" (indeed, he produced quite an impression on the rude and grim audience), and then he called upon Councillor Barlow to make a statement.

Councillor Barlow, on the Mayor's right, was a different

kind of man from the Mayor. He was fifty and iron-grey, with whiskers, but no moustache; short, stoutish, raspish.

He said nothing about manliness, pluck, history, or Auld Lang Syne.

He said he had given his services as Chairman to the football club for thirteen years; that he had taken up £2,000 worth of shares in the Company; and that as at that moment the Company's liabilities would exactly absorb its assets, his £2,000 was worth exactly nothing. "You may say," he said, "I've lost that £2,000 in thirteen years. That is, it's the same as if I'd been steadily paying three pun' a week out of my own pocket to provide football matches that you chaps wouldn't take the trouble to go and see. That's the straight of it! What have I got for my pains? Nothing but worries and these! (He pointed to his grey hairs.) And I'm not alone; there's others; and now I have to come and defend myself at a public meeting. I'm supposed not to have the best interests of football at heart. Me and my co-Directors," he proceeded, with even a rougher raspishness, "have warned the town again and again what would happen if the matches weren't better patronized. And now it's happened, and now it's too late, you want to *do* something! You can't! It's too late! There's only one thing the matter with first-class football in Bursley," he concluded, "and it isn't the players. It's the public – it's yourselves. You're the most craven lot of tom-fools that ever a big football club had to do with. When we lose a match, what do you do? Do you come and encourage us next time? No, you stop away, and leave us fifty or sixty pound out of pocket on a match, just to teach us better! Do you expect us to win every match? Why, Preston North End itself" – here he spoke solemnly, of heroes – "Preston North End itself in its great days didn't win every match – it lost to Accrington. But did the Preston public desert it? No! *You* – you haven't got the pluck of a louse, nor the faithfulness of a cat. You've starved your football club to death, and now you call a meeting to weep and grumble. And you have the insolence to write letters to the *Signal* about bad management, forsooth! If anybody in the hall thinks he can manage this club better than me and my co-Directors have done, I may say that we hold a majority of the shares, and we'll part with the whole show to any clever person or persons who care to take it off our hands at a bargain price. That's talking."

He sat down.

Silence fell. Even in the Five Towns a public meeting is seldom bullied as Councillor Barlow had bullied that meeting. It was aghast. Councillor Barlow had never been popular: he had merely been respected; but thenceforward he became even less popular than before.

"I'm sure we shall all find Councillor Barlow's heat quite excusable . . . " the Mayor diplomatically began.

"No heat at all," the Councillor interrupted. "Simply cold truth!"

A number of speakers followed, and nearly all of them were against the Directors. Some, with prodigious memories for every combination of players in every match that had ever been played, sought to prove by detailed instances that Councillor Barlow and his co-Directors had persistently and regularly muddled their work during thirteen industrious years. And they defended the insulted public by asserting that no public that respected itself would pay sixpence to watch the wretched football provided by Councillor Barlow. They shouted that the team wanted reconstituting, wanted new blood.

"Yes," shouted Councillor Barlow in reply, "and how are you going to get new blood, with transfer fees as high as they are now? You can't get even an average good player for less than £200. Where's the money to come from? Anybody want to lend a thousand or so on second debentures?"

He laughed sneeringly.

No one showed a desire to invest in second debentures of the Bursley F.C. Ltd.

Still, speakers kept harping on the necessity of new blood in the team, and then others, bolder, harped on the necessity of new blood on the board.

"Shares on sale!" cried the Councillor. "Any buyers? Or," he added, "do you want something for nothing – as usual?"

At length a gentleman rose at the back of the hall.

"I don't pretend to be an expert on football," said he, "though I think it's a great game, but I should like to say a few words as to this question of new blood."

The audience craned its neck.

"Will Mr Councillor Machin kindly step up to the platform?" the Mayor suggested.

And up Denry stepped.

The thought in every mind was: "What's he going to do? What's he got up his sleeve – this time?"

"Three cheers for Machin!" people chanted gaily.

"Order!" said the Mayor.

Denry faced the audience. He was now accustomed to audiences. He said:

"If I'm not mistaken, one of the greatest modern footballers is a native of this town."

And scores of voices yelled, "Ay! Callear! Callear! Greatest centre forward in England!"

"Yes," said Denry. "Callear is the man I mean. Callear left the district, unfortunately for the district, at the age of nineteen for Liverpool. And it was not till after he left that his astonishing abilities were perceived. It isn't too much to say that he made the fortune of Liverpool City. And I believe it is the fact that he scored more goals in three seasons than any other player has done in the League. Then, York County, which was in a tight place last year, bought him from Liverpool for a high price, and, as all the world knows, Callear had his leg broken in the first match he played for his new club. That just happened to be the ruin of the York Club, which is now quite suddenly in bankruptcy (which happily we are not), and which is disposing of its players. Gentlemen, I say that Callear ought to come back to his native town. He is fitter than ever he was, and his proper place is in his native town."

Loud cheers.

"As captain and centre forward of the club of the mother of the Five Towns, he would be an immense acquisition and attraction, and he would lead us to victory."

Renewed cheers.

"And how," demanded Councillor Barlow, jumping up angrily, "are we to get him back to his precious native town? Councillor Machin admits that he is not an expert on football. It will probably be news to him that Aston Villa have offered £700 to York for the transfer of Callear, and Blackburn Rovers have offered £750, and they're fighting it out between 'em. Any gentleman willing to put down £800 to buy Callear for Bursley?" he sneered. "I don't mind telling you that steam-engines and the King himself couldn't get Callear into our club."

"Quite finished?" Denry inquired, still standing.

Laughter, overtopped by Councillor Barlow's snort as he sat down.

Denry lifted his voice.

"Mr Callear, will you be good enough to step forward and let us all have a look at you?"

The effect of these apparently simple words surpassed any effect previously obtained by the most complex flights of oratory in that hall. A young, blushing, clumsy, long-limbed, small-bodied giant stumbled along the central aisle and climbed the steps to the platform, where Denry pointed him to a seat. He was recognized by all the true votaries of the game. And everybody said to everybody: "By Gosh! It's him, right enough. It's Callear!" And a vast astonishment and expectation of good fortune filled the hall. Applause burst forth, and though no one knew what the appearance of Callear signified, the applause continued and waxed.

"Good old Callear!" the hoarse shouts succeeded each other. "Good old Machin!"

"Anyhow," said Denry, when the storm was stilled, "we've got him here, without either steam-engines or His Majesty. Will the directors of the club accept him?"

"And what about the transfer?" Councillor Barlow demanded.

"Would you accept him and try another season if you could get him free?" Denry retorted.

Councillor Barlow always knew his mind, and was never afraid to let other people share that knowledge.

"Yes," he said.

"Then I will see that you have the transfer free."

"But what about York?"

"I have settled with York provisionally," said Denry. "That is my affair. I have returned from York today. Leave all that to me. This town has had many benefactors far more important than myself. But I shall be able to claim this originality: I'm the first to make a present of a live man to the town. Gentlemen – Mr Mayor – I venture to call for three cheers for the greatest centre forward in England, our fellow-townsman."

The scene, as the *Signal* said, was unique.

And at the Sports Club and the other clubs afterwards, men said to each other: "No one but him would have thought of bringing Callear over specially and showing him on the platform. . . . That's cost him above twopence, that has!"

Two days later a letter appeared in the *Signal* (signed "Fiat Justitia"), suggesting that Denry, as some reward for his public spirit, ought to be the next mayor of Bursley, in place of Alderman Bloor deceased. The letter urged that he would make an admirable mayor, the sort of mayor the old town wanted in order to wake it up. And also it pointed out that Denry would be the youngest mayor that Bursley had ever had, and probably the youngest mayor in England that year. The sentiment in the last idea appealed to the town. The town decided that it would positively *like* to have the youngest mayor it had ever had, and probably the youngest mayor in England that year. The *Signal* printed dozens of letters on the subject. When the Council met, more informally than formally, to choose a chief magistrate in place of the dead alderman, several councillors urged that what Bursley wanted was a young and *popular* mayor. And, in fine, Councillor Barlow was shelved for a year. On the choice being published the entire town said: "Now we *shall* have a mayoralty – and don't you forget it!"

And Denry said to Nellie: "You'll be mayoress to the

youngest mayor, etc., my child. And it's cost me, including hotel and travelling expenses, eight hundred and eleven pounds six and sevenpence."

The rightness of the Council in selecting Denry as mayor was confirmed in a singular manner by the behaviour of the football and of Callear at the opening match of the season.

It was a philanthropic match, between Bursley and Axe, for the benefit of a county orphanage, and, according to the custom of such matches, the ball was formally kicked off by a celebrity, a pillar of society. The ceremony of kicking off has no sporting significance; the celebrity merely with gentleness propels the ball out of the white circle and then flies for his life from the *mêlée*; but it is supposed to add to the moral splendour of the game. In the present instance the posters said: "Kick-off at 3-45 by Councillor E. H. Machin, Mayor-designate". And, indeed, no other celebrity could have been decently selected. On the fine afternoon of the match Denry therefore discovered himself with a new football at his toes, a silk hat on his head, and twenty-two Herculean players menacing him in attitudes expressive of an intention to murder him. Bursley had lost the toss, and hence Denry had to kick towards the Bursley goal. As the *Signal* said, he "despatched the sphere" straight into the keeping of Callear, who as centre forward was facing him, and Callear was dodging down the field with it before the Axe players had finished admiring Denry's effrontery. Every reader will remember with a thrill the historic match in which the immortal Jimmy Brown, on the last occasion when he captained Blackburn Rovers, dribbled the ball himself down the length of the field, scored a goal, and went home with the English Cup under his arm. Callear evidently intended to imitate the feat. He was entirely wrong. Dribbling tactics had been killed forever, years before, by Preston North End, who invented the "passing" game. Yet Callear went on, and good luck seemed to float over him like a cherub. Finally he shot; a wild, high shot; but there was an adverse wind which dragged the ball down, swept it round, and blew it into the net. The first goal had been scored in twenty seconds! (It was also the last in the match.) Callear's reputation was established. Useless for solemn experts to point out that he had simply been larking for the gallery, and that the result was a shocking fluke – Callear's reputation was established. He became at once the idol of the populace. As Denry walked gingerly off the field to the grandstand, he, too, was loudly cheered, and he could not help feeling that, somehow, it was he who had scored that goal. And although nobody uttered the precise thought, most people did secretly think, as they gazed at the triumphant Denry, that a man who triumphed like that, because he triumphed like that, was the right sort of man to be mayor, the kind of man they needed.

from THE CARD *1909*

The Matador of the Five Towns

ARNOLD BENNETT

Loring, who works in the British Museum, has gone to stay the week-end in Knype, one of the Five Towns, with Robert Brindley and his family. On the Saturday Mrs Brindley insists that the family go to her Grandmother's birthday party – so Brindley calls on his friend Dr Stirling to entertain Loring. Stirling, desperate for an idea, takes Loring to Hanbridge where he remembers a call he should have made. As he returns to the car he has a "second inspiration".

"We might go down to the *Signal* offices and worry Buchanan a bit," said the doctor, cheerfully, when he came back to the car.

Buchanan, of whom I had heard, was another Scotchman and the editor of the sole daily organ of the Five Towns, an evening newspaper cried all day in the streets and read by the entire population. Its green sheet appeared to be a permanent waving feature of the main thoroughfares. The offices lay round a corner close by, and as we drew up in front of them a crowd of tattered urchins interrupted their diversions in the sodden road to celebrate our glorious arrival by unanimously yelling at the top of their strident and hoarse voices:

"Hooray! Hoo – bl – dy – ray!"

Abashed, I followed my doctor into the shelter of the building, a new edifice, capacious and considerable, but horribly faced with terra cotta, and quite unimposing, lacking in the spectacular effect; like nearly everything in the Five Towns, carelessly and scornfully ugly! The mean, swinging double-doors returned to the assault when you pushed them, and hit you viciously. In a dark, countered room marked "Enquiries" there was nobody.

"Hi, there!" called the doctor.

A head appeared at a door.

"Mr Buchanan upstairs?"

"Yes," snapped the head, and disappeared.

Up a dark staircase we went, and at the summit were half flung back again by another self-acting door.

In the room to which we next came an old man and a youngish one were bent over a large, littered table, scribbling on and arranging pieces of grey tissue paper and telegrams. Behind the old man stood a boy. Neither of them looked up.

"Mr Buchanan in his – " the doctor began to question. "Oh! There you are!"

The editor was standing in hat and muffler at the window, gazing out. His age was about that of the doctor – forty or so; and like the doctor he was rather stout and clean-shaven. Their Scotch accents mingled in greeting, the doctor's being the more marked. Buchanan shook my hand with a certain courtliness, indicating that he was well accustomed to receive strangers. As an expert in small talk, however, he shone no brighter than his visitors, and the three of us stood there by the window awkwardly in the heaped disorder of the room, while the other two men scratched and fidgeted with bits of paper at the soiled table.

Suddenly and savagely the old man turned on the boy:

"What the hades are you waiting there for?"

"I thought there was something else, sir."

"Sling your hook."

Buchanan winked at Stirling and me as the boy slouched off and the old man blandly resumed his writing.

"Perhaps you'd like to look over the place?" Buchanan suggested politely to me. "I'll come with you. It's all I'm fit for today. . . . 'Flu!" He glanced at Stirling, and yawned.

"Ye ought to be in bed," said Stirling.

"Yes. I know. I've known it for twelve years. I shall go to bed as soon as I get a bit of time to myself. Well, will you come? The half-time results are beginning to come in."

A telephone bell rang impatiently.

"You might just see what that is, boss," said the old man without looking up.

Buchanan went to the telephone and replied into it: "Yes? What? Oh! Myatt? Yes, he's playing. . . . Of course I'm sure! Goodbye." He turned to the old man: "It's another of 'em wanting to know if Myatt is playing. Birmingham, this time."

"Ah!" exclaimed the old man, still writing.

"It's because of the betting," Buchanan glanced at me. "The odds are on Knype now – three to two."

"If Myatt is playing Knype have got me to thank for it," said the doctor, surprisingly.

"You?"

"Me! He fetched me to his wife this morning. She's nearing her confinement. False alarm. I guaranteed him at least another twelve hours."

"Oh! So that's it, is it?" Buchanan murmured.

Both the sub-editors raised their heads.

"That's it," said the doctor.

"Some people were saying he'd quarrelled with the trainer again and was shamming," said Buchanan. "But I didn't believe that. There's no hanky-panky about Jos Myatt, anyhow."

I learnt in answer to my questions that a great and terrible football match was at that moment in progress at Knype, a couple of miles away, between the Knype Club and the

Manchester Rovers. It was conveyed to me that the importance
of this match was almost national, and that the entire
district was practically holding its breath till the result
should be known. The half-time result was one goal
each.

"If Knype lose," said Buchanan, explanatorily, "they'll find
themselves pushed out of the First League at the end of the
season. That's a cert. . . . one of the oldest clubs in England.
Semi-finalists for the English Cup in '78."

" '79," corrected the elder sub-editor.

I gathered that the crisis was grave.

"And Myatt's the captain, I suppose?" said I.

"No. But he's the finest full-back in the League."

I then had a vision of Myatt as a great man. By an effort of
the imagination I perceived that the equivalent of the fate of
nations depended upon him. I recollected, now, large yellow
posters on the hoardings we had passed, with the names of
Knype and of Manchester Rovers in letters a foot high and the
legend "League match at Knype" over all. It seemed to me
that the heroic name of Jos Myatt, if truly he were the finest
full-back in the League, if truly his presence or absence affected
the betting as far off as Birmingham, ought also to have been
on the posters, together with possibly his portrait. I saw
Jos Myatt as a matador, with a long ribbon of scarlet necktie
down his breast, and embroidered trousers.

"Why," said Buchanan, "if Knype drop into the Second
Division they'll never pay another dividend! It'll be all up with
first-class football in the Five Towns!"

The interests involved seemed to grow more complicated.
And here I had been in the district nearly four hours without
having guessed that the district was quivering in the tense
excitement of gigantic issues! And here was this Scotch doctor,
at whose word the great Myatt would have declined to play,
never saying a syllable about the affair, until a chance remark
from Buchanan loosened his tongue. But all doctors are
strangely secretive. Secretiveness is one of their chief private
pleasures.

"Come and see the pigeons, eh?" said Buchanan.

"Pigeons?" I repeated.

"We give the results of over a hundred matches in our Football Edition," said Buchanan, and added: "not counting Rugby."

As we left the room two boys dodged round us into it, bearing telegrams.

In a moment we were, in the most astonishing manner, on a leaden roof of the *Signal* offices. High factory chimneys rose over the horizon of slates on every side, blowing thick smoke into the general murk of the afternoon sky, and crossing the western crimson with long pennons of black. And out of the murk there came from afar a blue-and-white pigeon which circled largely several times over the offices of the *Signal*. At length it descended, and I could hear the whirr of its strong wings. The wings ceased to beat and the pigeon slanted downwards in a curve, its head lower than its wide tail. Then the little head gradually rose and the tail fell; the curve had changed, the pace slackened; the pigeon was calculating with all its brain; eyes, wings, tail and feet were being co-ordinated to the resolution of an intricate mechanical problem. The pinkish claws seemed to grope – and after an instant of hesitation the thing was done, the problem solved; the pigeon, with delicious gracefulness, had established equilibrium on the ridge of a pigeon-cote, and folded its wings, and was peering about with strange motions of its extremely movable head. Presently it flew down to the leads, waddled to and fro with the ungainly gestures of a fat woman of sixty, and disappeared into the cote. At the same moment the boy who had been dismissed from the sub-editor's room ran forward and entered the cote by a wire-screened door.

"Handy things, pigeons!" said the doctor as we approached to examine the cote. Fifty or sixty pigeons were cooing and strutting in it. There was a protest of wings as the boy seized the last arriving messenger.

"Give it here!" Buchanan ordered.

The boy handed over a thin tube of paper which he had

unfastened from the bird's leg. Buchanan unrolled it and showed it to me. I read: "Midland Federation. Axe United, Macclesfield Town. Match abandoned after half-hour's play owing to fog. Three forty-five."

"Three forty-five," said Buchanan, looking at his watch. "He's done the ten miles in half an hour, roughly. Not bad. First time we tried pigeons from as far off as Axe. Here, boy!" And he restored the paper to the boy, who gave it to another boy, who departed with it.

"Man," said the doctor, eyeing Buchanan. "Ye'd no business out here. Ye're not precisely a pigeon."

Down we went, one after another, by the ladder, and now we fell into the composing-room, where Buchanan said he felt warmer. An immense, dirty, white-washed apartment crowded with linotypes and other machines, in front of which sat men in white aprons, tapping, tapping – gazing at documents pinned at the level of their eyes – and tapping, tapping. A kind of cavernous retreat in which monstrous iron growths rose out of the floor and were met half-way by electric flowers that had their roots in the ceiling! In this jungle there was scarcely room for us to walk. Buchanan explained the linotypes to me. I watched, as though romantically dreaming, the flashing descent of letter after letter, a rain of letters into the belly of the machine; then, going round to the back, I watched the same letters rising again in a close, slow procession, and sorting themselves by themselves at the top in readiness to answer again to the tapping, tapping of a man in a once-white apron. And while I was watching all that I could somehow, by a faculty which we have, at the same time see pigeons far overhead, arriving and arriving out of the murk from beyond the verge of chimneys.

"Ingenious, isn't it?" said Stirling.

But I imagine that he had not the faculty by which to see the pigeons.

A reverend, bearded, spectacled man, with his shirt-sleeves rolled up and an apron stretched over his hemispherical paunch, strolled slowly along an alley, glancing at a galley-

B

proof with an ingenuous air just as if he had never seen a galley-proof before.

"It's a stick more than a column already," said he confidentially, offering the long paper, and then gravely looking at Buchanan, with head bent forward, not through his spectacles but over them.

The editor negligently accepted the proof, and I read a series of titles: "Knype *v.* Manchester Rovers. Record Gate. Fifteen thousand spectators. Two goals in twelve minutes. Myatt in form. Special Report."

Buchanan gave the slip back without a word.

"There you are!" said he to me, as another compositor near us attached a piece of tissue paper to his machine. It was the very paper that I had seen come out of the sky, but its contents had been enlarged and amended by the sub-editorial pen. The man began tapping, tapping, and the letters began to flash downwards on their way to tell a quarter of a million people that Axe *v.* Macclesfield had been stopped by fog.

"I suppose that Knype match is over by now?" I said.

"Oh no!" said Buchanan. "The second half has scarcely begun."

"Like to go?" Stirling asked.

"Well," I said, feeling adventurous, "it's a notion, isn't it?"

"You can run Mr Loring down there in five or six minutes," said Buchanan. "And he's probably never seen anything like it before. You might call here as you come home and see the paper on the machines."

We went on the Grand Stand, which was packed with men whose eyes were fixed, with an unconscious but intense effort, on a common object Among the men were a few women in furs and wraps, equally absorbed. Nobody took any notice of us as we insinuated our way up a rickety flight of wooden stairs, but when by misadventure we grazed a human being the elbow of that being shoved itself automatically and fiercely outwards, to repel. I had an impression of hats, caps, and woolly overcoats stretched in long parallel lines, and of grimy

raw planks everywhere presenting possibly dangerous splinters,
save where use had worn them into smooth shininess. Then
gradually I became aware of the vast field, which was more
brown than green. Around the field was a wide border of
infinitesimal hats and pale faces, rising in tiers, and beyond
this border fences, hoardings, chimneys, furnaces, gasometers,
telegraph-poles, houses, and dead trees. And here and there,
perched in strange perilous places, even high up towards the
sombre sky, were more human beings clinging. On the field
itself, at one end of it, were a scattered handful of doll-like
figures, motionless; some had white bodies, others red; and
three were in black; all were so small and so far off that they
seemed to be mere unimportant casual incidents in whatever
recondite affair it was that was proceeding. Then a whistle
shrieked, and all these figures began simultaneously to move,
and then I saw a ball in the air. An obscure, uneasy murmuring
rose from the immense multitude like an invisible but audible
vapour. The next instant the vapour had condensed into a
sudden shout. Now I saw the ball rolling solitary in the middle
of the field, and a single red doll racing towards it; at one end
was a confused group of red and white, and at the other two
white dolls, rather lonely in the expanse. The single red doll
overtook the ball and scudded along with it at his twinkling
toes. A great voice behind me bellowed with an incredible
volume of sound:

"Now, Jos!"

And another voice, further away, bellowed:

"Now, Jos!"

And still more distantly the grim warning shot forth from
the crowd:

"Now, Jos! Now, Jos!"

The nearer of the white dolls, as the red one approached,
sprang forward. I could see a leg. And the ball was flying back
in a magnificent curve into the skies; it passed out of my sight,
and then I heard a bump on the slates of the roof of the grand
stand, and it fell among the crowd in the stand-enclosure. But
almost before the flight of the ball had commenced, a terrific

roar of relief had rolled formidably round the field, and out of that roar, like rockets out of thick smoke, burst acutely ecstatic cries of adoration:

"Bravo, Jos!"

"Good old Jos!"

The leg had evidently been Jos's leg. The nearer of these two white dolls must be Jos, darling of fifteen thousand frenzied people.

Stirling punched a neighbour in the side to attract his attention.

"What's the score?" he demanded of the neighbour, who scowled and then grinned.

"Two – one – agen uz!" The other growled. "It'll take our b——s all their time to draw. They're playing a man short."

"Accident?"

"No! Referee ordered him off for rough play."

Several spectators began to explain, passionately, furiously, that the referee's action was utterly bereft of common sense and justice; and I gathered that a less gentlemanly crowd would undoubtedly have lynched the referee. The explanations died down, and everybody except me resumed his fierce watch on the field.

I was recalled from the exercise of a vague curiosity upon the set, anxious faces around me by a crashing, whooping cheer which in volume and sincerity of joy surpassed all noises in my experience. This massive cheer reverberated round the field like the echoes of a battleship's broadside in a fiord. But it was human, and therefore more terrible than guns. I instinctively thought: "If such are the symptoms of pleasure, what must be the symptoms of pain or disappointment?" Simultaneously with the expulsion of the unique noise the expression of the faces changed. Eyes sparkled; teeth became prominent in enormous, uncontrolled smiles. Ferocious satisfaction had to find vent in ferocious gestures, wreaked either upon dead wood or upon the living tissues of fellow-creatures. The gentle, mannerly sound of hand-clapping was a kind of light froth on the surface of the billowy sea of heartfelt applause. The host of the fifteen thousand might have just had their lives saved, or their children snatched from destruction and their wives from dishonour; they might have been preserved from bankruptcy, starvation, prison, torture; they might have been rewarding with their impassioned worship a band of national heroes. But it was not so. All that had happened was that the ball had rolled into the net of the Manchester Rovers' goal. Knype had drawn level. The reputation of the Five Towns before the jury of expert opinion that could distinguish between first-class football and second-class was maintained intact. I could hear specialists around me proving that though Knype had yet five League matches to play, its situation was safe. They pointed excitedly to a huge hoarding at one end of the ground on which appeared names of other clubs with changing figures. These clubs included the clubs which Knype would have to meet before the end of the season, and the figures indicated their fortunes on various grounds similar to this ground all over the country. If a goal was scored in Newcastle, or in Southampton, the very Peru of first-class football, it was registered on that board and its possible effect on the destinies of Knype was instantly assessed. The calculations made were dizzying.

Then a little flock of pigeons flew up and separated, under the illusion that they were free agents and masters of the air, but really wafted away to fixed destinations on the stupendous atmospheric waves of still-continued cheering.

After a minute or two the ball was restarted, and the greater noise had diminished to the sensitive uneasy murmur which responded like a delicate instrument to the fluctuations of the game. Each feat and manœuvre of Knype drew generous applause in proportion to its intention or its success, and each sleight of the Manchester Rovers, successful or not, provoked a holy disgust. The attitude of the host had passed beyond morality into religion.

Then, again, while my attention had lapsed from the field, a devilish, a barbaric, and a deafening yell broke from those fifteen thousand passionate hearts. It thrilled me; it genuinely frightened me. I involuntarily made the motion of swallowing.

After the thunderous crash of anger from the host came the thin sound of a whistle. The game stopped. I heard the same word repeated again and again, in divers tones of exasperated fury:

"Foul!"

I felt that I was hemmed in by potential homicides, whose arms were lifted in the desire of murder and whose features were changed from the likeness of man into the corporeal form of some pure and terrible instinct.

And I saw a long doll rise from the ground and approach a lesser doll with threatening hands.

"Foul! Foul!"

"Go it, Jos! Knock his neck out! Jos! He tripped thee up!"

There was a prolonged gesticulatory altercation between the three black dolls in leather leggings and several of the white and the red dolls. At last one of the mannikins in leggings shrugged his shoulders, made a definite gesture to the other two, and walked away towards the edge of the field nearest the stand. It was the unprincipled referee; he had disallowed the foul. In the protracted duel between the offending Manchester forward and the great, honest Jos Myatt he had given another point to the enemy. As soon as the host realized the infamy it yelled once more in heightened fury. It seemed to surge in masses against the thick iron railings that alone stood between the referee and death. The discreet referee was approaching the grand stand as the least unsafe place. In a second a handful of executioners had somehow got on to the grass. And in the next second several policemen were in front of them, not striking nor striving to intimidate, but heavily pushing them into bounds.

"Get back there!" cried a few abrupt, commanding voices from the stand.

The referee stood with his hands in his pockets and his whistle in his mouth. I think that in that moment of acutest suspense the whole of his earthly career must have flashed before him in a phantasmagoria. And then the crisis was past. The inherent gentlemanliness of the outraged host had triumphed and the referee was spared.

"Served him right if they'd man-handled him!" said a spectator.

"Ay!" said another, gloomily, "ay! And th' Football Association 'ud ha' fined us maybe a hundred quid and dis-qualified th' ground for the rest o' th' season!"

"D—n th' Football Association!"

"Ay! But you canna'!"

"Now, lads! Play up, Knype! Now, lads! Give 'em hot hell!" Different voices heartily encouraged the home team as the ball was thrown into play.

The fouling Manchester forward immediately resumed possession of the ball. Experience could not teach him. He parted with the ball and got it again, twice. The devil was in him and in the ball. The devil was driving him towards Myatt. They met. And then came a sound quite new: a cracking sound, somewhat like the snapping of a bough, but sharper, more decisive.

"By Jove!" exclaimed Stirling. "That's his bone!"

And instantly he was off down the staircase and I after him. But he was not the first doctor on the field. Nothing had been unforeseen in the wonderful organization of this enterprise. A pigeon sped away and an official doctor and an official stretcher appeared, miraculously, simultaneously. It was tremendous. It inspired awe in me.

"He asked for it!" I heard a man say as I hesitated on the shore of the ocean of mud.

Then I knew that it was Manchester and not Knype that had suffered. The confusion and hubbub were in a high degree disturbing and puzzling. But one emotion emerged clear: pleasure. I felt it myself. I was aware of joy in that the two sides were now levelled to ten men apiece. I was mystically identified with the Five Towns, absorbed into their life. I could discern on every face the conviction that a divine provi-dence was in this affair, that God could not be mocked. I too had this conviction. I could discern also on every face the fear lest the referee might give a foul against the hero Myatt, or even order him off the field, though of course the fracture was a simple accident. I too had this fear. It was soon dispelled by the news which swept across the entire enclosure like a sweet smell, that the referee had adopted the theory of a simple accident. I saw vaguely policemen, a stretcher, streaming crowds, and my ears heard a monstrous universal babbling. And then the figure of Stirling detached itself from the moving disorder and came to me.

"Well, Myatt's calf was harder than the other chap's, that's all," he said.

"Which *is* Myatt?" I asked, for the red and the white dolls had all vanished at close quarters, and were replaced by unrecognizably gigantic human animals, still clad, however, in dolls' vests and dolls' knickerbockers.

Stirling warningly jerked his head to indicate a man not ten feet away from me. This was Myatt, the hero of the host and the darling of populations. I gazed up at him. His mouth and his left knee were red with blood, and he was piebald with thick patches of mud from his tousled crown to his enormous boot. His blue eyes had a heavy, stupid, honest glance; and of the three qualities stupidity predominated. He seemed to be all feet, knees, hands and elbows. His head was very small – the sole remainder of the doll in him.

A little man approached him, conscious – somewhat too obviously conscious – of his right to approach. Myatt nodded.

"Ye'n settled *him*, seemingly, Jos!" said the little man.

"Well," said Myatt, with slow bitterness. "Hadn't he been blooming well begging and praying for it, aw afternoon? Hadn't he now?"

The little man nodded. Then he said in a lower tone:

"How's missis, like?"

"Her's altogether yet," said Myatt. "Or I'd none ha' played!"

"I've bet Watty half-a-dollar as it inna' a lad!" said the little man.

Myatt seemed angry.

"Wilt bet me half a *quid* as it inna' a lad?" he demanded, bending down and scowling and sticking out his muddy chin.

"Ay!" said the little man, not blenching.

"Evens?"

"Evens."

"I'll take thee, Charlie," said Myatt, resuming his calm.

The whistle sounded. And several orders were given to clear the field. Eight minutes had been lost over a broken leg, but Stirling said that the referee would surely deduct them from the official time, so that after all the game would not be shortened.

"I'll be up yon, to-morra morning," said the little man.

Myatt nodded and departed. Charlie, the little man, turned on his heel and proudly rejoined the crowd. He had been seen of all in converse with supreme greatness.

Stirling and I also retired; and though Jos Myatt had not even done his doctor the honour of seeing him, neither of us, I think, was quite without a consciousness of glory: I cannot imagine why. The rest of the game was flat and tame. Nothing occurred. The match ended in a draw.

We were swept from the football ground on a furious flood of humanity – carried forth and flung down a slope into a large waste space that separated the ground from the nearest streets of little reddish houses. At the bottom of the slope, on my suggestion, we halted for a few moments aside, while the current rushed forward and, spreading out, inundated the whole space in one marvellous minute. The impression of the multitude streaming from that gap in the wooden wall was like nothing more than the impression of a burst main which only the emptying of the reservoir will assuage. Anybody who wanted to commit suicide might have stood in front of that gap and had his wish. He would not have been noticed. The interminable and implacable infantry charge would have passed unheedingly over him. A silent, preoccupied host, bent on something else now, and perhaps teased by the inconvenient thought that after all a draw is not as good as a win! It hurried blindly, instinctively outwards, knees and chins protruding, hands deep in pockets, chilled feet stamping. Occasionally

B*

someone stopped or slackened to light a pipe, and on being curtly bunted onward by a blind force from behind, accepted the hint as an atom accepts the law of gravity. The fever and ecstasy were over. What fascinated the Southern in me was the grim taciturnity, the steady stare (vacant or dreaming), and the heavy, muffled, multitudinous tramp shaking the cindery earth. The flood continued to rage through the gap.

Our automobile had been left at the Haycock Hotel; we went to get it, braving the inundation. Nearly opposite the stableyard the electric trams started for Hanbridge, Bursley and Turnhill, and for Longshaw. Here the crowd was less dangerous, but still very formidable – to my eyes. Each tram as it came up was savagely assaulted, seized, crammed and possessed, with astounding rapidity. Its steps were the western bank of a Beresina. At a given moment the inured conductor, brandishing his leather-shielded arm with a pitiless gesture, thrust aspirants down into the mud and the tram rolled power-fully away. All this in silence.

After a few minutes a bicyclist swished along through the mud, taking the far side of the road, which was comparatively free. He wore grey trousers, heavy boots, and a dark cut-away coat, up the back of which a line of caked mud had deposited itself. On his head was a bowler hat.

"How do, Jos?" cried a couple of boys, cheekily. And then there were a few adult greetings of respect.

It was the hero, in haste.

"Out of it, there!" he warned impeders, between his teeth, and plugged on with bent head.

"He keeps the Foaming Quart up at Toft End," said the doctor. "It's the highest pub in the Five Towns. He used to be what they call a pot-hunter, a racing bicyclist, you know. But he's got past that and he'll soon be past football. He's thirty-four if he's a day. That's one reason why he's so independent – that and because he's almost the only genuine native in the team."

"Why?" I asked. "Where do they come from, then?"

"Oh!" said Stirling as he gently started the car. "The club

buys 'em, up and down the country. Four of 'em are Scots. A
few years ago an Oldham club offered Knype £500 for Myatt,
a big price – more than he's worth now! But he wouldn't go,
though they guaranteed to put him into a first-class pub – a free
house. He's never cost Knype anything except his wages and
the goodwill of the Foaming Quart."

"What are his wages?"

"Don't know exactly. Not much. The Football Association
fix a maximum. I daresay about four pounds a week. *Hi there!
Are you deaf?*"

"Thee mind what tha'rt about!" responded a stout loiterer
in our path. "Or I'll take thy ears home for my tea, mester."

Stirling laughed.

In a few minutes we had arrived at Hanbridge, splashing all
the way between two processions that crowded either footpath. And in the middle of the road was a third procession of
trams – tram following tram, each gorged with passengers,
frothing at the step with passengers; not the lackadaisical trams
that I had seen earlier in the afternoon in Crown Square; a
different race of trams, eager and impetuous velocities. We
reached the *Signal* offices. No crowd of urchins to salute us this
time!

Under the earth was the machine-room of the *Signal*. It
reminded me of the bowels of a ship, so full was it of machinery.
One huge machine clattered slowly, and a folded green thing
dropped strangely on to a little iron table in front of us.
Buchanan opened it, and I saw that the broken leg was in it at
length, together with a statement that in the *Signal's* opinion
the sympathy of every true sportsman would be with the disabled player. I began to say something to Buchanan, when
suddenly I could not hear my own voice. The great machine,
with another behind us, was working at a fabulous speed and
with a fabulous clatter. All that my startled senses could clearly
disentangle was that the blue arc-lights above us blinked occasionally, and that folded green papers were snowing down
upon the iron table far faster than the eye could follow them.
Tall lads in aprons elbowed me away and carried off the green

papers in bundles, but not more quickly than the machine shed them. Buchanan put his lips to my ear. But I could hear nothing. I shook my head. He smiled, and led us out from the tumult.

"Come and see the boys take them," he said at the foot of the stairs.

In a sort of hall on the ground floor was a long counter, and beyond the counter a system of steel railings in parallel lines, so arranged that a person entering at the public door could only reach the counter by passing up or down each alley in succession. These steel lanes, which absolutely ensured the triumph of right over might, were packed with boys – the ragged urchins whom we had seen playing in the street. But not urchins now; rather young tigers! Perhaps half a dozen had reached the counter; the rest were massed behind, shouting and quarrelling. Through a hole in the wall, at the level of the counter, bundles of papers shot continuously, and were snatched up by servers, who distributed them in smaller bundles to the hungry boys; who flung down metal discs in exchange and fled, fled madly as though fiends were after them, through a third door, out of the pandemonium into the darkling street. And unceasingly the green papers appeared at the hole in the wall and unceasingly they were plucked away and borne off by those maddened children, whose destination was apparently Aix or Ghent, and whose wings were their tatters.

"What are those discs?" I inquired.

"The lads have to come and buy them earlier in the day," said Buchanan. "We haven't time to sell this edition for cash, you see."

"Well," I said as we left, "I'm very much obliged."

"What on earth for?" Buchanan asked.

"Everything," I said.

We returned through the squares of Hanbridge and by Trafalgar Road to Stirling's house at Bleakridge. And everywhere in the deepening twilight I could see the urchins, often hatless and sometimes scarcely shod, scudding over the lamp-reflecting mire with sheets of wavy green, and above the noises of traffic I could hear the shrill outcry: "*Signal*. Football Edition. Football Edition. *Signal*." The world was being informed of the might of Jos Myatt, and of the averting of disaster from Knype, and of the results of over a hundred other matches – not counting Rugby.

During the course of the evening, when Stirling had thoroughly accustomed himself to the state of being in sole charge of an expert from the British Museum, London, and the high walls round his more private soul had yielded to my timid but constant attacks, we grew fairly intimate. And in particular the doctor proved to me that his reputation for persuasive raciness with patients was well founded. Yet up to the time of dessert I might have been justified in supposing that that much-praised "manner" in a sick-room was nothing but a provincial legend. Such may be the influence of a quite inoffensive and shy Londoner in the country. At half-past ten, Titus being already asleep for the night in an arm-chair, we sat at ease over the fire in the study telling each other stories. We had dealt with the arts, and with medicine; now we were dealing with life, in those aspects of it which cause men to laugh and women uneasily to wonder. Once or twice we had mentioned the Brindleys. The hour for their arrival was come. But being deeply comfortable and content where I was, I felt no impatience. Then there was a tap on the window.

"That's Bobbie!" said Stirling, rising slowly from his chair. "*He* won't refuse whisky, even if you do. I'd better get another bottle."

The tap was repeated peevishly.

"I'm coming, laddie!" Stirling protested.

He slippered out through the hall and through the surgery to the side door, I following, and Titus sneezing and snuffling in the rear.

"I say, mester," said a heavy voice as the doctor opened the door. It was not Brindley, but Jos Myatt. Unable to locate the bell-push in the dark, he had characteristically attacked the sole illuminated window. He demanded, or he commanded, very curtly, that the doctor should go up instantly to the Foaming Quart at Toft End.

Stirling hesiated a moment.

"All right, my man," said he, calmly.

"Now?" the heavy, suspicious voice on the doorstep insisted.

"I'll be there before ye if ye don't sprint, man. I'll run up in the car." Stirling shut the door. I heard footsteps on the gravel path outside.

"Ye heard?" said he to me. "And what am I to do with ye?"

"I'll go with you, of course," I answered.

"I may be kept up there a while."

"I don't care," I said roisterously. "It's a pub and I'm a traveller."

Stirling's household was in bed and his assistant gone home. While he and Titus got out the car I wrote a line for the Brindleys: "Gone with doctor to see patient at Toft End. Don't wait up. – A.L." This we pushed under Brindley's front door on our way forth. Very soon we were vibrating up a steep street on the first speed of the car, and the yellow reflections of distant furnaces began to shine over house roofs below us. It was exhilaratingly cold, a clear and frosty night, tonic, bracing after the enclosed warmth of the study. I was joyous, but silently. We had quitted the kingdom of the god Pan; we were in Lucina's realm, its consequence, where there is no laughter. We were on a mission.

"I didn't expect this," said Stirling.

"No?" I said. "But seeing that he fetched you this morning—"

"Oh! That was only in order to be sure, for himself. His sister was there, in charge. Seemed very capable. Knew all about everything. Until ye get to the high social status of a clerk or a draper's assistant people seem to manage to have their children without professional assistance."

"Then do you think there's anything wrong?" I asked.

"I'd not be surprised."

He changed to the second speed as the car topped the first bluff. We said no more. The night and the mission solemnized us. And gradually, as we rose towards the purple skies, the Five Towns wrote themselves out in fire on the irregular plain below.

"That's Hanbridge Town Hall," said Stirling, pointing to the right. "And that's Bursley Town Hall," he said, pointing to the left. And there were many other beacons, dominating the jewelled street-lines that faded on the horizon into golden-tinted smoke.

The road was never quite free of houses. After occurring but sparsely for half a mile, they thickened into a village – the suburb of Bursley called Toft End. I saw a moving red light in front of us. It was the reverse of Myatt's bicycle lantern. The car stopped near the dark façade of the inn, of which two yellow windows gleamed. Stirling, under Myatt's shouted guidance, backed into an obscured yard under cover. The engine ceased to throb.

"Friend of mine," he introduced me to Myatt. "By the way, Loring, pass me my bag, will you? Mustn't forget that." Then he extinguished the acetylene lamps, and there was no light in the yard except the ray of the bicycle lantern which Myatt held in his hand. We groped towards the house. Strange, every step that I take in the Five Towns seems to have the genuine quality of an adventure!

In five minutes I was of no account in the scheme of things at Toft End, and I began to wonder why I had come. Stirling, my sole protector, had vanished up the dark stairs of the house, following a stout, youngish woman in a white apron, who bore a candle. Jos Myatt behind, said to me: "Happen you'd better go in there, mester," pointing to a half-open door at the foot of the stairs. I went into a little room at the rear of the bar-parlour. A good fire burned in a small old-fashioned grate, but there was no other light. The inn was closed to customers, it being past eleven o'clock. On a bare table I perceived a candle, and ventured to put a match to it. I then saw almost exactly such a room as one would expect to find at the rear of the bar-parlour of an inn on the outskirts of an industrial town. It appeared to served the double purpose of a living-room and of a retreat for favoured customers. The table was evidently one at which men drank. On a shelf was a row of bottles, more or less empty, bearing names famous in newspaper advertisements and in the House of Lords. The dozen chairs suggested an acute bodily discomfort such as would only be tolerated by a sitter all of whose sensory faculties were centred in his palate. On a broken chair in a corner was an insecure pile of books. A smaller table was covered with a chequered cloth on which were a few plates. Along one wall, under the window, ran a pitch-pine sofa upholstered with a stuff slightly dissimilar from that on the table. The mattress of the sofa was uneven and its surface wrinkled, and old newspapers and pieces of brown paper had been stowed away between it and the framework. The chief article of furniture was an effective walnut bookcase, the glass doors of which were curtained with red cloth. The window, wider than it was high, was also curtained with red cloth. The walls, papered in a saffron tint, bore framed adver-tisements and a few photographs of self-conscious persons. The ceiling was as obscure as heaven; the floor tiled, with a list rug in front of the steel fender.

I put my overcoat on the sofa, picked up the candle and glanced at the books in the corner: Lavater's indestructible work, a paper-covered *Whitaker*, the *Licensed Victuallers' Almanac*, *Johnny Ludlow*, the illustrated catalogue of the Exhibition of 1856, *Cruden's Concordance*, and seven or eight volumes of *Knight's Penny Encyclopædia*. While I was poring on these titles I heard movements overhead – previously there had been no sound whatever – and with guilty haste I restored the candle to the table and placed myself negligently in front of the fire.

"Now don't let me see ye up here any more till I fetch ye!" said a woman's distant voice – not crossly, but firmly. And then, crossly: "Be off with ye now!"

Reluctant boots on the stairs! Jos Myatt entered to me. He

did not speak at first; nor did I. He avoided my glance. He was still wearing the cut-away coat with the line of mud up the back. I took out my watch, not for the sake of information, but from mere nervousness, and the sight of the watch reminded me that it would be prudent to wind it up.

"Better not forget that," I said, winding it.

"Ay!" said he, gloomily. "It's a tip." And he wound up his watch; a large, thick, golden one.

This watch-winding established a basis of intercourse between us.

"I hope everything is going on all right," I murmured.

"What dun ye say?" he asked.

"I say I hope everything is going on all right," I repeated louder, and jerked my head in the direction of the stairs, to indicate the place from which he had come.

"Oh!" he exclaimed, as if surprised. "Now what'll ye have, mester?" He stood waiting. "It's my call tonight."

I explained to him that I never took alcohol. It was not quite true, but it was as true as most general propositions are.

"Neither me!" he said shortly, after a pause.

"You're a teetotaller too?" I showed a little involuntary astonishment.

He put forward his chin.

"What do *you* think?" he said confidentially and scornfully. It was precisely as if he had said: "Do you think that anybody but a born ass would *not* be a teetotaller, in my position?"

I sat down on a chair.

"Take th' squab, mester," he said, pointing to the sofa. I took it.

He picked up the candle; then dropped it, and lighted a lamp which was on the mantelpiece between his vases of blue glass. His movements were very slow, hesitating and clumsy. Blowing out the candle, which smoked for a long time, he went with the lamp to the bookcase. As the key of the bookcase was in his right pocket and the lamp in his right hand he had to change the lamp, cautiously, from hand to hand. When he opened the cupboard I saw a rich gleam of silver from every shelf of it

except the lowest, and I could distinguish the forms of cere-
monial cups with pedestals and immense handles.

"I suppose these are your pots?" I said.

"Ay!"

He displayed to me the fruits of his manifold victories. I
could see him straining along endless cinder-paths and high-
roads under hot suns, his great knees going up and down like
treadles amid the plaudits and howls of vast populations. And
all that now remained of that glory was these debased and
vicious shapes, magnificently useless, grossly ugly, with their
inscriptions lost in a mess of flourishes.

"Ay!" he said again, when I had fingered the last of them.

"A very fine show indeed!" I said, resuming the sofa.

He took a penny bottle of ink and a pen out of the bookcase,
and also, from the lowest shelf, a bag of money and a long
narrow account book. Then he sat down at the table and commenced accountancy. It was clear that he regarded his task as
formidable and complex. To see him reckoning the coins,
manipulating the pen, splashing the ink, scratching the page;
to hear him whispering consecutive numbers aloud, and
muttering mysterious anathemas against the untamable naughti-
ness of figures – all this was painful, and with the painfulness
of a simple exercise rendered difficult by inaptitude and incompetence. I wanted to jump up and cry to him: "Get out of
the way, man, and let me do it for you! I can do it while you
are wiping hairs from your pen on your sleeve." I was sorry
for him because he was ridiculous – and even more grotesque
than ridiculous. I felt, quite actuely, that it was a shame that
he could not be for ever the central figure of a field of mud,
kicking a ball into long and grandiose parabolas higher than
gasometers, or breaking an occasional leg, surrounded by the
violent affection of hearts whose melting-point was the
exclamation, "Good old Jos!" I felt that if he must repose his
existence ought to have been so contrived that he could repose
in impassive and senseless dignity, like a mountain watching
the flight of time. The conception of him tracing symbols in a
ledger, counting shillings and sixpences, descending to arith-

metic, and suffering those humiliations which are the invariable preliminaries to legitimate fatherhood, was shocking to a nice taste for harmonious fitness. . . . What, this precious and terrific organism, this slave with a specialty – whom distant towns had once been anxious to buy at the prodigious figure of five hundred pounds – obliged to sit in a mean chamber and wait silently while the woman of his choice encountered the supreme peril! And he would "soon be past football!" He was "thirty-four if a day!" It was the verge of senility! He was no longer worth five hundred pounds. Perhaps even now this jointed merchandise was only worth two hundred pounds! And "they" – the shadowy directors, who could not kick a ball fifty feet and who would probably turn sick if they broke a leg – "they" paid him four pounds a week for being the hero of a quarter of a million of people! He was the chief magnet to draw fifteen thousand sixpences and shillings of a Saturday afternoon into a company's cash box, and here he sat splitting his head over fewer sixpences and shillings than would fill a half-pint pot! Jos, you ought in justice to have been José, with a thin red necktie down your breast (instead of a line of mud up your back), and embroidered breeches on those miraculous legs, and an income of a quarter of a million pesetas, and the languishing acquiescence of innumerable mantillas. Every moment you were getting older and stiffer; every moment was bringing nearer the moment when young men would reply curtly to their doddering elders: "Jos Myatt – who was '*e*?"

The putting away of the ledger, the ink, the pen and the money was as exasperating as their taking out had been. Then Jos, always too large for the room, crossed the tiled floor and mended the fire. A poker was more suited to his capacity than a pen. He glanced about him, uncertain and anxious, and then crept to the door near the foot of the stairs and listened. There was no sound; and that was curious. The woman who was bringing into the world the hero's child made no cry that reached us below. Once or twice I had heard muffled movements not quite overhead – somewhere above – but naught else. The doctor and Jos's sister seemed to have retired into a sinister and dangerous mystery. I could not dispel from my mind pictures of what they were watching and what they were doing. The vast, cruel, fumbling clumsiness of Nature, her lack of majesty in crises that ought to be majestic, her incurable indignity, disgusted me, aroused my disdain. I wanted, as a philosopher of all the cultures, to feel that the present was indeed a majestic crisis, to be so esteemed by a superior man. I could not. Though the crisis possibly intimidated me somewhat, yet, on behalf of Jos Myatt, I was ashamed of it. This may be reprehensible, but it is true.

He sat down by the fire and looked at the fire. I could not attempt to carry on a conversation with him, and to avoid the necessity for any talk at all, I extended myself on the sofa and averted my face, wondering once again why I had accompanied the doctor to Toft End. The doctor was now in another, an inaccessible world. I dozed, and from my doze I was roused by Jos Myatt going to the door on the stairs.

"Jos," said a voice. "It's a girl."

Then a silence.

I admit there was a flutter in my heart. Another soul, another formed and unchangeable temperament, tumbled into the world! Whence? Whither? . . . As for the quality of majesty – yes, if silver trumpets had announced the advent, instead of a stout, aproned woman, the moment could not have been more majestic in its sadness. I say "sadness", which is the inevitable and sole effect of these eternal and banal questions, "Whence? Whither?"

"Is her bad?" Jos whispered.

"Her's pretty bad," said the voice, but cheerily. "Bring me up another scuttle o' coal."

When he returned to the parlour, after being again dismissed, I said to him:

"Well, I congratulate you."

"I thank ye!" he said, and sat down. Presently I could hear him muttering to himself, mildly: "Hell! Hell! Hell!"

I thought: "Stirling will not be very long now, and we can depart home." I looked at my watch. It was a quarter to two.

But Stirling did not appear, nor was there any message from him or sign. I had to submit to the predicament. As a faint chilliness from the window affected my back I drew my overcoat up to my shoulders as a counterpane. Through a gap between the red curtains of the window I could see a star blazing. It passed behind the curtain with disconcerting rapidity. The universe was swinging and whirling as usual.

Sounds of knocking disturbed me. In the few seconds that elapsed before I could realize just where I was and why I was there, the summoning knocks were repeated. The early sun was shining through the red blind. I sat up and straightened my hair, involuntarily composing my attitude so that nobody who might enter the room should imagine that I had been other than patiently wide-awake all night. The second door of the parlour – that leading to the bar-room of the Foaming Quart – was open, and I could see the bar itself, with shelves rising behind it and the upright handles of a beer-engine at one end. Someone whom I could not see was evidently unbolting and unlocking the principal entrance to the inn. Then I heard the scraping of a creaky portal on the floor.

"Well, Jos lad!"

It was the voice of the little man, Charlie, who had spoken with Myatt on the football field.

"Come in quick, Charlie. It's cowd [cold]," said the voice of Jos Myatt, gloomily.

"Ay! Cowd it is, lad! It's above three mile as I've walked, and thou knows it, Jos. Give us a quartern o' gin."

The door grated again and a bolt was drawn.

The two men passed together behind the bar, and so within my vision. Charlie had a grey muffler round his neck; his hands were far in his pockets and seemed to be at strain, as though trying to prevent his upper and his lower garments from flying apart. Jos Myatt was extremely dishevelled. In the little man's demeanour towards the big one there was now none of the self-conscious pride in the mere fact of acquaintance that I had noticed on the field. Clearly the two were intimate friends, perhaps relatives. While Jos was dispensing the gin, Charlie said, in a low tone:

"Well, what luck, Jos?"

This was the first reference, by either of them, to the crisis. Jos deliberately finished pouring out the gin. Then he said:

"There's two on 'em, Charlie."

"Two on 'em? What mean'st tha', lad?"

"I mean as it's twins."

Charlie and I were equally startled.

"Thou never says!" he murmured, incredulous.

"Ay! One o' both sorts," said Jos.

"Thou never says!" Charlie repeated, holding his glass of gin steady in his hand.

"One come at summat after one o'clock, and th' other between five and six. I had for fetch old woman Eardley to help. It were more than a handful for Susannah and th' doctor."

Astonishing, that I should have slept through these events!

"How is her?" asked Charlie, quietly, as it were casually. I think this appearance of casualness was caused by the stoic suppression of the symptoms of anxiety.

"Her's bad," said Jos, briefly.

"And I am na' surprised," said Charlie. And he tilted the glass. "Well – here's luck." He sipped the gin, savouring it on his tongue like a connoisseur, and gradually making up his mind about its quality. Then he took another sip.

"Hast seen her?"

"I seed her for a minute, but our Susannah wouldna' let me stop i' th' room. Her was raving like."

"Missis?"

"Ay!"

"And th' babbies – hast seen *them*?"

"Ay! But I can make nowt out of 'em. Mrs Eardley says as her's never seen no finer."

"Doctor gone?"

"That he has na'! He's bin up there all the blessed night, in his shirt-sleeves. I give him a stiff glass o' whisky at five o'clock and that's all as he's had."

Charlie finished his gin. The pair stood silent.

"Well," said Charlie, striking his leg. "Swelp me bob! It fair beats me! Twins! Who'd ha' thought it? Jos, lad, thou mayst be thankful as it isna' triplets. Never did I think, as I was footing it up here this morning, as it was twins I was coming to!"

"Hast got that half quid in thy pocket?"

"What half quid?" said Charlie, defensively.

"Now then. Chuck us it over!" said Jos, suddenly harsh and overbearing.

"I laid thee half quid as it 'ud be a wench," said Charlie, doggedly.

"Thou'rt a liar, Charlie!" said Jos. "Thou laidst half a quid as it wasna' a boy."

"Nay, nay!" Charlie shook his head.

"And a boy it is!" Jos persisted.

"It being a lad *and* a wench," said Charlie, with a judicial air, "and me 'aving laid as it 'ud be a wench, I wins." In his accents and his gestures I could discern the mean soul, who on principle never paid until he was absolutely forced to pay. I could see also that Jos Myatt knew his man.

"Thou laidst me as it wasna' a lad," Jos almost shouted. "And a lad it is, I tell thee."

"*And* a wench!" said Charlie; then shook his head.

The wrangle proceeded monotonously, each party repeating over and over again the phrases of his own argument. I was very glad that Jos did not know me to be a witness of the making of the bet; otherwise I should assuredly have been summoned to give judgment.

"Let's call it off, then," Charlie suggested at length. "That'll settle it. And it being twins—"

"Nay, thou old devil, I'll none call it off. Thou owes me half a quid, and I'll have it out of thee."

"Look ye here," Charlie said more softly. "I'll tell thee what'll settle it. Which on 'em come first, th' lad or th' wench?"

"Th' wench come first," Jos Myatt admitted, with resentful reluctance, dully aware that defeat was awaiting him.

"Well, then! Th' wench is thy eldest child. That's law, that is. And what was us betting about, Jos lad? Us was betting about thy eldest and no other. I'll admit as I laid it wasna' a lad, as thou sayst. And it *wasna'* a lad. First come is eldest, and us was betting about eldest."

Charlie stared at the father in triumph.

Jos Myatt pushed roughly past him in the narrow space behind the bar, and came into the parlour. Nodding to me curtly, he unlocked the bookcase and took two crown pieces from a leathern purse which lay next to the bag. Then he returned to the bar and banged the coins on the counter with fury.

"Take thy brass!" he shouted angrily. "Take thy brass! But thou'rt a damned shark, Charlie, and if anybody 'ud give me a plug o' bacca for doing it, I'd bash thy face in."

The other sniggered contentedly as he picked up his money.

"A bet's a bet," said Charlie.

He was clearly accustomed to an occasional violence of demeanour from Jos Myatt, and felt no fear. But he was wrong in feeling no fear. He had not allowed, in his estimate of the situation, for the exasperated condition of Jos Myatt's nerves under the unique experiences of the night.

Jos's face twisted into a hundred wrinkles and his hand seized Charlie by the arm whose hand held the coins.

"Drop 'em!" he cried loudly, repenting his naïve honesty. "Drop 'em! Or I'll—"

The stout woman, her apron all soiled, now came swiftly and scarce heard into the parlour, and stood at the door leading to the bar-room.

"What's up, Susannah?" Jos demanded in a new voice.

"Well may ye ask what's up!" said the woman. "Shouting and brangling there, ye sots!"

"What's up?" Jos demanded again, loosing Charlie's arm.

"Her's gone!" the woman feebly whimpered. "Like that!" with a vague movement of the hand indicating suddenness. Then she burst into wild sobs and rushed madly back whence she had come, and the sound of her sobs diminished as she ascended the stairs, and expired altogether in the distant shutting of a door.

The men looked at each other.

Charlie restored the crown-pieces to the counter and pushed them towards Jos.

"Here!" he murmured faintly.

Jos flung them savagely to the ground. Another pause followed.

"As God is my witness," he exlaimed solemnly, his voice saturated with feeling, "as God is my witness," he repeated, "I'll ne'er touch a footba' again!"

Little Charlie gazed up at him sadly, plaintively, for what seemed a long while.

"It's goodbye to th' First League, then, for Knype!" he tragically muttered, at length.

Dr Stirling drove the car very slowly back to Bursley. We glided gently down into the populous valleys. All the stunted trees were coated with rime, which made the sharpest contrast with their black branches and the black mud under us. The high chimneys sent forth their black smoke calmly and tirelessly into the fresh blue sky. Sunday had descended on the vast landscape like a physical influence. We saw a snake of children winding out of a dark brown Sunday school into a dark brown chapel. And up from the valleys came all the bells of all the temples of all the different gods of the Five Towns, chiming, clanging, ringing, each insisting that it alone invited to the altar of the one God. And priests and acolytes of the various cults hurried occasionally along, in silk hats and bright neckties, and smooth coats with folded handkerchiefs sticking out of the pockets, busy, happy and self-important, the convinced heralds of eternal salvation: no doubt nor hesitation as to any fundamental truth had ever entered their minds. We passed through a long, straight street of new red houses with blue slate roofs, all gated and gardened. Here and there a girl with her hair in pins and a rough brown apron over a gaudy frock was stoning a front step. And half-way down the street a man in a scarlet jersey, supported by two women in blue bonnets, was beating a drum and crying aloud: "My friends, you may die tonight. Where, I ask you, where—?" But he had no friends; not even a boy heeded him. The drum continued to bang in our rear.

I enjoyed all this. All this seemed to me to be fine, seemed to throw off the true, fine romantic savour of life. I would have altered nothing in it. Mean, harsh, ugly, squalid, crude, barbaric – yes, but what an intoxicating sense in it of the organized vitality of a vast community unconscious of itself! I would have altered nothing even in the events of the night. I thought of the rooms at the top of the staircase of the Foaming Quart – mysterious rooms which I had not seen and never should see, recondite rooms from which a soul had slipped away and into which two had come, scenes of anguish and of frustrated effort! Historical rooms, surely! And yet not a house in the hundreds of houses past which we slid but possessed rooms ennobled and made august by happenings exactly as impressive in their tremendous inexplicableness.

The natural humanity of Jos Myatt and Charlie, their fashion of comporting themselves in a sudden stress, pleased me. How else should they have behaved? I could understand Charlie's prophetic dirge over the ruin of the Knype Football Club. It was not that he did not feel the tragedy in the house. He had felt it, and because he had felt it he had uttered at random, foolishly, the first clear thought that ran into his head.

Stirling was quiet. He appeared to be absorbed in steering, and looked straight in front, yawning now and again. He was much more fatigued than I was. Indeed, I had slept pretty well. He said, as we swerved into Trafalgar Road and overtook the aristocracy on its way to chapel and church:

"Well, ye let yeself in for a night, young man! No mistake!"

He smiled, and I smiled.

"What's going to occur up there?" I asked, indicating Toft End.

"What do you mean?"

"A man like that – left with two babies!"

"Oh!" he said. "They'll manage that all right. His sister's a widow. She'll go and live with him. She's as fond of those infants already as if they were her own."

We drew up at his double gates.

"Be sure ye explain to Brindley," he said, as I left him, "that it isn't my fault ye've had a night out of bed. It was your own doing. I'm going to get a bit of sleep now. See you this evening. Bob's asked me to supper."

A servant was sweeping Bob Brindley's porch and the front door was open. I went in. The sound of the piano guided me to the drawing-room. Brindley, the morning cigarette between his lips, was playing Maurice Ravel's *L'heure espagnole*. He held his head back so as to keep the smoke out of his eyes. His children in their blue jerseys were building bricks on the carpet.

Without ceasing to play he addressed me calmly:

"You're a nice chap! Where the devil have you been?"

And one of the little boys, glancing up, said, with roguish, imitative innocence, in his high, shrill voice:

"Where the del you been?"

from THE MATADOR OF THE FIVE TOWNS
AND OTHER STORIES *1912*

The Black Diamond

FRANCIS BRETT YOUNG

The football season had opened with a flourish as far as Mawne United were concerned. In the North Bromwich League they had beaten all their principal rivals, Wolverbury, Dulston and even the Albion Reserves. Now, in the semi-final of the Midland Cup they were to meet the Albion again. The members of the team became more than ever popular heroes, and Abner, down at the works, was conscious of his share in the distinc-

tion. The winter had set in early with a November of black
frost that made the scrap-iron with which he was still engaged
under the same grumbling foreman harder and more icy to the
touch, and congealed the grease in the running guide-wheels
of the trolley railway. It was some compensation that the blast
furnaces, which were surrounded in summer by a zone of air
undulant with intolerable heat, now gave a sense of neigh-
bourly warmth to the centre of the works.

Abner, who knew that his position was more secure than
ever, managed to spend most of his day near the black towers,
talking football to the men who were engaged in making the
moulds of sand into which the molten metal would flow when
the furnaces were tapped. It was an idle and pleasant life; but
he enjoyed it, knowing, as did everyone else in the works, that
it was no more than a preparation for the sterner business of
Saturdays.

One Wednesday, in the middle of the afternoon, he was at
work loading some pigs of iron into a truck that stood waiting
on the siding near the furnace. It was good warm work for a
winter's day, and Abner had thrown off his coat, rolled up his
sleeves, and unfastened the neck of his shirt. He and his mate
had just hoisted the last of the pigs into the truck when the
furnace foreman gave the signal for the tapping of the nearest
tower. Abner watched the proceeding as he put on his coat
and wiped the sweat from his forehead. The men, stripped to
the waist, approached the vent of the furnace carrying a heavy
crowbar with which they loosened the plug of fireclay which
kept the contents of the furnace from escaping. They leapt
aside as the first stream of molten mineral gushed out. The
foreman watched them, shading his eyes from the heat. The
fluid that came first was the dross of the ore which had sunk
to the bottom of the furnace, and this was diverted so that it
flowed into a wide pan where it would cool into a cake of
brittle, iridescent slag. A moment later pure iron began to flow.
The puddlers closed the entrance to the pool of slag, and
molten metal crept, with the slow persistence of a lava-flow,
down the central channel and into the moulds of sand that

were ready to receive it. The damp air above the beds first steamed, then swam with heat. Not molten gold could have seemed more beautiful than this harsh, intractable metal. It ran into the moulds sluggishly and with a soft, hissing sound.

Someone tapped Abner on the shoulder and drew him aside. It was Mr Hudson, who had walked down delicately from the office, so delicately that he had not even disturbed the two pencils wedged above his ears. He shivered slightly, for he had been shut up all day with a coke stove. Drawing Abner aside behind the line of trucks he began to talk to him about the cup-tie with the Albion. With the utmost friendliness he discussed the prospects of Mawne United in the match, which was now only ten days ahead. Abner answered him respectfully. Mr Hudson had not only given him his present comfortable job, but also carried in his pocket the future of every man employed in the works, for Mr Willis, whose eager mind was always set on expansions of the monster that had been created out of the fortune which his father-in-law had made in the Franco-Prussian war, was far too busy to worry his head about such details.

"So you think we'll win?" said Mr Hudson, fingering the bronze cross on his watch-chain.

"It bain't no good playing any match if you don't think you'll win," said Abner.

Mr Hudson stroked his red moustache. "I may say that the Albion has offered us a hundred pounds to play the match at North Bromwich, on their ground. The club could do with the money."

"Don't you take it," Abner replied. "Don't you take it. The Mawne ground's worth a couple of goals to our chaps in a match of that kind. That slope down by the Royal Oak puzzled the Albion last time. Our forwards know how to use it."

"The Albion's particularly anxious to win," said Hudson. "What's more, the bookmakers are giving three to one against Mawne. That shows you which way the wind's blowing."

"Well, I hope to God it busts them!" said Abner. "I'm no friend to football bookmakers."

Mr Hudson blenched at this loose employment of the deity's name. He took Abner by the arm. "Look here," he said, "speaking in the strictest confidence, I can tell you that the club will accept Albion's offer to play at North Bromwich. What's more, if Albion win, I can safely say it will be worth ten pounds to you personally."

Abner shook himself free from Mr Hudson's friendly arm. If he had followed the inclination of the moment he would have laid Mr Hudson flat there and then on the cinders. His feelings had passed beyond the stage of words. But while he stood glaring at Mr Hudson's face, now weakly smiling and white with fear, he saw something that stopped him: the figure of a woman running towards them as fast as she could over the cumbered ground of the works. She was hatless and had a shawl thrown round her shoulders. He knew, even at a distance, that it was Alice. She ran straight up to Abner, with her hair blown loose and with a flush of excitement that made her singularly beautiful.

Mr Hudson snatched at the opportunity for retreat. "This lady wants you," he said. . . .

Abner was now in strict training for the cup-tie with the Albion, and went to bed early every night. The Mawne directors, as Mr Hudson had foretold, jumped at the big club's offer to play the match at North Bromwich, tempted not only by the welcome hundred pounds, but by the prospect of an even bigger share of gate-money. The team went through their training with the greatest earnestness. Every afternoon they turned out on the Mawne ground practising passing, shooting, and tactics, followed by the eyes of the trainer, an international long since retired, who walked about the field carrying always a black bag that contained lemons, elastic bandages, and a patent embrocation of his own that smelt like Elliman's.

Nobody who saw these men at practice could possibly have suspected that they thought of anything but winning their match, though each of them must have known that all the others had been offered ten pounds a head to lose it. In the dressing-room, where they stood rubbing each other down with flesh-gloves in the clouds of steam that the cold air condensed from half a dozen tin baths of hot water, they talked of plans and prospects just as if no shadow of corruption had ever approached them. Nobody had mentioned the subject to Abner since Hudson had tackled him at the works. That, no doubt, was the policy of those who had put up the money; to let the thought of it sink in over a period of ten days and to trust to the frailty of human nature on the eleventh. They knew their business, for the mere presence of such a disturbing problem was enough to demoralize the team.

On the day before the match the Mawne goalkeeper sprained his ankle at practice, and neither the bandages nor the embrocation of the trainer could restore him. In this emergency the committee called upon George Harper, who had retired four or five years before and was now a man of substance and landlord of a public-house, to take his place. Abner, who had always been on good terms with this idol of his boyhood, went up to him after the last practice game and told him of Hudson's offer. Harper listened to him in silence, nodding his head, but when Abner asked him if he, too, had been approached by Hudson, he only laughed. "Hudson?" he said, "that red-whiskered b . . . No fear of that! He dursen't come near me. He knows what he'd get, does Mr Hudson."

In spite of this, when the team was assembled in the dressing-room of the Albion ground on the day of the cup-tie, Abner saw the trainer take George Harper aside. He talked excitedly in a low voice, but Harper only went red in the face and said nothing. As they left the dressing-room, Abner winked at George, and George, solemnly, winked back at him. The captain kicked the ball into the middle of the field, and the Mawne team ran out after him, amid a spreading uproar of cheers.

The turf of the Albion ground was incredibly smooth and level after the rough field in which they were accustomed to play at Mawne. The place was, indeed, a vast oval amphitheatre, with high stands rising above the dressing-rooms on the west and on every other side a sloping embankment so packed with people that the ground on which they stood could nowhere be seen. The vastness of the white-faced multitude was imposing in its ugliness. Its pale, restless masses represented on a horrible scale the grimy flatness of the city complexion. From the crowd a low murmur arose like the noise of the sea breaking on distant shingles, and over all its surface floated a fume of tobacco smoke. A moment later the Albion team emerged; the crowd swayed, and the murmur swelled to a roar of welcome. The chocolate and yellow jerseys of Mawne so nearly resembled the Albion's colours that the home team turned out in white shirts and knickers. It was partly the spotlessness of this attire that made them seem like a company of athletic giants, swifter, more flexible and stronger than their opponents. Even Abner's six feet were dwarfed by the diverse colours of his clothes. It seemed a ridiculous thing to match this shabby team of stunted pitmen with eleven picked athletes.

The game began. Almost at once the white line of the Albion forwards was in motion. It was a lovely sight, a lesson in fleetness, elasticity and precision. The Albion, taking no risks, had introduced a number of their first league players in the team, and it looked as if Mawne must be nowhere. Abner, at centre-half, the pivotal position of the whole field, felt that he could do no more than play a spoiling game against this perfect machine. In the back of his mind he knew also that a certain number, probably the majority, of the Mawne players, were not anxious to win. It is not easy, however, to play deliberately a losing game, or indeed to play football with any degree of deliberation. The heat of the game seemed to inspire the Mawne team to a stubborn, almost desperate, defence. As a last barrier to the Albion attacks he knew that George Harper, even if he were an old stager, was incorruptible, and George Harper, in his prime, had never played a more marvellous game. Perhaps the feeling that he belonged to an older and more gifted generation of footballers helped him. Time after time, when the Albion forwards came swinging down the field in a perfect crescent, he saved the Mawne goal. His play was inspired, and when half-time came, no goal had been scored. The players stood sweating in the dressing-room. The trainer handed out lemons. Once again Abner saw him approach George Harper and take him by the sleeve; but this time the goalkeeper pushed him away. Mr Willis came down into the dressing-room to congratulate the players. He was smoking a big cigar, and evidently immensely pleased with himself. He, at any rate, was above suspicion. The referee called the players out again.

In the second half Abner worked as he had never worked before. The Mawne team was tiring; play grew scrappy and spiteful; but though the Albion players could do what they liked with the ball in mid-field, they did not seem able to score. Even if Mawne were equally ineffective it seemed probable that the match would end in a draw. The Albion crowd grew restless, and began to think that the referee was favouring their opponents. The Albion players, now a little rattled, tried to effect by roughness what they could not do by skill. Several free-kicks were given against them for fouls, and the crowd began to boo the referee. It was like the hollow voice of some sullen ocean monster. The Albion, encouraged by the support of the crowd, pursued these tactics. Two men were ordered off for fighting. A moment later the crowd regained its good humour, stimulated by the sight of a shot from the Albion centre-forward that hit the cross-bar above George Harper's head. If the shot had been three inches lower he could not possibly have saved it. The kick that followed transferred the play to the other end of the field. It was close on time and everybody was nervous. A centre from the Mawne outside right came to Abner's feet in front of the Albion goal. One of the Albion backs tried to trip him, getting cleverly on the blind side of the referee. Abner stumbled free, and since the goal was now open, the player lashed out at his ear. Abner's temper was up. He left the ball and closed with his opponent. The Mawne team held up their hands and called on the referee like one man. A violent fight had begun when the referee arrived, shaking

C

himself free from a gesticulating escort of Mawne players. The Albion men separated the fighters, and though the referee warned both of them that if anything more happened he would send them off, he gave a free kick to Mawne. The crowd howled. It seemed for a moment as if they would burst their barriers and swarm on to the field. Very grimly, his face streaming with blood, Abner took the kick. The Albion goalkeeper, making a high save, tipped the ball over the cross-bar. A corner. The players lined up, panting, in front of the Albion goal. The young outside-right, whose centre had been the beginning of the trouble, took the kick. The ball sailed high and fell slowly into the *mêlée* of players. Abner, who had proved his dangerousness, was carefully marked and charged as the ball fell but he butted his opponent aside, and making full use of his superior height, managed to head it into the top left-hand corner of the net. A shout of "Goal" rose from the crowd, but there was no applause. The strange thing about the whole business was the attitude of the Mawne players. These men, who had been playing a half-hearted game all afternoon, appeared to be overwhelmed with joy. They ran up to Abner and shook both his hands as if there had been no matter of ten pounds depending on his achievement. Even George Harper came running down the field and patted him on the back. George had his work cut out, for in the last three minutes of the game the Albion made a desperate effort to equalize, and subjected him to an incessant bombardment. Luck aided his skill, and when the whistle went for time Mawne had won their match.

Abner went home that night with a thick ear and a slowly closing right eye. He was tired and sore, but elated. He wanted to do nothing but sit in front of the fire and think over again the progress of the match. Alice, on the other hand, was terribly concerned with his injuries. She dressed his face with some ointment that Mrs Moseley had recommended her for the baby, and sat opposite to him burning with pain and indignation.

"I wish you'd give it up, Abner," she said. "One of these

days you'll get killed. It's downright brutal. It's worse than prize-fighting."

"That's what it was," Abner chuckled.

He pretended that he didn't want her to fuss over him; but all the same this devotion was very pleasant. As for Alice, the pain of seeing him so battered was almost equalled by her pleasure in tending him. And they were alone. She was thankful that they were alone. Time after time she returned to her pleading that he would give up football. "You've never come home in a state like this," she said.

"Give up football?" said Abner. "And what would we live on then? You couldn't manage, and that's straight!"

"I'd do it," she said. "I'd manage somehow."

He laughed at her intensity. "Don't you fret yourself about me," he said. "I'm all right." He went to bed and slept like a log. She brought him breakfast and clean dressings to his bedroom.

On Monday morning down at the works Mr Willis met him. "Good lad!" he said. "Good lad!" Later in the day Mr Hudson came down from the office to the place where he was working. He smiled to conceal his annoyance. "Well, I suppose we've got to thank you and Harper for the win," he said.

"I reckon we've not got to thank you!" Abner replied.

"H'm, that's it, is it?" said Hudson. "You'd better go up to the pay-office for your money."

"Time enough when I've finished," said Abner. Football always prevented him from collecting his pay on a Saturday morning with the other men. At the end of the day he went to the pay clerk. Instead of twenty-five shillings as usual he was given fifty.

"What's this for?" he asked.

"Lieu of a week's notice," said the clerk. "The gaffer says we have to cut down. Mr Hudson's orders."

"B . . . r Hudson!" said Abner angrily.

from THE BLACK DIAMOND *1921*

Football Lesson in the Park

HENRI DE MONTHERLANT

*Jacques Peyrony, fifteen and a half years old, captain of the "Junior I"
football team in a great Paris club.*

*The "inside-forward" of the third team of the same club, twenty-five
years old. (He has been to the war.)*

*On the outskirts of Paris, in a great public park, a vast field,
attached to a stadium. It is April, the end of the day. It has been
raining. The expanse is closed on the horizon by a mediterranean of
trees, overhung from a hillside by the peaceful houses of a little,
suddenly revealed market town, a pleasant thing to come on by surprise.
And the inside-forward sometimes bends on it the clear, cold look of a
conqueror of towns. Are they Partisans, exponents of the sudden raid,
who are camping in the plain? The football games are over. Some
players are returning to the stadium, with heavy step, a little wearied.
Grouped around the goal-posts, as though in bivouac, indifferent to the
rain-nourished soil, others are stretched out or sitting, in every attitude
of fatigue and repose. A fickle sun plays on the crowns of their heads,
laying on each of them a little tongue of fire. Time is suspended. Life
itself marks time.*

*The inside-forward goes up to Peyrony who is putting on his sweater,
the game over. The young captain's face is bathed in sweat, black with
the earth which his muddy hands have left on it. His features are wan
beneath this trickling patina, and his face is burning so much that he
blinks his eyelids. In weariness, his mouth remains half open, his gaze
has become dull, and his eyeballs strangely pale.*

THE INSIDE FORWARD: Hallo, little man. What, beaten 4-1?
Hum, hum! Did you know I was watching you for the
last twenty minutes?

PEYRONY: I saw you.

THE INSIDE FORWARD: Well, I like that! When the play
brought you over to the touchline, a yard away from me,
you looked at me as if I was a stranger. Fair enough!

There's a time for everything. But you looked awful –
like Achilles in the *Iliad*, "bearing in your eyebrows the
terrible mark of war". (PEYRONY *lets himself fall on to a
mound of grass planted with trees.*) Put this jacket on your legs,
so that the muscles don't catch cold. Put your head back:
you're quite black. . . .

(*He pulls down a low branch, whose raindrops* PEYRONY
*receives on his face, grimacing, wiping it afterwards with his
sleeve.*)

PEYRONY: I've something for you. (*He gives him a rather
muddy piece of lemon.*) I didn't have it at half-time. But I ran
over to the forest lodge, and drank half a cup of milk there.

THE INSIDE FORWARD: Half a cup! How wise of you!

(*He bites eagerly into the lemon, chewing it, then swallowing the
pulp.*)

*The man who is beginning the final season of his youth is sitting beside
the boy who is entering the flower of it. In one, strength is hidden in
weakness (for after all he is a child); in the other, nonchalance; and it is
moving that it should be so invisible both in one and the other, concealed
and secret like the fire in the earth or the juice in the fruit. Meanwhile,
the knees and the beginning of the thighs of the older man, in this
moment of relaxation, are knotted with muscle, bulging to the point
of being gross, one would almost say romantic. But with the younger,
everything is contained, like perfection in more exquisite arts: the
courageous legs which run and kick for six quarters of an hour are
smooth as a brown wax candle; there's nothing to blemish their clarity.
And, just as in both of them strength lies at the bottom of their languor,
so, in the frank countenance of the younger there is a slight, faintly
savage note, the eyes veined with blood. And they're stretched under the
good shade as though in the trough of a weariness that they've wanted.*

PEYRONY: I got the ball full in the face. It's given me a headache.

THE INSIDE FORWARD: Take an aspirin when you get home.

PEYRONY: That won't be necessary! It'll pass off after a
shower.

THE INSIDE FORWARD: I like the way you take care of

yourself. A week ago, when you had a cold, you told me, "Oh, with a good massage . . ."

PEYRONY: Well, what do you think of the team?

THE INSIDE FORWARD: Everything's possible: they obey you. All the more meritorious when several of them are better than you.

PEYRONY: I know that quite well.

THE INSIDE FORWARD: They've understood, then, that to be a good captain you don't have to be an outstanding player. But even if you make a mistake as captain, they still obey you, without comment. When you persisted in playing over-elaborately in the last quarter hour, against a team which had run out of breath – instead of forcing the play – you can be sure that players like Labbé, or that astonishing little fellow with the English head, realised you were wrong, yet they conformed to your tactics, out of discipline.

PEYRONY: The little fellow in question *is* English.

THE INSIDE FORWARD: Really? Ah, what a shame!

PEYRONY: Why?

THE INSIDE FORWARD: Because if I was in your place, I'd never keep him in my team.

PEYRONY: What? Him? He's our best player!

THE INSIDE FORWARD: All the more reason. You can't run the risk of a French team winning a championship thanks to a foreigner. And then, how can a foreigner share in all your feelings of team spirit? In the war, I could have led a well paid, comfortable, sheltered life as an interpreter in the English or American army. But I chose to remain a soldier in a French infantry regiment; I waited till the Armistice to join the Americans, because none of my great moments of the war would have been complete if I'd lived them with fellows different from our own. For me, the war would have been ruined. And one more last piece of advice: sack Guilhermet. He's thoroughly mediocre. Every time one looks at him during a game, he's sitting on his backside – like one of those trams that's stationary whenever one sees it.

PEYRONY: He's the only one in the whole team who's really a friend of mine.

THE INSIDE FORWARD: Remember there are two parts of your life; the first has nothing to do with your team and includes Guilhermet; spend as much time with him as you please. But second, there is the team, which has only one aim: to do what its motto says, its best. Guilhermet, who plays badly is taking the place of somebody who could play well. Sack him gently, but sack him.

PEYRONY: The team would suffer from his absence, because if he wasn't there I should feel less like playing.

THE INSIDE FORWARD: Are you quite sure? You think that Guilhermet, who hasn't any athletic value, has a moral value which makes him more useful to the team than a newcomer playing better?

PEYRONY: Yes, quite seriously.

THE INSIDE FORWARD: In that case, keep him. Usefulness is our touchstone, and here, sentiment is useful. Long live sentiment, so long as we remain the masters of it!

LESSONS OF A MATCH

PEYRONY, *with an ironic emphasis*: Tell me the "lessons of the match," the one that you've just played.

THE INSIDE FORWARD: One of their forwards had had a couple of pieces of bad luck, the blunderer. I saw that he was a sensitive boy, that he was susceptible. I wanted to dishearten him, and every time he came in contact with me, I made him look silly with a feint. After two of these displays, he was reduced to nothing; there were still eleven of them, but we were playing against ten. Well, while I was dealing relentlessly with this fellow, I noticed that I was encouraged, spurred on, excited, by a quite obscure part of myself, that I was playing against him with a sort of angry joy which doubled my skill. And this threw light for me on several comparable things. You know that a wild beast will throw itself on its trainer when he accidentally happens to fall. Until then, I used to think it was because it told itself, "Let's take advantage, here's a chance." I now believe that it's because he conceives a horror of the man, seeing him cut down in size. Thus, the brute who beats his wife doubles his blows if she covers her face and groans. Thus the god from Olympus loses interest in the warrior he protected when he sees him brought down. In the same way, I have three cats: the grandmother, her daughter, and the daughter's son. When he was a few months old, this son started attacking his mother, scratching her, and she, the imbecile, put up with it, with a piteous air. You know what happened? The grandmother, who'd been living very affectionately for years with her daughter (sleeping in the same basket, and all that), suddenly grew enraged with her and now chases her all day, to attack her. How do you explain that, if not because she was exasperated to see her put up with it so passively? Feebleness gives rise to hate; feebleness is the mother of fighting. There's one of the "lessons of the game".

PEYRONY: The orator, returning to his seat, receives his colleagues' congratulations.

THE INSIDE FORWARD: The second lesson began from an amusing little incident, and I must tell you about it, as you can profit by it. You know we're always told, "When you take a throw-in, pretend to throw the ball to one of your team mates, so that the other side concentrates on him, then quickly throw it to another man who is unmarked." It's a trick as old as the hills. Well, then, I picked up the ball, I stared into Beyssac's eyes and then . . . then threw it to Beyssac. What chaos among the Red Lions! By instinct, seeing me pick out Beyssac, they'd marked every one except him, and there was my Beyssac racing away. Well, this trick reminded me of a saying of Aristotle. . . .

PEYRONY: Ah, Aristotle, no, that's got nothing to do with it! Let's get on to the flood.

THE INSIDE FORWARD: Don't laugh at a saying of Aristotle. It's when we seem to be innovating something that we need above all to feel ourselves supported by the past. The only reason I've such a perfect passion for what we were doing here is that I know it's justified by the opinions of bygone men. I'm constantly consulting them, and if I find that we're in agreement, I go ahead with my mind at rest. Well, Aristotle asked the gymnast to create "a mind inventive of stratagem, a spirit hardy and prudent, enterprising yet accepting". Isn't that what our football gives us?

PEYRONY: What strikes me above all is that Aristotle asks the *gymnast* to create only *moral* qualities.

THE INSIDE FORWARD: That's true, I never took account of it. And this saying contains one quite beautiful word; an *accepting* spirit. Through an hour and a half's play, what else have I done if not accept? Accept with a free and masculine heart, that's to say accept with regret and with approval. I resigned myself that the sun should disappear when it would have affected our opponents, and reappear when it affected us. I resigned myself that the wind should blow when it was against us, and drop when it would have been with us. I resigned myself to playing my part in tactics which I thought doomed to frustration, as your Labbé and your Englishman resigned themselves to your tactics while condemning them. I resigned myself to effort and fatigue which I knew to be useless, like chasing a man faster than myself, for the sole moral satisfaction of having tried as hard as I could. I resigned myself to Beyssac scoring a goal, being shaken by the hand, earning the smiles of the ladies and having his name on the stadium score-board, when it was I and I alone whose switch of play let him score. I resigned myself to ten occasions when the referee forgot to use his eyes, or used them wrongly, to our disadvantage, and I said nothing. If I'd once begun to protest, Ramondou would have clapped his hand over my mouth. . . . Ramondou is eighteen years old, I am twenty-five, and I'd have accepted his casual brusqueness because as far as justice is concerned, I'd have been in the right,

C*

but as far as play was concerned, I'd have been wrong, and this is the place to repeat after Goethe, "I prefer injustice to disorder." I accepted my failings which I studied for half an hour, ah! I promise you, without letting one of them escape me. I know I lack wind, that I allow myself to be tackled, that my kicking isn't accurate. I know that there lies in me a power as mysterious as genius or electricity, my *form*; which comes and goes, returns for no reason, defying every common law; which gives me the capacity of a demi-god for ten hours, then weakens my legs for ten and a half and is suddenly reborn from the depths of a complete ruin; which disappears for days of the most strenuous training, so that it makes one think there's a *spirit of the body* quite independent of the other. And I look inside myself at this living person, who is at once a stranger yet myself and with whom I can do nothing. I know it, I accept it, and so must we all.

We are in the third team, which plainly means that we play better than the fourth team and worse than the second; we know this about our team, just as each of us knows that so and so is a better player, perhaps because he's younger and fresher to the game. And to know one's worth, to know one's place, helps one to know the worth and place of everything.

We honestly want to climb to a higher level, which is our duty, and to strive – we, too – to do our best, without believing on that account that there's anything serious or dishonourable in it if we don't succeed. For the connecting-rod in a car is the equal in dignity of the piston, and a back in a team is the equal of a forward, and the third team, weakest in the club, has its dignity and its pride like the first. This is what we all know, and we approve of it.

The rain has stopped. There has been a moment's sun, and the grass, the mud, the branches, the bark of the trees, suddenly give off a stronger scent because of the sun. Water falls from the branches with a rapid

rhythm, fuller than the twittering of sparrows. The chestnut trees shed
their leaves like great drops against the milky sky.
  And little by little, night falls.

I can't tell you how many times, here, the whole war
leaped into my mind. Like a unit going through the
countryside, the team sets off for unknown lands, cheerfully
crossing a whole town to get to the opposing club's
"strongpoint", testing the direction of the wind, as if it
were carrying gas. We play – and attack, defence, break-
through, wing, opening, bombardment of goal . . . you
only need to mention the technical terms to smell the smell
of war. But what you cannot know is the intensity with
which the body remembers, recovers its sensations: for
example, when a forward line starts moving and we run
a few paces apart from one another, how is it possible not
to believe oneself back in a wave of assault? When we
come off the field harassed, bathed in sweat, our big boots
heavy with mud, and cross with the fresh team coming to
replace us, how can we not think of relieving troops? And
the friendly commotion in the dressing-room, people who
don't put on any pretence because they've taken each
other's measure and aren't afraid of reality there. And
when night comes, the strolls along the quayside, with the
fellow who sits on his knapsack (just as it used to be, just
as it used to be!) with the craven civilians whom one
scornfully stares down. All that, my little friend, is war,
that war from which you've reaped all the horror, but
which still has something left that's tough and good.
Must I sum up again the – what can I call it? – the philosophy
of it, to see what it's all about?

Here, there are no moral victories, which one cannot
verify. There is certainty. No appeal by the undeserving.
It is: adorable words.

Man against man, and not against ideas, not against
shadows. You can go and have a look at him at the station,
when he arrives. "His wrists are bigger than mine." "When

we collide at top speed it's I who'll be bowled over," and all the rest of it.

No *sins* against the unreal, against laws which one breaks without infringing Nature. But offences against rules conceived with a precise aim in view – your victory – and if you break them, you are beaten. Continual contact with reality. One comes in contact with it and replenishes one's strength. Earth and Antée.

The selection: everyone young and healthy. No illnesses. A wound, and it's a clean one.

No illness, no sadness; those two Gorgons compared with which death is quite beautiful.

To stay silent. The team, too, is one great mute.

Self-sacrifice. I pass him the ball – and my own chance with it.

Confidence. The team which sees its goal in danger but doesn't drop back, confident that the three men in defence will do what's necessary. One's immobility when one's looking on at the play. And to feel in oneself this immobility, what a moving experience, how well worth having lived it makes one feel!

Where else can one find what one finds here? The comrade suddenly twisted with agony, doubled up on the daisy-strewn grass. You see into those dep hs of a human being which show only under physical shock. You know whether he is brave or not, and how important that is! You say to yourself: perhaps in five minutes it will be I.

CONCERNING ORDERLY VIOLENCE

Concerning calm and orderly violence, courage, healthiness, simplicity, something virginal and rough which takes no account of itself: that's what I liked in war, yes, liked, despite all the distress and the horror, and that's what I've found here, that's what I get from these three days a week, the only ones which meet my demands in a life that's too small for me. Everything here is tied up with nature;

the earth, the wind, the sun are pals who play for us or against us, and you can see that just now we were the brothers of the rain, just as in the last war I was the brother of the roots and of the starry night. There's no doubt that it's from this that this great benefit comes. I'm not talking to you about semi-professional teams, whose ways must be pretty crude, nor of the little local clubs, the kind under someone's patronage. I'm talking to you about an old club which isn't Oxford, but where all in all the members are of good quality: in its "soul" as in its dressing-rooms, there's an odour of clean skin and rich leather. When we have a frugal meal before giving battle, and I see you refuse wine, refuse coffee, refuse a liqueur, refuse cigarettes, when I see your disgust for our neighbours, the tennis players, rude to the waiter and putting their feet up on the chairs, when I see you so indifferent to the snares of the world, whether they be silk socks, liquorice-water, or sentimental refinements, really pure like bread and salt (and at the same time as full of mischief as young fox let loose in a chicken run), it seems to me that the genius of Nature has entered into you during our hours of fresh air, and that it's he, giving you this horror of deceit, who has also given you this horror of evil, without you knowing it. For it's true! We scarcely bother ourselves with being moral, and yet, when we see the townsfolk again in the evening, pusillanimous and feeble, with their "discontent", with their "needs", their "sins", their imbecile "problems", people who share with us only those functions we share with the animals, I believe I can really see that this life we lead is the life that was dreamed about by the wise men or by God. Peyrony! Peyrony! We can now imagine the Golden Age. . . . And if all that, as we must believe, is merely an introduction to greater things, the stern reflection of the iron century should be welcome in our Golden Age. Paradise lies in the shadow of the sword.

PEYRONY: I am happy, and you too. But we mustn't think about it.

THE INSIDE FORWARD: The night is made for us to say these things. One would never dream of saying them in the morning. (PEYRONY *coughs*.) Be careful not to catch cold. Let's go up.

PEYRONY: Cold? A sportsman? You go up, if you feel cold.

THE INSIDE FORWARD: And Fred Borotra, and Loren, who were better athletes than you, and who were carried off in only a few days by colds! Come on, up with you! I beg you! You can have a glass of grog up there.

PEYRONY: Pooh, a glass of grog! That's woman's stuff.

THE INSIDE FORWARD: Ah, how irritating you can be at times! Listen, it was enough for me to hear you cough once, one single time . . . and I couldn't maintain what I did a minute ago with the same assurance. If you were tossing on your bed with fever tomorrow, with your mother holding your hand, would we repeat the things we've been declaiming here, in the pride of life? Everything we think out here, we think in a sort of drunkenness. In youth and strength, in the midst of Nature, leaping, conquering the others with one's body, one doesn't see a single day, two days together, without seeing the world in another way from those who haven't tasted such wine. One sees it as if there existed only a super-race of men whom we can treat with the same rough frankness we accept for ourselves. And meanwhile the games come to an end and we must go back among the suffering, who need a bit of gentleness, and perhaps we'll be numbered among them tomorrow, if this be the hour of death.

PEYRONY, *with a suppressed smile*: You're in eloquent vein this evening. Unfortunately, this is quite the opposite to your usual harangues against weakness, maudlin sentimentality, and the rest. You're going over to the enemy.

THE INSIDE FORWARD: I know, I know. It's partly my fault if sometimes you're surly, cutting, unfair, cruel, with a deliberate lack of subtlety, possessed by some destructive spirit. I've spoken words that I'll retract only with the silence of the tomb, I've written words that I've washed out with my tears, tears which aren't tears of rage, and which I like you well enough to hope that you will shed one day. Believe me, when it's not a question of charity, but just of avoiding misfortune, follow the old advice of the Greeks; be prudent in triumph and fear excess, even in good times. I've never harmed as many people as when I was bursting with virtue. (*Looking at him.*) No, there's no reason to make a face as if I were fooling you. All I ask you is one thing: have you been listening to what I just said?

PEYRONY: More or less.

THE INSIDE FORWARD: Will you remember it?

PEYRONY. I can't promise.

THE INSIDE FORWARD: Remember it. If only to remind me of it myself, because after a quarter of an hour's play I shall perhaps have forgotten it.

PEYRONY, *after a while*: What would you say to kicking a ball about a bit, before we go? There's one free down there.

THE INSIDE FORWARD: But it's dark!

PEYRONY: One can see well enough. We've got a good five minutes.

THE INSIDE FORWARD: And your tiredness? And your headache?

PEYRONY: They were just talk.

THE INSIDE FORWARD: What do you mean, talk?

PEYRONY: I mean, it's all gone.

PEYRONY *has risen; the far off ball, lying in the middle of a seated group of boys, fascinates him. His eyes suddenly sparkle with excitement. His whole face quivers like water, showing that, beneath the surface, there is who knows what lively humidity, as if the night, the trees, the wind, the salt of the air had put it there, like the proboscis in the flowers. But the older man's face is abstracted.*

PEYRONY: I can see Labbé. We can attack in threes.

THE INSIDE FORWARD: No, no, it's stupid.

PEYRONY: Listen, please! I promise you it's sensible. (*With reproach.*) After all you've just told me!

THE INSIDE FORWARD: Let's go!

PEYRONY, *voice transformed with delight, and with the tone of command he has already acquired*: Hey, you lads down there, let's have your ball!

THE BOYS: What for? We're going in. It's night time.

PEYRONY: Let's have your ball, I tell you!

One of the shadows gets up, sends over the ball. PEYRONY *hurls himself forward, the inside forward following. Seeing them, a second shadow gets up and runs towards them. One hears a shout of, "To me!" "Right away!" A little farther off, three shadows bound to their feet, as if galvanized by seeing this leather globe return to life.* PEYRONY *takes possession, and passes to the inside forward, who passes to a figure which has come galloping up at his side. They disappear into the thick darkness, followed by anonymous footsteps, taking with them that ball which is taking them, their breath streaming before them like men. They're a troop of centaurs, drunk with themselves and with that great Everything which is rising up in them, challenging them. And it's* PEYRONY, *the youngest, who is leading them. And one sees his face, silent beneath the steady gaze of his wingers.*

VOICES, *curt, crisp, true, pass along the ground*: Come on, come on!

from PARADIS Á L'OMBRE DES ÉPÉES *1934*

Watching Bruddersford

J. B. PRIESTLEY

Something very queer is happening in that narrow thoroughfare to the west of the town. It is called Manchester Road because it actually leads you to that city, though in order to get there you will have to climb to the windy roof of England and spend an hour or two with the curlews. What is so queer about it now is that the road itself cannot be seen at all. A grey-green tide flows sluggishly down its length. It is a tide of cloth caps. These caps have just left the ground of the Bruddersford

United Association Football Club. Thirty-five thousand men and boys have just seen what most of them call "t'United" play Bolton Wanderers. Many of them should never have been there at all.

It would not be difficult to prove by statistics and those mournful little budgets (How a Man May Live – or rather, avoid death – on 35 Shillings a Week) that seem to attract some minds, that these fellows could not afford the entrance fee. When some mills are only working half the week and others not at all, a shilling is a respectable sum of money. It would puzzle an economist to discover where all these shillings came from.

But if he lived in Bruddersford, though he might still wonder where they came from, he would certainly understand why they were produced. To say that these men paid their shillings to watch twenty-two hirelings kick a ball is merely to say that a violin is wood and catgut, that *Hamlet* is so much paper and ink.

For a shilling the Bruddersford United A.F.C. offered you Conflict and Art; it turned you into a critic, happy in your judgment of fine points, ready in a second to estimate the worth of a well-judged pass, a run down the touch-line, a lightning shot, a clearance kick by back or goalkeeper; it turned you into a partisan, holding your breath when the ball came sailing into your own goalmouth, ecstatic when your forwards raced away towards the opposite goal, elated, downcast, bitter, triumphant by turns at the fortunes of your side, watching a ball shape *Iliads* and *Odysseys* for you. . . .

And what is more, it turned you into a member of a new community, all brothers together for an hour and a half, for not only had you escaped from the clanking machinery of this lesser life, from work, wages, rent, doles, sick pay, insurance-cards, nagging wives, ailing children, bad bosses, idle work-men, but you had escaped with most of your mates and your neighbours, with half the town, and there you were, cheering together, thumping one another on the shoulders, swopping judgments like lords of the earth, having pushed your way through a turnstile into another and altogether more splendid kind of life, hurtling with Conflict and yet passionate and beautiful in its Art.

Moreover, it offered you more than a shilling's worth of material for talk during the rest of the week. A man who had missed the last home match of "t'United" had to enter social life on tiptoe in Bruddersford.

As he moved slowly down Manchester Road, the press of fellow spectators still thick about him, Mr Oakroyd found himself brooding over the hollow vanities of this life. He felt unusually depressed. His physical condition may have had something to do with it, for he was hot, dusty and tired; there had been a full morning's hard work for him at the mill; he had hurried through his dinner; walked to the ground, and had been on his feet ever since. Manchester Road after a match had never seemed so narrow and airless; a chap could hardly breathe in such a crowd of folk.

And what a match it had been! For once he was sorry he had come. No score at all. Not a single goal on either side. Even a goal against the United would have been something, would have wakened them up a bit.

The first half had been nothing but exasperation, with the United all round the Wanderers' goal but never able to score; centres clean flung away, open goals missed, crazy football. The second half had not been even that, nothing but aimless kicking about on both sides, a kids' game.

During the time that it took him to progress 300 yards down the crowded road, Mr Oakroyd gave himself up to these bitter reflections. A little farther along, where there was more room, he was able to give them tongue, for he jostled an acquaintance, who turned round and recognized him.

"Na Jess!" said the acquaintance, taking an imitation calabash pipe out of his mouth and then winking mysteriously.

"Na Jim!" returned Mr Oakroyd. This "Na," which must once have been "Now", is the recognized salutation in Bruddersford, and the fact that it sounds more like a word of caution than a word of greeting is by no means surprising. You have to be careful in Bruddersford.

"Well," said Jim, falling into step, "what did you think on 'em?"

"Think on 'em!" Mr Oakroyd made a number of noises with his tongue to show what he thought of them.

"Ah thowt t'United 'a' made rings rahnd 'em," Jim remarked.

"So they owt to 'a' done," said Mr Oakroyd, with great bitterness. "And so they would 'a' done if they'd nobbut tried a bit. I've seen 'em better ner this when they've lost. They were better ner this when they lost to Newcastle t'other week, better bi far."

"Ay, a seet better," said the other. "Did you ivver see sick a match! Ah'd as soon go and see 'tschooil lads at it. A shilling fair thrawn away, ah call it." And for a moment he brooded over his lost shilling. Then, suddenly changing his tone and becoming very aggressive, he went on: "Yon new centre-forward they've getton – MacDermott, or whativver he calls hissen – he'll nivver be owt, nivver. He were like a great lass on t'job. And what did they pay for him? Wer it two thahsand pahnd?"

"Ay." Mr Oakroyd made this monosyllable very expressive.

"Two thahsand pahnd. That's abaht a hundred for ivvery goal he missed today. Watson were worth twenty on 'im – ah liked that lad, and if they'd let him alone, he'd 'a' done summat for 'em. And then they go and get this MacDermott and pay two thahsand pahnd for him to kick t'ball ower top!" Jim lit his yellow monster of a pipe and puffed away with an air of great satisfaction. He had obviously found a topic that would carry him comfortably through that evening, in the taproom of *The Hare and Hounds*, the next morning, in the East Bruddersford Working Men's Club and possibly Sunday, Monday and Tuesday nights.

Mr Oakroyd walked on in silence, quickening his pace now that the crowd was not so thick and there was room to move. At the corner of Manchester Road and Shuttle Street, both men halted, for here their paths diverged.

"Ah'll tell tha what it is, Jess," said his companion, pointing the stem of his pipe and becoming broader in his Yorkshire as he grew more philosophical. "If t'United has less brass to lake wi', they'd lake better fooitball." His eyes searched the past for a moment, looking for the team that had less money and had played better football. "Tha can remember when t'club had nivver set eyes on two thahsand pahnds, when t'job lot wor not worth two thahsand pahnds, pavilion an' all, and what sort o' fooitball did they lake then? We knaw, don't we? They could gi' thee summat worth watching then. Nah, it's all nowt, like t'ale an' baccy they ask so mich for – money fair thrawn away, ah calls it."

"Well, we mun 'a' wer teas and get ower it. Behave thi-sen, Jess!" And he turned away, for that final word of caution was only one of Bruddersford's familiar good-byes.

"Ay," replied Mr Oakroyd dispiritedly. "So long, Jim!"

from THE GOOD COMPANIONS *1928*

The Match

ALAN SILLITOE

Bristol City had played Notts County and won. Right from the kick-off Lennox had somehow known that Notts was going to lose, not through any prophetic knowledge of each home-player's performance, but because he himself, a spectator, hadn't been feeling in top form. One-track pessimism had made him godly enough to inform his mechanic friend Fred Iremonger who stood by his side: "I knew they'd bleddy-well lose, all the time."

Towards the end of the match, when Bristol scored their winning goal, the players could only just be seen, and the ball was a roll of mist being kicked about the field. Advertising boards above the stands, telling of pork pies, ales, whisky, cigarettes and other delights of Saturday night, faded with the afternoon visibility.

They stood in the one-and-threes, Lennox trying to fix his eyes on the ball, to follow each one of its erratic well-kicked movements, but after ten minutes going from blurred player to player he gave it up and turned to look at the spectators massed in the rising stands that reached out in a wide arc on either side and joined dimly way out over the pitch. This proving equally futile he rubbed a clenched hand into his weak eyes and squeezed them tight, as if pain would give them more strength. Useless. All it produced was a mass of grey squares dancing before his open lids, so that when they cleared his sight was no better than before. Such an affliction made him appear more phlegmatic at a football match than Fred and most of the others round about, who spun rattles, waved hats and scarves, opened their throats wide to each fresh vaccillation in the game.

During his temporary blindness the Notts' forwards were pecking and weaving around the Bristol goal and a bright slam from one of them gave rise to a false alarm, an indecisive rolling of cheers roofed in by a grey heavy sky. "What's up?" Lennox asked Fred. "Who scored? Anybody?"

Fred was a younger man, recently married, done up in his Saturday afternoon best of sports coat, gaberdine trousers and rain-mac, dark hair sleeked back with oil. "Not in a month of Sundays," he laughed, "but they had a bleddy good try, I'll tell you that."

By the time Lennox had focused his eyes once more on the players the battle had moved to Notts' goal and Bristol were about to score. He saw a player running down the field, hearing in his imagination the thud of boots on damp introdden turf. A knot of adversaries dribbled out in a line and straggled behind him at a trot. Suddenly the man with the ball spurted forward, was seen to be clear of everyone as if, in a second of time that hadn't existed to any spectator or other player, he'd been catapulted into a hallowed untouchable area before the goal posts. Lennox's heart stopped beating. He peered between two oaken unmovable shoulders that, he thought with anger, had swayed in front purposely to stop him seeing. The renegade centre-forward from the opposing side was seen, like a puppet worked by someone above the low clouds, to bring his legs back, lunge out heavily with his booted foot. "No," Lennox had time to say. "Get on to him you dozy sods. Don't let him get it in."

From an animal pacing within the prescribed area of his defended posts, the goalkeeper turned into a leaping ape, arms and legs outstretched, then became a mere stick that swung into a curve – and missed the ball as it sped to one side and lost itself in folds of net behind him.

The lull in the general noise seemed like silence for the mass of people packed about the field. Everyone had settled it in his mind that the match, bad as it was, would be a draw, but now it was clear that Notts, the home team, had lost. A great roar of disappointment and joy, from the thirty thousand spectators who hadn't realized that the star of Bristol City was so close, or who had expected a miracle from their own stars at the last moment, ran up the packed embankments, overflowing into streets outside where groups of people, startled at the sudden noise of an erupting mob, speculated as to which team had scored.

Fred was laughing wildly, jumping up and down, bellowing something between a cheer and a shout of hilarious anger, as if out to get his money's worth on the principle that an adverse goal was better than no goal at all. "Would you believe it?" he called at Lennox. "Would you believe it? Ninety-five thousand quid gone up like Scotch mist!"

Hardly knowing what he was doing Lennox pulled out a cigarette, lit it. "It's no good," he cursed, "they've lost. They should have walked away with the game" – adding under his breath that he must get some glasses in order to see things better. His sight was now so bad that the line of each eye crossed and converged some distance in front of him. At the cinema he was forced down to the front row, and he was never the first to recognize a pal on the street. And it spelt ruination for any football match. He could remember being able to pin-point each player's face, and distinguish every spectator around the field, yet he still persuaded himself that he had no need of glasses and that somehow his sight would begin to improve. A more barbed occurrence connected with such eyes was that people were beginning to call him Cock-eye. At the garage where he worked the men sat down to tea-break the other day, and because he wasn't in the room one of them said: "Where's owd Cock-eye? 'Is tea'll get cold."

"What hard lines," Fred shouted, as if no one yet knew about the goal. "Would you believe it?" The cheering and booing were beginning to die down.

"That goalie's a bloody fool," Lennox swore, cap pulled low over his forehead. "He couldn't even catch a bleeding cold."

"It was dead lucky," Fred put in reluctantly, "they deserved it, I suppose" – simmering down now, the full force of the tragedy seeping through even to his newly-wedded body and soul. "Christ, I should have stayed at home with my missis. I'd a bin warm there, I know that much. I might even have cut my-self a chunk of hearthrug pie if I'd have asked her right!"

The laugh and wink were intended for Lennox, who was still in the backwater of his personal defeat. "I suppose that's all you think on these days," he said wryly.

" 'Appen I do, but I don't get all that much of it, I can tell you." It was obvious though that he got enough to keep him in good spirits at a cold and disappointing football match.

"Well," Lennox pronounced, "all that'll alter in a bit. You can bet on that."

"Not if I know it," Fred said with a broad smile. "And I reckon it's better after a bad match than if I didn't come to one."

"You never said a truer word about bad," Lennox said. He bit his lip with anger. "Bloody team. They'd even lose at blow football." A woman behind, swathed in a thick woollen scarf coloured white and black, like the Notts players, who had been screaming herself hoarse in support of the home team all the afternoon was almost in tears at the adverse goal. "Foul! Foul!

Get the dirty lot off the field. Send 'em back to Bristol where they came from. Foul! Foul I tell yer."

People all around were stamping feet dead from the cold, having for more than an hour staved off its encroachment into their limbs by the hope of at least one home-team win before Christmas. Lennox could hardly feel his, hadn't the will to help them back to life, especially in face of an added force to the bitter wind, and a goal that had been given away so easily. Movement on the pitch was now desultory, for there were only ten minutes of play left to go. The two teams knotted up towards one goal, then spread out around an invisible ball, and moved down the field again, back to the other with no decisive result. It seemed that both teams had accepted the present score to be the final state of the game, as though all effort had deserted their limbs and lungs.

"They're done for," Lennox observed to Fred. People began leaving the ground, making a way between those who were determined to see the game out to its bitter end. Right up to the dull warbling blast of the final whistle the hard core of optimists hoped for a miraculous revival in the worn-out players.

"I'm ready when yo' are," Fred said.

"Suits me." He threw his cigarette end to the floor and, with a grimace of disappointment and disgust, made his way up the steps. At the highest point he turned a last glance over the field, saw two players running and the rest standing around in deepening mist – nothing doing – so went on down towards the barriers. When they were on the road a great cheer rose behind, as a whistle blew the signal for a mass rush to follow.

Lamps were already lit along the road, and bus queues grew quickly in semi-darkness. Fastening up his mac Lennox hurried across the road. Fred lagged behind, dodged a trolleybus that sloped up to the pavement edge like a man-eating monster and carried off a crowd of people to the city centre with blue lights flickering from overhead wires. "Well," Lennox said when they came close, "after that little lot I only hope the wife's got summat nice for my tea."

"I can think of more than that to hope for," Fred said. "I'm not one to grumble about my grub."

" 'Course," Lennox sneered, "you're living on love. If you had Kit-E-Kat shoved in front of you you'd say it was a good dinner." They turned off by the recruiting centre into the heart of the Meadows, an ageing suburb of black houses and small factories. "That's what yo' think," Fred retorted, slightly offended yet too full of hope to really mind. "I'm just not one to grumble a lot about my snap, that's all."

"It wouldn't be any good if you was," Lennox rejoined, "but the grub's rotten these days, that's the trouble. Either frozen, or in tins. Nowt natural. The bread's enough to choke yer." And so was the fog: weighed down by frost it lingered and thickened, causing Fred to pull up his rain-mac collar. A man who came level with them on the same side called out derisively: "Did you ever see such a game?"

"Never in all my born days," Fred replied.

"It's always the same though," Lennox was glad to comment, "the best players are never on the field. I don't know what they pay 'em for."

The man laughed at this sound logic. "They'll 'appen get 'em on nex' wik. That'll show 'em."

"Let's hope so," Lennox called out as the man was lost in the fog. "It ain't a bad team," he added to Fred. But that wasn't what he was thinking. He remembered how he had been up before the gaffer yesterday at the garage for clouting the mash-lad who had called him Cock-eye in front of the office girl, and the manager said that if it happened again he would get his cards. And now he wasn't sure that he wouldn't ask for them anyway. He'd never lack a job, he told himself, knowing his own worth and the sureness of his instinct when dissecting piston from cylinder, camshaft and connecting-rod and searching among a thousand-and-one possible faults before setting an engine bursting once more with life. A small boy called from the doorway of a house: "What's the score, mate?"

"They lost, two-one," he said curtly, and heard a loud clear-sounding door-slam as the boy ran in with the news. He walked with hands in pockets, and a cigarette at the corner of his mouth so that ash occasionally fell on to his mac. The smell of fish-and-chips came from a well-lit shop, making him feel hungry.

"No pictures for me tonight," Fred was saying. "I know the best place in weather like this." The Meadows were hollow with the clatter of boots behind them, the muttering of voices hot in discussion about the lost match. Groups gathered at each corner, arguing and teasing any girl that passed, lighted gas lamps a weakening ally in the fog. Lennox turned into an entry, where the cold damp smell of backyards mingled with that of dustbins. They pushed open gates to their separate houses.

"So long. See you tomorrow at the pub maybe."

"Not tomorrow," Fred answered, already at his back door. "I'll have a job on mending my bike. I'm going to gi' it a coat of enamel and fix in some new brake blocks. I nearly got flattened by a bus the other day when they didn't work."

The gate latch clattered. "All right then," Lennox said, "see you soon" – opening the back door and going into his house.

He walked through the small living-room without speaking, took off his mac in the parlour. "You should mek a fire in there," he said, coming out. "It smells musty. No wonder the clo'es go to pieces inside six months." His wife sat by the fire knitting from two balls of electric-blue wool in her lap. She was forty, the same age as Lennox, but gone to a plainness and discontented fat, while he had stayed thin and wiry from the same reason. Three children, the eldest a girl of fourteen, were at the table finishing tea.

Mrs Lennox went on knitting. "I was going to make one today but I didn't have time."

"Iris can mek one," Lennox said, sitting down at the table.

The girl looked up. "I haven't finished my tea yet, our dad." The wheedling tone of her voice made him angry. "Finish it later," he said with a threatening look. "The fire needs making now, so come on, look sharp and get some coal from the cellar."

She didn't move, sat there with the obstinacy of the young

spoiled by a mother. Lennox stood up. "Don't let me have to tell you again." Tears came into her eyes. "Go on," he shouted. "Do as you're told." He ignored his wife's plea to stop picking on her and lifted his hand to settle her with a blow.

"All right, I'm going. Look" – she got up and went to the cellar door. So he sat down again, his eyes roaming over the well-set table before him, holding his hands tightly clenched beneath the cloth. "What's for tea, then?"

His wife looked up again from her knitting. "There's two kippers in the oven."

He did not move, sat morosely fingering a knife and fork, "Well?" he demanded. "Do I have to wait all night for a bit o' summat t'eat?"

Quietly she took a plate from the oven and put it before him. Two brown kippers lay steaming across it. "One of these days," he said, pulling a long strip of white flesh from the bone, "we'll have a change."

"That's the best I can do," she said, her deliberate patience no way to stop his grumbling – though she didn't know what else would. And the fact that he detected it made things worse.

"I'm sure it is," he retorted. The coal bucket clattered from the parlour where the girl was making a fire. Slowly, he picked his kippers to pieces without eating any. The other two children sat on the sofa watching him, not daring to talk. On one side of his plate he laid bones; on the other, flesh. When the cat rubbed against his leg he dropped pieces of fish for it on to the lino, and when he considered that it had eaten enough he kicked it away with such force that its head knocked against the sideboard. It leapt on to a chair and began to lick itself, looking at him with green surprised eyes.

He gave one of the boys sixpence to fetch a *Football Guardian*. "And be quick about it," he called after him. He pushed his plate away, and nodded towards the mauled kippers. "I don't want this. You'd better send somebody out for some pastries. And mash some fresh tea," he added as an afterthought, "that pot's stewed."

He had gone too far. Why did he make Saturday afternoon such hell on earth? Anger throbbed violently in her temples. Through the furious beating of her heart she cried out: "If you want some pastries you'll fetch 'em yourself. And you'll mash your own tea as well."

"When a man goes to work all week he wants some tea," he said, glaring at her. Nodding at the boy: "Send him out for some cakes."

The boy had already stood up. "Don't go. Sit down," she said to him. "Get 'em yourself," she retorted to her husband. "The tea I've already put on the table's good enough for anybody. There's nowt wrong wi' it at all, and then you carry on like this. I suppose they lost at the match, because I can't think of any other reason why you should have such a long face."

He was shocked by such a sustained tirade, stood up to subdue her. "You what?" he shouted. "What do you think you're on wi'?"

Her face turned a deep pink. "You heard," she called back. "A few home truths might do you a bit of good."

He picked up the plate of fish and, with exaggerated deliberation, threw it to the floor. "There," he roared. "That's what you can do with your bleeding tea."

"You're a lunatic," she screamed. "You're mental."

He hit her once, twice, three times across the head, and knocked her to the ground. The little boy wailed, and his sister came running in from the parlour. . . .

Fred and his young wife in the house next door heard a commotion through the thin walls. They caught the cadence of voices and shifting chairs, but didn't really think anything amiss until the shriller climax was reached. "Would you believe it?" Ruby said, slipping off Fred's knee and straightening her skirt. "Just because Notts have lost again. I'm glad yo' aren't like that."

Ruby was nineteen, plump like a pear not round like a pudding, already pregnant though they'd only been married a month. Fred held her back by the wrist. "I'm not so daft as to let owt like that bother me."

She wrenched herself free. "It's a good job you're not; because if you was I'd bosh you one."

Fred sat by the fire with a bemused, Cheshire-cat grin on his face while Ruby was in the scullery getting them something to eat. The noise in the next house had died down. After a slamming of doors and much walking to and fro outside Lennox's wife had taken the children, and left him for the last time.

from THE LONELINESS OF THE LONG-DISTANCE RUNNER *1959*

The Footballers

BRIAN GLANVILLE

"*Hallo-my-dear!*" Franco never spoke on the telephone, he bellowed; a great lion's roar suggesting his scepticism that the instrument really transcended distance.

"Listen! This morning you come down with me to Rifredi: I make you see what I am doing! Lovely *boys!* Beautiful *play*ers! You have no idea! Just like young English players: you will see!"

It was the highest compliment he could pay, based on a strange Anglophilia which derived solely from his admiration for English football. I myself was a lucky beneficiary; friendship, goodwill, generosity rained down upon me, as on the son of some deceased national hero.

"I'll be delighted to come," I told him, in Italian, but Franco boomed back at me in his curious sing-song English, at once fluent and grotesque, a switchback of mistaken cadences, odd transliterations. "Very *well!* I see you at ten, in Cathedral Square." There were times when he went too far.

It was a clear, pale day in late October; the sun shone bright and heatless out of a God the Father sky, full of billowing cloud. Above the city, seen from my window, the villas of Fiesole stood out sharp and deceptively close from their dark green mounting of cyprus. Down river, the trees in the Cascine were less luxuriant now, and the Arno itself moved slow, on one of its ugly, khaki days.

Franco wasn't in the Piazza del Duomo at ten, but then I had not expected him to be. He was always late and seldom in haste, arriving at last with a casual, mattered apology.

With its great, swelling dome, its garish red, white, and green walls, the Duomo towered above the square in vulgar majesty, like a handsome woman in tawdry clothes. Outside the large bar, which was one of Franco's rendezvous, my hand was seized by a friend of his, a season ticket holder at the football stadium, curly grey haired, with the contrasting face of a cherub.

"*Ciào, caro! Prende un caffè?*"

To know Franco was a magic passport; previously this man had shown me only the detached hostility which the Florentine reserves for foreigners. I thanked him, and we went into the bar. "Waiting for Franco, eh?" he asked. I said that I was. He chuckled, as Franco's friends and pupils did when they talked about him, a chuckle of benign astonishment, shocked admiration; that of a parent with a loved, outrageous child. "*Ma che fenomeno,*" he said, shaking his head, "*che fenomeno.*"

I agreed, and conversation flagged, until – the eternal last resort – we began to talk about La Fiorentina. But within minutes, Franco himself had arrived – "*Oh! My* dear!" – great arms outstretched in a reflex gesture of delight and repentance, which dissolved at once as the arms dropped to his sides, and he turned to the three or four men who instantly surrounded him.

He radiated an intense, physical masculinity; a tall, outdoor man, vastly broad, his white shirt unbuttoned, despite the weather, to reveal his deep, bronzed chest. Over his shoulder, characteristically, he had slung his jacket, as though scornfully deferring to an ordinance of dress. His face still retained part of its summer tan, but the impression it gave was rather one of wind-whipped ruddiness. His nose was large and jagged, his chin strong, and his metallic blond hair was combed back thickly from his forehead. The men eddied about him, waves around a rock, half mocking, half his disciples.

"Eh, Franco!" they said, "What about the Fiorentina?" and looked at one another half giggling, like children, knowing each response.

"*Macche Fiorentina!*" Franco shouted, in the thick, rough Tuscan of the Florentine backstreets. "That team doesn't understand a —— about football!" He perorated on without looking at them, louder and louder, as though reciting a set piece which nothing they might say could modify. Names of players, names of managers, were fed gleefully by them into the machine, and each in turn produced its roar of contemptuous abuse, larded with obscenity. The man with curly hair turned to me, rolled his eyes in apology, and said, "You know how he always exaggerates. . . ."

"Who exaggerates?" Franco bellowed. "I tell you I've two boys in my team now who could. . . ." But here his remarks were lost in a tumult of jeers and mock applause. Again, he seemed unaffected, neither angry nor amused; he merely raised his voice still higher and shouted, with the strange, aspirated Florentine "C", "*Sanno giohare, sanno giohare,*" they know how to play. Then he put a hand absently on my shoulder and guided me out of the bar, like a casual sheep dog.

We took the *filobus* from Piazza del Duomo to the Industrial Zone. The journey began in Florence, in the shadow of the *duomo*; went by the fortifications, with their miniature lake, then passed speedily into No Man's Land. The city's perimeter might have been anywhere, functional, and shallow, a compound of ugly bypasses, garrisoned by numberless garish filling stations; of railway bridges, hurtling lorries, grey, anonymous side streets.

We got out, fighting our way down the narrow aisle of the 'bus, at Rifredi, where Franco trained his young players. This was the Industrial Zone, and it had always seemed right to me that the football ground should lie among this waste of factory buildings, one-storied, white walled; an ugly, half-hearted gesture at modernity. Industry and football belonged together, irrelevant alike to the nature of the city itself.

We walked into the little stadium. The stretch of grass – uncommon enough in Tuscany – was dark green and uneven, worn in front of the goals, at either end. Round it stood a fence of wire netting, a reminder of combustible passions. A small, compact grandstand with terraced blocks instead of seats stood apart as though abandoned there. Just outside the ground rose a workers' apartment block, a futuristic barracks, its outer stairways a maze of stone corkscrews, its terrace walls inlaid with shiny purple.

On the field, several boys in football kit were kicking a ball to one another, moving with the plasticity of the young Italian, and the young Italian's delight in his own virtuosity. They bounced the ball on their thighs, tried to flick it over their heads with their heels, or hurled themselves into the air in an attempted *rovesciata*, scissor-kicking backwards, high above their heads. Franco greeted them with an offhand cry of, "*Oh, ragazzi*," and for the second time that morning he was surrounded – "*Senti, Franco . . . Franco!*" the boys asking him a score of eager questions.

Here, too, Franco moved with a strange detachment; gentler, now, eyes still distant, moving a hand now and then in a gesture of deprecation. Suddenly, with a bellow, he was wide awake, seizing a ball, calling for another, dividing the boys into groups, marshalling them with the abuse of a drill sergeant. "*Bischero! Testa di cazzo!* What are you doing, standing there playing with yourselves?"

The boys seemed unresentful. They responded, brisk and alert, to his commands, as though the mastering of each skill, each exercise, were of ritual importance. And indeed, it was; their very lives were in prospect; proficiency in this game could make the difference between wealth and unemployment, mean wages and a life of fast cars, new flats, women, adulation. Through Franco and his training lay the path to the rich professional clubs, backed by millionaires – themselves in search of that corrosive goal of the Italian male, the making of the *bella figura*. A few of these boys would succeed, some would have mediocre careers with lesser professional clubs, others would fall by the wayside, forced to abandon their dreams.

Franco, then, for all his four-square masculinity, was a trader in dreams, holding in this sport a unique position. He had a prospector's eye for latent talent, could find his players in the streets and squares, kicking a rubber ball, in minor matches, in obscure teams run by priests. Then he would train and coach them, give them money to subsist on, play them in his own, junior team, and hope to sell them at last to one of the rich professional clubs in deals of labyrinthine complexity.

Once, I tried to leave the little stadium, but Franco caught sight of me at once. "No, no! You must see my centre-'alf! Lovely player!" and reluctantly I stayed.

The centre-half was tall, graceful, and feline, with a Grecian head and physique. Perhaps it was his very fluency and relaxation that made me remark, by contrast, another boy, heavier in build and movement, strained and alert, his thatch of fair hair resembling Franco's. If the centre-half received most of the praise and individual attention, this other player was obviously the butt. Franco abused them all from time to time, but the blond boy was more often the target than any of them, while the abuse, now I paid attention seemed sharper, and more sharply felt.

The consequence was inevitable: the boy tried too hard to do well, and accordingly did badly, the strong body tense, so that it resisted the ball, instead of yielding and persuading it.

"*You* can't play!" Franco shouted at him, on one of these occasions. "How can anyone as ugly as you are be a footballer? With a face like yours, you're only good for scaring women!"

There was sycophantic laughter at this, and from where I sat, the boy seemed almost to be in tears.

When Franco at last came off the field, and I strolled forward with relief to meet him, the boy was at his side, anxious and pleading. "But Franco, Franco, show me what I'm doing

D

wrong! I know I haven't got it yet, but show me!" Franco did
not turn to look at him, but merely growled, "I've shown you
a dozen times."

"But how can I improve? Tell me!"

"You can't improve. You're an idiot."

"But *Franco*!" Now I could plainly see tears in his eyes. His
face, as Franco had said, was ugly, yet it was not displeasing.
The jaw was long and heavy and blunt, like a trowel, the mouth
hung slightly open, as though drawn down irresistibly by the
weight below. Altogether the impression given was that of a
friendly, clumsy dog, a Newfoundland puppy, desperately
anxious to please.

"But Franco. . . ." he said.

"I'll show you tomorrow," Franco told him, in blunt dis-
missal. The boy went in with the others to change, and I felt
glad and relieved. Wanting to intervene, I had been held back
by knowing I had no real part in the scene, that my very presence
was no more than an accident.

"Who is he?" I asked. Franco shrugged. "One of my
players: Carlo Paolozzi. I find him in a street team when he
was thirteen."

"Is he good?"

Again a shrug: this time more a movement of the head than
of the shoulders; the subject clearly did not touch him. "His
ball control's quite good. He studies the game a lot. But he's
too much of an idiot: you saw his face?" And here Franco gave
a cruel parody of the boy, protruding his chin, opening his
mouth, rolling his eyes.

We waited for the players to change, they emerged dressed in
heavy woollen jerseys and cheap sports jackets, then together
we made our way to the *filobus* stop.

"What a woman!" Franco was saying now, while the boys
nudged each other and guffawed with delight. "Three times I
went with her, and she said to me, 'I've never come across a
man like you. You're the strongest man I've ever known'."

"Bravo Franco!" said one of the boys.

"But it's true!" Franco shouted, and his voice rose higher

still. "I'll show her to you. Brothel stuff, *roba da casino, ma bella, bella!*"

At the 'bus stop, the conversation returned to football. Franco began to expound tactics, to analyse the team's previous match, and Carlo, eyes shining with delight, spread his arms in a clumsy, touching gesture of joy and cried, "But Franco, you're great! *Tu sei grande!*"

Franco had invited me to lunch, and we left the 'bus a few hundred yards from the rough stone apartment house where his family lived, not far from Rifredi. He pressed the bell, a buzzer sounded, the door opened, and from high above, wafted faintly down the dark stair well, came a cry of, "*Chi è?*"

"It's me!" Franco shouted, and we began to ascend the endless stairs. As we climbed, he was no longer talking about his boys, of whom I'd expressed due admiration, but about English players. What did I think of Stanley Matthews? Had I ever seen Shackleton play? His knowledge of names and teams was astonishing, almost compulsive, the fruit of endless poring over a thousand books and magazines.

"It's not the same in England," he said, nostalgically, with a smile that envied me my innocence. "In English football, there's *serietà*."

His pale, thin, weary stepmother opened the door, and he gave her a cursory greeting. I tried to atone with a greater cordiality, knowing it was hopeless to try to change the pattern, to alter the facts of acceptance and defeat. I was Franco's friend, his appendage, and as such, she expected no more from me than she received from him.

In the little dining-room, with its glass-doored cabinet of china and its two worn, chintz-covered armchairs, his father sat, reading *L'Unità*, in his lap lay the plump black and white cat. As I came in, he put down the Communist newspaper and said, in rumbling Tuscan, "Well, then, what about the Americans?"

"I don't know," I said.

"Children," he answered, the old eyes full of gleeful malice, "all of them. But Stalin will take care of them, you'll see."

"Don't bother him with politics," Franco said, swinging out of the room again, to the bathroom.

"He's interested in politics," said the old man, "only cretins aren't interested in politics."

When Franco had washed, he called me into his room to show me a magazine article. It was more of a cell than a room, gloomy, cramped, and windowless, with a narrow bed hard up against one wall. Alongside it ran a bookshelf; I had looked at his curious collection of books many times while waiting for him to arrive. Several were about English football; there was a paper backed copy of *The Constant Nymph*, an English grammar and a little platoon of pamphlets about sex. In that room, in its contents, its very physical dimensions, there seemed to be expressed the whole tragedy of the Italian male.

In the dining-room, the bowls of *pastina in brodo* were already cooling on the table. Franco ate quickly and single-mindedly, less with greed than with a jungle appetite. Every now and again he emerged from a torpor of mastication to pour me some wine or ask me a question, then went back to his food again, crouched over the table, large elbows splayed on either side of his plate. We were cut off on three little islands; he and I, his stepmother, his father, and I felt the usual futile stirrings of discomfort. His father ate slowly, locked in a coma of his own, while the stepmother presided selflessly over the table, with her faint, tragic smile, moving, serving and offering plates with undemanding devotion.

Once, the old man said, "You see what that fool Mayor La Pira wants to do," and Franco responded, mouth full, with ready disgust, "What do you expect, then? He's a friar!"

"They're all friars," his father said, and began with sudden gentleness to feed the cat with scraps from his plate. Their anti-clericalism was one of the links that bound them oddly but unmistakably together. It was a flat without crucifixes, without Sacred Hearts, and their tiny, votary electric bulbs.

After the meal, Franco went with me, as usual, to the 'bus

stop. "My dear!" he cried. "There is nothing in the world greater than football."

"Well. . . ." I said, and at once he laughed. "Right you are! I like to go with women – like a beast! But after that – football!"

When the 'bus arrived he turned home at once, neither waving nor looking round as he walked back purposeful and heavy shouldered.

A few days later, I came across Carlo in the town. It was in Via Tornabuoni, outside the ochre, compact elegance of the Palazzo Antinori. He was wearing a blue mackintosh, and when he half raised his arms in greeting he seemed for a moment like some great, shy bird, about to fly away.

"*Oh! Buon' giorno, dottore!*" I returned the greeting and felt a vague stirring of guilt at the memory of his dismay, on the football ground.

"Have a coffee?"

I agreed without feeling much enthusiasm; between them, he and Franco had cast me for the rôle of prophet from afar, and on such an obstacle, conversation could only founder. His pleasure, besides, seemed excessive. "What luck, what luck!" he kept saying, as we went across the road, towards a bar. "I hoped to get a chance to talk to you, and now I have. I'm mad about English football: Franco's infected me!"

At the zinc counter of the bar, he forcibly prevented my attempt to pay. "You must come round to my house! I told my parents I met you! I want to learn all I can about English football! One of these days, perhaps I'll go there." At this, he became almost ecstatic. "Ah, what an ambition! It's my greatest dream!" As he talked, it seemed to me that he had not only acquired Franco's ideas, but some of his very physical mannerisms. A surface resemblance in their build, the colour of their hair, may partly have suggested this, yet the leonine voice – a surprise to me – was surely an echo of Franco.

I asked him feebly whether he enjoyed his training, and he was off at once on another panegyric. "Of course! Franco's

marvellous: magnificent! You don't know how intelligent
he is: there's nothing about this game that he doesn't understand!"

"And you'll join a professional club, I suppose?"

At this, exuberance seemed to drain away from him. His
mouth drew tight, and he shook his head in dissatisfaction.
"Who knows? Maybe yes, maybe no: it's a question of
temperament. I think I'm talented, but there are too many
things I understand in principle, and don't do right on the
field." He talked on, with the ornate, astonishing fluency of the
working-class Florentine. "With the help of the good Lord,
I'll manage, and if I don't. . . ." The life fled from his face
again; for a moment, despair overwhelmed him. "I don't
know what I'll do. I daren't even think about it. I don't know
anything except football. I read a lot, but I haven't any culture;
I'm ignorant. . . . But excuse me, excuse me, I'm boring you."

I told him he wasn't. "But how can you be interested in these
things; a footballer in a junior team who isn't even a professional yet . . . perhaps never will be."

"But Franco must believe in you," I said, awkwardly.

Carlo shook his great head, and I noticed the powerful,
footballer's neck. "Sometimes he doesn't treat me well. He
knows I'm sensitive. The other day at the ground when he
said those things to me, I didn't sleep all night. In front of
you, too. . . ."

"You'll succeed," I said, "I'm sure you will," but the
consolation seemed the emptier because he so plainly knew it
for the evasion it was.

"Let's hope so," he said, but he brightened when we
parted outside the bar and he said, "I'll 'phone you up, soon:
you must come to dinner."

For some reason, I never did, and it was not until July that
I saw him or Franco again, after a winter spent in Rome. In
the sun, the city had changed, so that it seemed unrelated to
the brooding, ingoing, rejecting Florence of the colder months.
Americans swarmed everywhere like a noisy, passive army:

cropped haired, gloomy young men on mopeds, in shorts, lurid shirts, and three-quarter length socks; girls in sleeveless dresses from Vassar and Radcliffe; legions of blue-haired, middle-aged, spectacled matrons. Everywhere one was followed by the high, harsh clamour of the American female voice. It was as though the native Florentines had been driven from their squares and narrow streets, into the surrounding mountains.

One morning, Franco telephoned to ask me to come with him to Viareggio. "I've got a car!" he shouted, this time in Italian. "I go like a madman, you'll see! I pass everybody on the road!"

It was hard to associate him with a car. For as long as I had known him, he had made his way about on a serviceable grey bicycle; how often had I waited in his flat, when he was late, for the ring of the bell and the tick-tick-tick of the slowly revolving wheel as he climbed the stairs, bicycle hoisted on his shoulder. I was sorry the bicycle had gone; it had somehow been a symbol of integrity, of his contempt for an over-monied sport in which the least of managers, the most banal of players, drove their mille centos and sei centos. This manager was a "blockhead"; that one "don't know nothing about football", but now, some of the sting seemed to be drawn from his contempt; buying the car was a step towards compromise.

Like the bicycle, it, too, was grey. It stood outside my pensione by the parapet of the Arno, sparkling in the early sunshine.

"Fine car, eh?" Franco asked, briefly. Haste consumed him, making him seem more remote and distracted than ever. Upstairs, he had paced about my tiny room, refusing the offer of tea. "*Andiamo, andiamo!* If we don't go now, we'll be caught in the queue; we'll never get there till after mid-day!"

The day was going to be another superb one. It was only twenty past six, and the sun was still low in a bright, cloud-tufted sky, its mellow light dappling the tall, cool palaces, playing without response on the sluggish summer river. Our side of the Arno was still protected by shadow, in a brief morning armistice.

Sitting in the back of the car was a tall, serious boy with wiry brown hair. In an aside, Franco told me, "My right-half: Bertuccini. *Lovely* player! I make a trial of him with Pisa."

He drove rapidly downriver, across the brute stone of the Ponte alla Carraia, through a city for the moment deserted and unspoiled, until at length we were on the white, anonymous stretch of road which would lead us to the coast.

I quickly understood his urgency. As we went on, Franco cutting ruthlessly past other cars, the traffic increased, till finally we were brought to a halt at the end of a line which wound out of sight, towards a toll gate. Franco swore quietly to himself, and drummed his big hands on the steering wheel. Though the windows of the car were open and he was wearing the inevitable open-necked white shirt, sweat was coursing down his red, flushed face in a network of tiny rivulets. "Bertuccini," he said, suddenly, without turning round. "How many cars have we passed?"

"Twenty-three."

"Keep the score, keep the score!"

The caravan moved slowly on until we reached the toll stage: with impatient generosity, Franco brushed away my offer of change. Then we were off again, faster than before, Franco hunched over the wheel, entering now into a private fantasy. He was Fangio, Musso or Stirling Moss, gloriously winning the Mille Miglia; mute, invisible thousands lined the road to cheer. "*Dio boia!*" he shouted, in thicker and thicker Tuscan, "God the hangman! God the dog! Did you see how I went past that one, Bertuccini?" And Bertuccini, he, too, in the fantasy, kept the score; a calm co-driver.

"Seventy . . . seventy-eight . . . Look out, there's that ward-robe behind us again." This for a large American car. And again, "Franco, there's a blonde driving that car in front. Shall I whistle?"

"Yes," said Franco, grimly between his teeth, "whistle," at

which the serious Bertuccini leaned gravely out of the window and let forth a sudden, terrifying blast of sound.

Once, we stopped for petrol. A tanned, attractive girl had got out of a car which already stood at the pump, and Franco prowled round her in a wide semi-circle, his lips pursed in a long, soundless whistle.

Past the cypresses we went, running the hideous gauntlet of coloured wooden advertisements which lined the road on either side – for coffee, petrol, motor tyres. Far off, to our right, one could just see the Apuan Alps swelling through cloud, huge, majestic, and contemptuous.

"How many cars, Bertuccini?"

"A hundred and three."

"And to think," he said, turning to me in proud delight, "that I've only been driving two months! If I'd started at 16, I'd have been another Musso!"

He edged out of the line of cars for another foray, but the advent of a massive truck on the other side of the road forced him to withdraw. Then he was out again, circling precariously round a Lancia, edging his way into a traffic gap, crying in half apology, "Because there's no discipline in Italy. . . ."

At last we were on the outskirts of the vulgar little town, among cool pinewoods, one of a line of cars that had slowed and faltered, now that the goal was in sight.

"Bertuccini!" Franco said. "What a woman I had last night. *Che donnuccia!* Six times, I promise you, six times!"

"*Bella roba*," Bertuccini dutifully said, but already Franco had left the subject, like a discarded toy, and was talking to me. "I have five of my boys here."

"Including Carlo?"

"Yes," he replied, indifferently, "he's here."

"Is he doing well?"

"A blockhead! He will never become a good footballer!"

"Then why do you keep him?"

A heave of the shoulders. "*Chi lo sa?*"

From behind us, Bertuccini said, "He's a good ball player."

Franco agreed with a grimace of indifference.

D*

"And your centre-half?" I asked.

"*Ottimo, ottimo;* always improving."

Slowly we made our way into the little town, bright and noisy and jerry-built, a summer colony of Florence. Each narrow street was indistinguishable from the next, with its pale stone houses, its chromium bars, its *rosticcerie*, its extinct neon signs, its shuffling morning hordes in sandals, shorts, and raffia hats. Across the streets, bright banners advertised the February carnival, but one could not visualize this town in winter. It had too strong an air of transience, a town run up by property-men for a season, which would be dismantled and carried away with terrible, ruthless speed as soon as that season was over.

Franco stopped the car in front of one of the featureless houses and got out, leaving me with Bertuccini. To break the silence, I turned to him and asked, "Will Carlo 'make it', do you think?"

"He may do," the boy replied. "*È un ragazzo serio:* he lives for football. But he doesn't get on with Franco; who knows why?" Who, indeed? "He reads a lot," Bertuccini said, gratuitously, "he's always reading."

At that moment, Franco reappeared, at the head of his boys, great voice thundering like a friendly sergeant major's. Carlo was there, greeting me with simple delight, so that again I felt guilty of a masquerade. The centre-half was there, too, a smiling Hermes, quite without problems, and there were several other boys whom I vaguely remembered from the football stadium. All of them wore shorts, all of them, even Carlo, were tanned and relaxed.

They bundled into the car and we drove on to the sea front, past the swollen abortions of the big hotels. The beach was a benign concentration camp, each section carefully partitioned from the next, each entered by a coloured wooden arch on which one read its name – "Italia", "Two Sisters", "Victory", "Miramare". Our beach was called "La Bella Speranza".

Franco swaggered through the arch as though it had been erected for his triumph, to be met at once by a fusillade of greeting. *"Ciào Franco! Oh, Franco!"* greeted by boys, by men, by toothless women bathing attendants, he himself smiling a smile so cheerful as for once to be almost self-conscious, shortly returning a salutation here, another there. It was at this beach that his young players spent the summer each year, financed by himself, while he scoured the country in search of *ingaggi;* contracts with professional clubs for the following season.

We changed in turn in a small, dark communal dressing room. When I came out, Franco was waiting for me at the end of the boardwalk, a huge, bronzed figure in his blue bathing slip, which seemed no more than a formal dash of colour at his loins. We moved out on to the hot, pale sand, moved between the beach umbrellas, the serried battalions of deck chairs that turned the beach into a congested, three sided square. Everywhere one looked there was noise and intimacy; people sat shoulder to shoulder – except for the grandmothers, wizened in their ugly black – gathered on the shore in talkative knots, moved up and down in phalanx.

Franco had scarcely gone five yards when he was stopped by a man almost as large as himself, whose camera, slung around his bare chest, showed him to be a beach photographer. The man greeted him with a robust mixture of banter and welcome. "What about these footballers of yours? They do nothing all day but go with women!"

"Not true, not true!" Franco roared, looking out to sea. "I've told all of them: no more than three times a week!" And he resumed his march, only to be stopped again by the blue jerseyed *bagnino* and again, seconds later, by a bald young man in bathing trunks.

And so it continued, Franco moving slowly, powerfully up and down the beach with his rolling, swaggering walk, a little posse of young footballers and boys at his shoulders, greeted by all with the amusement tinged with admiration which one might reserve for some faintly comic institution.

After a while, four of us took a blue bathing float and rowed out for a swim. The water was a pale, domesticated green. On it, a motor-boat with a loud hailer coursed tirelessly up and down, blaring its intrusions at the beaches; exhortations to go to this dancing place, to drink that orangeade.

Franco swum well, as one expected, moving through the water with the speed and power of a destroyer: around him, his players gambolled like acolytes about a sea god.

It was past two o'clock before we were back at the pensione for lunch, served *al fresco* on the cool, trellised *terrazza*. Franco sat shirtless at the head of the table, keeping up a roaring, straight faced monologue, fluent, ruthless, cynical, and at times immensely comic. The boys looked on, beaming, and nudging one another with delight, smiling at me from time to time as though to ask, "What do you think of him, eh?"

"Meneghini!" thundered Franco. "What a manager! That no good! *Quel cialtrone!* So he's going to Brazil to study training. And what's he going to find out when he gets there? That at Rio they've got a beach seven miles long, where everybody plays: women, children, old men, cripples!" He took an enormous forkful of spaghetti, and resumed.

When the explosion came it was from the blue, curiously under-determined. The meal was nearly over, we were eating fruit, and Franco was pillorying yet another manager. *"Un' testa di cazzo!* A half-wit! With an idiot's face – like yours!" he added, gesturing vaguely towards Carlo.

Carlo rose at once to his feet, his face contorted, and cried in a high, anguished voice, *"Franco: ma tu sei sadico!* You're a sadist! Why must you always persecute me? It's not fair! I know my own defects perfectly well: I try and do something about them – saying things like that all the time doesn't help me! Well, I can't put up with it any more. Maybe I am ugly. Maybe I never will succeed as a footballer. But you: what's going to happen to you? It's a weakness in you, that you have to keep treating me like this. You'll ruin yourself, Franco, I swear it; you'll ruin yourself!" He stopped for a moment, amidst dead silence. Franco was gaping at him in sheer astonishment, a banana half way to his mouth; as though he had gently prodded a dog which responded by leaping at his throat. The *signora* had come to the open door and was looking on with anxious astonishment. Carlo was crying in earnest, now; tears ran steadily down the tanned cheeks of his gentle, ugly face. He tried to speak again, gulped and stammered, then at last managed to shout, quick and hoarse, "You shouldn't treat me like that! It's not human!" Then he turned clumsily away from the table, upsetting his chair, and pushed his way blindly past the *signora*, into the house.

Silence continued for a full minute after his departure, then Franco said, in a grumbling voice without conviction, "*Ma quel cretino. . . .*"

Two days later, in Florence, Carlo telephoned me. His voice was hesitant and stuttering. "*Dottore*, if you wouldn't mind. . . . I'd like to see you: it's important for me." I agreed to meet him that afternoon, in the Piazza della Repubblica.

In these hot tourist months, the vulgar irrelevance of the piazza no longer gave offence: one did not grudge it to the invading armies; it was theirs as much as the city's, more than the city's, with its four brassy cafés, its air-cooled multiple store and its coloured advertisements.

I was five minutes late, and Carlo was waiting for me, as I knew he would be, sitting, white shirted, under a red umbrella, his crisp sleeves buttoned to the wrists. The café he had chosen was on the Oltrarno, less popular, side, gaudily placarded with English tourist menus, painted on shiny white boards. He rose to his feet, arms moving in the familiar, arrested gesture. "*Dottore . . . dottore . . .* I'm sorry . . . what will you have? A cognac?"

I said I would have a coffee, and made him sit down; his body trembled with agitation. He waited in anguished silence till the waiter came to take our order, then, when the man was barely three paces away, he blurted out, "I wanted to apologize!"

"But why? There's no reason. . . ."

His mouth contracted, he looked down at the table and he said, "I shouldn't have behaved like that. I'm ashamed. It was a great embarrassment for you."

"It wasn't. . . ." I said, ineptly, wishing he'd stop.

"I wanted to explain. There's no excuse: it was unforgiveable; but if you knew the things that had been happening, perhaps you wouldn't judge me too harshly."

I said I was in no position to judge him at all, but he scarcely seemed to hear. "I don't admire Franco any more," he said. "You understand – not as a man. As a coach, yes, he's great; great," and his eyes lit up, as though despite himself. "But I've thought a lot since I saw you, in the winter. I've read a lot, too; I've begun to understand things. And I've realized for one thing that I'm never going to be a great footballer, Franco's right about that . . . no, no, he's right: not because I'm ugly, that's got nothing to do with it; but because I'm not gifted enough: now I know it. And knowing it's made me less dependent on him. I became more objective, you understand; I saw things I didn't see before. As a human being . . . well, now I don't esteem him."

At the table behind us, a loud voice was saying, "So I told him, do you know I can get these things for half the price back home?"

"Since he got the car," Carlo said, in agitation, "I've told him, 'Franco, you'll destroy yourself. Always with women . . . Stick to football, or it'll be the end of you.' He used to spend hours with us, just talking football, but now it's different. He didn't use to care much about money, but now he talks about it all the time."

He leaned across the table earnestly and said, "Perhaps you don't believe me. He shows another side to you. . . . But it's all true, I swear it."

"Then I'm sorry," I said.

"I tell him," Carlo cried, "very well, I'm a failure, I admit it! *Un calciatore fallito!* But with you, Franco, where's it going to end?"

It was more than a year before I visited Florence again. Franco, when I telephoned him, greeted me with his usual roar of welcome. "OOH! *My* dear! You come my house for dinner!"

I came. Nothing had visibly changed, save the arrival of a television set. It stood in the far left hand corner of the dining room, a cynosure, monopolizing attention, strangling conversation. Franco watched it from his place at table, chewing slowly, half-hypnotized. If I spoke to him, he laid a hand on my arm, as though to reassure me of his sympathy, despite his evident distraction. After a while, I asked him what had happened to Carlo.

He shrugged, without taking his eyes from the screen. "That cretin! He doesn't play any more."

"Not at all?"

"He's got a job at a school." He laughed. "You know what he's doing? Teaching gymnastics to boys of six and seven."

"So he gave up football," I said.

"*Ma!* With a face like that."

I telephoned Carlo, and we met the following day, at the same café as before. Once more, he had preceded me, once more, he greeted me with embarrassing enthusiasm. And yet I could sense at once that a change had taken place, as though the very admission of failure, the abandoning of ambition, had given him a sudden independence.

"Franco told me you'd given up football," I said. "I wanted to tell you I was sorry."

"It's very kind of you, very kind." He shook his head, slowly and miserably. "It wasn't easy. You can't give up your greatest love easily. I keep away from football now: if I go to watch Fiorentina, or to Rifredi, it makes me want to cry. I've got a little job now at a school, teaching physical education. It isn't much, but it's a beginning. I'm working for my certificate."

In disillusion, he seemed to have gained not only maturity but authority; perhaps it came from his new job. Afterwards, we walked together through the darkening streets; beside a newspaper kiosk in the nearby *portico*, Franco was arguing loudly with a group of football fans.

When Carlo saw him, he shied, almost imperceptibly, like a

horse recovered from a recent fall; then he went on again and said, his face uncertain, "*Ciào*, Franco."

"*Ciào*, gymnast," Franco said, and greeted me more cordially, "One of my ex-pupils," he addressed the group. "He couldn't play football, so now he's trying to teach gymnastics to babies."

Carlo's face was tense, unsmiling, appallingly vulnerable. He did not reply, but he stared at Franco, now, with neither wonder nor admiration.

"What are you showing them, eh?" Franco asked, "how to get off with women – like you do?"

Carlo's face quivered, and for a moment I thought it was going to disintegrate, as it had at Viareggio. Then he said, "*Caro Franco*, you never change. You never change at all."

I left him at the corner of Via Strozzi; he did not speak again till then. Then he said, "I've failed as a footballer. I've failed."

"But Carlo, you've got your new job."

"I've failed once," he insisted, "in the thing I most wanted to do, most wanted to be. Who knows if I can ever succeed in anything else?"

"I'm sure you will," I said, as we shook hands.

He smiled then, a pale, sad smile and said, "You're too kind to me; but you don't know my deficiencies."

I watched him as he walked away, broad shoulders stooped in his blue mackintosh, moving joylessly among the passers-by. But I did not feel sorry for Carlo.

from A BAD STREAK *1961*

If he's good enough, he's big enough

BRIAN GLANVILLE

Johnny's great trouble was that he was small. Or rather, not so much that he was small, but that *being* small made people think about him as if he was just another small player, if you see what I mean. If he'd had one more stone and another couple of inches, there's nothing could have stopped him. But on the other hand, you never know; maybe if he'd been bigger he wouldn't have been the same player.

I'd known him ever since he came to the club. That's one of the things about being on a local paper, you can follow their careers all the way along. On the other hand a lot of them that are all over you in the beginning hoping you'll write them up don't want to know you as soon as they're there, so it cuts both ways, I suppose. I used to think Johnny would get like that once things started breaking for him, but he never did, he stayed just the same.

He came to the club from amateur football, Barking, but I'd already heard about him from friends who used to watch games on Hackney Marshes. That probably had a lot to do with developing his ball control; on the Marshes the pitches are so small that someone Johnny's size just has to become a ball player in self-defence, otherwise he'd never live in Sunday football.

He was a Stepney lad. He was sixteen when he joined United, and as soon as he came to his seventeenth birthday they signed him pro. I remember the first time I saw him what a shock I had. It was down at the ground and I'd been there to see Jack Dougan, the manager. Coming out, with one or two of the players, I caught sight of this tiny little bloke in the passage.

"Who's that?" I said, "he's not one of the ground staff boys, is he?" That was all I could think he might be, but even that would have been a surprise, he looked so thin and small. He was just a little shrimp of a fellow, as shy as a mouse, with sunken cheeks all hollow, and his face all red and chapped with the cold. He looked as if they were half starving him.

One of the first team players, I can't remember which it was, said, "No, that ain't no ground staff boy, that's the new professional. They've just gone and signed him on."

"Well, now that you've signed him," I said, "you'd better see that he gets something to eat, and all."

"You'd be surprised," they said, "he can do anything with a football."

It was true, too; I saw him in a third team game a few days later. And he wasn't just one of these players who can do it when nobody's treading on their toes or breathing down their neck. You get plenty of 'em will take the ball out on the practice ground and practically make it talk, but Johnny could do it in the middle of a match, with his half-back trying to kick him up in the air. Back-heels, flicks, lobbing the ball over his head, sending his man the wrong way, he could do the lot; and the big thing was that he wasn't just showing off, he always did it with a purpose. Anyway, you could see from his face that he wasn't getting much fun out of it. Dead serious, never smiling, always looking as if his bonus depended on it.

I never really got to talk to him much the first few seasons he was there. He was never in the first team, and he only played in the Combination side a couple of times before he went in the Army. Then they sent him off to somewhere like Hong Kong and that was it for the next two years; the only football he played was against Chinamen.

When he came back, he still hadn't got any bigger. The first time I saw him I said, just joking, "Hullo, Johnny, I thought they'd put a bit of weight on you in the Army. Don't they eat rice out there no more?"

"Yes," he says, very serious, "but it upset me. I couldn't take it. Made me ill, it did."

From then on I used to talk to him quite a lot, though he never said much at any time, and to most people that he didn't know, he wouldn't say a word, he'd just shut up and sort of edge away. Perhaps he spoke to me because I was an East London boy, too.

He got into the Combination team permanently after a couple of months, and whenever I saw him he was making the rest of them look silly. He couldn't only control a ball, he knew how to use it, too, every sort of pass; through balls, square balls, reverse passes and even cross balls; he could hit a ball so well it surprised me. I said to Jack Dougan one day, "Why don't you put him in the League team, Jack?"

"No," he said. "Too small."

"Well," I said, "if they're big enough, they're good enough, and he looks good enough to me in Combination football."

"Combination stuff's a different thing," he said, which you couldn't deny. "You've got time to trap a ball then look round and see what you'll do with it. They'd eat him alive in the First Division. What'd happen if he came up against a wing-half like Alex Forbes or Jimmy Scoular?"

"I think he'd give them the run-around," I said.

"*No*," he said, "he'd never live with 'em. And on the heavy grounds he wouldn't last beyond the first twenty minutes."

"Maybe," I said, because you don't argue with managers if you can help it, least of all if you're covering the local club. "Why don't you try building him up?"

"We've tried," he said, "it's useless. We thought he might strengthen up a bit in the Army, but you can see for yourself. We've sent him to doctors, put him on special diets, given him special exercises, and you might as well save your time. He'll never get any bigger than what he is."

I didn't say anything to Johnny, but I thought, if that's the way they feel about him here, he'd be better off trying somewhere else.

It was two years before he got a chance in the first team. Every now and then, one of the inside-forwards would drop out with an injury, and I'd think, Johnny'll go in, now; but it was always somebody else. If it had been in the middle of February and thick mud all the time you could have accepted it that Jack didn't want to risk him on a heavy ground, but when it happened in August or the end of March, you could tell there must be other reasons. Jack never said what they were in so many words, but it was obvious that what he *really* objected to was Johnny's style of play. He'd built up the team on this give-and-go plan; you pushed the ball to the man that was nearest you then you put your head down and ran like hell, hoping he'd give you a return.

Johnny didn't like to play like that. He liked to hold the ball and maybe beat a couple of men until he'd put someone in the clear. "It's no good, Don," he used to say, "my style don't suit him. Give it and run, that's what he wants, hurry, hurry, hurry all the time. That ain't football."

"You try and tell Jack that it ain't," I said. "What are you going to do, put in for a transfer?"

"I dunno," he said, and I'd say he looked sad except that he always did, and talking now he didn't look no sadder than usual. "It wouldn't do me no good; who knows me? I never been in the first team, not once."

"Yeah, but people have seen you," I said. "Other clubs' scouts are always watching Combination games."

"They haven't put in no bid, though, have they?" he says.

Well, about a month after that they gave him his chance. Jack couldn't help himself, with three of his inside-forwards out, but what made it funny was it was just the sort of pitch he'd said Johnny could never live on; thick mud right up to the ankles. Poor old Johnny, I thought, and I had an idea Jack might be choosing him out of spite, so he could turn round after the game to the people that had been knocking him and say, "There you are, what did I tell you?"

I saw Johnny outside just before he went in to strip. "Heavy pitch today, Johnny," I said, trying to be sympathetic.

"I don't mind that," he says, "stops 'em turning, see? A little feller like me can get in and out while they're still stuck there."

While he was telling me he was twisting and turning like he was already on the field; it was a habit he had, he liked to demonstrate things. Like I remember in a café once I said to him, "With ball control like you got, John, you must do a lot of ball practice," and he said, "Oh, yes, I take a ball out and throw it against the wall and then I . . . *kick* it!" and caught me a crack right under the table.

I'll always remember that game, and I'll always remember the first time Johnny had the ball. There was a sort of buzz in the Press Box when he came on to the field; none of them – at least the national boys – had seen him before, and hadn't heard of him either, which wasn't surprising if you had to sit next to them week after week like I did, telling them players' Christian names. But you could understand their being surprised. I'd got used to Johnny being so small, long ago, but out there on the field he looked like a little schoolboy among a lot of grown men. Somebody said, "He'll get murdered on a pitch like this," and I was half afraid of it myself.

Then, about a couple of minutes after the kick-off, the ball came through to him from a long clearance. Instead of heading it on, like he would have been entitled to do, with three great Sunderland oxes moving in at once, he let it fall on to his right foot, hooked it over his head, caught it on his thigh and then, before it could touch the ground, he'd volleyed it straight to his outside-left, without as much as looking in his direction.

For a moment everything was dead quiet, then it was like the whole stadium exploded. There was cheers and applause and clapping, but the sort of applause you could tell had surprise in it as well. People couldn't believe what they'd seen. Soon after that he got the ball again and this time he sent the bloke the wrong way with that body-swerve of his – nobody could swerve the same as Johnny, it was like a clockwork toy, snap-snap! first one way, then back the other – and they were cheering him again.

After that you heard a roar go up every time he got the ball. He was having a wonderful game, everything seemed to be coming off for him, swerves, flicks, backheels, the lot. At half-time in the Press room everyone was talking about him so hard they didn't even have time to complain about the tea, and I remember standing there and grinning like I was his brother or something and saying, "I told you so, what did I tell you?"

"He'll never keep it up," they were saying, "second half he's bound to fade," and I was a little bit afriad of that myself, though I didn't let on I was.

Second half though, he's as good as the first, and five minutes from time he dummied through on his own and scored a beautiful goal; sent the keeper one way and just flicked it in the other. I thought the stand was going to come down with the noise.

Of course, I was delighted for Johnny, though in one way I suppose I was just a little bit sorry as well, from my own point of view, because I'd sort of come to look on him as a private discovery.

After the match I got a lift in the same car as he did. He was very quiet, just the same as usual, in fact if you hadn't been there you might have thought he'd had a bad game, instead of a blinder. When everyone congratulated him he just said, "Thanks very much, thanks," in that way of his, as if he wished they'd let him alone.

"Cheer up, Johnny," I said, "you're a star now."

"*Nar*," he said, "I'm not a star. Who are you kidding?"

"Well, you look at the papers tomorrow morning," I said, "and see if I'm not right."

The next week you could hardly open a paper without reading about him. United find new soccer genius. Tom Thumb soccer star. Another Alex James. Soccer's mighty midget, and all the rest of it. Mind you, he was worth it in my opinion, but I was a bit worried for him, it was so much to live up to. You can finish a player with praise a lot easier than you can with blame.

For the next three weeks, he stayed in the team; after a debut like that, he couldn't very well be dropped and besides, Joe Edwards still wasn't fit. All the publicity just seemed to have made him shyer than ever and on the two away trips they had, he just sat in a corner of the carriage without saying anything to anybody. He didn't even join in the solo.

He only came out of his shell about once. I said to him one day, kidding like, "I been reading about you, Johnny, all about your constructive play. How do you do it?" But he thought I was serious because he tapped himself on the head and said, "You got to have it up 'ere, you know."

"Well, you've got it and all, haven't you?" I said.

I'd expected he wouldn't have much time left for me, now he was in the headlines and all the big boys wanted to say hallo to him, instead of which he seemed to think of me as a sort of protector. When someone came up to us, a journalist or just a hanger on, he'd say to me out of the corner of his mouth, "Who's 'e? Is *he* all right?" And sometimes I'd say yes and others I'd say, "You want to watch your step."

After those four matches, Joe Edwards was fit again and Johnny went out. "I expected it, Don," he said, "I expected it. Joe can't do nothing wrong for Dougan. Anyhow, you can't have two constructive inside-forwards, can you?"

Personally I thought Johnny was right. Jack's excuse was, "Can't have Johnny in every week, we don't want him to wear himself out, he's so frail," and mind you he hadn't been the same in his last two games as he was in the first two. But even when all the papers had been raving about Johnny and calling him a future international, Jack had been very guarded. Obviously he couldn't afford to knock the kid, but he was saying things like, "Yes, he's doing well, but he isn't strong, you know." Besides, he'd built his whole forward-line round Joe and I suppose you could understand him not wanting to change it.

Still, it was crazy to think of Johnny going back in the reserves after the sensation he'd made, and there was a lot of fuss about it in the nationals. Probably if there hadn't been, Jack might have let him go, but like it was he was going to look silly if he transferred him and Johnny took up at once where he'd left off with United. So although I believe there were one or two enquiries, nothing came of it.

Luckily for Jack, United got into a winning spell, so if anybody criticized him over Johnny, he could come back with the old one about not wanting to change a winning team. Johnny only had five more first team games the rest of that season, three of them good and two of them bad, and after a while the nationals found something else to make a fuss about, like they always do.

Johnny took it all as if it was what he'd expected. I used to go round now and again to Stepney, where he lived. His father had a little tobacconist shop in one of those very poor streets off the Commercial Road, and there were three other brothers and sisters. His mother used to take me aside and say, "Why don't you talk to him, Don? Make him do something about it. He don't think enough of himself, that's his trouble. He's always letting himself get pushed out of the way, always has." But it wasn't easy to get Johnny to *say* things, let alone *do* them. Even at home he'd sit in a corner with a magazine or a cowboy book and wouldn't open his mouth much and later, when there was telly, he'd just watch that.

"He don't say much," his mother said, "but he *feels* things, Johnny does. He's too sensitive." So when he did open up at all about the game, it always came as a bit of surprise to hear him talk such sense. He had all the others pretty well weighed up, on the field and off it, too. I remember him saying about Eddie Miller, the right half, who was always hanging on the whole time and never giving a good pass, "That other fellow . . . you'd think it was his ball."

He understood about Jack Dougan, too. "The longer he keeps me out the less chance there'll be of him putting me in. Old Jack don't like admitting he's wrong."

Next season he was in and out of the team again. One morning when I arrived he came up to me and he said, "I done it."

"Gone on the list," he said. "I asked him this morning and he said I could go."

"It's about time," I said, when I'd had a moment to digest it. "I hope you get a good club soon."

But he didn't. He didn't get any club at all. It was beyond me, I couldn't understand it. Here he was, the best ball player in the

First Division, he'd proved what he could do when they'd given him the chance, never mind how small he was; clubs were supposed to be crying out for inside-forwards and yet there wasn't one of them would take a chance with him.

It was about then he got married, which was another surprise to me. I'd never seen his fiancée, he hadn't brought her along to any matches as far as I knew, but then that was like Johnny.

One day he said to me, just like that, out of the blue, "Do you want to come to my wedding?" I thought for a moment he must be joking; with anyone else I'd have *known* they were joking.

"I didn't know you *knew* no girls," I told him, but all he said was, "Her name's Jill, we haven't got a house yet. It's going to be on Wednesday fortnight."

I went along, of course, and quite a few of the players were there, too. I was surprised by his wife, she wasn't bad looking at all, though very quiet and shy, just like him.

After a midweek reserve match a few weeks later he said to me in that way he had – all of a sudden without looking at you – "Come and have a coffee?" Most of the boys used to go to the "Green Dragon" round the corner but if you asked Johnny he'd always say, "Nar, you know I don't drink," and if he went at all it was only to keep them company.

In the café, he brought us a couple of cups of tea then he said, "I'm going to change me style."

"What do you want to do that for?" I said.

"I've got to stay here, haven't I?" he said. "There's no one else wants me. I've got me wife now, and I'm still on top money with United. Well, then, if they won't change for me, then I got to fit in, see? I got to change for them."

"I think you're wrong, Johnny," I said, "but I can see your point."

A week or two after that Jack Dougan came up to me and said, "Johnny's playing better."

"Oh, yes?" I said, pretending like I didn't know nothing.

"Yes," he said, "he's moving the ball quicker now, he's getting on with the game. He'll fit in better in the League side than what he did."

It broke my heart whenever I saw him play now. He was getting rid of the ball as if it was red hot, you wouldn't have recognized him for the same player, and of course not being his natural game, he couldn't even do it as well as the rest. When he did get into the first team, now and again, he was just so-so, not good, not bad, and it was inevitable that people started to say, "Johnny hasn't got it no more; he's been in the reserves too long."

One day he was giving me a lift home – he'd gone and bought a car – when all of a sudden he said, "I'm going back again."

"I'm glad to hear it," I said, because I knew what he meant. To understand Johnny, you've always got to use a bit of telepathy.

"It's me Mum," he said. "She came down here to see the last game and she cried all over the week-end. She said to me, 'You'll never be nothing so long as you go on playing like that. You might as well get 'ung for a sheep as for a lamb.' "

"That's what I always thought about it myself," I said.

"I should of listened to you," he said, "but there's times you get in a tangle."

Perhaps it was as well he was in the reserves for the next couple of games, so Jack couldn't see him up to his old tricks again, because two weeks later Joe Edwards got an ankle done, and Johnny was in the semi-final team. They'd had a good Cup run that season, after nearly going out in the first round at Stockport of all places.

"Well done, Johnny," I said, "make a name, son," but he said, "Villa Park's an unlucky ground for me, Don. I never done well there."

You certainly wouldn't have thought it in the first half. Johnny had 'em going all ways, it was as good as that first game of his, against Sunderland. You know how big that Bolton defence is, they just towered over Johnny, but he was making them look silly every time he had the ball. United were two up inside the first quarter-of-an-hour. I was enjoying every minute of it, as you can imagine, and thinking that even if Jack left Johnny out for the Final, which would be difficult after a show like this, he could go to any club in the country after today.

Just before half-time he got the ball and suddenly started going through on his own, wiggle one way, wiggle the other, feinting to pass then keeping on, until all he'd got in his way was the goalkeeper. The 'keeper slung himself at his feet, it was all he could do, then they were both of them rolling all over the turf. I could tell it was something bad from the way Johnny kept moving and twitching, as if he couldn't keep still in any position, it hurt him so much.

They carried him off on a stretcher and up to half-time I was so worried I could hardly write. It was true he hadn't often been injured in the past, but that was because he was so quick he could keep out of trouble. At half-time the word came up – broken leg, suspected multiple fracture.

United hung on to win 2—1, but Johnny didn't go back to town with them; they kept him in hospital in Birmingham and it was three weeks before they sent him home. I went to see him the second day he was back.

His wife opened the door and her eyes were all red from crying. Johnny was lying there in bed with his leg in plaster and you'd never have thought a little thin bloke like him could lose so much weight. "Hullo, me old friend," he said, and it was terrible seeing him trying to smile.

"Hullo, John," I said, "you're a nice one, pulling out like that just when the team needed you."

"I know," he says, "ain't I?"

"Well," I said, still trying to make a joke of it, though it wasn't easy, "going to be ready for the Final?"

"No, Don," he says, "this is the end. I may play again, but I won't never be the same."

"Don't say that, John," I said, "you'll be all right," but he just gave me a smile and didn't even answer. After ten minutes I couldn't stand it in that room any more.

"Don't worry, John," I said, "you'll set 'em alight again, you'll see."

Then I ran down the stairs and out of the door and I was practically crying myself, because all I could see was him smiling that smile, and I knew even then that he was right.

from A BAD STREAK *1961*

Playing Away

HAROLD PINTER

GUS: What town are we in? I've forgotten.

BEN: I've told you. Birmingham.

GUS: Go on! (*He looks with interest about the room.*) That's in the Midlands. The second biggest city in Great Britain. I'd never have guessed. (*He snaps his fingers.*) Eh, it's Friday today, isn't it? It'll be Saturday tomorrow.

BEN: What about it?

GUS (*excited*): We could go and watch the Villa.

BEN: They're playing away.

GUS: No, are they? Caarr! What a pity.

BEN: Anyway, there's no time. We've got to get straight back.

GUS: Well, we have done in the past, haven't we? Stayed over and watched a game, haven't we? For a bit of relaxation.

BEN: Things have tightened up, mate. They've tightened up.

(GUS *chuckles to himself.*)

GUS: I saw the Villa get beat in a cup tie once. Who was it against now? White shirts. It was one-all at half-time. I'll never forget it. Their opponents won by a penalty. Talk about drama. Yes, it was a disputed penalty. Disputed. They got beat two-one, anyway, because of it. You were there yourself.

BEN: Not me.

GUS: Yes, you were there. Don't you remember that disputed penalty?

BEN: No.

GUS: He went down just inside the area. Then they said he was just acting. I didn't think the other bloke touched him myself. But the referee had the ball on the spot.

BEN: Didn't touch him! What are you talking about? He laid him out flat!

GUS: Not the Villa. The Villa don't play that sort of game.

BEN: Get out of it.

(*Pause.*)

GUS: Eh, that must have been here, in Birmingham.

BEN: What must?

GUS: The Villa. That must have been here.

BEN: They were playing away.

GUS: Because you know who the other team was? It was the Spurs. It was Tottenham Hotspur.

BEN: Well, what about it?

GUS: We've never done a job in Tottenham.

BEN: How do you know?

GUS: I'd remember Tottenham.

(BEN *turns on his bed to look at him.*)

BEN: Don't make me laugh, will you?

(BEN *turns back and reads.* GUS *yawns and speaks through his yawn.*)

GUS: When's he going to get in touch? (*Pause.*) Yes, I'd like to see another football match. I've always been an ardent football fan. Here, what about coming to see the Spurs tomorrow?

BEN (*tonelessly*): They're playing away.

GUS: Who are?

BEN: The Spurs.

GUS: Then they might be playing here.

BEN: Don't be silly.

GUS: If they're playing away they might be playing here. They might be playing the Villa.

BEN (*tonelessly*): But the Villa are playing away.

(*Pause. An envelope slides under the door, right.* GUS *sees it. He stands, looking at it.*)

GUS: Ben.

BEN: Away. They're all playing away.

from THE DUMB WAITER *1960*

His Normal Game

HAROLD PINTER

OLD MAN: Compressed. I thought he was looking compressed, didn't you, Fred?

BARMAN: Depressed. He means depressed.

SEELEY: No wonder. What about that game on Saturday, eh?

KEDGE: You were going to tell me. You haven't told me yet.

BARMAN: What game? Fulham?

SEELEY: No, the firm. Firm's got a team, see? Play on Saturdays.

BARMAN: Who'd you play?

SEELEY: Other firms.

BARMAN: You boys in the team, are you?

KEDGE: Yes. I've been off sick though. I didn't play last week.

BARMAN: Sick, eh? You want to try one of my sausages, don't he, Henry?

OLD MAN: Oh, ay, yes.

KEDGE: What happened with the game, then?

They move to the bench.

SEELEY: Well, when you couldn't play, Gidney moved Albert to left back.

KEDGE: He's a left half.

SEELEY: I know he's a left half. I said to Gidney myself, I said to him, look, why don't you go left back, Gidney? He said, no, I'm too valuable at centre half.

KEDGE: He didn't, did he?

SEELEY: Yes. Well, you know who was on the right wing, don't you? Connor.

KEDGE: Who? Tony Connor?

SEELEY: No. You know Connor. What's the matter with you? You've played against Connor yourself.

KEDGE: Oh – whatsisname – Micky Connor.

SEELEY: Yes.

KEDGE: I thought he'd given up the game.

SEELEY: No, what are you talking about? He plays for the printing works, plays outside right for the printing works.

KEDGE: He's a good ballplayer, that Connor, isn't he?

SEELEY: Look. I said to Albert before the kick off, Connor's on the right wing, I said, play your normal game. I told him six times before the kick off.

KEDGE: What's the good of him playing his normal game? He's a left half, he's not a left back.

SEELEY: Yes, but he's a defensive left half, isn't he? That's why I told him to play his normal game. You don't want to worry about Connor, I said, he's a good ballplayer but he's not all that good.

KEDGE: Oh, he's good, though.

SEELEY: No one's denying he's good. But he's not all that good. I mean, he's not tip-top. You know what I mean?

KEDGE: He's fast.

SEELEY: He's fast, but he's not all that fast, is he?

KEDGE (doubtfully): Well, not all that fast . . .

SEELEY: What about Levy? Was Levy fast?

KEDGE: Well, Levy was a sprinter.

SEELEY: He was a dasher, Levy. All he knew was run.

KEDGE: He could move.

SEELEY: Yes, but look how Albert played him! He cut him off, he played him out the game. And Levy's faster than Connor.

KEDGE: Yes, but he wasn't so clever, though.

SEELEY: Well, what about Foxall?

KEDGE: Who? Lou Foxall?

SEELEY: No, you're talking about Lou Fox, I'm talking about Sandy Foxall.

KEDGE: Oh, the winger.

SEELEY: Sure. He was a very smart ballplayer, Foxall. But

what did Albert do? He played his normal game. He let him come. He waited for him. And Connor's not as clever as Foxall.

KEDGE: He's clever though.

SEELEY: Gawd blimey, I know he's clever, but he's not as clever as Foxall, is he?

KEDGE: The trouble is, with Connor, he's fast too, isn't he?

SEELEY: But if Albert would have played his normal game! He played a game foreign to him.

KEDGE: How many'd Connor get?

SEELEY: He made three and scored two.

from A NIGHT OUT *1961*

Note: For two other football stories see "The Mine in the Goal" (page 353) and "Goalkeepers are Crazy" (page 358).

PART II

Great Games

"Follow the crowds to where the turnstiles click.
The terraces fill. *Hoompa*, blares the brassy band.
Saturday afternoon has come to Ninian Park. . . ."

DANNIE ABSE *The Game*

Arsenal v. Huddersfield Town, 1930

ROLAND ALLEN

Sometimes it is necessary to insist that the Cup Final is primarily a football match. There are the build-up, the drama, personalities, the poignant and emotional singing of *Abide With Me,* the massed bands, the community singing, the tall sailor in front of the Navy band, the thrill of getting there and getting away again. In this particular final there was the queer twist of fate which brought it about that the team which Mr Herbert Chapman was guiding through the first stages of a spectacular run of success should meet and beat the team which he had taken to the top, and then left, to score a second personal triumph in London.

Under the managership of Chapman, Huddersfield Town had won the League Championship for three successive seasons from 1924 and had beaten the famous Preston North End in a Cup final. The team had created a new football style, based on the roving forward and the stopper centre-half-back. It had been criticized and debated, but Chapman had persisted with it and had slowly and patiently built up an Arsenal team on the same pattern – a team which also won the League championship three times in succession and played in three Wembley Cup finals under his managership. Herbert Chapman had every reason for being a proud man that day. No doubt some of his pride was in the fact that Huddersfield Town put up a great battle, and played football of such tenacity and quality that Arsenal did no more than scrape home.

There were bits of unusual drama even in the game itself. Alex James scored a goal. That was unusual. The short Scot with the long shorts made a speciality of creating the opportunities for others to score. The goal itself was unusual. James was fouled and fell. He bounced up like a piece of rubber, shuffled for a few steps, placed the ball at the spot where the rules had been infringed and took the kick without waiting to straighten himself up again. He sent a short pass with the side of his boot to Clifford Bastin, his outside-left, trotted into position for the return pass, and scored. Some discussion as to whether he took the free kick before he had been signalled to do so by the referee was disposed of by Mr Tom Crew, the official in charge, who said later on that James made a raised-eyebrows appeal for permission to take the kick and Mr Crew waved him on. Quick thinking. James was good at that.

Once upon a time I was discussing with a world famous international inside-right the men we would pick for a world football team. We agreed upon Alex James as the inside-left, but my friend made the reservation that "You could not afford to have more than one of him in any team". It was a great compliment. If there was one quality James possessed it was his individuality. There never has been another footballer like him. There never will be. He was short, stocky, puckish looking, impudent in the daring with which he ambled and shuffled and held on to the ball until he had the other side baffled and exasperated and wondering what he was going to do with it. He was the supreme football jester. Only a genius can get away with that. I met him at the 1946 final and he had not altered a lot. There was the same shy grin, the same shrewd comment on the game, in the same broad accent which it took years to master.

Having scored the one goal, James flung ahead the long, raking, perfectly judged pass into the wide open space he had created to make it inevitable that Yorkshireman Jack Lambert should score the second goal to win a final everybody there will always remember – those behind the scenes not entirely for the football.

Arsenal, who had many talented forwards during their sensational run in the thirties, probably had their greatest forward-line in this match. Joe Hulme, professor of controlled speed who would make crowds sway like ripe corn in a half gale, cultured David Jack, "Honest" Jack Lambert, James, and Clifford Bastin, the boy from Devon with the football brains of a grown and experienced footballer who read James like a book and took the little Scot's word for it that if he remained in his place on the wing he would be certain of getting the ball, at the right time and in the right place.

Preddy, a daring goalkeeper, was well covered by shrewd Tom Parker, captain and master of positional play and Eddie Hapgood, young in the service of the Arsenal and destined in the years that followed to achieve world-wide fame as a footballer, break the record for caps for England and play for his country in fourteen other countries in Europe. Baker, Seddon, and Bob John, a clockwork half-back line, made up a great football machine.

Huddersfield Town, too, had their outstanding personalities. I should start the wrong way round, with W. H. Smith, the outside-left, in sorting them out. He had been with the club for seventeen seasons. He played all the way through with the speed and spirit of a man half his age. He had much to do with the fact that during a storming second half Huddersfield Town had us wondering which team Herbert Chapman would congratulate at the finish.

Turner, in goal, was sound rather than spectacular. Goodall, the right-back, was in the 1928 Cup final and was captain of England that same season in the match of the Scottish wizards, in which the Scots forwards put up a show which is still talked about as the greatest ever seen in any football match. Spence, his partner, had been a centre half-back. The centre half-back was the famous Tom Wilson and, by way of coincidence, Campbell, the left half-back, was a member of the Blackburn Rovers team which beat Huddersfield Town in that same 1928 Cup final.

On the opposite wing to W. H. Smith was that laughing cavalier, Alex Jackson. He was the star of that 1928 Wembley Wizards Scottish forward line. He had scored nine of the eleven goals which his team had obtained in the Cup competition. An elusive footballer, he was liable to steal inside as if on his tip-toes and bob up unexpectedly in a place where he was not supposed to be and take a defence completely by surprise.

Bob Kelly, the inside-right, had played thirteen times for

England – again including that 1928 affair – and it was not an unlucky number for either the player or his country. He knew how to hold a ball and when to let it go. One of football's craftsmen, Davies, the centre forward, had come from Stoke, and Raw, the inside-left, held down the tricky job of taking over from Clem Stephenson, who had played for Huddersfield Town, and for Aston Villa *against* them and been on the winning side each time. It should now be clear why it is said of Cup finals that there is also some football.

Just to round off an extraordinary day, a sinister, cigar-shaped monster, the German Graf Zeppelin, floated lazily low over the ground while the match was going through its most lively and exciting phase. Few people took more than a glance at this ominous portent of the future. So far as I saw not a player did more than raise his eyes for a split second to look at the thing. They were all too busy.

ARSENAL: Preedy; Parker, Hapgood; Baker, Seddon, John; Hulme, Jack, Lambert, James, Bastin.

HUDDERSFIELD TOWN: Turner; Goodall, Spence; Naylor, Wilson, Campbell; Jackson, Kelly, Davies, Raw, Smith.

from ALL THE CUP FINALS *1947*

$\mathcal{N}$ewcastle United v. $\mathcal{A}$rsenal, 1932

ROLAND ALLEN

If the camera cannot lie – an assertion which is open to challenge – it can inspire argument and controversy. When Richardson, the inside-right of Newcastle United, centred the ball for Allen to score the equalizing goal from the centre-forward position, a discussion was begun which lasted for several weeks. Some people said the ball was over the goal line when Richardson hooked it over towards Allen. Others as vigorously asserted that the ball was just in play. The Laws of the game state that the ball is out of play "when it has wholly crossed the goal-line or touch-line whether on the ground or in the air."

In this case the ball was in the air. It had bounced. Davidson, the centre-half of Newcastle United, had nipped in to intercept a long clearance by Eddie Hapgood, the Arsenal left-back and had, without hesitating, sent the ball swinging down the right wing, some little way inside the touchline. Richardson, the Newcastle United inside-right, had moved out to the wing a few seconds earlier when his partner Boyd had cut inside. He went on what looked like a desperately speculative chase after the ball. He got to it, anyhow, and made what was, in the difficult circumstances, an extremely accurate centre. The Arsenal defenders were appealing to the referee. He kept play going on. After he had pointed upfield to indicate that his decision was for a goal Mr W. P. Harper of Stourbridge disregarded further protests from the Arsenal players. In which, so far, as the principle of the thing goes, he was undoubtedly right.

The referee is the sole judge of what is right or wrong in a football game of which he has been given charge. "His decision on points of fact connected with the game shall be final so far as the result of the game is concerned," says the law. Mr Harper, who was one of a select few referees who got a cheer all to themselves when they trotted on to a football pitch decided that it was a goal. That is a question of fact. Therefore it was a goal. Press pictures and, later on, slowed down cinema shots, were produced and shown to support the assertion that the ball had been over the line. Taking no sides in this matter I might mention that I made a careful study of all the available press pictures and saw the film slowed down and actually stopped at the crucial point, and I still would not be prepared to assert as dogmatically as a lot of people did that the ball had been over the line at the moment when Richardson sent over his centre. Press and film pictures are taken from queer oblique viewpoints. They can lead you astray as I know from many years of experience in dealing with them. Perhaps the ball was, or perhaps it was not in play according to the letter of the law. There may be argument about that. There still is. Mr Harper having given it as a goal, it was a goal. There can be no argument about that. Allen also scored the other for Newcastle and the great Welsh International half-back Bob John, playing at outside-left, scored for Arsenal.

If any Cup final was a classic this was one. Arsenal were just into their stride on a run of successes which lasted ten years and during which they won the Cup twice and the League Championship five times. In this particular season they not only lost the Cup when they seemed to have one hand on it, but they missed the championship by a couple of points to Everton. Newcastle United have always been noted for the culture of their football. In this game they also proved that they had the right reaction to a big occasion, for Arsenal had scored first and it is said that the side which scores first in the Cup final wins the Cup. That is actually no more true than the statement that all the goals at Wembley have been scored at the same end.

It cannot be decided whether, and how far, the incident of the doubtful goal affected the Arsenal players. I knew nearly all of them and have never heard one of them complain that it did. Footballers rarely squeal, and they do not like the few who do. Arsenal fought every second of the way. The contrast in the style of the two teams and the clever things they did at top speed were a rare football feast and even the hardiest partisans were prepared to praise and cheer the skill of the other side.

One of the most skilful players on the Newcastle side was Sam Weaver, the left half-back, who achieved a reputation for sending a throw-in farther than almost any other player and keeping within the law. It could be said that he would have played more often than he did for England if this accomplishment had not distracted attention from the extremely high standard of the rest of his football. Nelson, the Newcastle right full back, who strode like a guardsman and played football with similar disciplined accuracy had a lot to do with the Newcastle victory. But this is not a match in which any particular player should be picked out. In the best sense of the term it was the victory of a team.

NEWCASTLE UNITED: McInroy; Nelson, Fairhurst; McKenzie, Davison, Weaver; Boyd, Richardson, Allen, McEnemy, Lang.

ARSENAL: Moss; Parker, Hapgood; Jones (C.), Roberts, Male; Hulme, Jack, Lambert, Bastin, John.

from ALL THE CUP FINALS *1947*

Arsenal v. Walsall, 1933

CLIFF BASTIN

When the draw was made for the Third Round of the F.A. Cup of 1932-33, the red, numbered ball which represented Arsenal came out of the little green bag together with that which denoted Walsall. Walsall were to play at home.

There seemed to be little doubt over the outcome of the game. Arsenal at the time were coasting smoothly along at the head of the First Division, while Walsall were buried deep among the obscure clubs of the Third Division South. Admittedly, the Midland team were the proud possessors of a hundred per cent record at home that season, but the opposition against which the record had been achieved was hardly of the highest calibre. Besides, Walsall had not managed to win away from home that season, and a team which could not even bring off a victory on the ground of a Third Division opponent would hardly seem to have much chance of holding the mighty Arsenal – even if they were playing at home.

Thus reasoned the sporting public of England, when it perused the Third Round draw.

At Highbury, we were all exceptionally keen to make up for last season's heart-breaking defeat in the Cup Final, and it did

E*

not seem to us that Walsall were likely to prevent us from breaking through to the Fourth Round. Nevertheless, we were not too happy about our draw.

We never liked to play against Third Division teams. Such teams, when pitted against the glamorous Arsenal, found themselves in a position of having everything to gain and nothing to lose. Consequently, they would fling themselves into the game with reckless abandon, and, win, lose, or draw, the gashed, bruised legs of the Arsenal players, after the game was over, would bear grim testimony to their misguided enthusiasm. The Third Division footballer may not be a Soccer artist, but when it comes to a heavy tackle, he ranks with the best.

As was now the Arsenal custom, we went down to Brighton to tune up for the Cup tie. Whether the opposition was to be Walsall or Aston Villa made no difference to this routine.

At this period, a severe influenza epidemic was sweeping the country, and three of our regular team – Eddie Hapgood, Bob John, and Jack Lambert – fell victims to it, shortly before our match was due to be played. Further, Joey Hulme was in the middle of one of those bad periods which come to even the greatest of footballers at one time or another, and, in consequence, Mr Chapman had some team selection problems on his hands.

In an endeavour to solve them, he chose Tommy Black, who had recently joined Arsenal from a Scottish junior team, to replace Eddie Hapgood. Norman Sidey, our reserve centre-half, took over at left-half, from Bob John; while to take over from Lambert and Joey Hulme, Mr Chapman chose, respectively, Charlie Walsh and Billy Warnes. In doing so, he made two of his very rare mistakes.

Warnes, an amateur international who had come to us from the Isthmian League club, Woking, was entirely the wrong kind of player for such a match as we were going to play. Essentially an artistic footballer, robust methods were liable to shake him off his game, and he was very chary of involving himself in a full-blooded tackle.

Charlie Walsh had long been trying to bring Chapman round

to his own way of thinking – that he was the best centre-forward on Arsenal's books – so far, without success. In this match, however, Chapman gave him his chance. He missed it, all too emphatically.

Almost as soon as play had started, on the microscopic Walsall ground, it became quite clear to me that all our fears about the tactics our opponents might employ were fully justified. As soon as the ball came out to me on the left wing I was blatantly fouled by the Walsall right-back, who bowled me over without ceremony. No foul was given, however. Throughout the game, the referee was curiously lenient.

Walsall could not have complained had five of their men, at least, been sent off the field in the first quarter of an hour. Arsenal were awarded ten free-kicks in as many minutes after the first whistle. Compared with this apology for a football match, the replayed Semi-Final against Hull City, three seasons back, had been child's play.

Soon after the kick-off, big Herbie Roberts sustained a cut eye, in a violent aerial collision, and was handicapped accordingly. Do not misinterpret me. I don't want to level an indictment at the Walsall players. They played, a little too vigorously, perhaps, the game which was right in the circumstances. If David had worn heavy armour against Goliath, the Philistine might have lived to a ripe old age! But it was rather disconcerting for Arsenal.

Yet for all Walsall's crude tactics, and for all the difficulties imposed by the tiny pitch, and the proximity of the spectators who sat around it, I still say we should have won. We had quite enough chances to have banged in half a dozen goals. Not one was accepted.

Charlie Walsh was the chief offender. His nervousness was pitiable to behold. On one occasion, during the first half, I crossed the ball right on to his head, with not one Walsall defender standing within yards of him. He misjudged the centre hopelessly and missed the ball completely. It bounced off his shoulder, to be pounced on by a thankful Walsall defence.

Half-time came without any score. The Walsall supporters cheered their team to the echo, as it came off the field. It had held the mighty Arsenal for fully three-quarters of an hour! How this had been done was a matter that did not need to be discussed.

For the second half, Charlie Walsh was switched to inside-right. David Jack took over from him as centre-forward. Perhaps, we thought, this switch would do the trick. We were wrong.

Walsall took the lead after fifteen minutes. Gilbert Allsop, their centre-forward, headed in a corner taken by the outside-right, Lee. The resultant clamour was heard fully two miles away. (This, incidentally, is a fact.)

Far from converting the Walsall players to less vigorous ways, this goal only served to encourage them to further excesses of zeal. Alex James, who was literally knocked off his game, was a particularly bad sufferer. The gravest casualty of the second half was, however, left-half Norman Sidey. Norman – a sound player, but always inclined to be a little slow – was moving in leisurely fashion for a ball which he seemed to have plenty of time to bring under control, when a Walsall player appeared on the scene, and kicked him very scientifically on the knee. Sorry as I was for Norman, I must confess that I had to laugh at his resultant antics. He doubled up with pain, then sank slowly, very slowly, to the ground. If he had collapsed at once, it would not have been in the least amusing. But the sight of Norman sinking to the earth in slow motion brought a ray of humour even into this evil-tasting game. Still, isn't it said that humour is always just a step away from tragedy?

If Arsenal had had plenty of chances in the first half, we could not complain of lack of opportunities in the second. On one particular occasion, we would almost certainly have equalized, had it not been for the presence of one Charles Walsh.

I gave David Jack a head-high centre. It was a golden chance, and I could sense that David was picking his spot in the Walsall net. But just as the ball was about to reach him, who should come thundering up from behind like a runaway tank but . . . Charlie Walsh!

The astonishing leap through the air with which he ended his run deserved a better fate than it actually received. Alas, all Charlie did was to divert the ball away from David Jack, far, far from the Walsall goal. I can remember vividly to this day the look which David Jack gave Charlie.

Walsall ultimately made things sure by converting a penalty. It was, I felt, rather curious that we, and not they, should give away a spot-kick, after the manner in which some of their players had behaved. However, there was no doubt at all that the penalty award against us was thoroughly deserved.

It came as the climax of a long series of duels between one of our defenders and a Walsall forward. Relations between these two had gradually been becoming more and more strained, until it ultimately came to a point at which the question was which of them would be the first to vent his feelings on the other. Unfortunately for us, it was our man. The incident was almost followed by a free fight in the Arsenal penalty area, but eventually wisdom prevailed.

Sheppard, the Walsall inside-right, took the penalty. His hard, low shot gave our goalkeeper, Frank Moss, no possible chance of saving.

As soon as the ball was safely in the back of the net, a factory chimney near the ground suddenly began to belch thick clouds of black smoke, with the result that the pitch was obscured for several minutes. I felt a little amused at the time. I sensed that the chimney was saying to itself: "Well, we won't let Arsenal score any more goals now, anyway!"

Arsenal didn't. The final whistle blew, with the score Walsall 2, Arsenal 0; and, as the frantically happy crowd chaired the Walsall players from the pitch, newspaper correspondents rushed to the telephones to tell the world of Arsenal's sensational defeat.

We certainly were an unhappy team as we changed slowly and moodily in the dressing-room. It was all the more infuriating because we knew we ought to have won. True, the Walsall players had at times behaved more like steamrollers than footballers. True, Charlie Walsh and Billy Warnes had been misfits. Nevertheless, granting all this, we had still been presented with enough chances to have won.

Never have I seen Herbert Chapman look so miserably unhappy. He made a brave, desperate, but unavailing effort to cheer us all up. "Never mind, boys," he said, "these things do happen." But we were all inconsolable, and so, for that matter, was he. I think he felt the blow more than any of us. Here was the team which he had come to when it was struggling pathetically at the bottom of the First Division; the team which he had made one of the greatest in the history of football, beaten by a fifth-rate side. Napoleon must have felt like that in Russia, a hundred and twenty-one years before.

Of all the players, I think I felt the effects of the defeat most deeply. At twenty years old, I was the youngest of the side, so perhaps this was only natural. On my way home to my lodgings that night, in the Underground Railway, I felt positively suicidal. Visions of the Arsenal goals that might have been rose up before my eyes; hopes that the events of the afternoon had been nothing but an evil nightmare would delude me for a brief moment, only to be banished away by the cold, grim reality.

Walsall 2, Arsenal 0. Nothing could change those figures.

Yet Walsall could hardly be denied some credit for the amazing manner in which they had risen to the occasion. Their tactics, it is true, had been, to say the least of it, somewhat rough and ready, yet it had been obvious that they could not hope to match us with skill, and their only chance lay in putting us off our game, by bustling methods. This they had done with astonishing success.

A sequel to this game was the transfer to another club of the man who gave Walsall their penalty. His foul was undoubtedly the result of great provocation, but Mr Chapman would not suffer behaviour like that from any player at Highbury.

They say that every cloud has its silver lining, and I suppose there were advantages to our Walsall defeat – though nothing would have convinced me of the fact at the time.

The season before we had, of course, fallen between two stools, coming second in the League Championship, and losing to Newcastle in the Cup Final. If we had beaten Walsall, we might easily have done the same again. As it was, we were left to concentrate on the League, and eventually carried it off with several points to spare.

That was certainly some consolation, but the Walsall defeat still rankles in my mind. I believe it always will.

ARSENAL: Moss; Male, Black; Hill, Roberts, Sidey; Warnes, Jack, Walsh, James, Bastin.

WALSALL: Cunningham; Bennett, Bird; Read, Leslie, Salt; Coward, Ball, Allsop, Sheppard, Lee.

from CLIFF BASTIN REMEMBERS *1950*

Italy v. Czechoslovakia, 1934

VITTORIO POZZO

Italy has won the World Cup. Won it by pursuing just the same path they had been obliged to follow in the quarter and semi-finals: that of the match which is a species of battle. So keen, so fierce was this battle as to tire out and exhaust half the men on the field, and to make extra time necessary to reach a result.

There were no easy games for anybody in this edition of the World Cup, but Italy was without doubt the international team which met the greatest and most arduous difficulties on its way. Spain, Austria, and Czechoslovakia were three veritable boulders to remove from our path, three obstacles which produced the three hardest, spikiest, most difficult and exhilarating matches of the whole tournament. Italy certainly didn't find the path strewn with roses. Neither the draw nor the type of game played by our opponents favoured us in any way. The normal playing time laid down for a team which got to the Final was 360 minutes, and Czechoslovakia, apart from yesterday's extra time, would have played those 360 minutes; extra time brought them up to 390. The knocked-out semi-finalist which played the longest was Austria, with a total of 300 minutes, which would have risen to 390, had they qualified for the Final. Now, the Italian team ran up a total of 510 minutes of play, with the eighth-finals, the quarter-finals, extra time, a replay, the semi-final, Final and more extra time. Which means that, in terms of time, the "azzurri" played two tournaments, while their opponents played only one. 510 minutes play, 420 of them made up of hard fighting, fierce and enervating.

The Italian team had to undergo a miniature Calvary on its way to success. Yesterday, too, that Czech team which had excited nobody, let alone impressed them, in the course of the tournament, showed its claws and a style of play to confound the sceptics. Tough, spiky, leathery, the representatives of Bohemian football never for an instant admitted the possibility of defeat. It needed extra time to bring them to their knees. When they crumbled, it was essentially through lack of stamina after the immense effort of 120 minutes of extremely fast play.

This Bohemian team is a fine one. It has a unity and cohesion guaranteed by the fact that the players which form it come from only two clubs: seven men from Slavia and four from Sparta of Prague. It has experience, ability, its subtlety assured by the age of its players, all men with a long international career behind them, all of them old foxes, all men who know their job backwards.

For team play, pure combination, it must be said that there were marked periods when the Czech team was superior to the Italian.

There was a moment in the second half when the Czechs almost overran our players with their play, based on intricate movements and short passes. In midfield they manœuvre and advance in a way which makes it difficult, highly difficult, to stop them. This type of play has its Achilles' heel in the fact that movements develop largely in a line, in a uniform and even a monotonous way. Always the same thing, always the same approach, always the same execution. So that when, fired by the unfavourable score and their period of nervous depression over, our men set out to put the situation right, their understanding of their opponents' methods enabled them almost wholly to neutralize the movements the Czechs built up.

But the Czech team is of high technical merit. Their captain and goalkeeper is a Colossus – not in physique but precisely in technical merit. It was said that he was on the decline. Yesterday there was a time when he gave the impression of being as unbeatable as Zamora had seemed in the first match at Florence.* In terms of goalkeepers, this was the fate of the "azzurri" in the World Championship: escaping the grasp of Zamora, to fall into that of Platzer; escaping from Platzer, to fall into the hands of Planicka! A great goalkeeper, of great resource, Planicka! It needed the two formidable broadsides of Orsi and Schiavio to force him to capitulate.

The two backs have for years had a special reputation for no more than their energy and decisiveness. Yesterday they did justice to that reputation and Meazza and Schiavio paid the price of that decisiveness: Orsi, on the other hand, and to some extent Guaita, managed to find the weak spot in their system – their decisiveness often – transforms itself into simple recklessness – and turned the situation in their own favour.

Of the visitors' half-back line the best, beyond doubt, was the man in the middle. They'd said that Cambal was quite incapable of standing up to ninety minutes' hard play. Yesterday he did not last in extra time, but in ordinary time he gave a full account of himself. Cambal is a great technical player. A close-playing technical player – he rarely passes to the wings – but a man of constructive tendencies. There's nothing in him of that safety-first third back play which is in vogue today, everything in him of the sort of game which backs up, helps,

* When Spain held Italy to a draw.

sets moving and gives ideas to the attack. Cambal yesterday
was, in the first and second half, one of the most dangerous
players in the Bohemian attacks. In extra time he was physically played out.

By contrast, the wing-halves deserve no special mention –
players barren of personality. Personality is to be found, by
contrast, in the forward-line. Three men stand out: Svoboda,
Nejedly, and Puc, the inside-right, inside-left, and outside-left.
Svoboda, the old man, seemed to be finished a year ago. He
didn't even appear in the ranks of his club team. He'd almost
stopped playing. It needed the World Cup to revive him. In
Rome he was the intelligence and mainspring of his attack.
Wily, cunning, able, he controls the ball in such a way that it is
difficult to take it away from him. Svoboda, who has never
been in two minds about what means to use, was yesterday a
very fount of problems for our defence. Nejedly, by contrast,
is more of a doer than a thinker. He was unlucky with his shots,
but his ball control is of the most polished. Puc, the outside-
left, was a pure finisher, the fastest of the Bohemian forwards.
He scored his team's goal and forced Combi to make some
very difficult saves. One degree below his old level is the
outside-right, while the centre-forward, Sobotka, seems a class
inferior to his colleagues.

Such being their opponents, the "azzurri" had to do some
hard thinking to overcome them. They ended the first half
with the score at 0–0, but showing a slight superiority, because
they had had the wind against them. At the beginning of the
second half they allowed the visitors to take the initiative, and
then came trouble. For twenty minutes one seriously feared
for the outcome. Czechoslovakia scored first when Puc, taking
one more through pass, went on a few strides and then
unleashed a powerful shot low to Combi's left hand corner.
The visitors' lead was very nearly increased when Combi
managed to turn a strong, high shot against the post, and clear
the danger soon afterwards.

But from that moment, our team rolled up its sleeves. Puc's
goal was like a smart blow of the whip to a good horse. It

needed that wound to self-respect, that intimation of supreme risk, to bring out the physical and moral qualities stored up by our men during the period of preparation.

The revival of the "azzurri" was a model of force and will. Wave after wave of attacks beat on Planicka by a forward-line in which the change of position between Guaita and Schiavio had given new force and drive. When Orsi succeeded in equalizing, after a highly individualistic run, crowned by a superbly strong, accurate shot, all anxiety about the final result suddenly vanished. It was clear that, barring accidents, we could no longer lose. Yet the Bohemians still had two or three of their most dangerous chances when all seemed safe for Italy. It was Combi who, in this crisis, saved the situation.

Then came Schiavio's goal, fruit of a combination with Guaita. The Bologna man's shot was a cannon-ball. Planicka touched the ball but could not stop it, so strong was the shot, and from then on the Czechs no longer managed to look really dangerous.

Orsi had a great day. With Planicka, he was the best man on the field. The rest of the team must all be given great praise for the proud way they bore themselves, even if at times they looked disorientated and nervous.

Our team was in a period of nervous depression, after the last, terrible week, a week of four matches in eight days and 420 minutes' play in four days. After the nervous tension, there came the nervous relapse; a natural thing for those who have lived such a life. It needed what the doctors call a "whiplash" to the nerves to restore the organism to efficiency. And it regained its efficiency in a grandiose, impressive way.

From the point of view of excitement, the World Championship could not have had a more worthy epilogue. A remarkable crowd; the play varied, fast, sometimes clever, sometimes even resplendent with beauty; the Italians momentarily in danger of seeing forty days' labour ruined, swift reaction, recovery of the situation, success. It was a sort of apotheosis of the game of football, with our players moved to tears, the crowd mad with joy, the Duce expressing fully, with face and voice alike, his satisfaction.

A virile bearing, that of the "azzurri". Their success constituted the fullest reward to which they could aspire, the highest ambition they could cherish. A coveted success, rewarding dedication, moral strength, the spirit of self-sacrifice and the firm will of a platoon of men who so that they might worthily defend the colours of Italy, did not hesitate to cut themselves off from the world for forty days, deprive themselves of everything and bend themselves to every discipline. No international team has ever done what our "azzurri" did in their period of preparation. It is poetic justice that victory should have crowned their labours.

Say what one will, nothing in the world rivals the satisfaction of duty done conscientiously, faithfully, stubbornly if necessary, studiously, prudently, and successfully. It is a profound, an intimate satisfaction, which makes up for everything.

ITALY: Combi; Monzeglio, Allemandi; Ferraris IV, Monti, Bertolini; Guaita, Meazza, Schiavio, Ferrari, Orsi.

CZECHOSLOVAKIA: Planicka; Zenisek, Ctyroky; Kostalek, Cambal, Krcil; Junek, Svoboda, Sobotka, Nejedly, Puc.

from LA STAMPA *11/6/34*

The Battle of Highbury, 1934

VITTORIO POZZO

The England v. Italy match of November 1934 *has gone down in* [British] *football history as "The Battle of Highbury". Seven of the England team afterwards required treatment; Eddie Hapgood, the captain, who described it as "the dirtiest game I ever played in" had his nose smashed by an Italian. The Italian view, seldom encountered over here, is somewhat different, and is given in the following account.*

Winners of the World Championship, we now had to pass beneath the grim gallows of England, who at that period did not take part in international tournaments. They stood aside, not running the risks of the eliminators, quarter-finals, semi-finals and the Final. They stood aside, tranquilly. And when it was all over, they challenged the winner of the tournament to play them on their own ground, in the conditions which best suited them. It was a very convenient way of determining the question of world leadership. A sincere admirer of many of the qualities to be found in England, I am an equally ruthless critic of others, which represent the English mentality in its dealings with the foreigner. In this particular case, the Italian Federation accepted the invitation which their English counterparts didn't fail to send them after our success. And when it came to agreeing on the details of the game, I myself was sent to London. Relationships could not have been closer. I spoke the language, I knew the men and the environment. It was up to me.

In London, when I heard, as I had feared, that we would have to play at once, in October, and on Arsenal's ground, I objected. I telephoned Rome, advising against acceptance. In vain. Somebody in Rome at top level – a political interference – had at once gone ecstatic. We had to accept: without wasting too much time on details of organization, details which I, from experience, knew to be of the highest importance to our task. "We'll beat them just the same," I seemed to hear them murmur, far away as they were. I was in a position in which I couldn't mark time: it would look as if I wanted to be difficult, devious, pretentious, after the World Championship success. Disciplined, I stood symbolically to attention, and agreed to everything. Rome wanted me to arrange that both our usual anthems should be played on the field, before the match, and I arranged it.

On the field, it seemed at once that the Devil had planted his hoof on us. And even now, no one will convince me that the hoof of that influential person – from a neutral country, but morally biased – wasn't in evidence. Silently, everyone at once picked on Monti. Monti had a great personal feud with the Danubians – he considered all of them to be tarred with the same brush, and said that all of them made him see red – but apart from that, he was the cleanest player in the world. (*An opinion open to serious doubts, in view of incidents in the* 1930 *World Cup, and Chelsea's tour of South America.* Ed.) He played the ball, not the man. The fact remains that, right at the beginning of the game, Monti received a kick from Drake, the centre-forward, which broke a bone in his right foot. Luisito was a stoic, who never gave way to anything; his resistance to pain was incredible. He stayed at his post. But he could no longer move.

The first goal against us came from a back pass which Bertolini sent him almost automatically, and which in fact he couldn't reach. In twelve minutes, we let in three goals: scorers Brook, Brook, and Drake. It was tough getting Monti off the field. First he went to right-half, then to outside-right, and at last into the dressing-room. He was not used to beating a retreat. In the dressing-room, our doctor didn't arrive in time. There came instead a Scots doctor who looked, saw and then said to me, "Broken. To the hospital." They say that the fracture of this bone is the most painful that can happen to the human body: agonizing. I don't know, from personal experience. I only know that Luisito begged me to stuff a hand-kerchief in his mouth, so he shouldn't scream, and left for hospital with our trainer, Angeli. I went back to the field, to that wire cage which is reserved at Arsenal for team managers. At half-time, I hid from our men the seriousness of Monti's injury. I had many reasons for being saddened and angry that day: private reasons. I restored the players' morale with the energy that comes from grief, and they responded by wiping out in four minutes – from the thirteenth to the seventeenth – two thirds of the deficit, with two goals by Meazza. In the final minutes of that half, a *quid pro quo* between Guaita and Meazza prevented us from gaining the draw that lay within our grasp.

At half-time that day, I remember, His Excellency Signor Grandi, Italian minister in London, whom I already knew from military life, came into the dressing-room. He heard me talk to the players, and summoned me the following day to a private audience. The English players had complained after the match of the tone of violence brought into the game by some of our players, especially Serantoni, Allemandi, Ferraris, and Monzeglio. The injury sustained by Monti they called "an incident in the game", "an accidental happening". I still think from time to time of that accidental happening. When I go to London, I meet Drake every now and then in an Italian restaurant, between Piccadilly and Oxford Circus. Every time I bring the conversation round to the fracture suffered by Monti. He answers me that it was "a sad thing". It was, indeed, very sad, for Luisito physically, for me and for all of us, morally. Drake is now manager of Chelsea, the old London club, and behaves towards me in the most sporting and courteous manner imaginable. That spiteful match at Highbury left its traces for quite a while. None of those who took part in it directly, or who were present, have forgotten it.

ENGLAND: Moss; Male, Hapgood; Britton, Barker, Copping; Matthews Bowden, Drake, Bastin, Brook.
ITALY: Ceresoli; Monzeglio, Allemandi; Ferraris IV, Monti, Bertolini; Guaita, Serantoni, Meazza, Ferrari, Orsi.

from CAMPIONI DEL MONDO *1960*

Italy v. Hungary, 1938

VITTORIO POZZO

The World Cup is over. The greatest football trophy which exists on this terrestrial orb, the most sought after of honours, remains with Italy.

When, at 7.52 p.m., the referee signalled the end of the contest, the players stood a moment as though they had only been pulled up. Because that instant a clash between an Italian and a Hungarian had taken place in midfield, several of the

players believed that the noise which came from Signor
Capdeville's whistle signified a foul against one of the two
contestants. No, instead it was the end, that end which for so
long had seemed so distant – like the victory it implied – as
to take on the form of a mirage. For a moment, the "azzurri"
looked at one another, motionless, dazed, abstracted, as though
their feelings were so strong that they were unable to move.
One moment, as though joy had stricken every one of them.
Then, enthusiasm and delight found free expression. Arms
raised high, cries sticking in the throat, they looked round for
those who had shared their exertions, sacrifices, and emotions;
they kissed, embraced. And, all round them were thousands of
Italians, apparently crazy, shouting, yelling, and waving little
flags.

They certainly made themselves heard, those people, while
on the field there were several who were crying. It is no
weakness on anyone's part, including the athlete whose body
is exhausted and whose face is crumbled by fatigue, to give his
feelings that intimate expression which we call emotion. The
great Final, so far as the Italians were concerned, was similar
to the semi-final, the quarter-final, the first round, in the type
of difficulty met and overcome. That is to say, the difficulties
in all the matches of this intensely fought competition turned
out on the field to be of a single kind: negotiable from the
technical point of view, but complex from the point of view
of setting and psychology – as is the way of Cup matches, where
playing the better is not enough; proving oneself superior is
not everything; where a slip, any little error, a moment of
distraction or weakness, can compromise everything, absolutely
everything.

In fact this last exertion, this battle which would decide
everything, the issue of two months' work, the good name of
Italian football, the question of prestige, the title, was already
won by our team when the referee sent the players into the
dressing-room for half-time. Indeed, to be accurate it was won,
some time earlier, at the moment when, thanks to an un-
stoppable shot by Colaussi, it went ahead to 3–1. A lead of

two goals in the hands of the "azzurri", in normal form; at a time, that is to say, when the emotion roused by the importance of the prize at stake did not tip the balance and weaken the limbs, would have meant that the game was won beyond doubt. Holding such a lead, the representatives of our colours had never been caught; nor even with a lead that was not as big. But here it was a different story.

At half-time the team was unsettled. It faltered in the dressing-room. One must know it, to understand it. It had got where it had thanks to a strength of will and physique of quite a special character. It had been caught up in a crisis which could have taken on the dimensions of a grave illness, at the very first step of the tournament. It had recovered to fall out of the frying-pan into the fire, that is to say, into the most difficult moral situation that the great competition could present for any of its competitors.

Emerging triumphant from this complex predicament, it had found the way barred by the most technically formidable opposition in the whole tournament, by the very "bogey" of that tournament: Brazil. In an *ambiance* openly and fiercely hostile, it had beaten that opposition, raising its own play to the highest level. And with this physical and moral weight on its shoulders and behind it, it had come to the Final, where, steadfastly awaiting it, was a team which had behind it no burden of fatigue at all.

Dashingly, six minutes from the start, the "azzurri" took the lead. Too quickly, too quickly. It is never good for our team to score at the opening of hostilities: for, just as in the match with France, they lost this lead immediately. Only to regain it ten minutes later. Only to increase it before half-time. Only to confirm their clear technical and tactical superiority in forty-five minutes of open, honest, decisive play. At half-time, let us repeat, the game could logically have been considered won. Here the team fell into the snare of emotion. It saw the winning-post clearly, it sensed release of tension almost as though that were a scent, felt success to be within its grasp, and faltered. Faltered, for one thing, at the thought that any error, the simplest of mistakes, could dash away the victory it so deserved. Consequently there came the moment of crisis, the moment that made the watching Italians suffer. Hungary, spurred on by desperation, went into the attack in impressive style. And what they had failed to do at the beginning of the second half, they managed to do when about half of it was gone. They reduced the deficit: they brought it down to the smallest possible margin: three–two.

It was now that our men's force of will re-awoke. As though a sudden shiver swept through it, the team pulled out of that sort of slight hysteria which had been allowed to overcome it, returned to the attack, and re-established its lead. The match which the "azzurri" had already won in the first half, they won again in that moment: in plain and decisive style.

Re-establishing their lead, as has been said, thanks to a goal scored by Piola after a run by Biavati, the "azzurri" ended in full command, confident, dominant, masterful, firmly controlling the play. They finished in glory.

There is not the smallest doubt that, with this final effort, they fully merited victory. The best play was theirs; the most limpid movements were developed by them, the most effective style and the best technique were their theirs too.

Sarosi's team showed itself in this match to be thoroughly combative and fast and much improved by comparison with the teams they have lately opposed to us. But it was always inferior, by and large, to the potential of an Italian team functioning and playing its normal game. The Hungarians' improvement is almost exclusively limited to the work of the attack. Here things are certainly going better than they once were. Sarosi is no great finisher, but he is the true intelligence of the line. Those two periods of the second half in which the Hungarian attack, unleashed, battered our defensive lines, belong to the finest moments of the whole match.

In all that regards defensive play, however, the team has remained what it was. With backs who have no great speed, half-backs with no great positional sense, this defence looked vulnerable every time our men went into the assault. Open movements, attacks carried out by the wingers, particularly caught the backs in an embarrassing position. So much so that, if our outside-right had only been able to throw into the balance the weight of that experience which years alone can confer on a footballer, the lead with which the Italians finished the game would have been much more pronounced. Apart from that justifiable nervousness and hysteria which impeded their play in certain periods of the second half, our team played the match in the same high, praiseworthy style as the matches against France and Brazil.

That state of convincing technical superiority over every other contestant, which had emerged in the other matches, was fully borne out by the Final at Colombes. None – none, we say – of the 50,000 spectators present left the stadium with the shadow of a doubt not only of the result of the match, but of the whole competition.

The first to say so were the Hungarians themselves, who sportingly came to congratulate the Italians. Iron defence, with a Rava who at times gave the impression of being quite unbeatable, a mobile and consistent half-back line, with a Locatelli always on the ball and a Serantoni tenacious as a mastiff; a forward line eminently practical in style, thanks to methods derived from the intelligence of Meazza and Ferrari and to the penetrative capacity of spearhead players like Piola, Colaussi, and Biavati.

The field in which the Italian national team has surpassed every other contestant, not just in the final match but in every other game in the competition, is that of developing its play in a practical, progressive style. Beginning with the game against France – the milestone at which the team found itself once more – the side has played to win, only to win and exclusively to win. It has excluded from its repertory every number that was not indispensable, was not strictly useful in gaining victory, and, with a style reduced to the expression of the utmost simplicity, has ended by carrying the day. This simplicity of style was the technical weapon with which it overcame its crisis – one can talk of no other weapon in this series of upheavals: a simplicity which never made its play dull, devoid of content and of beauty. The style of the Italian team has been defined, here in Paris, as the purest expression of the modern game.

The labour is over. In the hearts of all those who took part, there is an intimate satisfaction, a joy so lively and intense that no word, no phrase, could express it. It makes up for everything, this joy which throws directors and players into one another's arms, which wrings the heart, makes the eyes swell and cannot be properly put into words. There is no satisfaction in the world as great and fine as having done one's duty with success.

ITALY: Olivieri; Foni, Rava; Serantoni, Andreolo, Locatelli; Biavati, Meazza, Piola, Ferrari, Colaussi.

HUNGARY: Szabo; Polgar, Biro; Szalai, Szucs, Lazar; Sas, Vincze, Sarosi, Szengeller, Titkos.

from LA STAMPA *20/6/38*

Portsmouth v. Wolverhampton Wanderers, 1939

ROLAND ALLEN

Mr Jack Tinn did a little step dance on the green and velvety Wembley pitch when the English Cup final of April 1939 ended. Wolverhampton Wanderers, hottest favourites in any final of my time, had been beaten by four goals to one.

Youth will tell, say the wise men. In this case youth was told. The oldest player on either side was Worrall, the Portsmouth outside-right. He never put a foot wrong all through the match – right from the time that he had adjusted Mr Jack Tinn's spats until the time when he proudly walked up the steps to take his medal.

Mr Jack Tinn's spats had by now become almost as much a football institution as the Cup itself. He wore them on every occasion on which Portsmouth football club, of which he was the manager, played in a football match. I saw the ceremony of fixing them and adjusting them carried out by Worrall, in Mr Jack Tinn's office at Portsmouth, a few minutes before the start of a match there, a few weeks before Portsmouth won the Cup.

Jack Tinn unlocked the safe and almost reverently produced the spats. Worrall bent down and fixed and fastened them, then leaned back to look at and admire his work. It was laid down, I do not know when, by whom, or for what reason, that the left foot should be the first to be clothed in these symbols of football superstition. Yes, there was a lot of that in football.

The spats were the mascot of the club. Actually, of course, Mr Jack Tinn and his footballers were entirely responsible for the considerable success which Portsmouth football team achieved. Perhaps it was superstition, or it may more probably have been his knowledge of how important a part the state of mind of footballers plays in big football games, which persuaded Mr Jack Tinn to include Mr Albert Burdon among the coach-party of Portsmouth players from the London arrival station to Wembley for this final.

Mr Albert Burdon was a famous comedian who had been a Portsmouth fan for many years. His job was to keep the players suitably amused, and if you know Mr Burdon I do not need to tell you that he made a great job of it. The white spats, by the way, were ceremoniously fitted to the ankles of Mr Albert Burdon before he started the run of a show called *Eve On Parade* at the Garrick Theatre.

Mr Jack Tinn's spats were far from being the only notable factor in this notable Cup final. On the Wednesday before the match both teams had the final dose of gland treatment. They had been given this treatment for several weeks before the match. Mr A. Menzies Sharp, the Australian who introduced gland therapy into football, said that all the twenty-two footballers would go on to the field neither excited nor overawed, which at least would be unusual in a Cup final.

Both teams would play football of the highest class. I would hardly agree with that, leaving out one or two exceptions. "Both teams," said Mr Menzies Sharp, "have been receiving exactly the same treatment. Each has benefited to the same extent from my gland extract from special bulls, rabbits, and other animals. The Wolves began the treatment first. Portsmouth came under treatment later. There will be no last-minute gland injections. The substances do not act as a temporary stimulant."

Gland therapy was and is the subject of medical discussion into which I am not qualified to enter. I merely mention it as one of the unusual factors in this unusual football match. "You would be surprised," Mr Menzies Sharpe concluded, "if I mentioned to you the names of some of the eminent statesmen and men distinguished in other walks of life who are prolonging their lives and mental vigour with the help of this treatment."

Although the incalculable factor intruded itself into every Cup final, indeed every big soccer occasion, which came under my notice, I could quote few clearer examples of its application than this 1939 final. For weeks before the match it was a generally accepted conclusion that the Wolves, a team of very young players gathered and welded together by football impresario Major Frank Buckley, were merely going through a customary formality in playing at all in this final.

Ever since they had beaten the mighty Everton, Football League champions that season, in the sixth round, they steadily developed into the biggest "certainty" there had been in a final during the many years I had been following the game.

As I visualized the match in print before it took place I anticipated that we should go to Wembley to find the Wolves a trifle apprehensive about the responsibilities of the position of hot favourites, which had been thrust upon them. I visualized the older men of Portsmouth rather resenting the suggestion – and it should be said in fairness that the suggestion was never made or supported by anybody connected with the Wolves or their club – that they were to be there merely because it took two teams to make a football match.

There was a set-up, which those of us who looked for the human rather than the mechanical and mathematical factors to guide our sport prophecies, often encountered, especially in the scramble for a rather ordinary-looking piece of silver. On the one hand a team almost placed, not by themselves but through circumstances over which they had no control, under a moral obligation to win and, on the other, a team with nothing to lose in the matter of dignity so far as concerned this particular occasion.

It happened not quite so often, and this was one of those occasions, that the side with apparently nothing to lose was inspired to show everybody, including in this case Wolverhampton Wanderers, how wrong and foolish it is ever to suggest that there is such a thing as certainty in any game.

I had, by then, discovered that one had to look beyond mere football efficiency, tradition or reputation for the factors which decided this sort of football game, with its over-dramatization and general atmosphere, likely to throw the most experienced of the footballers off his game. If it were possible to forecast the reactions of the respective players to what is a nerve-testing occasion, starting from the moment they wake up in the morning – if they sleep at all – right up to the last kick I would guarantee, with the mathematical information which a forecaster always has available, to tell you the result of almost any Cup final before it has been played.

In the match under discussion the Wolves came to Wembley having gone through calmly, unruffled, almost majestically through the ties which brought them there. The side they selected had never previously been beaten. That is a habit from which eleven footballers take a lot of shaking. It also gives them a tremendous moral advantage.

On the other hand Portsmouth had shown an extraordinary capacity for producing an irresistible quarter of an hour in the course of each of their Cup games. I had seen them do this against West Ham United and again against Huddersfield

Town, after they had on both occasions been played more or less right out of the first two-thirds of each game.

It was that which caused me to expect that Portsmouth might easily, as it were, sweep even such an imperturbable lot of people as the Wolves out of the Stadium, across into the handsome Wembley swimming pool, and sink them. It happened like that.

PORTSMOUTH: Walker; Morgan, Rochford; Guthrie, Rowe, Wharton; Worrall, McAlinden, Anderson, Barlow, Parker.

WOLVERHAMPTON WANDERERS: Scott; Morris, Taylor; Galley, Cullis, Gardiner; Burton, McIntosh, Westcott, Dorsett, McGuire.

from ALL IN THE DAY'S SPORT *1947*

Britain v. Europe, 1947

CARLO PAROLA

I don't think I have any doubt about it. If I am asked to recall the finest day of my sporting career I must return in memory to that afternoon of 10 May, 1947, when at Glasgow, as a member of the Continental team – also known as The Rest of Europe – I faced the "great white team" of England.* It may seem strange, at least to the very young, that I should want to recall a football match which saw the team, for which I was playing centre-half, beaten 6–1. And yet I remember that I never felt so pleased with myself as on that day. I had learned in the course of my football career that one cannot always win. Yet one can have a great day oneself when the team as a whole has a bad one, when circumstances or skill or exceptional fitness enable one player to rise above all the rest, to prove himself before the crowd and the critics.

On that far-off Saturday twelve years ago, faced by the

* Great Britain in fact played in blue.

greatest centre-forward of the day, the brilliant Lawton, I felt
that I had won my sporting battle as completely as could be,
and that I had done honour to Italy. I was the only Italian
chosen, at a time when post-war quarrels and resentments were
still in the air.

Before telling what happened on the very green turf of
Hampden Park, let me give a sketch of the happenings great
and small which preceded that unforgettable afternoon. They
will enable you to understand my state of mind, and justify
my enthusiasm. I would even say that the description of the
preliminaries is as important to me as that of the match which
crowned me "Continental Carletto". In 1947 the position of
football in Italy was very different from today. There was no
shortage of great footballers in Europe, especially Britain,
and in Italy, for example, my friends of the great and unforgettable Torino team were still alive, players of the class of
Rigamonti, Mazzola, Gabetto, Loik, Menti, Carapellese,
Maroso, Ballarin. To be chosen to fill a position as important
as centre-half in a team allegedly representing the "best" of
Continental Europe seemed to me in itself a tremendous
honour. I considered it the highest recognition of my professional career since I had first put on – with an emotion I
cannot begin to describe – the black and white shirt of "my"
Juventus.

When Rimet, the President of F.I.F.A., cabled me that I had
been chosen, ordering me to put myself at the disposal of the
team managers and begin training, I confess I was overcome
by an unspeakable feeling of pride. Yet I did not feel nervous.
I had already put my qualities of temperament to the test – I
never have been the nervous kind – in various international
matches. Besides, I knew I had been carefully watched in the
last two internationals played by the "azzurri".

Ten minutes after the cable arrived, I was already at the
Juventus offices to tell the directors and my team mates. I was
happy. Several bottles of *spumante* were broached in my honour.
I remember, too, an old director saying to me in more or less
these words, "Carletto, it's going to be pretty tough there in

F

Glasgow against Britain and their stars. You'll be playing against a team that represents the best in international football. Not only that, but you'll have people with you whom you don't know. You'll never have seen one another before and you'll be talking a completely different footballing 'language'. Yet I'm sure that you're still going to cut a fine figure in this conglomeration of individuals. In this sort of match the result is perhaps the least important thing. What matters is to be able to come off the field with your head held high."

It was true; the result of the game was the thing that mattered least. The important thing at Hampden Park, in front of 150,000 spectators, was to pass an important test as an individual. And I must say that every one of us players in the Continental side acquitted himself well, against the footballers of the British Empire [sic]. I myself had the fortune to be the best on the field.

Unfortunately, when I enthusiastically accepted my selection for Europe, I forgot a detail of the highest importance. The Sunday after the great match in Scotland, Hungary and Italy were due to play an international game in Turin. It is true that every coin has its reverse side. But I have no regrets. Indeed, I still think that I rendered a fine service to Italy by upholding her prestige in that charged atmosphere, against the great British team itself.

The Press of that time, busy describing and dealing with international problems of quite a different character, said little about the preparations for the Glasgow match – if anything devoting the limited space it had to the coming match between Italy and Hungary. The long preliminaries – in fact a far longer period of training was necessary to play the British – went by almost in silence. The sporting dailies alone had "special bulletins", while the political dailies merely gave brief paragraphs of news now and then. I must admit, too, that not every newspaper approved my preferring the Glasgow match to being picked for Italy. Even though they knew that a player of Rigamonti's class would play against Hungary, many critics were unhappy, preferring me on the grounds that

I was younger. These few criticisms did not make me change my mind or perturb me, and I continued to prepare myself "morally" for the great day.

The collective training sessions were of little use. We strove in vain, first in Amsterdam, then in the quiet little Scottish village of Troon, to understand each other. I met players of exceptional class. I remember how I was impressed, from the very first training sessions, by the Swedes Nordahl and Gren, the Dane Praest, the Dutchman Wilkes, who was later signed by Inter, and the Irishman, Carey. I thought I would do a good turn to "my" Juventus, trying at once to talk Nordahl, the centre-forward, and the left-winger, Praest, into playing in our black and white shirt. I was successful only in the case of Praest, who in fact was signed the following year by Juventus, where he played for many seasons, always proving himself the finest winger in the whole League. Nordahl, however, went through a series of mishaps, to another big Italian club, Milan. My other brave comrades were the French goalkeeper Da Rui, the full-backs Petersen and Steffen, Danish and Swiss respectively, the Czech wing-half Ludl (the other was Carey) and the Belgian outside-right, Lemberechts. They were good, but they did not reach the class of Nordahl, Gren, Praest, and Wilkes.

I soon became aware of the difficulties we faced. In a football team, the harmony and friendship of its players is of the utmost importance; they should get to know one another as well as they possibly can, both inside and outside the purely sporting context. But in the space of a few days we could not hope to show our strengths and weaknesses and, after our training sessions, the interpreters alone could not keep our conversation going. There was, alas, a feeling of coldness between us all. I was at once complimented by the managers and by my team mates for my famous "flying bicycle kick", which had the effect of putting an opponent off his stroke, the ball being whipped away from under his nose when he thought he had full control of it. I was young then, 26 years old, and I was also very good in anticipation, and in guessing my opponent's moves in advance.

I remember being very unhappy because I had to change my way of life. I was always in search of meat and *pastasciutte*, each of which – along with many other foods – was still rationed at the time in Holland and Scotland: everyone called me "Parola Pastasciutta". We played our public trial on May 6th. in Rotterdam, against the Dutch international team and won 2–0, with two goals scored by Wilkes. But we all felt that our team was in essence a beautiful mosaic, a talented mixture of individuals, struggling to find a common tongue.

We spent the last days of waiting, peacefully, at Troon. The Scottish and English newspapers "splashed" the game every day, saying that the second meeting between the Rest of Europe and the English international team [*sic*] was going to eclipse every other sporting event, including the great spectacles of the Derby, the Cup Final, and even the Oxford and Cambridge Boat Race. Finally we got to Glasgow. In the middle of the town one could scarcely move, and the outskirts swarmed with people; Hampden Park was sold out. None of us had any illusions about the result; I felt quite calm.

The moment I had been waiting for so long arrived. When I came on to the field, I was almost dazed for a moment by the impressive sight of the crowd. I had never seen so many people in a single stadium till then. But it lasted only a moment; when the English referee, Reader, blew the whistle to begin the game, my attention was immediately fixed on my formidable opponent, Lawton. This was how we lined-up: Da Rui (France); Petersen (Denmark), Steffen (Switzerland); Carey (Ireland), myself, Ludl (Czechoslovakia); Lemberechts (Belgium), Gren (Sweden), Nordahl (Sweden), Wilkes (Holland), Praest (Denmark). Our manager was Mr Carver. The British team was made up of the best professional players, exceptionally rich in common experience. They played this team: Swift; Hardwick, Hughes; Macaulay, Vernon, Burgess; Matthews, Mannion, Lawton, Steel, Liddell.

Our heterogeneous mosaic-side could not withstand the British avalanche. After the first exchanges, I could see that we were disintegrating. I was busily involved in studying my direct opponent, Lawton – a demon. Very mobile, astute, powerful. We held out for half-an-hour and, little by little, I found myself better able to anticipate Lawton's plans. Tireless, urged on deafeningly by the crowd, he led his companions in attack in one dangerous movement after another on the goal of the highly nervous Da Rui. I had no real help, alas, from my colleagues in defence, who were far too busy trying to stop the wingers and inside-forwards to spare a moment's attention for my rampant opponent. Lawton stepped-up his pace, as though annoyed by the fact that I was frequently beating him in the air and taking precious chances away from his feet. But his forward colleagues almost surrounded me. After 22 minutes' play Mannion, the inside-right, succeeded in breaching our defence, but after 25 minutes, in a breakaway, Nordahl, the centre-forward, got the equalizer, beating the massive Swift. A few minutes later a Continental defender committed a foul in the area in a defensive mix-up, and the English scored from a penalty, again through Mannion.

I seemed to be building my house on sand. I could not understand why my team mates were losing all their poise, allowing dreadful gaps to open in our defensive system. I felt full of energy, but I could not, logically, be everywhere at once when danger threatened. The crowd sportingly began to applaud me after my numberless duels with Lawton – and with Steel and Mannion, too. Every now and then, I even tried to set my forward-line going, but I was forced to drop back to fill the great gap in front of Da Rui; a task I find it hard to describe. Yet I knew that I was fully succeeding in containing the dashing Lawton; perhaps with a little more calm and organization on the part of my backs and half-backs, the result might have been quite different. Instead the English wingers and inside-forwards had practically a free hand, and were able to give my direct opponent chance after chance to score. Almost all the danger came from the outside-right and the outside-left. Undaunted, I went on fighting, sending Praest and Lemberechts ball after ball. From the terraces they continued to applaud me, and I saw a great many Italian flags being waved there.

The minutes seemed like hours. At the thirty-fifth and the thirty-seventh two more goals yet went into Da Rui's net. Steel scored the first, after easily getting past Ludl, while the second went to Lawton himself. But, honestly, it was not my fault, because at that moment I was involved in dealing with another opponent.

In the second half, the superiority of the British side was almost unbroken. My own work was doubled. Realizing that I had managed to "neutralize" Lawton (the expression used by almost the whole of the British Press) they kept on playing down the wings. In the twenty-eighth minute, alas, Da Rui, tired, demoralized, and not anticipating my intentions, allowed my very easy pass-back to escape him: an own goal. I could have cried and yelled with rage. But once again I took a grip on myself and continued to play "guardian angel" to Lawton. But again he managed to get away, in the thirty-eighth minute, cleverly flicking into the net with his head a cross by Mannion – who astoundingly had been left unmarked. In the remaining minutes, I tried to inspire the Continental team to fight back; but my team mates were too depressed and devoid of energy to be able to appreciate my efforts. The game was drawing to an end; they were shouting my name on the terraces.

Half-an-hour after the end of the match the football editions came out in Glasgow. They spoke of me as the true protagonist of the match. They remembered my bicycle kick and called me "The first centreback of Europe" [*sic*]. At last I shed my usual composure, weeping tears of joy. The Chelsea directors wanted to offer me a £15,000 signing-on fee, but I refused without hesitation. I knew that my place was with Juventus, where I had first played for the League team at only eighteen, against Novara. I was obliged to play against my "Juve" only once, at the end of my career, when just for a year I went to Lazio, on a free transfer granted me by the President, Gianni Agnelli. If Glasgow is the finest memory of my footballing life, the match in which I had to play against the black and white is certainly the saddest. Now, at the age of thirty-eight, I have gone back to Juventus as manager, with Cesarini – and I am happy.

from LA SETTIMANA INCOM *24/10/59*

Arsenal v. Newcastle United, 1952

H. D. DAVIES

Even in the rain the stadium was gloomily impressive during the F.A. Cup Final, in which Newcastle United, the holders, beat Arsenal 1–0 here today. Gone for the most part were the colours and the favours. Drab raincoats and waterproof capes were the only wear. But there was plenty of animation and singing, including a fine rendering of the old favourite *Abide with me*, a hymn which must have been sung with particular fervour by Mr Tom Whittaker, the Arsenal manager, in view of his experiences in recent weeks. As a hundred thousand white handkerchiefs fluttered at the call of the song-leader it was plain that the spirit of George Borrow was abroad on the terraces – "Life is sweet, brother. Who would wish to die?" And when the familiar square bowler and broad shoulders of Mr Churchill were seen moving on to the arena for introduction to the gladiators a long roar swept across the home shires and, as it seemed, along the corridors of time itself. Here was a festival and a setting Augustus himself would have recognized. Across the centuries Wembley called to Rome.

Recent newspaper articles by Mercer and Forbes, written in a spirit of noble forgiveness for those who cannot, or will not, appreciate the sublime purity of Arsenal's methods – they don't know the difference between toughness and roughness, poor fish! – had somehow prepared us in advance to see certain of the Arsenal players wearing, metaphorically, the crown of martyrdom. But few of us guessed how near the truth we were. With only 22 minutes gone Barnes hurt his right knee in tackling Milburn. He was strapped up, was hurt again in tackling Robledo, withdrew for further repairs, and, after struggling gamely to help in a minor way as outside right for a while, was forced in the end by a badly strained ligament to limp despairingly from the scene. This left eight fit men and two doubtfuls, Logie and Daniel, to face the punishment alone. Here was martyrdom indeed. All seemed set now for the Newcastle lions to tear Arsenal to shreds.

But something had gone wrong with the lions. Never before had one seen Milburn so hesitant, so clumsy, so erratic in his passing. The close attentions of Daniel were no doubt partly responsible for this, as well as the tight defensive cordon which Arsenal threw round him whenever he got the ball. Stride for stride, Milburn could give Daniel little in the way of speed, and even when he tried the old trick of beating him on the turn by slipping the ball past him on one side and charging past him on the other he found that Arsenal's covering was too swift for him, and that discovery seemed to breed progressive mistrust. Of course, from Milburn the footballing public has grown to expect nothing less than ideal standards. It is with him as it used to be with Bradman. Anything less than a century for Bradman was considered a failure; anything less than a hat trick for Milburn is a failure too. Yet, even though playing under a cloud, Milburn struck twice in a fashion which made 70,000 hearts, at least, miss a beat – once when a magnificent left-foot shot scudded narrowly wide of a post and again when a superb back-header, during a goalmouth struggle, was rescued by Smith's long neck even as it shaped to cross the goal line.

Yet one of the cleverest scoring attempts had been made by Lishman for Arsenal within two minutes of the start. A brilliantly speculative overhead kick just grazed the Newcastle post on the wrong side. A success at that moment might have yielded miraculous fruits. But soon came Barnes's injury, and a drastic, not to say heart-breaking, reshuffle. Roper, outside left, crossed over to right back, and Cox, outside right, became outside left with a roving commission to wander anywhere and everywhere and try to create the impression in Newcastle minds that three sound forwards and a gallant invalid, Logie, could have the same impact as five good men and true. It was magnificent no doubt, but it was scarcely practical politics. The loss of Barnes, of course, threw a tremendous burden on the ten survivors generally and on the five defenders in particular, and the main interest of a game which was never technically first rate centred on the ability of Arsenal to follow Mercer's heroic lead and hold out. At times even Arsenal came within an ace of stealing the match. It was as though an old Roman circus promoter had billed up the following: – "Saturday's special attraction at the Colosseum. Come and see the Martyrs mauling the Lions!"

Slowly, very slowly, Newcastle recovered their lost touch and in the closing twenty minutes or so Arsenal were called to enter upon their last agony. Mitchell, on whom Newcastle's main hopes depended, twice appeared to have the match within his grasp. The first time after beating two men with subtle body swerves he let fly savagely, and when his shot was charged down he hurled his body at the ball and watched it scrape the post on the wrong side. Again Mitchell danced his way through, then stood petrified, a prey to mistrust, until a brusque tackle put an end to his dalliance. But, just when it seemed that Mitchell's near misses and the cruder blunders of G. Robledo and Walker had committed Newcastle to a further trial of strength, fate decided that Arsenal, whom it has scourged unmercifully during recent weeks, should finally go under. A beautiful centre from Mitchell drew Swindin out of goal and curled teasingly away from his finger-tips. The swarthy head of G. Robledo connected and a goal of historic significance to English football, scored by a Chilean, bounced in off a post. After an interval of 61 years the Cup had been won by the same team in two successive seasons, this time by Newcastle United.

One noted that the merry-making of the "Geordies" after the match was subdued and restrained, and to some extent even wry-faced. They could not shake off the feeling that their own pets, Newcastle, though victors, had not been the day's real

F*

heroes. That distinction went to Mercer and his men. Mercer has rarely played so finely and never with a more infectious courage. It was as though the challenge of the hour had given him strength to cast off the burden of the years and find his youth again. With arms outstretched, and with his long legs and big feet plying, he sailed into his tackles with a bold Tennysonian vigour – "Clang, battle-axe, and flash brand!" – and his example brought a like response from the others, notably Smith, Daniel, and Forbes. It was only when Logie and Roper lay prostrate, one at each end of the field, that Newcastle were able at long last to work their will. Teams:

ARSENAL: Swindin; Barnes, Smith (L.); Forbes, Daniel, Mercer; Cox, Logie, Holton, Lishman, Roper.

NEWCASTLE UNITED: Simpson; Cowell, McMichael; Harvey, Brennan, Robledo (E.); Walker, Foulkes, Milburn, Robledo (G.), Mitchell.

from THE BEDSIDE GUARDIAN I *1952*

Yugoslavia v. Russia, 1952

A. J. LIEBLING

On the morning following the opening of the Olympic Games I found myself on a train bound from Helsinki to the much smaller city of Tampere, about a hundred miles north of here, to see a soccer game between Neuvostoliitto, which is the Finnish name for the Union of Soviet Socialist Republics, and Jugoslavia, which is what the Finns call Yugoslavia.

I had some herring sandwiches and an ice-cream cone on the platform at Riihimäki, and discovered that a couple of football experts from English papers of large circulation were on the same train. I met them again in midafternoon on the platform at Tampere, and as we set out for the football field one of them, a thin fellow with a North Country accent, informed me that

the Yugos had fair outplayed Brazil in Rio and had far too
much experience for the Russians. Our way led through the
main street of the town and across a bridge adorned with four
huge and explicit nudes. (This explicitness is a feature of
Finnish public sculpture; my football man told me that there
was only one thing to compare with Finnish statuary in
London, and that in a place where one wouldn't ordinarily
notice it, high up on a government building.) The two Englishmen lingered to admire the statues, and I went along to the
field.

Soon after finding myself a seat in the press row, I was
enveloped by Iron Curtain football correspondents. On my
left was a merry-looking young woman, red-cheeked, plump,
and with amazingly tufted black eyebrows, who told me in
French, after a few unsuccessful passes in other languages, that
she represented the Bulgarian press agency. On my right was a
Russian youth with an ovoid, olive face and grey-blue eye – a
knowledgeable and authoritative man, from his appearance,
who looked at me in a challenging and disillusioned way, as if
to defy me to try any of my capitalistic dialectics on him. I
asked him in English if he wanted to sit next to the girl, as they
had begun talking across me. He said, "Don't bother you,"
and gazed at me broodingly from under long Circassian
eyelashes.

"Who do you think will win?" I asked him.

"Who you think?" he parried unerringly.

"I don't know," I said, eager to disclaim *parti pris*.

"That's what I don't know also," he said, and we lapsed into
silence. He had a camera that looked complex enough to shoot
actinic rays or automatically vend Coca-Cola. He didn't use it
once during the game, from which I surmised that it was either
a tommy gun or a coop for a carrier pigeon, if not a piggy bank.

The game was to start at seven; it stays light until well after
ten in Tampere at this season. Despite the long wait ahead, the
field, locally referred to as a *stadion*, was filling up. Tampere
has a population of a hundred thousand, and the paid attendance
was eighteen thousand, of which at least ten thousand were

standees. There were wooden bleachers on both sides at mid-field, but most of the crowd stood on banks of earth at the ends. The town band tried its best to fill in the interval pleasantly for us, and succeeded very well as far as I was concerned. It played a more extensive version of "The Merry Widow" score than one hears in the usual capsule medley, and was surprisingly accomplished in Sousa marches. The bandsmen wore ordinary civilian clothes, but they all had white yachting caps. I asked the Bulgarian girl if she didn't think they were good and she said that the town was culturally undeveloped. A slip of paper giving the names of the referee and the linesmen was passed along our row; the referee was an Englishman and the linesmen were Finns. Then the Russian team came out for a bit of practice. They were big fellows in red jerseys and light-blue shorts, and they passed the ball about among themselves, kicking it with the sides of their feet and bouncing it off the tops of their heads with considerable adroitness. The Yugoslavs, believers in applied psychology, scorned practice and did not appear on the field until time to line up. They wore dark-blue jerseys and white shorts, and had many more tall men than the Russian side but were in general less chunky. Both teams were well received by the crowd. Newspapermen here have been trying to develop a new science of determining the political tone of an athletic cheer in Finnish, which is a Finno-Ugric language closely related to Estonian. Having lagged in this department, I can report only that the crowd cheered good and loud for both sides. Each team had brought a small but taut cheering section of its own, recruited from its Olympic and press delegations, and these were decidedly partisan. The Russian cheer, as nearly as I could make it out, was "Bra! Bra! Bra!," repeated as long as lungs and throats lasted. I am not even sure that it wasn't an unusually short, choppy rendition of "Rah! Rah! Rah!" About the Yugoslav yell I am equally uncertain, but it sounded to me like "Slahvee! Slahvee! Slahvee!", with a strong accent on the second syllable. This, I guessed, meant "Slavs", which seemed a likely thing for Slavs to shout. When things were going well, they would also shout "Haida!" I asked my Bulgarian newspaperwoman what this meant, and she said, "*Ça veut dire, 'Allons!'* "

Punctually at seven, the two teams, of eleven men each, lined up, and play began. Soccer, I might point out, is a game whose main object is brilliantly easy to understand, similar in some respects to ice hockey and polo. There is a goal, something like a netted lean-to, at each end of the field. All you have to do is kick the ball into your opponents' net or bump it in with your head, and you get one point. But the speed and intricacy of the play is something else again. Good players pass and dribble almost as accurately as if they were allowed to use their hands. They know how to be almost as rough as if they were allowed to tackle. And they have to have practically superhuman endurance, since they play two forty-five-minute halves without any substitutions. The weather was favourable to these exertions, being just under sixty degrees, but the turf was wet and slippery. (It has rained several times a day in Finland since the opening of the Games, and when the cold sun does shine through, it does not say long enough to dry out the ground.) Another thing about soccer is that it is a game whose subtleties the spectator quickly begins to think he understands – the despair of the man who goes down the field for a pass and doesn't get it, the *légerdepied* of the dribbler who seems to offer the ball to his charging opponent and then takes it away, leaving the opponent prone. It was not difficult to keep track of the individual players, since they wore numbers on their jerseys. Two especially caught my eye – the husky, barrel-chested Russian No. 7, named Trofimov, one of those hustling players, always tearing off somewhere at great speed, whom you see in every field sport and who impress you until you realize that they are usually going nowhere in particular, and the extremely tall Yugoslav No. 11, named Zebec, as fine a pantomimist as we have had since the days of the silent movies, who transmitted all his emotions to the crowd by a fine sequence of Yugoslavian gestures and kept leaping high into the air to receive the ball on his apparently cast-iron potato, while the Russians writhed in baffled fury at the lesser altitudes that were all they succeeded in attaining.

For the first half hour, neither side scored, although the Yugos had the ball in Russian territory at least two-thirds of the time. My Russian neighbour with the camera was already making me feel sorry for him, because of the emotional tension I could see he was suffering. He was one of those sotto-voce cheerers, a type I recognized from my race-track experience. They are afraid to cheer out loud because they feel it may jinx the outcome, a feeling whose origins are undoubtedly somewhere in Frazer, if one cared to look for them. "Cheep, cheep!" he would begin softly when a Russian player got the ball and started a run; then, imploringly and with accelerated enunciation, "Cheep *cheep!*" as the player hesitated, looking for somebody to pass to; "*Cheep cheep!*" – with wild hope, as the player moved on again; and, finally, "Cheep *cheep* CHEEP!" But the last "cheep" was always followed by a gusty sigh – "Oo – ah!" – as the cove lost the ball.

Ivanov, the Russian goalkeeper, who looked like Chaliapin in a peaked cap, made some splendid stops, once flying horizontally to his right, his body exactly parallel to the ground, as he stopped the ball with his chest and hugged it. (The goalkeeper is allowed to use his hands.) I shouted "Bra!" and drew a glance of tender gratitude from beneath the Bulgarian girl's right eyebrow. Then a Yugo named Mitic scored the first goal, and I impartially shouted "Haida!" The crowd cheered unanimously – the special Russian rooting section excepted – denoting, I suppose, either a diminution within half an hour of the Communist faction in the local metalworkers' union (Tampere is a factory town) or simply excitement. Four minutes later, a Yugo named Ognjanov scored another goal. By this time, the Bulgarian girl was crying, although I should have thought that since Russia had put Bulgaria out of the tournament in an earlier game, she might harbour some resentment toward the team. My Russian looked so glum that I feared he would reveal the true nature of his camera and possibly blow up the stadium. Then Zebec, the mimetic giraffe, kicked in a third goal. "Slahvee!" I shouted happily, and then "Haida!", for I am always for the underdog when he is on top. That was how the score stood at half time, 3–0. *"Il est bon, votre Ivanov,"* I remarked – unkindly, I'm afraid – to my Balkan colleague. *"Mais il a trop de travail."* Her sobs prevented her from answering coherently.

The second half opened catastrophically for my neighbours. Ognjanov scored again in the first minute. Eight minutes later, a player named Bobrov scored the first goal for Russia. The man with the camera showed a slight flicker of animation, but he relapsed into his cataleptic state a bit later, when Zebec scored once more for the Yugos. The score stayed at 5–1 until fifteen minutes before the end of the game. Then the Russians scored two goals close together. The Yugos were obviously rattled. The man with the camera began his "Cheep, cheep!" again, like a robin reappearing with the spring.

Soon, however, the Yugos pulled themselves together and became cagey. They decided to play a defensive game and freeze the ball. The politically unstable crowd was now hysterically on the side of the Russians. I could sympathize with their switch to anti-deviationism, for it was plain to me that, in purest Finno-Ugric, they were shouting, "Cut the stalling!" I began to discern repulsive characteristics in even the heroic Zebec. When the Yugos had been well ahead, the Russian goalkeeper had come out of his net to snatch the ball virtually off Zebec's toe and Zebec had magnanimously jumped clear over the stooping man's head to avert a collision, landing asprawl on the turf ten feet away; now, in a similar situation, Zebec went into the goalie with both feet and then kicked himself free of the presumed cadaver. The crowd howled its disapproval so vociferously that for a moment I began to fear that Finland had followed the path of Czechoslovakia. The stalling lasted for ten minutes, and then somehow the Yugos lost the touch. Russia scored after eighty-seven minutes of play, with three minutes to go. And suddenly I sensed that everybody, including the Yugos, had the feeling that the Russians were going to get the tying goal. In international

soccer, a goal within three minutes is an unlikely proposition
(a team seldom gets more than half a dozen goals in a ninety-
minute game), but I would have bet even money the Russians
were going to get it. And in some mystic way they did, with
one minute to play. The marsh-fire of Communism now played
incandescently around the periphery of the *stadion* and the
welkin rang with the clarion of subversion. It sounded like
Ebbets Field in the days of Babe Herman. A Russian named
Petrov had banged the ball in with his head, which is the way
Herman used to field them.

One minute – a panicky one for the Yugoslavs – passed and
the whistle blew, ending the regular game with the teams tied
at 5–5. I turned to my Russian for information. He had
collapsed across the typewriter bench in front of him and was
sobbing. I gently touched his shoulder and in time brought
him back to an awareness of his surroundings. "What happens
now?" I asked. He sat up. "Fifteens minutes overtimes this
way," he said, sweeping a hand from right to left. "Then
change sides and fifteens minutes that way" – and he swept the
hand from left to right. "And if it's still tied?" I asked. "Play
again," he said. I could tell from his tone that he didn't have
any doubt that his team would careen on to victory, since it
was now, as the sportswriters would say, on the crest of a
surge. It seemed logical that a team like Yugoslavia, which had
allowed four goals in fifteen minutes, was played off its legs.
But the two extra periods produced neither scores nor drama,
and the game ended at 5–5.

On the way out, I encountered the thin English football man
again, and he said that the whole theory of the Yugoslav game
suffered from excessive finesse, although he did not phrase it
quite that way. I think he said, "They ran about too bloody
much." "Let the ball do the work, they always say in England,"
he told me. "Take more shots." I asked him if he thought the
Yugos would win the playoff, and he replied, "They've had a
nasty knock." He added that in all his life he had never seen
such a collapse, or such a rally, depending on how you wanted
to look at it.

The two teams played again in Tampere last night, and this time Yugoslavia beat Russia, 3–1. The Russians scored first; it was Bobrov again, according to the score card. But after that it was all Yugoslavia. Mitic, Bobek, and Cajkovski made the goals. Haida! Slahvee! Slahvee!

YUGOSLAVIA: Beara; Stankovic; Crnkovic; Tchaicowski, Horvat, Boskov; Ognjanov, Mitic, Vukas, Bobek, Zebec.

RUSSIA: Ivanov; Krijevski, Nyrkov; Netto, Bachachkine, Petrov; Trofimov, Nikolaiev, Bobrov, Beskov, Marjutin.

from THE NEW YORKER 2/8/52

Blackpool v. Bolton Wanderers, 1953

GEOFFREY GREEN

The Cup Final of 1953 will live in memory. It will live with that 100,000 crowd compressed within the stately curve of a Wembley Stadium once more bathed in the spring sunshine of a Saturday; it will live with that other countless multitude that viewed it second-hand upon the magic screen of television. It will live not only because of its highly colourful and emotional climax, that saw Blackpool emerge from a losing position of 1–3 twenty-five minutes from the end to pluck a glorious victory by four goals to three as the last seconds were being drained from the afternoon. It will live largely because here in the presence of the Queen and the Duke of Edinburgh the game of football, the game of the people, was crowned with all felicity in this year of Coronation and national rejoicing.

So Blackpool at the last came from the blue to gain their place in history for the first time. But where to begin the story of such an afternoon of contrast; of light and shade, of tragedy and error, of mediocrity and supreme quality? The thoughts go round in one's head as though they were coloured beads in a box.

First, perhaps, one should say, with a passing and kindly thought for Bolton, that seldom can there have been a more popular victory. Certainly there has never been one quite so dramatic. And never before has the lush stage of Wembley been so dominated by the performance of a single player. This popular sentiment and this performance embraced but a single subject – Stanley Matthews. This was his finest hour, and that it should come with such timing at such a moment at Wembley, when the eyes of the country were upon him in his third Cup Final, was a rightful consummation of a great career.

It is by the power to call souls out of the abyss into life that greatness is judged. So can Matthews be judged, for that exactly is what he achieved on this memorable Saturday. With twenty-five minutes left Bolton led by three goals to one and seemed assured of their fourth Wembley victory. Few then could cavil at their apparently unassailable position, for while two of their goals could be tabulated as gifts from a strangely hypnotized and unnerved Farm under the Blackpool crossbar – ever has Wembley been the graveyard of goalkeepers! – against this there could be set the sad fact that from the opening quarter of an hour Bolton had been reduced to ten effective men through a leg injury to Bell, their left-half.

Thus, with a disorganized team, they had taken what chances the gods had to offer, had played an open, fast game – with the long through pass to the dangerous Lofthouse as their sharpest dagger – and had worked themselves into a winning position, while their opponents time after time frittered away the openings Matthews created with deft artistry.

To understand the ending one must begin at the beginning. Within ninety seconds of the kick-off there came the first shaft of tragedy, Lofthouse lashed in a powerful low drive from twenty-five yards and Farm, perhaps taken by surprise and certainly beaten by a slight swerve off the pitch, allowed the swift-moving shot to glance off his arm into the net as he dived. Thus Blackpool, having scarcely touched the ball, at once gave Bolton a goal start. When Moir put Lofthouse clean through at the twentieth minute and the centre-forward, angling his shot past the advancing Farm, hit the far post a resounding thud the Blackpool fires were all but extinguished. But not quite, for in spite of everything, the fates were storing up their smiles for them until the climax, and this Lofthouse shot, as it proved, may well have been a turning point.

Certainly it looked like it when Blackpool, after some inept finishing by Taylor and Mudie, drew level for the first time ten minutes before half-time. Again the imp of Wembley produced a freak goal, for now as Mortensen, who had a fine match in every way, broke loose through the middle past Barrass and Ball and slammed a left-foot shot to the far post, the unfortunate Hassall, fast in retreat, ran straight across the line to divert the ball helplessly into his own net.

There is no defence against this sort of thing. But within four minutes Bolton were ahead again, and again Farm, still dazed by his error, was at fault. Langton curled a lob into the goalmouth where Moir, with quick perception, leapt across the face of Farm to divert the ball by perhaps the barest shade into the net. It was swift thought and action, no doubt, but a goal-keeper, especially of international standing, should never be caught in this way.

So Bolton led 2–1 at half-time in a match that thus far had produced too many moments of flat mediocrity. The goals were there, of course – and all the world loves a goal – but each was untidy. Bolton, with Bell limping at outside-left, Langton inside him, and Hassall playing finely at left-half, clearly were the more workmanlike, for Blackpool as yet withheld in their finishing the promise of some cultured approach play, where the ball was stroked along the ground. Matthews, as opportunity offered, tempted each of his forwards to rise above himself at the crux, but with no response.

So it was that when Bell, soaring off like some gull with a stricken wing, gallantly headed Holden's cross past Farm to give Bolton a 3–1 lead ten minutes after the interval it looked all over. But it was now that the afternoon suddenly took on a new quality. The colours became brighter, the outlines sharper. It was Matthews the artist who effected the transformation.

And so we came to the last breathless stage that will live on into history. The story book ending was at hand.

Matthews is a superb artist, a football genius beyond compare. He paints, as it were, in water-colours and not oils. His work always has had that beautiful bloom that oils cannot give. He has it within him to turn mice into horses, and nothing into everything. Now in those last twenty-five minutes he turned Blackpool into giants at a time when all his inspiration might well have drained away after earlier disappointment. Blackpool, in a word, began to hum like a machine in top gear – with the young Robinson at last recovered from his early anxiety – and suddenly the ten gallant men of Bolton were no longer sufficient to stay the hand of events.

As Matthews suddenly took an acutely measured pass from the diminutive Taylor there were twenty-two minutes left. Once again he left the bewildered Ball stranded; not this time with a lazy inside swerve, or that famous shuffling outward flick, but by pure acceleration. In a flash he was gone and at top speed he chipped a perfect centre spinning unpleasantly under the far corner of the Bolton cross-bar. Hanson no more than got his fingers to the ball and as it fell loose, about to pass outside the post, Mortensen, straining forward at full stretch, just managed to squeeze the ball home through the only space left to him. It was through the eye of a needle.

That was 2–3, and now there came a new hope as rising excitement flooded the arena like light, with Matthews reaching the heights of his creative instinct. Outside and inside, he kept bewildering opponent after opponent as a torrent of noise swelled up from the vast crowd. But still Bolton hung on bravely, with Wheeler, Barrass, and Hassall their heroes. Once Perry missed a "sitter" from Matthews, so did Mudie and then Hanson saved brilliantly from Mortensen at point blank range.

Three minutes remained. Surely it was over now for all that Matthews, Johnston, Mortensen, and little Taylor had tried to to do. But no. Suddenly there came an infringement against Mortensen on the edge of the penalty area, and before one could realize it there lay the ball in the back of the Bolton net, shot home like some red-hot thunderbolt by Mortensen himself from twenty yards; 3–3 and now extra time. But no again. With time measured in seconds Taylor again gave Matthews a lovely pass. Matthews, with supreme balance and control, now went inside Ball. As Barrass challenged he left the centre-half on the outside, streaked in to the by-line, cut back a diagonal pass and Perry, putting away all past sins, shot home low past a defence cut to ribbons.

Blackpool had won unbelievably. Almost at once came the whistle to create an unforgettable last scene, for there, amidst all the roar and the clatter, and the long shadows of the Band of the Brigade of Guards in the centre of the sunlit field, was Matthews being carried shoulder high with his captain Johnston from the place of triumph, each with his hand upon the Cup.

Poor Bolton, they were left with the red hot cinders. But what a finish, and the most goals ever scored at Wembley!

BLACKPOOL: Farm; Shimwell, Garrett; Fenton, Johnston, Robinson; Matthews, Taylor, Mortensen, Mudie, Perry.

BOLTON WANDERERS: Hanson; Ball, Banks; Wheeler, Barrass, Bell; Holden, Moir, Lofthouse, Hassall, Langton.

from THE TIMES 4/5/53

England v. Hungary, 1953

GEOFFREY GREEN

Yesterday by 4 o'clock on a grey winter's afternoon within the bowl of Wembley Stadium the inevitable had happened. To those who had seen the shadows of the recent years creeping closer and closer there was perhaps no real surprise. England at last were beaten by the foreign invader on solid English soil. And it was to a great side from Hungary, the Olympic champions, that the final honour fell. They have won a most precious prize by their rich, overflowing, and to English patriots, unbelievable victory of six goals to three over an England side that was cut to ribbons for most of an astonishing afternoon. Here, indeed, did we attend, all 100,000 of us, the twilight of the gods.

There is no sense in writing that England were a poor side. Everything in this world is comparative. Taken within the framework of British football they were acceptable. This same combination – with the addition of the absent Finney – could probably win against Scotland at Hampden Park next April. But here, on Wembley's velvet turf, they found themselves strangers in a strange world, a world of flitting red spirits, for such did the Hungarians seem as they moved at devastating pace with superb skill and powerful finish in their cherry bright shirts.

One has talked about the new conception of football as developed by the continentals and South Americans. Always the main criticism against the style has been its lack of a final punch near goal. One has thought at times, too, that perhaps the perfection of football was to be found somewhere between the hard hitting, open British method and this other more subtle, probing infiltration.

Yesterday the Hungarians, with perfect team work, demonstrated this midway point to perfection. Theirs was a mixture of exquisite short passing and the long English game. The whole of it was knit by exact ball control and mounted by a speed of movement and surprise of thought that had an English team ground into Wembley's pitch a long way from the end. The Hungarians, in fact, moved the ball swiftly along the ground with delicate flicks or used the long pass in the air. And the point was that they used these variations as they wished, changing the point of attack at remarkable speed. To round it off – this was the real point – they shot with the accuracy and speed of archers. It was Agincourt in reverse.

One has always said that the day the continental learned to shoot would be the moment British football would have to wake up. That moment has come at last. In truth, it has been around the corner for some time, but there can no longer be any doubt. England's sad end on the national stage now proclaims it to the skies.

Outpaced and outmanoeuvred by this intelligent exposition of football, England never were truly in the match. There were odd moments certainly when a fitful hope spurted up, such as when Sewell put us level at one all at the quarter hour and later during a brave rally that took England to half-time 2–4 down. Yet these were merely the stirrings of a patriot who clung jealously to the past. The cold voice of reason always pressed home the truth.

Indeed from the very first minute the writing loomed large on Wembley's steep and tight-packed banks. Within sixty seconds Hungary took the lead when a quick central thrust by Bozsik, Zakarias, and Hidegkuti left the centre-forward to sell a perfect dummy and lash home, right foot, a swift rising shot to the top corner of Merrick's net. The ball was white and gleaming. It could have been a dove of peace. Rather it was a bird of ill-omen, for from that moment the Hungarians shot ten times to every once of England.

Just before England drew level a sharp move of fascinating beauty, both in conception and execution, between Czibor and Puskas was finished off by Hidegkuti. But the Dutch referee gave the centre-forward offside, which perhaps was charitable as things ended. Yet the English reply when it did come also arrived excitingly, for Johnston, intercepting in his own penalty area, ran forward to send Mortensen through. A quick pass to the left next set Sewell free and that was one all as a low left-foot shot beat Grosics.

But hope was quickly stilled. Within twenty-eight minutes Hungary led 4–1. However disturbing it might have been, it was breathtaking. At the twentieth minute, for instance, Puskas sent Czibor racing down the left and from Kocsis's flick Hidegkuti put Hungary ahead again at close range, the ball hitting Eckersley as he tried a desperate interception. Almost at once Kocsis sent the fast-moving Czibor, who entered the attack time after time down the right flank, past

Eckersley. A diagonal ground pass was pulled back by Puskas, evading a tackle in an inside-right position – sheer jugglery, this – and finished off with a fizzing left-foot shot inside the near post: 1–3.

Minutes later a free kick by the progressive Bozsik was diverted by Puskas's heel past the diving Merrick, and England, 4–1 down with the half-hour not yet struck, were an army in retreat and disorder. Certainly some flagging courage was whipped in that rally up to half-time by Matthews and Mortensen, both of whom played their hearts out, crowded as they were, but though it brought a goal it could no more turn back the tide of elusive red shirts than if a fly had settled on the centre circle.

After an acrobatic save by Grosics to a great header by Robb it was Mortensen, dashing away from a throw-in, losing then recovering the ball and calling up some of his dynamic past, who now set Wembley roaring as he sped through like a whippet to shoot England's second goal. But 2–4 down at half-time clearly demanded a miracle in the space left after some of the desperate escapes at Merrick's end that had gone hand in hand with the telling Hungarian thrusts and overall authority.

Within ten minutes of the interval the past was dead and buried for ever. A great rising shot by Bozsik as the ball was caressed back to him on the edge of the penalty area after Merrick had turned Czibor's header on to the post made it 5–2, and moments later Hidegkuti brought his personal contribution to three within a perfect performance as he volleyed home Hungary's sixth goal from a lob by Puskas. It was too much. Though Ramsey said the last word of all for England with a penalty kick when Mortensen was brought down half an hour from the end, the crucial lines had been written and declaimed long since by Hungary in the sunshine of the early afternoon. Ten minutes before the end Grosics, with an injured arm, surrendered his charge to Geller, his substitute, but by now a Hungarian goalkeeper was but a formal requirement.

So was history made. England were beaten at all points, on

the ground, in the air, and tactically. Hidegkuti, a centre-forward who played deep in the rear supplying the midfield link to probing and brilliant inside-forwards and fast wingers, not only left Johnston a lonely, detached figure on the edge of England's penalty area but also scored three goals completely to beat the English defensive retreat. But Johnston was not to blame: the whole side was unhinged. The speed, cunning, and shooting power of the Hungarian forwards provided a spectacle not to be forgotten.

Long passes out of defence to five forwards who showed football dressed in new colours was something not seen before in this country. We have our Matthews and our Finney certainly, but they are alone. Taylor and Sewell, hard as they and the whole side now fought to the last drop, were by comparison mere workers with scarcely a shot between them at the side of progressive, dangerous artists who seemed able to adjust themselves at will to any demand. When extreme skill was needed it was there. When some fire and bite entered the battle after half-time it made no difference.

English football can be proud of its past. But it must awake to a new future.

ENGLAND: Merrick; Ramsey, Eckersley; Wright, Johnston, Dickson; Matthews, Taylor, Mortensen, Sewell, Robb.

HUNGARY: Grosics; Buazanszky, Lantos; Bozsik, Lorant, Zakarias; Budai, Kocsis, Hidegkuti, Puskas, Czibor.

from THE TIMES *26/11/53*

West Bromwich Albion v. Port Vale, 1954

J. P. W. MALLALIEU

Just as Liverpool looks down on Lancashire, so Birmingham looks down on the Black Country. Birmingham's skilled workers affect to think that you can look after yourself in, say, West Bromwich, provided you know how to hit something with a hammer. They make fun of the sing-song Black Country accent, so barely distinguishable from their own – it is said that when a Smethwick man reported that his "mate" had fallen in, the police dragged the canal, only to find later that the man was talking about the "mate" in his sandwich. They make fun of the Black Country's detectable ignorance – only a week ago a policeman in court accused someone of removing a "cewit" of coal. This delighted Birmingham which knows a cwt. when it sees one.

But, with the fun-making, there is mingled some respect. Though a man from the Black Country seldom appears to know anything, it is suspected that much of his "ignorance" is just the adopted camouflage of an area where one's attitude to the law is somewhat informal, and that it would be unwise for anyone who owes money to a Black Country man to presume on it.

This somewhat ungenerous attitude to the Black Country pervades even the football life of Birmingham. It happens that West Bromwich Albion at the moment are the finest team in the country. They lead the First Division by several points and have the best chance of any team in years of winning the Cup-and-Championship double. But, to Birmingham, they are just hammer-hitters. Worse, they are uncomfortably near-neighbours – the Albion Ground at The Hawthorns is half in Birmingham so that, during a match, the ball passes to and fro across the municipal boundaries – and, if there is one thing that a Birmingham man dislikes more than the Black Country

186

as a whole, it is his immediate neighbour in it. After a home
match, a crowd of Villa supporters stand expectantly in front
of the score-board where the full-time results are to be shown,
and if they find that Wolves, West Brom, or, of course,
Birmingham itself, have been beaten, they find no trouble in
concealing their satisfaction.

All this made Villa Park a perfect background for Port Vale
when, last Saturday, they came to face the mighty West Bromwich in the semi-final of the F.A. Cup. Port Vale are from the
Potteries, an area of skilled labour – unlike the roughnecks
from just down the street. Even more important, they come
from full forty miles away, and so cannot, by any stretch of the
term, be called neighbours. So the people of Birmingham, to a
man, were on their side. So, too, was everyone else in the 69,000
crowd – except, of course, the regular West Brom supporters –
for Port Vale are the little team from the Third Division with
six locally-born players in their side; and the instincts of every
neutral sportsman in the country yearns to the little man.

So, though the crowd before the match was soberly dressed
and decorously spoken, as befitted a great occasion in the red-
brick, fusty, Victorian ground of Aston Villa, when the teams
came out the decorousness continued only for West Brom.
Port Vale were given a wild, expectant ovation of uncontainable
goodwill. In one tragic second they were to dissipate this goodwill and so, I believe, to lose the match. But that is a story for
the second half.

The first half was a story of first-time tackling. Territorially,
West Bromwich had much more of the game; but it was little
use to them. If they got the ball near the Port Vale penalty-
area, they found that all the Port Vale players, except the
centre-forward, were there too. Even the wing-forwards came
back in defence, going like bullocks at who ever had the ball,
robbing him and then belting it away upfield. Throughout the
half the brilliant West Brom forwards only twice had a sight of
goal, and each time King, the Port Vale goalkeeper, saved
brilliantly. Then just as we were saying that this Port Vale
defence, effective though it was, was not really football, and

could not be expected to stand up to ninety minutes' battering, the Port Vale attack suddenly broke away and, after a beautiful cross from the left wing, all but scored. This shook West Brom. They began to make mistakes; and suddenly, after what might be called a loose scrum on the Albion goal-line – there was the referee pointing to the centre, and Port Vale, somehow, had scored. The exultation did not subside until the teams had left the field for half-time.

Poor Albion! I felt. They had had the burden of playing a Cup-tie every Saturday – for every team is out to beat the League leaders. They had tried to play class football, even in this match. But they were a goal down against a team which has specialized in holding to a snap-goal lead, and they had most of the Villa Park crowd and the whole of the rest of the country against them. You could see in the first ten minutes of the second half that the strain had already told, that the team was near to breaking. Their passing went wrong, their tackling went wrong, their shooting went wrong. It seemed that their heart had gone wrong. Then came one of those flukes. Dugdale, the West Brom centre-half, kicked a long curving ball towards goal. He probably meant it as a centre, but it was too far for that, and was going comfortably into the Port Vale goal-keeper's arms when it touched the head of a defender. It glided into goal.

You could have heard the silence miles away.

This, of course, put heart into West Bromwich; but it did not markedly depress either Port Vale or their supporting millions – for West Brom did not look like scoring another goal, and Port Vale sometimes did. But then came the tragedy.

A West Brom forward was tackled on the edge of the Port Vale penalty area, probably just inside it. Forward and defender fell together as the ball went loose; but, as the forward rose to follow it, the defender, still lying on the ground, in that split second between sensible civilization and madness, jabbed both feet into the forward's stomach.

Everyone on the ground, bar the referee and the linesman, seemed to have seen that vicious foul; and, at the sight of it, all the bursting goodwill towards Port Vale evaporated. Booing burst from the ground, but what was even more marked was the inward transfer of support, as silently audible as the look on a woman's face when she catches her man out. Port Vale, who, in the later stages of the Cup have been carried through by their tackling, but even more by a bubbling sea of emotion, could not stand the bump when suddenly they were dropped.

All spirit left them as if it had been switched off at the main. Within two minutes there was another incident on the edge of their penalty area which this time the referee swooped on with hardly concealed relief. Allen, the West Brom centre-forward, stood for a second or two peering into the ground as though trying to wipe the vision of Wembley from his eyes. Then a sliding run, a bang, and there was Allen, left hand thrown wildly upright, relief and joy bursting from his body; and there was the end.

There was the end, even for the Brummagen crowd who wanted to see a neighbour lose. There was the end for Port Vale. There was the end for people like me who, when our own team is not at the stake, like to see the little man win. But there was not the end for the little, red-faced Port Vale defender, who, in a second, saw everything that the Five Towns had recently been fighting for appear to be slipping between his legs; who had half a second to think about it and still lunged; who knows, and will know to the end of his day, that a half-instinctive action of his cost his team, not only the chance of Wembley, but also goodwill from nearly all men.

WEST BROMWICH ALBION: Heath; Rickaby, Millard; Dudley Dugdale, Barlow; Griffin, Ryan, Allen, Nichols, Lee.

PORT VALE: King; Turner, Potts; Mullard, Cheadle, Sposson; Askey, Leake, Hayward, Griffiths, Cunliffe.

from SPORTING DAYS *1955*

West Bromwich Albion
v. Preston North End, 1954

ALAN ROSS

In a match that had many changes of character and fortune, West Bromwich Albion finally acquired the F.A. Cup, that choicest and most robust of sporting blooms, with a goal scored by Griffin just over one minute from the end. When the Cup and medals had been presented by Queen Elizabeth the Queen Mother, Millard, the West Bromwich captain, in a voice rough with the strength, smoke, and endurance of the Midlands, called for three cheers for Her Majesty. His voice, almost more than anything else, produced the right epitaph for a season in which both the great prizes have gone to Midland clubs.

In the event West Bromwich deserved their triumph, not only for the beauty and sweep of their play throughout the season, but on the afternoon. With a team lately and rudely knocked from what had seemed a remote pedestal, and further upset by a spate of injuries, they took a long while to find their confidence and to recapture their understanding.

Five minutes after half-time they were 2–1 down, but, gradually gaining strength and carried for some vital moments on Barlow's great shoulders, they discovered the old resources still there, and moved on to their final climax. Preston, who had looked the merest shade the more dangerous side, if only for the persistent threat of Finney, never quite realized their powers near goal.

Dugdale held the Albion defence together as firmly as a nail, and even Finney's persuasions, not quite as bewitching as usual, could not create that extra man over.

The start neatly crystallized the style of both teams, Barlow picked up a pass in midfield, slid the ball hard and fast down the central gap, and Allen, gliding in after it, flicked it out to Lee. The winger's shot, from an open position, skidded a yard or so wide. It was the strategy of the direct pass, swept along the ground, made for the roving Allen or Nicholls to slip through the opening almost before it was made and before the defensive net could haul them in.

Next Preston. Marston pushed the ball on to Docherty, Docherty held it, turned inwards, and with the West Bromwich defence moving with him suddenly sent it outwards to Finney, standing motionless, a lone barracuda well away from the swarming pilot fish.

In the first five minutes Finney made three successive runs, beating four men each time, and his easy acceleration past Millard looked ominously impressive. Subsequently, though Millard and Barlow were often left sprawling by him, Finney never got completely clear, for someone either came across from the other side or his colleagues were so well marked that he was forced into waiting too long for his final pass.

It was, on an uncertain, occasionally sunny, afternoon, a remarkably cool opening. Few mistakes were made, no nerves betrayed. The tackling was so hard, however, and the marking so mercilessly close that none of the lovely *arpeggios* of which both these sides are capable was apparent for a long while. The phrasing was subtle, but necessarily hurried.

After Thompson had moved well to save a good header from Allen, West Bromwich took the lead in the twenty-first minute. Cunningham, the Preston right-back, went to kick hard up-field, the ball rebounded off the oncoming Lee, and as Lee flashed it wide of Thompson across goal, Allen was up to tap it into an empty net.

Within a minute Preston were level. From the kick-off they attacked on the right, and the ball was pushed back to Docherty. Docherty swung the ball hard towards goal, and Morrison sailed up near the left post to nod it in.

The rest of the first half was moderate, but equally fought. Thompson once saved finely from Lee, Ryan twice moved strongly through the centre to catch the Preston defence standing square, and Wayman's taking of some difficult passes was miraculously deft. Just on half time there was a delicate

West Bromwich attack in which five men stroked the ball diagonally from corner to corner without interruption.

The second half began with a run by Finney the whole length of the field, an effortless scale by the master as if to keep his hand in, and then Preston went ahead. Docherty, feinting to pass to Finney, instead put a sharp diagonal pass down the middle where Wayman loitered, apparently high and dry off-side.

Play seemed to stop, but no whistle blew and methodically though rather in the manner of a man idly doodling on paper Wayman dribbled formally round Sanders, who made a token resistance, and shot into goal. But a real goal it was.

For a quarter of an hour Preston seemed likely to hold, if not increase, that lead. Then, after a clever Allen-Lee move had broken up, Barlow brushed his way through right into the penalty area, where Docherty upset him not more than five yards from goal. Allen scored with the penalty kick, though Thompson, getting a hand to a hard drive, all but brought off an incredible save.

Now West Bromwich took on their true stature. Again, Barlow, a Colossus gathering strength and pace with each step, strode up-field and flicked out a pass to Lee standing unmarked. Lee centred and Walton, tearing back in defence, nearly cracked it into his own goal.

Five minutes from the end, in one of the less-frequent Preston attacks. Foster shot hard for the left-hand corner of the West Bromwich goal, but Sanders, anticipating smartly, soared up and turned the ball away.

That, if any, was the vital moment. West Bromwich came back full of spirit, though there was barely a minute and a half to go, when Kennedy pushed the ball up to Ryan and Ryan chipped it on to Griffin. Up till now Griffin had looked the weakest forward on the field. This time he took his chance in the grand manner. He slipped round Walton and, from what seemed an impossible scoring angle, drove the ball past Thompson and an inch inside the far post.

PRESTON NORTH END: Thompson; Cunningham, Walton; Docherty, Marston, Forbes; Finney, Foster, Wayman, Baxter, Morrison.

WEST BROMWICH ALBION: Sanders; Kennedy, Millard; Dudley, Dugdale, Barlow; Griffin, Ryan, Allen, Nicholls, Lee.

from THE OBSERVER *2/5/54*

Hungary v. England, 1954

GEOFFREY GREEN

We came and although we did not conquer we saw here in the People's Stadium this evening how football in its new world conception should be and is played. Hungary 7, England 1. That was the sad outcome of a continental trip that crystallized itself at the last into another ninety minutes of Magyar magic. Two crowns now sit triumphantly on the Hungarian brow. At Wembley, last November, they became the first national side from across the Channel ever to win on English soil. And now they can claim the greatest score ever achieved in history against England on a football field.

The day is now faded. The lights of Budapest city are winking. The streets are choked with bustling, excited people. Bells and klaxon horns intrude noisily as one tries to gather one's thoughts of yet another remarkable exposition of the game. It was one certainly as great as, if not greater than, we saw at Wembley. Then, on that distant November day, the unexpectedness of it all took our breath away. But now we should have been prepared. And we were not prepared.

The question now is sharp and clear. What is English football to do? The first hard fact to digest, if one can even swallow it, is that we are no longer a major world power in the game. We must reshape our whole outlook. The WM tactical formation against a team such as these Hungarians, with its new ideas, is as out-dated as the horse-drawn bus.

G

This, no doubt, is neither the time nor the place for a theoretical discussion, but as one of the England players remarked after the cruel execution was all over, "I have never seen anything like it. They were men from another planet." One remembers clearly writing almost those very same words about the will-of-the-wisp Hungarians in their maroon shirts when they exposed the bankruptcy of our football six months ago.

As a match today's affair was dead at the end of the opening half hour. By then, Hungary already were three up and within a space of five minutes, around the quarter hour after the interval, they hit the English net three more times, so that, just as they had done at Wembley, it took them but sixty minutes to score six goals. It needs no profound mathematician to work out that horribly simple divisional sum.

Still, for all the cruel trend of events, here was football one could sit and watch until old age finally overcame one. Here was a cultural expression, a game which, even if it was not on this occasion hurtling with sharp conflict, was yet passionate and beautiful in its art. The Hungarian attack, in all its imaginative conception, was like light passing through a prism. It had all the colours of the rainbow and constantly the combination of those colours were changed.

It all seemed so easy, looking down upon the pattern from the steep side of this breath-taking stadium. But no doubt it is very different being an Englishman in a white shirt down in the heart of that rich green battlefield where the blazing sun cast its lengthening shadows. The English side, straining every sinew and fighting to the last breath, were simply outclassed. There is no other word to use. As a team they were outpaced, outmanoeuvred, and outthought. Defence, as one has seen before, was drawn into the most grotesque shapes by the fiendishly clever decoy work of a superbly swift Hungarian team.

Once more one saw that these Hungarians have probably achieved at this point of time as great a mastery over a football as any team in history. By a perfect mixture of the short

Continental game and the long pass English style they have found the best of two worlds, all this based upon quintessence of controlled speed and quick thinking. Their shooting, too, from all angles once more was deadly when it mattered. Merrick, indeed, faced a shower of arrows.

By comparison with Puskas and the rest of his scintillating forward line Harris, Sewell, Jezzard, Broadis, and Finney were single units, moving separately and only occasionally thinking along co-operative lines. True they might have scored more than once in a second half, which saw some sudden sparks from Finney and Broadis, but by then it mattered nothing, for the battle was already over, England long since had been reduced to an army in retreat, a defiant one certainly, but in retreat.

Defensively one can point at once to a real hero, Byrne. Wright, Dickinson, Staniforth, and Owen all played till their lungs must have been near to bursting, but Byrne stood alone for his poise and quality in a position that so soon began to disintegrate. The basic trouble, of course, quite apart from the difference in fundamental skills, was our tactical inefficiency. The whole structure was torn apart by the Bozsik-Hidegkuti stratagem, the link in midfield between the roving right-half and deep-playing centre-forward. These two were at the heart of most Hungarian attacks, and out of their subtle insinuation the rest of the forward line moved and worked out their incisive patterns like lightning.

It was exactly as it happened at Wembley, Hidegkuti was able to detach himself at will because there was no plan, so far as one could see, to stop him. From him little close passing triangles were formed. This was the decoy stage. Suddenly the long through pass was loosed either to the wingers or to Puskas and Kocsis going through the wide gaps created. Thus time after time Merrick and his backs were faced with almost hopeless situations. If England should have scored more than once the Hungarians themselves might well have reached the round dozen.

The Hungarians so far from passing their peak as some have suggested are still a wonderful side and quite clearly made

England look poorer than perhaps they truly were. In Puskas and Kocsis they have two great attacking inside forwards. Puskas, strong and square of build, is perhaps the more dangerous, achieving his effects with a broader, more obvious sweep of the brush. Kocsis, lean and subtle, is the more delicate artist who works with a greater subtlety but with equal effect, for he, too, like his captain, scored two fine goals.

The bell first began to toll for England at the tenth minute when Dickinson was penalized, harshly one felt, for a tackle on Hidegkuti twenty yards out and straight in front of goal. Puskas called up the powerful Lantos to take the kick and the next moment the ball had hit the far corner of Merrick's net like a thunderbolt. Decision or no decision that opened the floodgates. Twelve minutes later Staniforth blocked a swift cross from Kocsis and Puskas hit home the rebound from close range. At the half-hour the brilliant Kocsis, returning to the field after repairs for an injury when he crashed into massed photographers, at once volleyed in a chipped pass from Puskas. It was deadly artistry.

So it was 3–0 at the interval, with only one shot from Broadis which brought Grosics full length to show as any reply from England. In the middle of that opening half the Hungarians, turning on their full speed as if from a tap, moved with a brilliance that would have turned and dazzled any defence in the world. Once more, after an opening rally by England at the change of ends, which saw a shot from Harris blocked on the line, that tap was opened again. At the twelfth, fifteenth, and seventeenth minutes Kocsis, Toth, and Hidegkuti beat the helpless Merrick from moves that achieved their ends with the long defence-splitting ground pass following opening decoy work. Each time the whole forward line, with a rhythmic flow, were concerned in this form of infiltration.

As the score mounted so too did the appetites of the huge crowd – over 90,000 strong. Triumphantly and with a pounding beat the roar smote the heavens rá-rá-hajrá. How they loved this banquet! And when at last one tiny crumb for England was picked up by Broadis as he shot home finely, following a free kick by Dickinson, even that was not allowed to go unpunished. For once more, with some twenty minutes left, Puskas again raced clean through unchallenged from Hidegkuti's long through pass to snatch Hungary's seventh and final goal.

Though Finney, Broadis, and Sewell showed some touches and Finney once missed a sitter none of this really mattered, not even the fact that the Hungarians substituted Gellert for Grosics in goal before the end. It was over long ago. But what a feast, attended by representatives from over twenty nations, to remember and digest.

HUNGARY: G. Grosics; J. Buzanszky, M. Lantos; J. Bozsik, G. Lorant, J. Zakarias; J. Toth, S. Kocsis, N. Hidegkuti, F. Puskas, Z. Czibor.

ENGLAND: Merrick; Staniforth, Byrne; Wright, Owen, Dickinson; Harris, Sewell, Jezzard, Broadis, Finney.

from THE TIMES *24/5/54*

Germany v. Hungary, 1954

J. L. WEINSTEIN

Nothing that could have happened in the Final will alter the view that the Hungarians proved themselves the pick of the footballing nations in 1954.

The Germans at last had to be taken seriously; their victory over the Austrians proved their stability, the excellence of their defence, the punch of their attack. They steadily advanced in confidence from their first thrashing by the Hungarians, and were at the peak of their form at just the right moment.

In the Final, Germany undoubtedly played their best football of the tournament. Under pouring rain, before a 60,000 crowd in the Wankdorf Stadium, Berne, jammed round the slippery surface, it was to be expected that Germany's simple and direct approach would suffer less than the more cultured style of Hungary, which depended on delicacy of touch and pin-point accuracy.

Germany had already shown one outstanding quality: their appreciation of their own limitations. They had already scored from an enormously high percentage of their hard-won opportunities. How important this now proved to be is shown by the fact that out of five or six clear chances in the Final, Germany scored three goals. The Hungarians created their usual crop of openings, but for the first time in this Cup, they were denied the full reward.

Certainly Hungary had some appallingly bad luck; on any other day they might have had half a dozen goals and more. But granted all this, the fact remains that Germany were two goals down after eight minutes and went on to win the Final. To achieve this required more than luck, conditions more favourable to them than to their opponents; it demanded football character.

Above all else, the Germans were incredibly fit; this showed up the more because the Hungarians were manifestly feeling the strain of meeting both Brazil and Uruguay in the space of six days before the Final. We shall see that this fitness provoked some nasty aftermaths. In addition, Herberger had organized his defence in remarkable fashion. At times one wondered how it could survive. Twice Hungarian shots hit the post and bar, Hidegkuti in the first half, Kocsis in the second; yet again Kohlmeyer was there to save on the line; thrice Turek made superhuman saves, to say nothing of his glorious stop from a slashing drive by Czibor in the last critical minutes of the game. One will never forget how he deflected Hidegkuti's volley on the turn from five yards; it is from such saves that a team gains the inspiration to rise above itself.

History is made of small events, and three may be cited in connection with this most unexpected of finals. All concern human judgements. Firstly there was the question of whether Puskas should play. It was certainly a difficult decision to take. The team had beaten both Brazil and Uruguay without him, and there had long been friction between him and his wingers, Budai and Czibor, both on and off the field. At no time did it seem that the team were really happy at his return. In the event he was clearly troubled by his injury. He lacked the speed off the mark and above all, perhaps, the pin-point accuracy and efficiency he had always shown. A fit Puskas, one said afterwards, and the Hungarians would have won.

The second judgement was that of linesman Mervyn Griffiths of Wales in the last minute. Here was a point which will be discussed not only by those present, but also by those who watched the match on television, for years to come.

Finally, there was the recall of Helmut Rahn to join the World Cup party at the last minute, for it was Rahn who was to score the two goals which gave Germany their victory. Rahn, right-winger of Rot-Weiss Essen, was in South America when the list of twenty-two players for the World Cup was communicated by Germany to F.I.F.A. He had a brilliant club tour in Latin America. When Rot-Weiss startled a 50,000 crowd in Montevideo by beating Penarol 3–1, the newspapers reported that Rahn was one of the greatest forwards they had ever seen, and begged local initiative to snap him up with an offer. In fact Rahn was offered a contract by Penarol, and by all accounts a very substantial one. He might have accepted had not the Germans recalled him urgently for duty in Switzerland. He proved the most dangerous of the German forwards, and the judgement that he should be recalled was vital to our story.

Out of the beginning none could have expected such an end. In the sixth minute Boszik sent Kocsis through with a perfectly measured ground pass; his shot was charge down, and there was Puskas to ram the ball home to give Hungary the lead. Within two minutes another central thrust, and when Kocsis was blocked, trying to reach a misplaced back-pass from Kohlmeyer to Turek, in nipped Czibor, switched to the right wing, to increase the lead.

Less than three minutes later, however, the Germans struck when Morlock got a foot to a fast cross by Fritz Walter and diverted the ball past Grosics. The game was alight, and before long the Hungarians were further shaken when Rahn drove home a corner-kick to level the scores.

For the first time the Hungarians seemed visibly worried. Turning to the attack, they met Turek making the first of his fantastic saves, from a header by Kocsis – the kind which had already brought him so many goals in the World Cup – and Hidegkuti's drive hit the post.

Within the first half-hour of the second half Turek make two miraculous stops from Puskas, and Kohlmeyer kicked Toth's shot off the line after the last beautifully flowing linked movement between all the Hungarian forwards. Then Kocsis headed Czibor's centre against the cross-bar, and this seemed to have the effect of strengthening the Germans. Eckel and Mai began to get a firmer hold on the inside-forwards, relentlessly tackling, searching out the *chef d'orchestre* Fritz Walter, or launching their fast wingers at every opportunity.

As the end drew near the vast sections of German supporters grew quieter; everyone was expecting that there was something dramatic reserved for the end. The moment came through a misplaced pass by Boszik, perhaps one of the very few he had made during the years in which he had established himself as one of the greatest wing-halves in the world. It was a costly error. Schaefer in a flash had the ball through to Fritz Walter, and as the latter's centre was pushed clear, there was Rahn with steady aim to shoot home from fifteen yards past a despairing Grosics.

With only five minutes to go, amidst remarkable scenes, Germany were in the lead. In what time was left Hungary fought to the last ditch. Suddenly there was Puskas, who had faded completely from the game, darting on to a perfect diagonal pass from Toth behind Posipal to flash the ball past Turek. It looked a magnificent goal, of pure Hungarian vintage. But the flag of Mr Griffiths, the linesman on Puskas' side of the field, was up for off-side, and the last drop of succour was dashed from Hungarian lips. It seemed a doubtful decision, though angles can be difficult to judge, but it was perhaps the speed of the movement that deceived Mr Griffiths. It was tragic that so much hung on such a decision. Then, as the hands of the clock had almost reached their target, there came Turek's dramatic save from Czibor.

It was all over. The Cup was presented for the last time by Jules Rimet; the band played *Deutschland über Alles* – the 1954 World Cup had ended on a totally unexpected note.

GERMANY: Turek; Posipal, Kohlmeyer; Eckel, Liebrich, Mai; Rahn, Morlock, Walter (O.), Walter (F.), Schaefer.

HUNGARY: Grosics; Buzansky, Lantos; Boszik, Lorant, Zakarias; Czibor, Kocsis, Hidegkuti, Puskas, Toth.

from WORLD CUP *1954*

Manchester City v. Birmingham City, 1956

H. D. DAVIES

There is a story of how Philip of Macedon on one and the same day, realized three ambitions. He himself was proclaimed Supreme Victor in the Olympic Games. One of his generals routed a dangerous enemy in the field. His wife bore him a son. Philip, overwhelmed, is said to have flung himself to his knees and to have prayed Jove to send him at once a little misfortune!

Paul, captain of the Manchester City team which defeated Birmingham City 3–1 in the F.A. Challenge Cup Final here today had a somewhat similar experience. He, too, realized three ambitions. He kept his promise, made in an unhappy hour last year, to lead his team back to Wembley and receive the Cup from the Queen. He added a cup-winner's medal to his own forty-three caps and sundry other trophies. He did his duty to his adopted City of Manchester by adding City's Cup to United's Championship and so completing a brilliant double. But he showed no disposition after the game to kneel down and pray for any more misfortunes. He and his colleagues had had enough of those, beforehand, and to spare.

Paul's leadership throughout the competition has been based on the conviction that to reach Wembley two years in succession gives to a team an advantage over its opponents equivalent almost to an extra man. New-comers are more apt to be put off balance by pre-match strain and ballyhoo; by the long-drawn-out formalities; by the sight of the huge bowl lined by 100,000 spectators; by the presence of royal patrons; and by the chafing to begin. Above all, they are apt to think that Wembley's lush green turf is as innocent as it looks. Old hands tell us that the soft spongy surface can turn the legs of the fittest of men into leaden aching limbs at the end of an hour's running; and that the secret of playing there is to learn how to alternate intensive effort with periods of comparative ease.

If such, indeed, were Manchester City's ideas today they worked out admirably. Their forwards set about the Birmingham defence at once before it had time to settle down, and a superb opening goal by Hayes, in the third minute, was at once a tribute to their skill and their timing. Then a great equalizer by Kinsey seemed to restore Birmingham's poise, and for the next half-hour it was the turn of the Manchester defenders to take the shock. That they were able to do so and indeed hold out to the end, without conceding another goal, was due first to the matchless skill and reckless daring of Trautmann, and after that to the willingness of Ewing, Paul, and Little, and to a lesser degree Barnes, each to do two men's work in order to lighten the burden of those whose fitness was suspect.

To the general surprise, and to Manchester's relief, Leivers, on whom Birmingham naturally exerted the greatest pressure, got through a tremendous amount of work apparently without discomfort. Not so Johnstone. The little Scot, heavily bandaged, hobbled about, and dodged tackles during the first half in a most painful manner. Many, including the writer and the Birmingham defenders, wrote him off as a complete passenger. We ought to have known better!

Though Manchester City made a great leap forward in the second half, when Dyson and Johnstone scored admirably for them, and were thus encouraged to spread their fine feathers in a manner rarely seen in cup finals, it should not be forgotten how often the Manchester goal itself appeared to lie at the mercy of the Birmingham forwards. How else shall we explain the prodigies of skill and pluck and dogged effort whereby Ewing and Trautmann, the real heroes of the last tense phase, repulsed desperate attacks?

Twice Trautmann made what appeared to be suicidal dives at the feet of Brown and Murphy; and on the second occasion received for his pains a purely accidental, but none the less frightful blow on the back of the neck or head. This left him reeling and swaying with pain and concussion and how in this state, and with twelve minutes to go, he contrived to make two further saves of the last-ditch variety, even he cannot explain. But he does remember vaguely, hearing a large portion of the crowd singing "For he's a jolly good fellow": a novel way of showing sympathy, anyway, to a man, who, as it later turned out, had a broken neck.

Revie, brought in at the last moment as a substitute for Spurdle, the hapless victim of boils, chose the occasion to give one of the finest performances of his career, and so added another vivid chapter to one of the strangest stories in professional football. His skilful assortment of long and short passes, timed and measured to perfection, probed ceaselessly into the Birmingham defences; while his shrewd positioning in deep midfield enabled him to collect, re-label, and re-despatch Trautmann's constructive throws and clearances to his fellow-conspirators' lurking up-field.

Johnstone, by his quiet behaviour in the first half, was perhaps conserving his energies for the second. Certainly, when he scored his decisive goal, and again when he beat three men almost in the space of a hearthrug, he seemed to shake off his physical disabilities absolutely. To such purpose that one or two of the more cynically minded accused him of "putting it on." If that were so then Sir Laurence Olivier ought to be told about Johnstone. He would be glad to meet a mime of such first-rate quality.

For Birmingham Brown, the sprinter, strove zealously and perhaps a little monotonously, to break through along the left wing. Occasionally he did so, but he rarely found Murphy uncovered for the return pass: and if he tore on himself he met either Ewing charging in to kick the ball or, as once happened Trautmann diving down to roll the ball from his questing instep.

All in all Manchester City richly deserved their victory. In a game which was pleasantly free from all save minor infringements and excepting the injury to Trautmann, which no one could help, they had the greater number of exceptionally gifted and experienced artists. What is more, they had been at Wembley twelve months before.

MANCHESTER CITY: Trautmann; Lievers, Little; Barnes, Ewing, Paul Johnstone, Hayes, Revie, Dyson, Clarke.

BIRMINGHAM CITY: Merrick; Hall, Green; Newman, Smith, Boyd; Astall, Kinsey, Brown, Murphy, Govan.

from THE BEDSIDE GUARDIAN 5 *1956*

Corinthian-Casuals v. Bishop Auckland, 1956

H. E. BATES

I am very devoted to April Saturdays when rosetted legionaires invade London in their thousands and Trafalgar Square is full of men with a fine "never-been-beaten-yet" look on their sharp, lean Northern faces.

They add a new touch to the capital, robbing it of that

rather stern week-day commercial air of bowler hats and
malacca cane umbrellas, and tired typists running for trains.

Suddenly you feel that there is stern true business to be done,
and I never drive up through the high North London suburbia
of yellow forsythia and pink almond without hoping that the
football at Wembley will match the capital's fresh taut air.

Today, when Corinthian-Casuals held a ferocious Bishop
Auckland to a 1–1 draw after extra time, I need not, as it
turned out, have doubted it would be otherwise. It was one
of those matches which began shakily as if Wembley, rather
than either team, would be the victor, and ended with fine
flash and flare of trumpet for both sides.

From the kick-off it seemed as if a removal van I had seen in
the morning, bearing in loud blue letters the deadly slogan
"Bishops Move", might contain in it the worst of omens for
London's amateurs who, for ten minutes, dithered against
Auckland's opening attacks like a bevy of prep school-boys
over-inflated by ginger beer on a wet Wednesday afternoon.

For this first opening spell you could faintly hear the creak of
early doom. It was exactly as if the boys were playing the
masters, and twice in four minutes the ball was skimming
fiercely, as it was to do so often afterwards, over the Casuals'
bar. But nervous athletes are often the best athletes and
presently Casuals weathered the whip lash, pulled themselves
together, grew up, became completely adult, and began to ask
themselves who, after all, these North-eastern invaders
were.

They began to show their weakness and their strength.
Their weakness lay in the fact that their forwards were always
a fraction slower off the mark and in the tackle than Bishop
Auckland, and their strength in that their defence, which was
to end the match in pure triumph, was a pack of lionhearts
prepared to fight it out just beyond the crack of doom.

All this time it was really mostly Bishop Auckland's game.
Superbly generalled, as always, by Hardisty they hardly ever
fooled a pass, and their forwards, with O'Connell and Lewin

always prominent, were like a pack of hounds snapping and jabbing into any hole they could find. Then, just before half-time, the whole Casuals forward line woke out of a soporific daze and gave us a taste of that clean, open, sweet football that men remember when they speak of the Corinthians of old.

Kerruish, always fast and dangerous, put in a long run; all the forwards moved like lions in a swoop on the Auckland goal: and suddenly I sensed that the battle was a long, long way from over.

So it turned out to be. The second half was only just over ten minutes old when Casuals, swooping down again, forced a corner on the right-wing from which Sharratt made a fantastically good save, almost identical with one he had made just before half-time.

The ball went straight back to Insole for a second corner and the Essex cricket captain put over a close swinging ball that fell in the middle of a whole circus of players and a second later was in the net, put there by heaven knows whom, but probably by Citron.

The Bishop Aucklanders, hitherto as cold and tough as lumps of North Sea coast rock, did not care very greatly for this reverse and they showed signs, I thought, that pressure might even darken their hearts a little further.

Then, as so often happens, Hardisty began to pull them together. It is no bad business for a man to be playing at thirty-five as well as he played at twenty-five, but Hardisty disdains these trivialities and not only plays as a half-back but for a great part of the time as a sixth forward too – and there he was, prompting, weaving, scheming, pushing the ball through with immaculate beauty until, after seventy-seven minutes play, the reward came.

The Casuals defence got itself for a second or two in one of its few painful tangles and the ball went screaming for goal. Ahm, of whom we still had not seen the last, made a magnificent save, but in a flash McKenna had the ball back in the net.

Extra time started with the same guise of impending doom for Casuals as the game itself had begun.

Oliver shot marvellously only to see Ahm bring off another splendid save, the first of so many that in the end my April-chilling fingers could no longer applaud them. From then it was no longer every "Bishops Move".

The whole chess board was alive. The Aucklanders looked surprisingly good, and they got, if anything, better and better. But football is not, of course, all brains and feet; and the better they got the more the Casuals' spirits rose and heightened until they, too, were equally magnificent in quite another way. Ahm, in goal, the two backs, Alexander and Newton, Cowan, and the red-haired Vowels, all played, as they say, "blinders".

During this period Citron went off with a leg injury and McKenna joined him shortly afterwards. And then the strangest thing happened. In a spirited burst of inspiration every Casual forward, with Citron back, joined in a lovely movement that took the ball down to a spot that seemed as if selected by divine providence for Laybourne, just in front of goal.

Sometime in 1984 he will probably still be sitting in some Orwellian chimney corner sadly trying to remember what happened, and "look upon himself and curse his fate".

It was the golden chance every schoolboy dreams about and few men are ever given. In a moment it was lost.

"It would have been sheer robbery," said a gentleman with a large and ferocious ginger moustache who sat next to me, but I could not help feeling that both sides had had, in a sense, a victory as flaming as his own wide and splendid bristles.

CORINTHIAN-CASUALS: P. Ahm; F. C. Alexander, D. W. Newton; G. M. Suttleworth, R. Cowan, R. C. Vowels; D. J. Insole, J. Sanders, J. S. Laybourne, G. C. Citron, N. Kerruish.

BISHOP AUCKLAND: H. Sharratt; R. Fryer, T. Stewart; J. R. E. Hardisty, C. Cresswell, J. Nimmins; F. McKenna, D. J. Lewin, R. Oliver, S. O'Connell, B. Edwards.

from SUNDAY TIMES 8/4/56

Sweden v. Brazil, 1958

GEOFFREY GREEN

The summit meeting of football is over. Brazil are the new world champions and a long awaited ambition has at last come true for them. In the first final between the New and the Old worlds it was they, the lordly representatives of the New, who brought a lustre, a magical quality that dazzled Sweden. It was a climax that had a 52,000 crowd holding its breath in wonder from start to finish here in the Rasunda Stadium—from the moment when Sweden took a swift lead through Liedholm, only to find themselves finally bewildered by a brand of football craft beyond the understanding of many.

Here were dark, expressive sportsmen of a distant continent. When the moment of triumph finally was sounded by the whistle, in an excited, demonstrative and kindly way they broke into triumphal circuit of the soft battlefield scarred by rain, brandishing above their heads a huge Swedish flag – a gesture of appreciation for their reception. The stadium stood to them as if it were the host nation herself who had won, and at the end the King of Sweden himself posed for photographs with the victors while many of them were openly overcome by their achievement.

After twenty-eight years of effort Brazil were the World Champions. To the Briton, perhaps, such scenes might seem far-fetched. But warmth, and an undisguised emotionalism, gushes out of the Brazilians. So it was as Mr Drewry, president of F.I.F.A., presented the gold statuette to Bellini, Brazil's captain, that he said in echoing terms: "Here indeed was a match to remember, a clean, sporting struggle between two great teams." Every word was true. None could disagree with that, for here indeed *was* a match to remember. Perhaps one of the finest ever played in history came four years ago in Switzerland when Hungary overcame Uruguay in the semi-final round. This, perhaps, lacked the fire of that other occasion, but for sheer skill it was little behind. The cycles of the game, unfortunately, seldom coincide. If only it were possible to put Puskas and his Hungarians of 1954 on the field with the Brazil of today. But that must be something for one's dreams.

The bones of today's performance were these: at the fifth minute Liedholm, completing a slick penetrating move with Bergmark, Borjesson, and Simonsson, beat two men on a sixpenny piece and shot home low to put Sweden one up. On a slithery green pitch, as glistening as the rooftops of Stockholm after a night and morning of rain, it now looked as if the favourites were in for trouble. The Swedes had got the first blow and the South Americans, so rumour has it, are unhappy in the wet.

But rumour was now put to flight summarily as Vava, at centre-forward after all, with goals in the ninth minute and then again at the half-hour, put Brazil 2–1 ahead by the interval. After that Pelé and Zagallo made it 4–1, and though Simonsson brought Sweden back to 4–2, the swarthy Pelé, leaping like a black panther, headed Brazil to 5–2 as the last seconds of a breathtaking exposition ran out. Brazil, in fact, proved that they could play in the wet.

Thus Sweden, a fine side by any standards, were finally run into the ground by a brand of footballing dexterity that knew no bounds. Strongly and bravely as the Swedish defenders faced the surging tide – Gustavsson, Bergmark, and Borjesson in particular – they were at times left spinning like tops. Gren, especially, Simonsson and Liedholm too worked heroically in attack, threading many a subtle central move. But where they were stifled was out on the flanks and that, if nothing else mattered, finally settled their fate. Hamrin and Skoglund, their match winners in the past were now blanketed by the majestic covering of D. Santos and N. Santos at full-back and Sweden's sharpest fangs were drawn.

Not so Brazil. Didi, floating about mysteriously in midfield, was always the master link, the dynamo setting his attack into swift motion; and, besides Didi, with Vava and Pelé a piercing double central thrust, they had the one man above all others to turn pumpkins into coaches and mice into men – Garrincha, at outside-right. Rightly has he been called the Matthews of the New World. His methods are the same: the suggestion of the inward pass, the body-swerve, the flick past the defender's left side, and the glide to freedom at an unbelievable acceleration. Poor Axbom stuck to him the best he could, but time after time he was left as lonely as a mountain wind. Garrincha, in fact, and the subtle use made of him by Didi in a swiftly changing thread of infiltration, was beyond control and that was that. There lay the most sensitive nerve-centre of the whole battle and so Brazil stretched out and grasped their ambition.

This Brazilian side was greater than their combination of eight years ago because of its defence: and it was in another world to the side that lost 2–4 to England at Wembley in 1955. England alone held them here in the World Cup. It seems incredible to think of it now, but over the last fortnight the Brazilians have been growing in stature and today they reached their zenith. They showed football as a different conception; they killed the white skidding ball from all angles as if it was a lump of cottonwool. From Gilmar in goal, the giant Bellini at centre-half, right through the team they were fused in swift, intimate thought and execution at changing tempos. They combined the theatrical with the practical and Sweden too often were left chasing dark shadows.

It was in fact a performance of superlatives and Brazil came to life that moment at the ninth minute when Garrincha, receiving from Didi, left Axbom stranded, swept into the by-line for Vava to flash in his diagonal cross. That was 1–1 and a moment later Pelé nearly uprooted the Swedish post with a left foot shot from twenty yards. But there was no holding Garrincha and again, at the half-hour, it was the old echo, Pelé, Didi, Garrincha, the flick, the by-line, the diagonal cross, and Vava striking again at close range. Ten minutes after the change of ends, Pelé with sleight of foot jugglery, flicked up a cross from Zagallo, balanced the ball on his instep, chipped it over Gustavsson and leapt round the centre-half to volley home. Who can live with this sort of stuff?

That was 3–1 to Brazil and the signal for individual exhibition in all corners of the field. Then it was 4–1 as Zagallo, cutting in on a rebound punished a mistake by Bergmark. Liedholm, with a long through pass, put Simonsson beautifully in for 4–2; and there might have been a penalty at each end as Sweden rallied fiercely and momentarily. But all hope was gone, and a swift header by Pelé from Zagallo's cross wrote the last word.

SWEDEN: Svensson; Bergmark, Axbom; Borjesson, Gustavsson, Parling; Hamrin, Gren, Simonsson, Liedholm, Skoglund.

BRAZIL: Gilmar; D. Santos, N. Santos; Zito, Bellini, Orlando; Garrincha, Didi, Vava, Pelé, Zagallo.

from THE TIMES *30/6/58*

PART III

The Titans

"There's music in the names I used to know,
And magic where I heard them, long ago."

THOMAS MOULT *The Names*

Alfred Lyttelton

EDWARD LYTTELTON

Alfred Lyttelton, the first double international at soccer and cricket, was a K.C. and an M.P. He was the father of Lord Chandos.

The newspaper writers who recorded Alfred Lyttelton's successes at other games have never known what he was as a "flying man" at the Eton game, or a centre-forward in the very early days of the Association game. He was over six-foot-one, and his onrush was like a tornado. There have been other players more deft at dribbling, there have been a few, very few, of greater speed, and there have been heavier players, but I never knew one who combined the three great essentials, and added to them a surprising accuracy at kicking goals and "bunting" his opponents. This last faculty he exercised by dint of a jerk of his hips, not as ordinarily by lowering the shoulder, and so the aggressor could see no signs of the terrific impact coming. Once playing against the Royal Engineers I saw him make a run down from one end of the field to the other and floor four last men on the way – the last two having charged him simultaneously from opposite sides, and both rebounding on to their backs – and shoot the goal at the end. Added to which he was generally in exactly the right state of irascibility, during most of the game, except when a successful "bunt" dissolved him into a loud merry laugh, in which the prostrate victim not infrequently joined. His method of securing a goal was peculiar and seldom failed, especially in the Association game, at which in those days a great deal more individual play was allowed than is now. He would run towards the corner and then swiftly turn inwards, running parallel to the back line, and some ten yards from it. At this point he was pursued probably by three of the opponents, barely keeping up. This continued till he got opposite the further goal-post, and then one huge foot was smartly dropped on to the ball, stopping it dead, and of course the pursuers all ran a yard or so too far, not suspecting the sudden pull up: thus he had a clear shot at the goal. When things grew to be exciting and his ardour rose to a formidable heat, he would come thundering down with the heavy knees far advanced and all the para- phernalia of a Homeric onset. Thus it was no wonder that he was adored by the Black Country and Kennington Oval crowds, who used to shriek ecstatically every time he got a run down. Once in the dingiest purlieus of the Oval Pavilion, when we were playing a University cricket match, about 1876, a diminutive unwashed tapster hailed me with cordiality, "Ha Lyttelton, I'm glad to see you – but it's your brother we all love so – to see him knock 'em down at football, oh it does my 'eart good, it does!"

from ALFRED LYTTELTON *1923*

W. N. Cobbold

ALFRED GIBSON and WILLIAM PICKFORD

If one were to ask, who were the three greatest forwards of all time, no matter what other two were named, W. N. Cobbold would perhaps come first to the lips. This is placing the Old Carthusian on a pedestal indeed, but there are few who knew Cobbold in his prime who would not agree. One may doubt, of course, whether the famous Cambridge forward would be able to cope with the modern half-back – the *enfant terrible* of the football field. One could almost see Ernest Needham smile if he had to oppose Cobbold as we knew him. An individualist, as Cobbold undoubtedly was, might conceivably receive short shrift from a smashing half-back of the type of Alf Leake. There are those who think that the Cobbold type of forward would thrive even in these days of a scientific trio of halves who play the modern game; but the mere fact that there are no players of the Cobbold type is at least a negative proof that they might not be successful under the prevailing conditions of defensive play.

Bethel Robinson, who used to partner Nick Ross in the Preston North End club in the old days and was known as a versatile player of a very high order, could play at half and at full back equally well. He played against Cobbold frequently in 1884, when both men were in their prime, and Robinson's opinion is that there never was, and never would be, a forward so clever and deadly as Cobbold. He regarded him as the greatest forward of all time.

It is very difficult for a man who has retired from the game for nearly twenty years to compare the men of his day with the players of modern times. The tendency is to glorify the past at the expense of the present. I feel sure that Cobbold, had he played at any time during the past three years, would have had to alter his style to excel as he did in the old days. His methods were the correct and effective methods at the time he played, but I am certain in my own mind that they would not meet with anything like the same success today. All the same, such was the masterly mind of the man, I believe he would have adapted himself to modern conditions and still have held his place as a prince of forwards.

Judging him, however, by what he was and did, Cobbold must rank as a giant. He was individualistic in style, but he also had the power of combining in a high degree. In those days "dribbling" was the great game, and one only passed the ball when one was completely hemmed in, and not always even then. The chief difference between the forward play of the old days and the present day might be described in this way: the old forward only passed when he could not do anything else; while the new forward passes because he cannot do anything else.

Cobbold was not the last of the dribblers, for he passed the tradition on to the younger generation of the Corinthians, and R. E. Foster in particular was a magnificent exponent of the art. Of the present generation S. S. Harris is a very able dribbler, but he too finds that passing forms the major part of the forward game. Amongst modern professionals, J. Walton, of Tottenham Hotspur, is the only dribbler of note, and clever though he is, he does not find dribbling pay against a really good half-back. Dribbling, like back-heeling, must be used with great discretion against anything like a powerful defence.

W. N. Cobbold, however, was not a mere dribbler. He was essentially a scoring forward, and one, too, that made most of his own chances. One could not, for instance, conceive a greater contrast in style than Cobbold and Bloomer, both inside-forwards. The former was almost continuously on the ball, while the Derby man seems to be doing nothing, and doing it well, for the greater part of the game. When Cobbold got possession of the ball he seemed to keep it glued to his toe, darting hither and thither as he pursued a tortuous course towards goal. One man was practically powerless to stop him. Two men might stay his career by dividing their attentions between the man and the ball, but they were not always successful even then. Very frequently Cobbold would shoulder his way through a whole crowd of the opposition, and emerge triumphant with the ball at his toe. He was built for hard, strenuous play, but he did not go to work like a battering-ram. He seemed to possess the knack of following what Herbert Spencer calls the line of least resistance. If anyone got in his way he would try to get round him, but if not, his opponent usually felt the weight of a ponderous shoulder, and he did not ask, "By your leave?"

In one respect at least Cobbold had no superior, if, indeed, he ever had an equal – I mean in shooting at goal. He could shoot in any position, and he sent the ball in like a charge from a hundred-ton gun. He could shoot with several opponents clinging round him, and if only he had two feet of daylight to aim at, he seldom missed the mark. In this respect modern forwards have a lot to learn. For shooting there is no Cobbold nowadays, nor any one approaching him. Why is it? Why is it? Must we again put it down to the prowess of the modern backs and goalkeeper?

Cobbold was powerfully built, strong on his legs, and with

determination written all over him. It was probably this latter
quality that exalted him above his fellows. It is amazing what
one strong determined man can do. Cobbold knew his own
strength, and he never gave up. He always fought till the last
gasp, and it is curious how, if one can survive the "last gasp",
one's adversary fades away, for he too at this time has usually
shot his bolt. Great, daring, original, plucky, fierce, chivalrous,
the Old Charterhouse boy has passed out of the arena of
football conflict, but those who saw his great deeds some twenty
years ago will always be inclined to repeat the scriptural
reflection that – "There were giants in the land in those
days".

from ASSOCIATION FOOTBALL AND
THE MEN WHO MADE IT *1906*

John Goodall

IVAN SHARPE

The death of John Goodall, on May 20, 1942, at the age of
78, removed from Association Football a figure-head of the
playing field of the days when the game's artistry was being
created. An inside-forward – mainly inside-right – he played
a prominent part in the triumphs of the Preston "Invincibles"
whom he helped to capture Cup and League Championship
in 1888–9, appearing often also as centre-forward.

Later he assisted Derby County with similar success,
Glossop and Watford, occupying positions in management
with the last two clubs. Capped by England fourteen times he
helped in his Derby days to bring out Steve Bloomer and to
act as guide, philosopher, and friend to many a young player.

Goodall was the footballer perfect – as near as the title can
be claimed. He was gentlemanly always in method, and owed
much of his success to cool judgement, marked ever by

masterly control of the ball. His control, like that of Colin
Veitch of Newcastle United, was so complete that the ball was
seldom bounding out of his reach – it seemed tied to his toe.
Hence he had those extra moments of time that enable the
great player to plan the next move.

Coolness and gentility were his other names; they were
equalled by his judgement. Like Vivian Woodward and other
stars of simple style, he made the game appear easy. There were
times when his vigorous centre-half-back brother Archie . . . a
man of steel muscle . . . played behind John in the Derby
team. And Archie could be heard calling to rattled opponents
who were "bumping" John: "What's the matter, sonny?
Trying to play rough? I'll *lean* against you in a minute!"
It was a warning no wise opponent failed to heed.

John Goodall believed in the natural footballer – he was one
himself. He was also one of the pioneers who created and
developed team-work and combination.

He fell foul of the moderns soon after the offside law was
amended in 1925–6 by decrying the rush and tumble of current
soccer, by declaring in *Athletic News* that the Preston ("Proud
Preston") of his day would give any of the existing teams "six
goals start and a beating". Probably his words were taken too
literally. What he meant was that the modern game was all too
hectic and short of genuine skill.

John Goodall's parents were Scotch, but his father – a
corporal in the Scottish fusiliers – was on the move so much
that John was born in London, Archie in Belfast, and a sister
in Edinburgh.

John learned his football in the Kilmarnock area. In 1883,
he went for a time to Great Lever near Bolton, and there was
"kidnapped", as he put it, from Bolton Wanderers by the
North End, whose representatives bundled him into a cab and
had him on the way to Preston – by a roundabout route –
before he really knew what they wanted.

He closed his career with Mardy in South Wales in the old
Southern League Second Division, and in January 1913,
played for them against Swansea in his fiftieth year.

He held that football had deteriorated in quality, and cited as the principal cause: "The players think of the manager, the directors, the Press and the spectators. Between the four they come to the ground. They try to suit everyone and they end by pleasing no one."

He has left a name in Association Football that no player can surpass – he was a pioneer of supreme skill and always his sportsmanship was of the highest standard.

from ATHLETIC NEWS FOOTBALL ANNUAL *1942-3*

Archie Hunter

ALFRED GIBSON and WILLIAM PICKFORD

There was only one Archie Hunter. There will never be another, so far as first-class football is concerned; indeed, it is difficult to see how another could arise. After all, men are products of their times. You would require lost conditions to be restored before you could get another Archie Hunter. The young professional of twenty-one, in receipt of £4 per week, is not going to be a leader of men; he is not going to act as an inspiration. Archie Hunter was great mainly, if not solely, because he loved football. Men do not love football in the same way nowadays; the professional does not always look forward with intense longing to the week-end to come. Often he would shirk the weekend task if he could.

Archie Hunter was the product of the old amateur spirit. Because a great many Scots came to England for football purposes long before the legalization of professionalism, it has often been assumed that Archie and Andy Hunter migrated to Birmingham with the specific object of playing football with Aston Villa. But that was not so. As a matter of fact, Archie Hunter did not know where the Aston Villa ground was when

he came to the Midland capital. In the season before Archie
came to Birmingham to fill a business position, the Calthorpe,
then the leading Birmingham team, had undertaken a Scottish
tour. They met Ayr and Mauchline, and Archie Hunter, who
was a playing member of the Ayr Thistle club, had met them.
Accordingly in the first few hours' leisure he had he went in
search of the Calthorpe ground, but failed to find it. He told
a fellow-worker of his unsuccessful quest, and that fellow-
worker happened to be an Aston Villa enthusiast. They were
few in number then, were Aston Villa enthusiasts, but they
were ever a keen set. He promptly invited Archie to look up
the Villa players, and told him of the association of George
Ramsay, a fellow Scot, with the club. Archie turned out for the
Villa, and who shall say what his accession meant to them?
But for his coming it is conceivable that the Villa might have
remained a purely local team, indeed, they might have gone the
way of hundreds of other clubs of moderate strength. St.
George's or Aston Trinity might have gone ahead instead of
the Villa.

What a sensation Archie's play caused! Hundreds of new
adherents came each week to watch a forward the like of
whom had never been seen in Birmingham games. I do not
believe there has ever been quite such a fascinating player.
Some men may have dribbled as well; others may have shot
as hard or as straight, but no forward that I have seen ever
dominated a game as Archie Hunter did. It was a black afternoon when he could not get off, and as he had an employer who
had small sympathy with football, he was never certain as to
his movements on Saturday afternoons. Often he left business
in bare time to catch the brake in which the rest of the team
were waiting round a convenient corner close to the place where
Archie was employed, and on one occasion the Villa chartered a
special train in order that their captain might reach Nottingham
in time for a match. That was an unheard-of thing in those
days, but whatever had to be done, Archie's presence must be
secured if that were humanly possible. Often in the early days
Archie used to play as "A. Centre", in order that it might

appear to certain of the outside world that he had not spent his Saturday half-holiday on the football field.

Archie Hunter was a born leader. He had a subtle influence on the Aston Villa team, and he was the idol of the crowd. What a roar there used to be as, just when it looked as though the Villa were destined to begin the game with ten men, Archie would leap into the arena. When he first came to Birmingham he always wore the regulation football cap, a kind of skull cap terminating in a point and a tassel. What a picture of health he looked! He was a well-built and indeed powerful man; like many young Scots he was raw-boned, and he was prodigiously strong about the hips. When Archie turned round and put his base into the ribs of an opponent the latter realized that there was a man about. Archie knew how to charge, too; he was a nasty player to adopt rough-and-tumble methods against. Occasionally unscrupulous opponents used to court a return charge, and usually they wished that they had not opened the debate.

Archie was a mild-mannered man; indeed, his bright, boyish face was wreathed in perpetual smiles, but he was a man in earnest. Like Nick Ross of later times, Archie Hunter went on to the field "to play fitba'," not to loll and dawdle about. He was loved by all honourable and sportsmanlike opponents, and even the few less reputable adversaries he met did not like to risk a second exhibition of that manly scorn which used to flash from Archie's eye when an illegal and underhand trick was played upon him.

Archie Hunter was a prince of dribblers. It was not an unusual performance of his to start at the half-way mark, and dribble through the whole of the opposing team! He would not lose the ball until he had literally dribbled it between the posts. I have seen him do that many times. The way in which, when apparently circumvented, he would turn round and keep the man off with his hindquarters while he adroitly put the ball back to a colleague, used to mystify every one; his opponent seemed at a loss to know what to do. Archie was a deadly shot too, while he knew all the tricks which made for effective combination. People marvelled last year at the skilful way in which Hampton, the young Villa centre, screwed the ball out to the wings. Why, Archie Hunter did that as no man has ever done it since. A dozen times in the course of a single game have I seen Archie, when going at full speed, suddenly swing the ball out to Andy or Eli Davis. It would go to an inch where it was intended that it should do.

But great as he was as a placer, he was much greater as a captain. "Now, lads!" was his invocation, and it seemed able to transform a mediocre performer into an enthusiastic expert. He seemed to know how to treat everyone, and he got the maximum amount of work out of every colleague. I often wonder what modern defenders would say if they had to deal with a dozen shots in the course of a match such as Archie and Olly Whateley used to get in? Goals are harder to get today than ever they were, I admit, but the shooting is paltry compared to what it was in Archie's day. There is no player in Great Britain who has any conception of the pace and directness with which Whateley used to shoot.

Earnest, terribly earnest, was Archie when leading an attack, but what a grand fellow he was at the festive board! There used to be a convivial gathering after every match in those days; that was part and parcel of the art of football. Whatever friction had occurred on the field of play, it was never (or rarely) carried further. Archie was not a great singer, but, like most men of character, he could make his hearers feel that he was interpreting something to them. He could sing many good old Scotch melodies well, but who among his friends of those days will ever forget Archie's great song, *Where are all those bright hearts now?* Let me give you a stanza; the words and sentiment are a shade above some of the modern ditties one hears at festive gatherings. It was sung to the tune of *Do you ken John Peel*. Here is a verse of Archie's favourite contribution:

> "Whaur are a' these bright hearts noo
> That were then sae leal and true?
> Some hae left life's troubled scene,
> Some still are struggling through,

And some hae risen high
In life's changeful destiny;
For they rose wi' the lark in the morning."

Some of the men who heard that song were rough in their way, but the voice of levity was hushed when Archie was on his legs giving that in true Scottish style. There was more pure enjoyment in the football and the football gatherings of that day than there is today or ever will be again. We are all too mercenary now.

Poor Archie lies at rest in the Villa Corner at Wilton Cemetery, Birmingham. Eli Davis lies there too, so do other Villa worthies. There is a handsome tombstone to the memory of the greatest leader the Villa have ever possessed; it was erected by the Villa club in conjunction with the Old Villan's Society. Archie died at the Royal Exchange, High Street, Aston.

From his window could be seen the crowds making for Perry Barr. Gaunt as a skeleton, he was an Aston Villa man when he could scarcely draw a breath. He would have his bed wheeled to the window on Saturday afternoons, and there he would watch the eager throng bustling towards the scene of his many triumphs. It was infinitely pathetic to see that wasted frame and to think what an indomitable spirit it confined. Archie played with the Villa until he was a long way behind his best form. He played until he had a species of stroke while acting in a League match at Everton. That was the warning-note that he must give up the pastime; he accepted the hint and became a member of committee, but he was not the power in the council room that he had been on the field.

The refusal of the Scottish Football Association to recognize the claims of the Anglo-Scots deprived Archie of his international cap; it also deprived Scotland of a great player; still it must be admitted that Scotland's need was not acute then. There were plenty of giants in the land in Archie's day. But what would Scotland say to a centre of Archie's class today!

from ASSOCIATION FOOTBALL AND
THE MEN WHO MADE IT *1906*

G. O. Smith

C. B. FRY

Corinthians and Cricketers, full of interest and information about an important period in the history of field-games, is in the nature of a Pindaric ode in prose. Its central subject is one man – his fame and prowess in football. But that select personality is a theme song, as it were, that introduces, among kindred topics, a great Public School, a great University, a great Club, and a great formative area of what is now a great national and international entertainment. Some would say an industrial entertainment . . .

The elegant and blameless football now seen on occasions, e.g. at Wembley, did not come from the Midland and Northern industrial towns, though of the skill a good deal did, but from the now supposedly obsolete Old Boys teams. Indeed, but for the Old Boys clubs – Carthusians, Etonians, Westminsters, Salopians, Reptonians and the like – the world of soccer would never have seen the Corinthians, in their day the greatest of all amateur football clubs yet known or likely to be known.

This epoch-making club came into being through the selective and organising ability of N. L. Jackson. He saw that if he avoided cup-tie competition he could skim off the cream of the Old Boys clubs into a quasi-international amateur team. This he did, and in 1886, he being on the Selection Committee, ten Corinthians and one professional appeared at Hampden Park to represent England v. Scotland. There has never been a stronger England team.

But let us now consider G. O. Smith,* our hero, and his compeers, if any, and his times. A genius in football he was. Like all geniuses he rose on stepping-stones of his real self by taking infinite pains in terms of his natural gifts.

He came up to Oxford from Charterhouse with as big a

* See also "A Visit to G. O. Smith", page 494.

name as any Freshman ever in Association football. He was
not alone as a Carthusian eminent – E. C. Bliss, E. Farquhar
Buzzard, R. J. Salt and C. D. Hewitt were all Blues with him.
In the 1893–4 Varsity match when I was captain we had the
strongest team that ever played for either University, but we
lost.

The ground was frozen at Queen's Club and was more
suited to skating than football. We had five internationals, but
not for skating. G.O. played extremely well all the same, and
he was as good a centre-forward then as ever afterwards.
A gem.

His rating as the finest man in his place who ever played for
England is generally accepted. But such rating cannot be
proved correct. *De gustibus* comes in. So do changes of con-
ditions of play. Anyhow he was the cleverest centre-forward
I saw between 1888 and 1903 – my years of first-class football.
Clever is not the word. He was inspired.

He was of medium height, slight and almost frail in build.
He was a quick mover but not a sprinter. He was uncannily
prehensile of foot and almost delicately neat. What made him
was his skill in elusive movements, his quickness in seeing how
best to bestow his passes, his accuracy and his remarkable
penetrative dribbling. He swung a marvellously heavy foot in
shooting – always along the turf and terrifically swift.

The yarn that he was a weak shot in his early first-class
seasons is just a yarn. I played often with and against him, and
he was as straight and hard a shot as I have ever met except
perhaps only Steven Bloomer of Derby County, on one of
Steve's special days. G.O.'s was every day.

The Corinthian players of the eighties used to say that
Tinsley Lindley of their great forward-line was at least as good
a centre. Theirs was a great line – Bambridge, Cobbold,
Lindley, Brann and either Aubrey Smith or Spilsbury. Lindley,
like G.O., was slim and elusive, with a knack of slipping in
unexpected shots, but he did not shoot as hard as G.O.

G.O. was, you might say, an epitome of Charterhouse football. He was an emanation of a hot-bed of skill in the game

produced by a long tradition and a fast sandy field where delay meant loss of the ball and inaccuracy a troublesome bounce.

Charterhouse, originally buried in London near Smithfield Market, was transferred to Godalming by Doctor Haig-Brown – its factor Headmaster. He selected a convenient table-land, built fine buildings and laid out fine grounds. He could say with Dido – *Urbem quam statui, vidi; mea moenia vidi* – The City I founded I have seen; my city walls I have seen. No wonder Dr. Haig-Brown was naturally annoyed when some idiot in a complimentary speech said that the Doctor's only defect was that he was not a Carthusian! The Doctor had a beard, and it positively stood out every hair at right-angles.

There were many fine footballers bred on the hill at Godalming. The brothers Walters, A. M. and P. M., were the best pair of backs who played for England in my time; C. Wreford Brown and Blenkiron were two excellent centre-halves; and among the earlier Carthusian footballers were two fine cricketers: Major E. G. Wynyard, D.S.O., and Sir C. Aubrey Smith, the actor and film hero. Yet the strange thing was that Charterhouse cricket, though of course good, was not at that time up to the standard of the football. They had no cricket master at all. I was a classical master there for two years and only just escaped being taught by the head boy, Lord Beveridge. But I did not teach cricket – I was not allowed.

G.O. in his schooldays was a great run-getter, but he had a peculiar short-handle lean-down style. He was a formally correct off-driver and cutter with an excellent defence, but although he scored a famous match-winning century for Oxford v. Cambridge he was not a good model for the average young batsman. Not upstanding enough and not free enough in his driving. No left arm swing. In fact he batted like a very good putter at golf. Nevertheless, a useful man on any side, he would have collected stacks of runs in Australia.

By the way, he had curiously fine grey eyes and grey eyelashes such as any girl would envy. He read History at Oxford and the Keble Dons thought well of him. I guess he taught well as a schoolmaster; he was kind, quiet, and peculiarly patient.

He is worth reading about, as also are many of his contemporaries, and much of his conspicuous context.

from Introduction to CORINTHIANS AND CRICKETERS *1955*

Billy Meredith

PERCY M. YOUNG

Like Caesar's Gaul the career of William Meredith was divided into three parts. He was of Wales, of Manchester City, and of Manchester United, with each affiliation interlocking. The argument as to who is or was the greatest footballer in the world will continue for ever; it is unlikely, however, that Meredith's claim will ever be disallowed before any neutral and informed tribunal.

A genius requires certain parental co-operation: he must be born at the right time. So it is that an apparent equality of talent as between two contestants for the honours of posterity must be subjected to an Aristotelian scrutiny. Thus we begin to consider the hero, heroically, as within the classical unities – of time, place, and action. The invasion of the north-west of England by Welshmen of the northern counties of the Principality had been in sporadic progress for six centuries before Meredith's intention to storm Manchester was fulfilled; but seldom, if ever, were such incursions so beneficial to all parties. Meredith's journey was in two stages, and at the end of the first he camped in mid-Cheshire.

In 1894 Northwich Victoria, one of the oldest teams in England, were in dire straits, having fallen out of the Second Division. The club was much involved in Welsh affairs, generally participating in the Welsh Cup, and for ever inviting promising young Welshmen to join its ranks. This time it was a pale-faced youth from Chirk, near Wrexham. Meredith came from a fine school of football, for he, like Di Jones, Lot Jones and Charles Morris, had been tutored by T. E. Thomas, treasurer of the Welsh Association for years. Thomas was a schoolmaster in Chirk with a particular aptitude for educating in the broadest sense: therefore he rescued the unacademic Meredith from the coal-pit to which he had been consigned and taught him how to capitalize his unique talents.

In Northwich they were sceptical. An echo passes down the years. "He is," remarked one sage in the hearing of a boy on the edge of the field, "too bloody slow for us." The point was: Meredith feinted and teased, kept the ball attached to his person by invisible bonds, and lured unwitting opponents to distraction and destruction, not seeking his end with the crude demonstrations that won easy acclaim. In Cheshire, clearly, he was before his time. The old ways died hard there, and, besides, Meredith was at first as enigmatic to his friends as to his foes. He was also too much of a showman. The toothpick, adopted in the first place to supplant the messy habit of chewing tobacco, but rapidly seen as a gimmick and readily exploited as such by its possessor; the habit of running outside the touch-line with the ball correctly grooved just within the field of play: these were commented on disparagingly. Anyway Meredith, always deceptive in the run, was too bloody slow. He played six matches or so for Northwich and then went to Manchester. Or, to be academically precise, he went as a City player to Newcastle.

"The first League match between these teams was played this afternoon at St. James's Park, Newcastle. The City eleven included W. Meredith, an amateur from Chirk, who partnered Finnerhan on the right wing. Nash was put in the centre-half position, and Dyer, having now sufficiently recovered from his severe injury, took the former's place. On account of the long and tiring journey, the players left Manchester yesterday and stayed at Roker overnight.

"The weather had been very wet and stormy since yesterday and when the game commenced there was only a small gate.

Thompson started for Newcastle, the City playing downhill.
Meredith was the first to show up and McReddie was just
robbed by Creilly. A rush by Thompson was dangerous, Smith
relieving at a critical moment. Corners were uselessly taken by
each side, and a free kick was shot over, but Finnerhan opened
the scoring with a splendid shot after ten minutes' play. A
grounder from McKane equalized the score a minute later. A
fast run and centre by Meredith ended in Sharpless scoring
again for the City. Another goal followed, Dickson heading
through from a free kick taken by Jeffrey. Excellent play by
the visitors' forwards came next. Halftime score: Newcastle,
two goals; City, two goals;

"McReddie was the first away on restarting, but Dickson
got the ball in an apparently offside position, Thompson with
a curling shot giving the homesters the lead. From a grand
centre from Meredith McReddie headed past Lowrey. A
moment later the latter player was hurt and left the field.
Sharples added another beauty for the visitors, and Graham
equalized. Sharples had a great goal disallowed.

Newcastle United: 5
Manchester City: 4"*

Meredith's first match at Hyde Road was on 3 November,
against – Newton Heath. Although Newton Heath won by
5–2 the new boy was again reputed to have shown promise.

Meredith was the complete footballer. He was a superb ball
player. It often seemed that his feet were endowed with the
sensitivity and suppleness in manipulation of another man's
hands. In this mastery he was a pioneer; his subtleties were of
intellectual provenance, natively Welsh, and the pity of British
football is that he has had too few disciples. There was,
however, more to it than mere jugglery. "A player," wrote
Meredith,† "is always fairly master of the situation so long as
he feels that he has the ball completely under his control. Now
it is not necessary that to accomplish this he should have the

---

* *Manchester Evening News*, 27 October 1894.
† *Association Football*, II, p. 12-13.

ball within a few inches of his toe or almost tied to his feet. I admit that a fast man who can reduce the space between himself and the ball, to bring it always within say, a couple of feet while yet travelling at top speed, will possess a big advantage, but the art of wing play is to have a definite idea of what you intend to do with the ball, presuming things go all right, and also to maintain direct sympathy with the ball, even whilst it is some yards in front of one." In an essay of technical brilliance (which loses none of its point in modern setting) Meredith gives more than a hint of his psychological attitude to the well-rehearsed improvisations that so often caught the defence in two minds. He lives in the memory on account of dazzling bravura movements down the wing and to the corner flag, whence he would centre with unerring accuracy. The staple of early twentieth-century journalism was: "Meredith centred and Turnbull headed into the net".* He scored, on the average, one goal in every three matches in which he played,† and his own comment is relevant: "A wing man who never attempts a shot, and who always requires to 'shake hands' with the corner-flag before centring, will soon find that he invites far closer attention than he would if he left the defence in complete ignorance whether he intended to shoot, centre, or pass. It is the player of originality and initiative, the man with cool self-possession, who knows just what he can do, and just what he ought not to attempt to do, but can measure up, not only his own speed and capabilities, but those of his opponent to a nicety – this is the type of player who will make his mark."

Meredith's powers of divination often left his opponents as figures of comedy. On one muddy day at Clayton Meredith bore down on goal with none but the goalkeeper to frustrate him. The ball was heavy, and the goalkeeper, so certain that a low shot was inevitable, dived. Meredith held the ball until the goalkeeper was in descent, and then coolly lifted it over his helpless arms into the net. The crowd roared with laughter.

* See *Western Mail*, 22 April 1958.
† In 1898–99 he set up an English record for a wing-forward by scoring 36 goals in 33 matches.

As to Meredith's use of the pass, this led to frequent fantasy, for he constantly allied himself with the supporting half-back, who was at the ready to receive the back pass and to return the ball to the departing winger. Half-backs accustomed to Meredith and in harmony with his thoughts were made to appear larger than life-size, as also were inside-forwards apt to his intentions.

Meredith won the F.A. Cup for Manchester City (whom he captained in the 1904 Final) by direct means. He scored the only goal. He won it for the United by indirect means, as has been shown. To Wales he was Wales. As was Lloyd George in one sphere so was Meredith in another; but whereas the former was all eloquence the latter was as silent, it was written, as a Trappist monk. On occasion, however, he was known to speak. But only in extreme neglect. If he received no pass for ten minutes he would call up his captain, "Charlie, you'll need me before the game's out". In 1912 Meredith's services to his country were marked by the organization of a Welsh National Testimonial (or Meredith's "Shilling Fund"), and at the same time Manchester United gave him a benefit match, and a complimentary dinner. The Great War soon supervened, and with it surely the final curtain for Meredith. But no, the man was indestructible. He continued methodically to train, and at the end of hostilities was in his old and accustomed place.

On Thursday, 26 February 1920, Wales played Scotland at Ninian Park, Cardiff. Before the match – which ended in a draw – Mr S. H. Nicholls presented Meredith with a silver epergne, subscribed for by members of the Welsh F.A. to mark his fiftieth appearance in the red of Wales. The artist was still superb. He "contributed a dazzling run which was greatly admired by the crowd. Obtaining possession in midfield, he cleverly evaded all would-be tacklers, and dribbled the ball to the Scottish goal-line. He then cut in and delivered a high drive from a difficult angle". So it continued, from time to time. "The evergreen Meredith," concluded the *Western Mail*, "gave glimpses of his one time brilliance, and despite his years it is very doubtful if Wales possesses a player who is worthy to

H*

step into his shoes." Less than a month later Meredith played
in his last international at Highbury, against England. Here,
indeed, generations overlapped. With Meredith in the
Welsh side was Vizard, against him Frank Bowen and Charles
Buchan.

In August 1921 Meredith retraced his steps and once again
became a City player. On 25 August Hyde Road was thronged
with 35,000 spectators all intrigued by "the reappearance of
Meredith, who played his first game for City exactly twenty-
seven years ago. Meredith's hair has become iron-grey, but his
footwork is as good and his figure as lithe as ever, and if he is a
bit slower his great experience enables him to nurse himself
carefully and to call up at the critical moment his old dash.
His game on Saturday – and he had the honour of being
largely responsible for City's first goal – showed that there is
still a good deal of football left in him."* The visiting team
that day was Aston Villa, who were beaten by 2–1. The
United, bereft of genius, concluded that season gloomily at the
foot of the First Division.

In Meredith's Indian summer one last match lingers in the
memory, especially of habitués of Ninian Park. This was in
1924 when Meredith was approaching his fiftieth birthday. It
was a Cup-tie between Manchester City and Cardiff City. The
match ran its normal time without any goals having been
scored. In extra time the young full-back responsible for
Meredith's supervision found his stamina wasted; he could
no longer keep pace with the master. Meredith ran loose,
"and his centre led to the vital goal for Manchester City."†
The City reached the Semi-final, which they lost, at Birmingham, to Newcastle United – against whom Meredith had
played his first game for the City almost thirty years before.
During this year Meredith virtually retired; but his swan-song
was in the testimonial match, at Maine Road, on 29 April 1925,
in which a team selected by Meredith played against a combined
Rangers and Celtic side. The result was a 2–2 draw. This was

* *Manchester Guardian*, 27 August 1921.
† *Western Mail*, 21 April 1958.

immaterial; what was not was the fact that the football graced the occasion and charmed the connoisseurs.

Like everyone else – although this is often overlooked – a footballer is a many-sided personality. On the field Meredith was the supreme craftsman, utterly devoted to his vocation and indifferent to public praise or blame. His paleness accentuated by his dark moustache, he appeared as something of a melancholic, and his occasional sallies of football wit sardonic; but there was, to the seeing eye, more than showed on the surface. The records show that off the field Meredith, like many men of genius, was a problem to the conventional. His early misadventures have already been reported, in which the prevailing factor was Meredith's inconvenient habit of demanding what he considered as his rights. At the beginning of the 1919–20 season there was a recrudescence of earlier obstinacy. The Management Committee of the Football League suggested that Meredith should be granted a free transfer. The Board of Manchester United were not prepared to accept the suggestion. After much argument it was reported on 22 December 1919 "that the Football Association had agreed with the figures as submitted by the Club and that that amount (in respect of benefit) £762 18s. 3d. was due to W. Meredith, also that he was still the Club's player and that he could not demand a free transfer so long as the maximum wage (of £9 a week) was offered to him, which the Secretary was instructed to do".* At this point Meredith asked for his back pay – against the period in which he had not resigned, pending a conclusion of negotiations. The Club agreed, but not the League, who declared such action against the rules. At the end of the 1920–21 season it was resolved by the United Directors "not to engage (Meredith) unless he is willing to sign at £5 per week, or to give him a free transfer to any club except Manchester City F.C."

Meredith fought hard throughout his career because he possessed the artist's reluctance to submit to anything that seemed like exploitation. The problem is perennial and applies

* Minute book, 1919–24.

not only to football. But Meredith, while proud of, but modest with, his unique skill, was not only concerned with himself. He was a powerful supporter of the Players' Union from its inception and took part in its affairs until the end of his life, and so he contributed to the well-being of the whole profession.

In spite of occasional discordant episodes Meredith was essentially a United man, returning in 1931 – at a time of great trouble at Old Trafford – to act as coach.* In later years he visited the ground, viewing silently the distinguished heirs to his own tradition. Sometimes he appeared at the Annual General Meeting,† and was frequently in the public parks happy to spot budding talent among the schoolboys. In 1950 he owed a small sum in respect of house-purchase. With the consent of the Football Association this was paid by the United Club; a last, graceful gesture to a great footballer.

Meredith died at the age of 81 on 19 April 1958, at Withington, Manchester.‡ The record books note that he played fifty-one times for Wales (Meredith's own estimate differs by one from that of the Welsh F.A.); he scored 281 goals in 857 League matches, and fifty-six in 166 Cup-ties. Such statistics, however, are irrelevant. The man bestrode the world of football like a Colossus – a Colossus with bandy legs.

from MANCHESTER UNITED *1960*

* Minute book, 9 September 1931.
† E.g. 28 October 1942 when he 'seconded the re-election of Messrs Gibson and Newton as directors'.
‡ See Obituary notices in *The Times*, *Western Mail*, and *Manchester Guardian*, 21 April 1958.

Vivian Woodward

ALFRED GIBSON and WILLIAM PICKFORD

Is there anything essentially different between the style of a professional forward and an amateur forward? One is inclined to believe that there is. The professional is as a rule more mechanical and less individual in his methods. He has learned his football in a school where experiments are frowned upon. The paid player, as a class, has learned that certain methods are regarded with favour, and that these methods frequently meet with success. He therefore cultivates this manner until he arrives at a state of mechanical perfection. In theory, at least, he is master of the conventional style. It is obviously the business of his opponents to upset his theories, and the forward who has no native ingenuity – no resource of his own – is a pitiable object. An amateur forward of the highest class has usually all the knowledge of the orthodox game and also the ability to play it; but if he be a football genius he also possesses a style of his own, with brains enough to improvise on the moment a new mode of attack or an original method of defence.

Speaking in broad and general terms one may say that the professional forward is the exponent of certain well-known methods of attack which have become mechanical, while the amateur adopts methods which include the professional theory, and adds an individual style of his own creation. G. O. Smith used what I have called the professional methods very largely, and no one put them to better use. But these methods by no means exhausted the *repertoire* of the greatest forward of modern times. His mechanical passing was perfection in its accuracy. No professional could have bettered it, but Smith had always something else up his sleeve. If he and his men were checkmated by the opposition, he had always an alternative plan.

W. N. Cobbold did not adopt the modern mechanical methods, partly because in his day they had not been sufficiently developed and partly because he was himself a man of infinite resource. He was a powerful dribbler with a pair of shoulders like an ox and a deadly intensity near goal that few defences knew how to cope with. How Cobbold would have fared with a modern defence one cannot say with any certainty, but the chances are that against three of our strongest half-backs he would have had to considerably modify his methods.

Vivian Woodward, England's most modern centre-forward, is a happy blend of G. O. Smith and W. N. Cobbold. Without possessing all the genius of the one or the other he knows the modern passing game well enough to utilize the best services of his professional comrades, while he is sufficiently individual in style to make the final single-handed dash on goal with a big chance of success. He is not quite heavy enough to "shoulder off" his opponents in the style of Cobbold, but what he lacks in respect of weight he makes up for in sheer skill. The ease and fluency with which he escapes the "attentions" of opposing forwards is hardly less marked than his strong single-handed run which carries the ball half the length of the field. Woodward is essentially a brainy player. He has no set style. An opponent watching Woodward can never argue that because he has once done a certain thing he will repeat it when the same set of circumstances recur. Because Woodward has acted in a given manner once is a fairly good reason for thinking that he will not repeat himself. The fact is that Woodward has the rare power of thinking on his legs. Many a man with a mind stored full of good things straightaway forgets them all when he rises to address a public meeting. Woodward is like the trained orator. His mind is full of ideas which he is constantly putting into shape, and he has the rarer power of suddenly altering his mind at will. He frequently acts on the inspiration of the moment with splendid results to his side. He can develop a plan as he runs, and while the defence is anticipating the conventional pass out to the wing he will swing towards the centre, feint to pass to a comrade, and go sailing on with the ball at his toe. And then heaven help the goalkeeper!

In looking at Woodward he does not impress me as a

centre-forward who could stand the rough wear and tear of weekly League matches, but then his physique is not robust. He is strong on his legs, and can take an honest "charge" without wincing. A modern centre-forward of any class is at once a marked man. It is a good many years since James Oswald declared that he had to retire from Notts County and the game because of the almost undivided attentions of the opposition, who were determined to stop him by hook or by crook. The crooks had it. Fortunately the football of today, if not less strenuous than that of, say, twelve years ago is less open to the charges of unfair play. At any rate, here is Vivian Woodward, week after week, playing with nothing but professionals around him, and after a good many years he has not got a surfeit of the game. It is rather curious that we hardly ever hear a first-class amateur complain of rough play. Woodward is certainly not built to be used as a battledore or shuttlecock, but he is quite man enough to look after himself and take his share of the hard knocks that invariably fall more upon the expert than upon the moderate players.

Woodward is easily recognized in a crowd. He is built rather after the greyhound pattern, and moves with great speed and freedom on the field. His is a pleasant face to look upon. To a clear complexion are added a firm mouth, strongly-marked eyebrows, and a keen, clear eye that takes in the situation at a glance. One could not mistake him for other than an amateur, and though he has now played many times as centre-forward for England, he is not averse to assisting his old original club, Chelmsford, nor does he object to turn out for his beloved county of Essex. It is, of course, as centre-forward to Tottenham Hotspur that he is best known. Week in week out, when fit and well, he is found at his post, and when Cup-ties call him for mid-week matches he is never absent. He is by profession an architect, and besides being a great footballer, he is also an expert cricketer, who can make hundreds in good company. In these days, whilst the game in its most highly developed stages is passing largely into the hands of the paid player, it is well to know that we have still an amateur of the class and calibre of Vivian Woodward, who would scorn to do a mean action, and who is incapable of an unfair one.

from ASSOCIATION FOOTBALL AND
THE MEN WHO MADE IT *1906*

Charlie Roberts

ALFRED GIBSON and WILLIAM PICKFORD

"Charlie" Roberts is not a Welshman, though Wales would like to claim him. Fortunately for England, and perhaps fortunately for Manchester United, the nimble little centre-half was born near Darlington.

He has never been anything but a footballer; indeed, it would be wonderful if he had.

One frequently hears of nature endowing a man for a particular sphere of work, but one seldom sees so complete an article so well applied as is Roberts to his soccer.

You see him in the street and you are told it is the famous Roberts. You are disappointed. He does not wear the healthful, lusty, muscular habit of the average ball manipulator. You would hint that he was delicate; his very sparseness puts activity out of your mind, and his lack of beam suggests a restful holiday trip as the best means of rescuing him from permanent illness.

But see him on the field! There you are presented with bottled essence of agility, the personification of unending activity, and a veritable spring-heeled jack. Acrobatics would appear to have been the particular study of this slim youth of twenty-two; and we imagine that should football fail him he might readily acquire fame on the music-hall stage as an expert in legmania.

Just as he jumps at the ball in most unpromising situation

and secures it, so he jumped at fame and snatched it when it seemed unlikely to be caught. He has represented England thrice, but it must be confessed that on none of these occasions did he play his best. He did not satisfy himself, and still less did he satisfy his admirers and his club. He will tell you quite candidly that the International games did not show him to be worthy of a place, but he is equally sure that he did not play badly. He places a high standard.

His admirers expected a blaze of triumph every time he turned out for his country; his club lost his aid on three occasions, and with it the points that would have taken them into the First Division – so it will be seen how thorough the disappointment was. But Roberts is only waiting another opportunity of showing the critics that he is the man his friends represented him to be.

When Grimsby secured Roberts from Darlington they were not long in discovering how great a "capture" they had made. Other clubs, too, were quick to realize his worth, and offers in plenty poured in on his employers. They would not, however, part with him till the affluence of Manchester United dazzled them. Full £400 was dangled before their eyes, and they fell. Roberts removed.

Those who know Grimsby and Manchester will appreciate that this was no small change for Roberts. He went from the bracing atmosphere of the German Ocean to the insalubrious environment of chemical manufactories. The change may have had something to do with his present pallid appearance, for it is reported that in the same district an unwary journalist once attended a match accompanied by a silver-mounted umbrella; he retained the umbrella, but the silver evaporated!

Roberts apparently realizes the danger he is in, for he devoted his summers to an exposure to the winds and spray of the North Sea. At the end of the football season he hies him to Grimsby, berths aboard a trawler, and roughs it for weeks at a time. Last summer he was accompanied by Walter Whittaker, the Brentford goalkeeper. Whittaker's first trip to the Iceland region was not of the pleasantest description, and

Roberts loves to tell of the discomfiture of his burly companion in the height of a storm in the North Sea. But even Whittaker is ready to grant that Roberts's idea of keeping fit has something more than novelty to commend it.

Close upon twenty-three years of age, Roberts strips a handy 12 stone 2 lb., and sticklers for proper proportions will gather his build from the fact that he is 5 feet 10½ inches in height. Manchester United is now a member of the First Division of the League, and no man has done more to get the club there than Charles Roberts.

from ASSOCIATION FOOTBALL AND
THE MEN WHO MADE IT *1906*

Steve Bloomer

IVAN SHARPE

The goal-scorers always steal the stage. So do batsmen. Stephen Bloomer became the English football hero of his time because he so often got the winning goal. That's why Scotland feared him. When I met him in season 1911–12 he had just returned from Middlesbrough to his beloved Derby County, the club which had brought him out. He had received from the crowd at Derby a welcome home such as no other footballer has known.

The star did not look the part. Bloomer was called "Pale-face". In the dressing-room his limbs lacked the ruddy glow of the players round him. His build was slim, yet, at inside-right, he was the master of them all. He was the driving-wheel of the Derby County eleven. Returning in 1910–11, he led them back to the First Division, as Second Division Champions, in 1911–12.

I was the outside-left of that eleven, and so was able to study his methods. He was not a subtle or really scientific player.

But he had the golden gift of splitting a defence with one arrow-like, pin-pointed pass. Just as he could make this pass while the ball was moving, so he could shoot with sudden touch. He scored most of his goals by *sudden* shooting. His great haul of 380 goals in first-class football – then a record – came principally from first-time shots. His was instantaneous marksmanship aimed at beating the goalkeeper's *eye*. It follows that he could use both feet.

But our Stephen was a tyrant. He said what he thought, and if things were going wrong his partner had no easy Saturday afternoon. "What d'ye call that? A pass? I haven't got an aeroplane!" This was a fair sample of a Bloomer explosion.

He would extend his activities to the opposite flank of the forward line. I was there. I know.

If, after a breakdown in attack, one studied the crowd, the sky, or any other useful object out of the line of Bloomer's glare – as was the rule in the Derby ranks of that day – he would stand stock still, in the centre of the field, strike an attitude by placing his hands on his hips, and fix the offender with a piercing eye. If this glare, as was the rule, etc., was still ignored, he would toss up his head, as if beseeching the recording angel to make a note of this most awful blunder, and stamp back to his position in a manner intended publicly to demonstrate his disapproval.

Quite wrong, of course. Not good for the side. Not good for the alleged offender. Not good for the game. But those who knew Bloomer knew that he was really quite harmless, quite a peaceable person, who meant well and got the best out of the players because of his inspiring example, his great unselfishness and his tremendous devotion to his team on the field of play. So harmless, in fact, that within a week or so of joining the ranks of the great Bloomer's club the budding juniors selected Bloomer for their dressing-room pranks.

A curious personality, but genius runs that way.

How did he shoot? With power, of course, but the shot came from nearer the toe than the instep. This gift enabled him to make the effort a moment quicker than the man who has to raise the foot a few more inches to bring to bear the curve and fuller power of the instep.

A magnet, but not a magician. Bloomer had few tricks, and plenty of players have excelled him in the dribble. Rare judgement, inspired raiding and passing, and sudden shooting sum up the story of Steve Bloomer in football. When he was asked to explain it all he said: "That's an easy one. I try to get there first." Most people do, but Bloomer usually succeeded.

from 40 YEARS IN FOOTBALL *1952*

Alan Morton

IVAN SHARPE

"Come away, the wee society man!" A voice on the terraces floating over the crowded ground at Ibrox Park, Glasgow. "Come away, the wee society man!"

"Until I found the appeal was intended for me," said Alan Morton, "I wondered what it was all about. Now I know this Rangers supporter had seen me on the way to business in bowler hat and lightweight overcoat, and carrying a rolled umbrella. Thus 'society man' perhaps meant insurance man, the man from the Prudential," he laughed. "I have always been a mining man, an engineer."

Alan Morton's honours and achievements? Look at the list: Ninety-two caps and medals. . . .

"The Wee Society Man", the "Wee Blue Devil", the star of only 5 ft. 4½ ins. and 9½ stone who had more honours than any other Scottish footballer, now was telling me his story. In the alcove of a restaurant in Gordon Street, Glasgow. Alan used sherry-glasses as goal-posts, cold toast as penalty-area, knives and forks as touchlines and a small bread-roll for a ball. We started at five and finished at 8 p.m., dinner table thrust into a corner and chairs pushed aside as he demonstrated tricks and traps and pivots; and continually complained, "We haven't really enough room."

Yet elbow-room was the need he mastered as a player. He had to do so in order to dodge and defeat the challenge of men big enough to bend, bruise and break him. How he did it, how he became the greatest of Scottish wing-men, the Stanley Matthews of his country, with neither height nor weight to help him, this chapter will explain.

We will set it down in chapter and verse. His secrets, the foundation-stones of his twenty years of uninterrupted triumph in first-class football at outside-left were:

1. Confident use of both feet, notably of the right foot on the left wing.
2. Body-balances to give him his all-important pivoting powers and his weaving, dancing-master run.
3. Ball-control, and
4. Speed off the mark.

1. *Use of both feet*. . . . "I was really an outside-right," Alan said, "but I became an outside-left. It is a change of position any moderate wing player or worried club manager might try. The outside-left who is able to dribble and pass with his right foot makes it a cock-eyed world for the opposing full-back, who doesn't know which way you are going with the ball. Of course, you will centre as a rule with the left foot."

How did Alan Morton gain this gift of using both feet? In youth. By fun. Really, by accident. As Don Bradman developed wrist and eye by batting, for fun, with a stump and golf ball, so Alan and his brothers, Bob and Jack, spent hours, day by day, playing with a "tuppeny" ball or a football. As with Bradman, it really amounted to first-class practice.

"There was a hole a little larger than a football in our cellar door. Why, I don't know. Perhaps to let light into the cellar. Anyway, we used to try to shoot or lob or half-volley the ball through the hole. Day after day we did it."

It helped young Morton to develop mastery over the ball. As Wilfred Rhodes bowled for hours as a boy at chalk-marks in a barn, for fun, so the feet of the Morton boys chivvied and chased a little ball. "Sometimes, we used to practise with a twopenny ball. I would kick it against the garden wall, and trap or collect it before it rebounded over the footpath. Although I was not aware of it at the time, this was helping me to develop a quick touch and speed off the mark. You have to be nippy to gather a small ball before it bounces off the footpath."

In after years this nip got him out of many a tight corner with 50,000 people wondering how it was done.

"Constant play of this kind gave me confident use of both feet. I cannot understand why our Scottish footballers cannot use both feet. Comparatively few of them can, you know. Perhaps ten per cent. I mean the use of both feet in a manner worthy of first class football. Only ten per cent! If, as I am told, this is also true of English football, there is something radically wrong with the national game. It argues lack of thoroughness and keenness, and without both the professional should quit."

Now *corner kicking*. . . . Use of both feet, of course, enables the outside-left to take a corner-kick with the right foot, and from the corner-line side of the flag. "This," Alan Morton confirms, "is the ideal way. This way the ball first curves outwards in flight and then swings in towards the far goal-post. Such a corner is more difficult for the goalkeeper, and yet no more difficult for the forward to head the ball into the net. I aimed at the far post and, in the absence of a goalkeeper, of course, I could curl the ball into the net four times in half-a-dozen efforts. Not that a corner should swing so close to the goalkeeper. It should pass him farther out. I quote the figures in order to show how dangerous such corner-kicks can be."

Morton's centres also were placed to the far side of the goal: this fact helped Alex Jackson to score three times from outside-right for Scotland at Wembley in 1928.

2. *Balance*. . . . Alan Morton declares with emphasis that "a footballer must learn to pivot. Otherwise he will get nowhere."

"I used only three studs on the soles of my football boots: one in the toe and two under the ball of the foot. Four studs, including two in the toe, may cling to the turf, interfere with pivoting, and also threaten to twist the cartilage in the knee. Three studs are easier on the muscles of the legs."

Weaving on the run he practised with Queen's Park and Rangers clubs. "Every Tuesday and Thursday I used to dribble the ball right round the field. Then I would prance some steps, as in shadow-boxing. Visitors to the grounds have said, 'What is that crazy stuff?' They may have wondered whether the little chap was quite right in his head. The idea was to build-up weaving and wobbling while running with the ball. Balance is necessary in order to change direction at speed. Mind and feet in due time synchronize. Weaving and swaying then come automatically."

Balance includes switching body and ball from one foot to the other – a trick of his own. Pivoting gave Morton one great asset. He could take a short step with one foot and then suddenly switch the other way, carrying the ball along with him. Thus, if near the touch-line on the left-wing, he might take a short step to the left as if to move along the touch-line and then, directly his opponent moved that way, Morton could switch to the right and carry away the ball *inside* the defender. Again, this short step got him out of many a spot at close quarters. It gave him speed off the mark. All this involves:

3. *Ball-control*. This he obtained in youthful practice. It is necessary for every football player of whatever standard. It is really the first essential.

"Harold Fleming, the English International of Swindon Town, came to Ibrox Park," said Alan, "and took a film of my run down the wing. When I saw the film I found, to my surprise, that I was dribbling and controlling the ball with the inside of my feet. It was obviously the right way, but the knack had arrived unknown."

4. For *speed off the mark* Morton practised short steps, after the style of a sprinter getting out of his holes. "This short step got me away with a spurt. At my weight, I needed acceleration to escape charges.

"In another respect I was fortunate," he added. "I had a

side view not unlike the view a mirror gives a motorist. Somehow I got this unusual view of what was happening beside and immediately behind me, so that more than once defenders have told me they wondered how they missed me."

Yes, he was the one that got away.

His training routine, then, was: attend the ground each Tuesday and Thursday . . . dribble the ball round the field . . . a few thirty-yard sprints . . . side-stepping and swaying, or corner-kicking. In the gymnasium: skipping or punch-ball or Indian clubs, followed sometimes by games with a tennis ball.

Alan Morton has a retentive memory. He could "play a match over again" weeks after, although other games had intervened. His playing career closed in 1933, yet, nearly twenty years after, he could quote details of the goals and incidents of great occasions:

"Perhaps my most memorable match was Scotland's 5–1 win over England in 1928 at Wembley, but the best English players of my time certainly included Sam Hardy of Aston Villa in goal. Unfortunately I did not see much of him but he was always so safe and sound in his goalkeeping.

"At full-back, Roy Goodall of Huddersfield Town always impressed me. We had many battles, and in all our duels there was only one rift. His foot came near my head during a clearance at Hampden Park, and when the ball went out of play I claimed 'Our shy!' The linesman disagreed and while I was in the process of explaining what I thought had happened, Roy chipped in with something about cutting it out and getting on with the game. I was a bit bothered at the time but it was a minor matter which really emphasized the friendliness of our struggles, even in front of excited crowds of 100,000 people. Ernest Blenkinsop of Sheffield Wednesday was another bonny full-back. His kicking and volleying were so clean.

"At half-back I remember with respect and pleasure Jack Hill, six-footer from Burnley. He was strictly fair with me. So was Willis Edwards of Leeds United, a really grand all-round player. So firm on the ball, yet so light on his feet and accurate in his passing. Arthur Grimsdell of Tottenham Hotspur I remember for the thunderbolt shooting which brought him two goals in the Victory International match with England in 1919 at Glasgow. But he was a half-back so sure and assertive in his play that he was far above average standard.

"Among centre-half-backs I liked best of the Englishmen George Wilson of Sheffield Wednesday. He seemed to me to have everything. He could tackle well and yet could follow-up an attack by dribbling the ball like an inside-forward. I am sorry that centre-half-back play after the Second World War failed by far to approach this standard.

"In the English forward lines I enjoyed the flying raids of Joe Hulme, the Arsenal outside-right, who could also centre dangerously on the run. So could Sam Crooks of Derby County, who was perhaps more versatile in method.

"Stanley Matthews, of course, is a genius, but I should have admired him more if he had been quicker to centre the ball. I don't like to see a defence given time to reassemble its forces and cover-up. The man on the opposite wing – and that was my position – will know how the quick centre often gives him a better chance of getting a goal.

"Tom Finney of Preston North End is a splendid example of the player who can use both feet expertly and confidently. How well he played against Scotland at Wembley in 1951 when Mannion was injured and Finney moved into the inside-forward position. That is the mark of the high-class player. It is my opinion, however, that the modern outside-forward often fails to use the full width of the pitch. Why should he wait for the ball in the *inside*-forward position? Why move nearer to the opposing full-back? Why handicap yourself by reducing your elbow-room? Why help your opponents by getting yourself marked?"

Now a director of Rangers F.C., Alan Morton showed concern about the game's slow recovery after the Second World War. During the 1951–2 season he said to me: "In Scotland today there is only one International eleven. Between the wars there were sufficient stars for several International teams. England has been more fortunate but is also feeling the pinch, so I have been told.

"Something should be done about the schoolboys. I see boys of the highest promise in schools games and they appear to be players of natural ability, yet a good many of them fade out of the picture. Maybe they sink their individuality and enterprise when they step into a higher grade of play. That is a mistake. The youth should not be talked out of his knacks and tricks. He should be encouraged to try them out and develop them, to show the will-power necessary to ignore crowd influence. He must learn to ignore the crowd. The star in action does not hear the crowd any more than he sees the goalkeeper when he is shooting and scoring.

"I have seen such promising schoolboy players that I have come to the conclusion that selected schoolboy elevens should be formed and kept together. Clubs or organizations should take a whole team under their wing and keep them there until the players are well into their teens. Something of the kind is done, I believe, in South America."

Such are the impressions and advice of an accepted master, of the man who overcame handicaps of height and weight and, throughout his playing career, also continued in his profession.

The story of Alan Morton, and the heights he reached, show that the day-by-day routine of the professional clubs is not always necessary.

from 40 YEARS IN FOOTBALL *1952*

Frank Barson

PETER MORRIS

For Aston Villa supporters waiting impatiently for the second half of the 1920 F.A. Cup Final against Huddersfield Town at Stamford Bridge, the interval talking point was not so much the goalless state of the game but the subdued manner in which

Frank Barson had been playing. In fact, the Villa following was finding it difficult to believe it was Barson at all. It was certainly not the Barson they were used to seeing back at Villa Park.

They did not know that, only a few minutes before the teams had come on to the field, the referee, Mr Jack Howcroft, had stalked into the Villa dressing-room, walked straight up to the famous centre-half, and cautioned him thus: "The first wrong move you make this afternoon, Barson – off you go!" This was *before* the game had started. Such was Barson's reputation that referee Howcroft, a martinet in the middle, had thought it necessary to give him prior warning that any rough stuff would see him back in the dressing-room.

Hardly fair, perhaps . . . but Frank Barson, never a man to mince words, was always the first to admit that he was rough, that he was tough, and that on occasions the crowd were justified in calling him downright dirty. Barson was also one of the greatest centre-halves football has known. Certainly he ranked with James Cowan as the finest ever to wear the colours of Aston Villa.

It was little wonder that this stern introduction to the Cup Final of 1920 for once completely floored him.

Barson was no respecter of referees as a rule – but Jack Howcroft was no mean disciplinarian, respected by the toughest of the tough. Barson, who fell into this category, was no exception. After half-time, Barson recovered his confidence and towards the end was playing with all the great verve and skill which had made him what he was. He won his one and only Cup medal in that Final.

The curious thing is that, although Barson's name is always associated with the Villa, he actually spent only three seasons with them – from October 1919 to August 1922. Then he left for Manchester United, helped the Old Trafford club to win promotion in 1925, and moved on to Watford, Hartlepools United, Wigan, and Rhyl Athletic. In his last game for Rhyl, long past the age of forty, Barson was sent off for the umpteenth time to maintain his record of being the most suspended player in football. But everywhere he went he was the dominant personality, the man who could take on the opponents single-handed if need be.

Frank Barson may have been one of football's strong-arm characters, but he was a magnificent player in his day; superb heading power and complete control of the middle made him worth two men.

In the autumn of 1919, Barson came to Villa Park, transformed a hopeless losing team into a confident winning combination in just a few months and helped to take the same team on to win Aston Villa the F.A. Cup for the sixth time.

That was Barson – dynamic, controversial, argumentative, constantly the centre of violent disputes with clubs, players and officials – but a born leader who feared no one. No one, that is, save perhaps Jackie Whitehouse of Derby County who was even harder than Barson – if such were possible.

Barson was brought up the hard way in Grimesthorpe, right in the heart of the Sheffield steel country. Here football was mostly played with a rubber ball or with a handy tin can. It was in these early knock-about games that Barson learnt his football, kicking his shoes to pieces, tearing his clothes and playing truant from school. Occasionally he saved enough money to get in at near-by Hillsborough to watch his great hero, centre-half Tommy Crawshaw of Sheffield Wednesday – the player on whom the young Barson modelled his style.

From junior football circles, where Barson rapidly proved himself the hardest nut of all, he became an apprentice blacksmith in Sheffield and received the first of many cautions for arguing with the referee in a local works league match.

Frank Barson might have landed up at Birmingham at that stage of his career. They were interested in the powerful young Yorkshire lad, but so were Barnsley – and it was Barnsley who stepped in and turned Frank professional for the princely wage of thirty shillings a week!

A dispute with Barnsley involving travelling expenses from his home in Sheffield ended his career at Oakwell in 1919. That same stubborn insistence on living in Sheffield also indirectly led to him leaving the Villa three years later.

But before his move to Villa Park he had fallen foul of the
"boo boys" on nearly every football ground in the country.
It was an incident in a Cup-tie between Barnsley and Everton
at Goodison Park that landed Barson with his first suspension.
He received a month but he was glad to get away from
Liverpool in one piece. An angry crowd waited menacingly
outside Goodison Park but Barson had been smuggled to the
station by taxi!

Later, in a war-time game against Birmingham, Frank
collected another suspension – this time for two months.
Punishments were extremely severe in those days. There were
some formidable characters about who should have been
discouraged but usually were not.

It was Sam Hardy who recommended Barson to Aston Villa
in the autumn of 1919 when the club urgently needed new
blood to pull the side together. Sam, who lived at Chesterfield,
knew all about Barson's prowess – and his reputation. But
Frederick Rinder and George Ramsay realized that here was
the one man who could lift the Villa out of trouble and so they
went after him.

It was after a 2–4 home defeat by Preston that George
Ramsay travelled north to Barnsley, saw Barson and asked him
if he fancied joining Aston Villa. Strangely enough, Barson
did not think he was good enough for the Villa – an unexpected
admission from a footballer who abounded in self-confidence.
But Villa wanted Barson and so Barson signed – for a fee of
£2,850. A player of his calibre today – and there is no one
remotely like him – would fetch something like £40,000!

Barson's first game was at Middlesbrough, where the Villa
won 4–1 and subsequently began a sensational recovery. It is
on the record that before that game Barson told his new
colleagues that he could not understand why the Villa were
doing so badly. "Wait until you've played with us – then you'll
know why," the players told him. Afterwards, someone asked
Barson: "Well, what do you think now, Frank?" Replied
Barson: "It was the easiest game I've ever had in my life."

The stories surrounding Barson are legion. There was, for

instance, the occasion on which he and Sam Hardy had to walk seven miles to catch a train to Manchester where the Villa were playing.

A collision had disrupted the rail service and the Villa pair had to footslog it through snow and hail to pick up a connexion. It got them to Old Trafford only a few minutes before the kick-off, soaked through, tired, and hungry. Barson miskicked to give the United their first goal, then settled down to play such a storming game that the Villa won 2–1.

This incident led to Barson getting into hot water with the Villa club. They were anxious that he, Clem Stephenson, Sam Hardy, Jimmy Harrop and Andy Ducat, all of whom lived away from Birmingham, should reside nearer the ground.

At the end of his first season with the club Barson was told that the directors wanted him to move his home to Birmingham. He had set himself up in business in Sheffield and refused to do so. There was some argument before he re-signed for the 1920–21 season, then again he was informed that he must comply with the club ruling.

Clem Stephenson was another Villa player who refused to live in Birmingham, and on the opening day of the season, when the Villa met Bolton, neither player turned up for the match – which the Villa lost. The pair of them were summoned before a Villa board meeting, told that their conduct was inexcusable and suspended for fourteen days. But in the end neither Barson nor Stephenson moved to Birmingham and Barson was actually appointed captain of the club in succession to Andy Ducat. It was about this time that he headed his incredible goal from thirty yards out against Sheffield United.

He was still incurring the wrath of crowds up and down the country and at one stage issued a statement defending his vigorous tactics on the grounds that he had been brought up to play hard and there was surely nothing unfair in the honest-to-goodness shoulder charge!

But Barson was a marked man. Several times he was really "roughed up" by opposing players and spent various periods in hospital, as well as breaking a nose that had already been smashed three times before he became a Villa player.

It was not always Barson who suffered though. He was such a nasty customer that the Villa's opponents would try and take it out of his colleagues if they could not get the centre-half himself. It was then that Frank would jut out his chin, roll up his sleeves and exact vengeance. His reputation alone often influenced the crowds to howl for his blood when he was the innocent party.

There was more trouble behind the scenes at Villa Park too. An unpleasant episode in the Villa dressing-room at Liverpool, when Barson invited in his pal Stan Fazackerley to wait for him while he dressed, drew a rather petty rebuke from a Villa director which resulted in a stand-up row between Barson and Mr Rinder who came in to find out what the trouble was about. Barson was called on to apologize at the next board meeting, but never did, and it was obvious that his days as a Villa player were numbered.

That was the era when, no matter how great the player, he never stayed long a Villa man unless he behaved in accordance with the club's traditional reputation for sportsmanship and dignity. The incident with Mr Rinder and his colleague on the Villa board led to another seven day suspension and eventually Frank decided to ask for a transfer.

Even then, the Villa were reluctant to let him go. They offered him good terms for the following season but Barson would not re-sign this time. He spent his Saturday afternoons watching football at home in Sheffield, turned down an offer to go to Burnley, and then, when Manchester United approached the Villa for his transfer in the late August of 1922, agreed to go to Old Trafford.

The Villa were asking £6,000 for Barson but Manchester would not pay it. Eventually the Villa knocked £1,000 off the transfer and the United got their man. As a condition of his move to Manchester, Barson had sought – and received – permission to live and train in Sheffield but there still remained the question of his percentage of the transfer fee in lieu of benefit from Aston Villa. This led to another headline-storm.

Barson had been told by the Villa secretary George Ramsay that he would certainly be paid his percentage, but as the weeks went by and Barson still had not received his dues, he protested so strongly that the Football League Management Committee started an investigation.

In fairness to the Villa, it must be said that they had been quite willing to pay Frank the money but had been prevented from doing so by the Management Committee who ruled that, since Barson had persistently refused to re-sign after being offered maximum terms, he had forced the club to transfer him and so had forfeited his rights to any share of the fee.

It was typical of Frederick Rinder that he should personally take Barson's claim to the League. But, after two hearings, the decision not to pay Barson his money remained unaltered and so scotched the rumours flying around Birmingham that the player had made a good thing out of his transfer.

Barson's career at Old Trafford was almost as colourful as it had been during his great days with the Villa. He continued to fall foul of players, referees, and crowds, nearly had his career prematurely ended by injury but survived to help Manchester United back to the First Division. He was always the popular hero in Manchester, where his famous hot-pot suppers for playing colleagues and his parrot have not been forgotten among an older generation of United supporters.

But Barson did not welcome flattery, nor could he be "kidded" into anything. His hard upbringing had made him too wily a bird for that. There is a story that, after United's promotion year, Barson, who had been promised a pub, got so fed up with all the back-slapping and compliments at the opening ceremony that he gave the pub away to the head waiter!

Now in his late sixties, a mellow and bespectacled Frank Barson is back again in Birmingham, living not far away from Villa Park and the club I suspect he still holds dearest to his heart.

from ASTON VILLA *1960*

Vittorio Pozzo

ANTONIO GHIRELLI

He had lived for some time abroad, especially in Switzerland and England, and was therefore able to bring with him a less narrow view of sporting problems. In him, the Fascist régime singled out the ideal man to "divert" the "emotional drive of the masses" into football, for he himself firmly believed in sport as being at once a sort of religious and patriotic myth, while from his knowledge of English civilization, he had learned the lesson of discipline, if not democracy. Rigid, authoritarian, paternalistic, he was the tutor of the international team, its austere mentor, a man who took his own job terribly seriously, as the Fascist leaders pretended to do in their own sphere, but in fact never did. He was a master in the ethical, in the sentimental, rather than the instructional sense of the word, an inspiring force following in the classic tradition of the Piedmontese Alpine officer; in a word, the typical figure of a gentleman of the old school. His good fortune was that of seeing his own particular mission coincide with the individual and collective flowering of Italian football; and the Fascist régime, whatever its ends, had the merit of supporting the work of their international team manager unreservedly, with an intensity, a dedication, which, had it been applied to national life, would have assured a very different fate for Italy. . . .

Pozzo had absolute power over the training programme of the Italian (1934 World Cup) team, comparable to that of a proconsul. It is true that when the thirty players he had chosen were brought together on 1 May at the retreat of Alpino, on Lake Maggiore, the technical and psychological situation was not easy. Three months previously the "veterans" had failed their test against Austria, while the Championship had opened up an abyss between the players of Juventus and those of Ambrosiana, the latter caught and overtaken by the Turin team "right on the post" and "in a manner and in circumstances which made them look almost foolish". But Pozzo was not discouraged and he approached the problem in a way that was half paternalist, half militarist. He refused all leave, "strategically" divided up his men in bedrooms, banished the thought of the championship from every mind, and set "the whole brigade to a healthy and restful régime of life: baths, massage, walks, short periods of recreation, long sleeps".

In other words the thirty "possible *azzurri*" were reduced to a state of pure infantilism, shrewdly concentrated on the single thought of the World Cup and the "moral" responsibility they bore. One free day was given them, after a training session at Novara, so that they might fleetingly renew acquaintance "with pastimes and pleasures which the retreat at Alpino had almost made them forget", then they were brought together again, this time at Roveta, above Florence. After a few hours of "long faces", the boys were reconciled to their team manager. They were now, as Pozzo himself said, "malleable to a degree, living only for the events which lay before them; and they wanted to win". Ready, then, for use. And the use was splendid, even if arduous. . . .

from STORIA DEL CALCIO IN ITALIA *1954*

Raich Carter — the Great Horatio

ROLAND ALLEN

One by one the great soccer personalities have come on to and gone from the smooth, green pitch at Wembley. In the case of International matches it has been by design, but in the case of Cup finals – because there are so many and incalcuable factors outside football which bring teams there – rather by accident.

Horatio Carter got there both ways. First time was in 1934,

when he was on the England side which won over Scotland by three goals. In this (1937) Cup final he was captain of the Sunderland team when they won the Cup for the first time in a long and brilliant career. The only previous Cup final in which they had played had been in 1913, when Aston Villa beat them by the only goal scored.

Carter came into football very young. As a schoolboy he played for England. As a young man he got as far as an International Trial, but it looked as if an obviously great player was going to be lost to his country because, in those very early days, there was a hesitation and nervousness about his football on big occasions which it took him a long time to conquer. He did get the better of it. That was perhaps the greatest victory of his football career. It was thereby made possible for thousands of us to have the privilege of watching the many delightful football exhibitions which Carter served up for us during the five or six years immediately before 1939. One of his minor distinctions was that he was a Sunderland born man and played for the Sunderland team. That was unusual. Another was that he played in two Cup finals at Wembley, nine years apart, and for different teams.

He was a straightforward, orthodox sort of inside right. He knew all the fundamentals and exploited them with brilliant efficiency. He had no mannerisms to speak of. It was, in his earlier days, necessary to watch him very closely to notice the way in which he tried to do everything correctly. There was lots of thought at the back of his football. He was not one of the showmen. He kept well over the ball, so that he rarely lost it until he decided it should go. He rolled his passes, made his swerves at the right time, in the right direction, and not too often. He had all it takes to make the complete inside forward and he still had it when he played in another Cup final, and again for England, after the 1939 war, and when his hair had slight streaks of grey running through it.

from ALL THE CUP FINALS *1947*

Stanley Matthews

MAURICE EDELSTON and
TERENCE DELANEY

'You mean to say you actually saw Stanley Matthews?"

We are advanced in years, chatting with a young man who is waiting to take our granddaughter to the pictures, and we suspect he has been told to say this.

"Oh, yes," we say, "yes indeed – many times."

"What was he like?" he asks. His expression is tolerant and politely sceptical.

What are we to tell him that he cannot read for himself in the record books? He already knows that Matthews was twenty-three years in international football, and played over fifty games for England – over eighty, if you count wartime and Victory internationals and tours; that he was made a C.B.E. in the New Year's Honours of 1957; that he played in three great Cup Finals, and eventually won a winner's medal when he was thirty-eight. He has seen pictures of Matthews, frozen in the act of rounding a groping full-back, and perhaps recognized him as he flickered for a few seconds in an old newsreel. He knows, in theory, that he was a "wizard"; but it all means nothing because he never saw him.

We, though, have seen Matthews, with the ball at his feet – seen him as often as possible in the past twenty years. What shall we remember? First, as he runs out on to the field, our feeling of surprise. Here he is again, the incomparable master of English football, the man of talent and reputation – and how little aware of it he seems. As we stand near the touch-line, waiting for the kick-off, he is only a few yards from us. His face is spare; his skin is neither ruddy nor brown, as you might expect of an athlete, but pale – tight over his cheek-bones and forehead – a high smooth forehead with the thin hair drawn well back. His eyebrows are raised, and his eyes hooded; he has an almost Chinese impassivity. He holds himself nervously, with a kind of brittle stiffness, his hands closed and his arms slightly bent. He tries his legs, shifting his weight from one to the other – but carefully; as if he were taking an inventory of his muscles; confirming that he has overlooked nothing in his methodical preparations. There is a tension in him, a restrained anxiety. For all his experience and confidence, he suggests the serious excitement of a schoolboy who hopes he will do well. He pays no attention to the crowd.

As the whistle goes, and the ball moves upfield, he jogs forward, with that same careful movement, wasting no energy, but with his cool eyes shifting, watching intently. He is a little behind the rest of the forward line, with a clear space ahead of him, when the ball comes to him for the first time – as he likes it, straight to his feet. The ball comes fast, but he stops it dead as it reaches him. It is already perfectly controlled as he turns, and, at little more than a fast walk, takes it towards the back. The back, like every other in the game, has heard all about Matthews. He knows that Matthews likes to beat his man by going outside him; he knows that if he rushes his tackle, Matthews will be round him; so he stays near the touchline, watches, and retreats. Matthews continues, in his leisurely way, to bring the ball to him; retreat becomes dangerous. The back holds his ground. Another man comes across in support. Matthews is now very close; the back is within a stride of the ball. Matthews shrugs his shoulders and sways to the left.

In that second, with a kind of desperate clarity, we can read the back's mind. It comes to him in a flash that this time Matthews is going inside. The ball is held in the curl of Matthews's right foot, and that lean, wonderfully balanced figure has swayed so far to the left that it is almost too late to catch him. But not quite – he is a quick strong back, and he goes across in a swift lunge. There is no one there. Matthews is gone – on the outside again – flying past him, already yards beyond him, imperturbable as ever; slowing down now to his jog-trot as he shows the ball, obligingly, to the next crouching defender.

The speed of that sudden sprint, over those few yards, is

amazing, and it is his essential secret. Without it, with all his other gifts, Matthews could still outwit and wrong-foot his opponents, but he would not leave them grotesquely and completely beaten, staggering off-balance, or sitting helplessly facing in the wrong direction. He has done this, over and over again, to the best defenders in the world, and he can still do it in his forties.

There are dozens of footballers who can out-race Matthews over sixty yards: but how often does a footballer need to run with the ball for sixty yards or even thirty? A good long pass will do the work better in a tenth of the time. Fifteen yards is another matter. Speed over that distance is priceless, and – over that distance – there are very few who can touch Matthews, *when Matthews has the ball*. Matthews knows the value of his gift, and a great part of his training is devoted to improving it – quick starts and short sprints, over and over again. He is a perfectionist, obsessed with physical fitness, disciplined to self-denial and hard training since he was little more than a baby.

His father was a boxer – Jack Matthews, "The Fighting Barber of Hanley", with a record of 350 fights, and good enough to appear at the National Sporting Club. He, too, was a lean, smallish man, a feather-weight, quick and skilful and, by all accounts, exceptionally fast and neat on his feet. He drank no alcohol, he never smoked, and he wore waxed moustaches. Matthews remembers that when he was only ten years old, the clothes were pulled off his bed at six o'clock every morning, and he had to join his father and two brothers at their dawn exercises; first, deep breathing at the open window, and then a spell with the chest expander. Jack Matthews had begun the athletic education of his youngest son even before that. He decided the boy was a sprinter, took him out for training on Saturday mornings, with a stop-watch, and entered him, when he was only six, for the 100 yards handicap at the Stoke-on-Trent sports. Stanley cried all the way there, and was so overcome by the occasion that he had to be withdrawn. His father's pride was saved the following year. Stanley was entered again, with a forty yard start against boys twice his age, and won the final and a gold watch. Matthews says now that, looking back, he is grateful for his father's severity. As a footballer, he has every reason to be; his wonderful durability is the direct result of that foundation of rigid physical habit – but it must have been hard going at the time.

Learning football, however, was a private pleasure; endless tapping of a rubber ball against a wall, hours of dribbling of a rag or paper ball between and over chairs, fierce after-school games on a piece of waste land – six-a-side in the bad weather, twenty a side on the fine evenings. What happened to all the other boys? How odd it is that, in any noisy disorganized crowd of small boys, there may be one, apparently just like the others, who has some extraordinary talent in him, some name that may soon be familiar all over the world, though it is still only an undistinguished collection of syllables – like Stan Matthews.

Matthews's unusual quality was discovered early. He was a centre-half when he played for his school at eleven years old – certainly not a defensive one, because he scored eight goals one afternoon – but they soon made him into an outside-right, and within a year of the change he was a schoolboy international. At fourteen he was an office-boy at Stoke City football club; at fifteen he played two games with the reserves; at sixteen, twenty-two games; on his seventeenth birthday he signed as a professional. Through these years he was still under the severe eye of his father. The physical training continued; when he was an office-boy his father took charge of his money. The boy walked the two miles between Hanley and Stoke four times every day – no bus fares, because the exercise was good for him; when he became a player, half his wages went into a post office savings account. At eighteen he was in the first team, Stoke City were promoted, and young Matthews won a Second Division Championship medal; at nineteen he played for England.

That first international, against Wales at Cardiff, was played in September 1934; his last was against Scotland in April, 1957, when he was over forty. On merit alone he might have gone on playing for England; a player in his twenties who was as good as Matthews was in 1958 would certainly have been picked for the World Cup. Even now, one is reluctant to believe that Matthews has played his last international; there were England sides without him before, for long periods, but he came back. He was "too old" ten years ago. We took him too much for granted. England's opponents in Europe and South America, in all the countries who learnt their football from England, never understood why, having a genius like Matthews, we did not use him, automatically and gratefully, in every England game through all his best years.

"Matthews is playing?" said the Frenchman – or Italian, or Dutchman, or Austrian.

"No," we said, "not this time."

"Ah, I am sorry – he is injured?"

"No. He was not picked this time."

Your visitor raises his eyebrows.

"You have someone *better* than Matthews?" he asks.

It was a difficult point to explain, but we all tried to explain it. One favourite theory was that, while Matthews was a great individual, he had his weaknesses as a team man; he held up the forward line; defences had time to assemble while he was holding the ball; he was old-fashioned; we needed direct, goal-scoring wingers. Maybe – but this explanation took no account of the magical effect of the mere name of Matthews, the moral advantage of his presence. A team facing Matthews – particularly a foreign team whose players had not seen him bundled about in League matches on muddy Saturdays – expected the impossible. They thought so hard about stopping Matthews that they forgot to give proper attention to the rest of the forward line. It is true that he gave the defence time to assemble its forces; but often the assembly took place around Matthews himself. Wide open spaces were left in the middle and, Matthews always knew exactly where those spaces were.

He was never a purely ornamental dribbler. He would stop the game sometimes, standing still over the ball, or tap-tap-tapping it with three men round him, but it was more than ball-control: it was command. With all his certainty of touch, he could look away from the ball, watch the other man's feet, take in the disposition of the field with one cool flickering glance, and place his passes to an inch. He came on to the field unobtrusively, physically unimpressive; but for the crowd, and for his opponents, the knowledge of his mastery and the prestige of his reputation sounded a silent fanfare. The crowd waited to be amazed; the opponents were already anxious and uneasy. No other player in English football ever carried such an atmosphere with him. In itself it is a weapon; Matthews knew it, and used it mercilessly. With his diffidence and modesty, his skill and delicacy, he is a ruthless player. He will never foul a man, he is never vicious, but he will beat a man, expose his inferiority, beat him again, coldly, and destroy his confidence.

To the English crowds he has always been the incomparable player. To them he is not a mystery, a superman, as he is abroad, but a familiar, admired favourite, whose mannerisms, tricks, and weaknesses are well known. If he is left without the ball for a quarter of an hour, the crowd becomes impatient: when a pass goes to him at last, there is a loud ironic cheer. "About time, too," says the man on the terraces, and waits to see what Stan will do with it. A young back who reaches the ball before Matthews is marked down as a coming man – but the crowd waits happily to see him taught his lesson. Once in every two or three games, when the ground is hard, Matthews heads the ball – a sharp forward nod, to bring it down to his feet where it belongs. More laughter and cheers. The English like traditional jokes, and Stan's reluctance to use his head, except for thinking, has become one of them. Institutions are cherished here; Matthews is a proud possession, and the attitude to him is protective and affectionate. If he is deliberately fouled and sent sprawling, there is an outraged roar of protest all around the ground – as if someone had thrown a ripe tomato at the Coronation Coach. Matthews himself remains unmoved. If he is put down, he gets up again, with no change of expression, and looks to see where the ball is. He has no time for theatricals; he never hides his face with his hands, or

i*

raises his hands to heaven in protest. These demonstrations, harmless, and often sympathetic, in other places, are irrelevant to Matthews. If the man who has fouled him offers to shake his hand afterwards he will shake it, but without interest. Discipline and under emphasis are as much a part of him as the ordinary clothes he wears off the field, and his flat native accent.

Matthews has given a great deal to football and made few demands in return. He has changed clubs only once, and has had little to say about his private affairs in public. He has been the world's greatest football star, at a time when football was crossing frontiers and becoming the most popular game in the world, yet he has always been the least flamboyant, the least assertive of players. What sensational headlines he might have made had he been otherwise; but on the whole he made his news on the field of play. For all this, Matthews has always known his own worth. He began work in the office at Stoke in 1931, and stayed with the club as a player for sixteen years; the first sign of any clash of interest came in 1938, when Matthews asked for a transfer. The effect this produced locally was extraordinary. Thousands of handbills and posters appeared all over the city, circulated by a group of business men, "STANLEY MATTHEWS MUST NOT GO!" they said, and called a public meeting to "urge the retention of Stanley Matthews". Three thousand people attended the meeting, and another thousand paraded with placards outside. Matthews stayed – for nine more years. Then, in 1946, injuries put him out of the team for a few weeks. Stoke were doing well and when he recovered the manager did not want to change a winning forward line. It was suggested that Matthews should turn out with the reserves. Matthews refused; not because of any inflated idea of his own importance, but simply because he thought he was worth a place in the League side – if not Stoke's, then somebody else's, and he was right. A few months later he was transferred, for the first and only time.

Matthews is thrifty, as might be expected from his upbringing, and by then he was the proprietor of a hotel in Blackpool. He had been training on the Blackpool ground for some time, and he made it clear that no matter how many other clubs were interested in him, Blackpool was where he intended to go. This meant that there was no competitive bidding for his signature. The fee was fixed at £11,500 – from Blackpool's point of view, one of the best football bargains ever made.

How many games of first-class football has Matthews played? Eighty-six internationals, twenty years of League football, five or six years of wartime games – unit games, services representative matches, exhibitions – games for the Football League, off-season tours with F.A. teams, invitation games, testimonials, cup-ties; he must have forgotten many of them himself, yet all over the world there are people who remember one particular unimportant football match because it was the time they saw Stanley Matthews. How can one do justice to a player like this? In simpler days his exploits would have been celebrated by ballad-singers – and long ballads they would have been, even if the minstrel cut himself down to one verse per game.

For the benefit of his unsophisticated audiences, accustomed perhaps to "The Ballad of Tom Lawton", the singer would have had to devote a stanza or two to explaining why Matthews scored so few goals. He used to be a goal-scorer in his early days with Stoke. He scored in his first international, and he had a hat-trick against Czechoslovakia in 1937 – three goals in a 5–4 win for England – but after a few years he changed his tactics. He decided, he says, that a winger who makes goals for the three inside-forwards is more valuable to the team. There is much to be said for the argument that the Matthews type of winger is in fact far more deadly than the type that cuts in and drives for goal. Matthews, out on the touchline, will take the ball right down to the corner-flag, and work in towards the goal. His characteristic high centre curves across to drop just beyond the far post, or out of the reach of the goalkeeper; his ground pass is angled back to the edge of the penalty area. In both cases the forwards are running on to the ball, and meet it as it comes to them; the defenders have to turn. Matthews is so far forward with the ball that it is almost impossible for the man receiving it to be offside; his control is so extraordinary that he can hold the ball until a clear opening is made. He is not rushed into bad passes; he does not pass at random. He not only makes goals, he makes easy goals. The scoring winger, on the other hand, is often forced to encroach on the ground of the inside men – to crowd the middle, instead of stringing out the defence – otherwise he must shoot from an angle, at a narrow mark. This, of course, is not the whole of the argument. If it were, the old-fashioned type of winger, with his mazy dribbles, would be commoner nowadays. The Matthews method, in modern football, requires a certain kind of temperament, complete confidence in its principles, and a technical skill that amounts to genius – in fact it requires Matthews. He is a school of football in himself.

With most great players it is possible, looking back over the records of their careers, to pick out one match and say: "That was his game, that was his peak – the day when he showed us everything he knew". With Matthews this is impossible. One might ask a dozen of his devoted admirers, and each one would choose a different wonderful game. There was the game against Germany at Wembley in 1955; Matthews had been in the England team that beat Germany in Berlin in 1938 – seventeen years before – yet at Wembley, when he was forty years old, it was Matthews who was light-footed, the young men who seemed tired and clumsy. He danced and glided his way through them, and sent them home to think over their lessons. In the same season England beat Scotland 7–2 and Matthews made five of the goals; no one could touch him that day. On the field was Duncan Edwards – it was his first game for England, and Matthews had been an international before he was born. He has had so many great games – but Matthews is by now an English institution rather than simply a footballer, his name is known to people who have never seen a professional match and, looking at him in that light, one day stands out as the peak of his career: Cup-Final day, 1953.

Wembley is a ground set aside for great occasions, and something in the air of the place seems to bring out the best in

Matthews. By 1953 he had been a professional footballer for over twenty years – twenty years of triumphs all over the world – but the great prize of English football, a cup winner's medal, had escaped him. He was thirty-three when he played in his first Final, in 1948; Blackpool were leading Manchester United by two goals to one twenty minutes from the end, but United scored three more, and that chance was gone. "I would have liked the medal," he said afterwards, with his usual absence of rhetoric, "I wanted to give it to my son Stanley. It's always been my great ambition." On the eve of that Final, the Football Writers' Association, newly formed, had named him as their first "Footballer of the Year" – a great compliment, but small consolation. Against the odds, Blackpool were back at Wembley three years later, this time against Newcastle. Matthews was the outstanding player on the field that afternoon, good in the first half, better and stronger minute by minute as time ran out in the second, as if driven on by the knowledge that his second – and probably his last – chance of that medal was slipping away. He contrived openings, but no one took advantage of them; he ranged all over the field, he fired in fierce shots himself, but it was Newcastle's day, not Blackpool's. Jackie Milburn scored two fine goals and Blackpool were out. That was 1951, and Matthews was 36.

By this time Matthews's medal, like Gordon Richards's Derby, had become an object of popular mythology. When Blackpool reached the Final again in 1953, with Bolton Wanderers as their opponents, the most unexpected people seemed to be emotionally involved in the result. Matthews appeared the calmest man in the stadium when the teams lined up before the Royal Box; no fidgeting, no sign of nerves or excitement. He stood in the curiously slack attitude that is characteristic of him at such times, his feet slightly apart, his shoulders slumped, his hands hanging by his sides. He looked his age, some of us thought, but then the game began, and within minutes we saw that Matthews, the unequalled, was at the peak of his form and style, tuned and trained to a hair. . . .

There were less than thirty seconds to go when, once again,

Taylor slid a pass to his partner, Matthews, and Matthews picked it up on the run. Banks came in to tackle, knowing that Matthews was going outside him; Matthews went inside this time, and left him. Barrass came out of the pack of defenders in the goal-mouth to block his way. Matthews feinted to the left, shifted his weight and went to the right, racing round him, leaning far in, like a racing cyclist taking a tight turn, the ball perfectly with him, as always. Then, within feet of the line, with the defence wheeling to face him, he cut back a hard ground pass – behind them all, behind Mortensen, running in, but straight into the space where Perry, the left-winger, was ready to meet it, and did meet it, and drove it in. Blackpool had the Cup, and Matthews had his ambition. As for us, we had seen Matthews again, on one of his great afternoons. Once you have done that, you can afford to be tolerant towards those who have never seen him – after all, there is a great deal about football that they will never know.

from MASTERS OF SOCCER *1960*

Stan Cullis

MAURICE EDELSTON and
TERENCE DELANEY

Mr Stanley Cullis has been manager of Wolverhampton Wanderers for ten years; only four times in those ten years has his team been out of the first three in the First Division of the League; three times they have been Champions. He is in his early forties now; a successful man, fit and business-like. His hair, not luxuriant in his playing-days, has receded to leave him a smooth high dome of a forehead; his chin is still long and aggressive; his small mouth shows a man who means to have his own way, and is accustomed to having it; his eyes are coldly observant. He is a man of determined, rigid principles,

who works hard, believes in hard work, and has little patience
with anyone who does not share that belief. He has been called
an iron man, a tyrant, a Napoleon – admiring, rather than
affectionate descriptions. He is unquestionably one of the great
managers and he commands respect.

It was in 1947 that Stan Cullis the player became Mr Stanley
Cullis the manager. Not being a man to be satisfied with anything less than success, he retired from playing when he was
only thirty-two. Many men would have put off the decision,
knowing that for a few seasons yet there would be clubs glad
to have them; but it is hard to imagine Cullis in Third Division
sides, being outpaced by younger men, trying to impose his
knowledge and his will on second-class games. In his thirteen
years of first-class football he never played out of the First
Division; in seven years he played over thirty times for
England. His reputation was still high when he determined
on his new career; only two years after he left the playing staff
he was manager of Wolverhampton – the club he had joined as
a nineteen year old boy fifteen years before.

With this unmistakable strain of single-mindedness and
determination in his character, the last thing one would expect
of Cullis is that he should be an artist; yet as a player that is
what he was – a strong, even ruthless artist, but still an artist,
and of an old-fashioned kind. In the early days of football, the
centre-half was a second centre-forward, playing a little
behind, and looking after the business of pushing the ball
through to the inside-forwards, while the wing-halves and the
backs did the defensive work. The great change in the function
of the centre-half came about ten years before Cullis began his
career; the "new" offside law was introduced, and the effect of
it was that teams playing in the old style were suddenly vulnerable to swift direct attacks down the middle. The "stopper"
centre-half appeared – the "policeman", the third back; the
names invented showed clearly enough what his duties were.

Cullis was great enough to play his own style, even though
it was against the fashion; he knew too much about the game,
and cared too much about it, to be content with defence alone.

To confine himself to marking the centre-forward would make him simply another man's shadow; some men could accept it, but not Cullis. He had the ideal of the complete footballer in his mind: the men who could both attack and defend, and do both efficiently, intelligently, and according to correct principles. Like all the great ball players, he could not bear to waste a ball; he would rather be caught with it than make a bad pass.

In this sense Cullis was a stylist, in the sense that style is the man – his manner was his own and no one else's; but if by style is meant stylishness, grace of movement, that was no part of Cullis. He was a beautiful player in every way but that. He was strongly built, but not unusually thick or tall; he treated the ball as if it were his precious private property, like a child with a balloon at a party. He stood over it, or moved with it, in a tense crouch, his knees bent, his back and shoulders curved over it; his arms were held out, his elbows jutted protectively. Until he had thought out his move, plotted exactly where the ball should go, no one else was going to have it. With all his concentration, his cherishing of the ball occupied only part of his attention; he raised his head quickly from time to time to give a hard and piercing look about the field; swinging his arms, he gestured his players urgently into position; his lips moved continually in an undertone of instruction, criticism and encouragement. Being something of a puritan, he is said to have been extremely annoyed when it was once carelessly reported that he was "swearing at his men"; there is a great driving force in puritanism – no amount of swearing could have had the effect he achieved by his dogged insistence on work and sound principles.

"The last of the great attacking centre-halves," Charles Buchan called Cullis – and the best, many people would add. Yet before attacks can be built the ball must be won; a centre-half sees it coming to him – especially in international football – in the possession of fast clever, and determined forwards. It switches from one to the other; if a centre-half allows himself to be drawn out of position, and fails to get the ball, he leaves an open pathway to the goal. He must be quick – but he must choose his moment. In this defensive part of his work, Cullis's judgement was unerring. He knew how to wait, to resist the temptation to be drawn. He would crouch and watch; he saw an inaccurate pass almost before it started, and was already moving to pick it off; if a forward held the ball just a second too long, Cullis was in – and he was a bitter tackler.

When the attack was checked, and Cullis held the ball, one saw the quality that made him an outstanding and memorable player. Near his own goal, and under pressure, he might have been excused if he had merely kicked for safety; but he would not do it. Here one saw the compulsion of the artist. The ball was to be used, immediately if possible, but if his men were not in position, then he would hold it until they were; if there was no proper opening, then – whatever the crowd or anyone else thought – he would not loose the ball until he had made one. "There is a proper way to play this game," Cullis seemed to say by his actions, "and whether you like it or not, that is all you're going to see from me." Considering the pace of first-class football, it is impossible to play like this without enormous confidence in oneself, and extraordinary coolness. Cullis had both; his confidence was entirely justified by his skill; as to his coolness, there were times when it worried even his own side; but it was a weapon in itself – if Cullis was so imperturbable, then the situation could not be as serious as it seemed. His calm was good for the morale of his own team, and bad for the confidence of his opponents.

Cullis was a builder, and he began building from wherever he happened to be; if necessary, from his own goal-line. From there, his characteristic pass was the one pushed out diagonally to his wing-halves. Upfield, as he followed the attack he had himself begun, his most dangerous move was the quickly seen and quickly executed through pass, thoughtfully placed, that sent a forward clean away. There are wing-halves nowadays with a comparable constructive gift, but there are no centre-halves like Cullis.

He did not begin as a centre-half; neither did he begin, as so many others seem to have done, with the exclusive ambition of becoming a professional footballer. He came from Cheshire, from Wirral; he, Joe Mercer and Frank Soo were in the same Cheshire Schoolboys' team, and he went on, as Joe Mercer did, to play as an amateur for Ellesmere Port – at inside-right. He was making his living as an assistant in a grocery shop, with the idea in the back of his mind of becoming a journalist. He was seriously set on improving himself; in his spare time, and at night school, the subjects he chose to study were shorthand and book-keeping, French, and Esperanto. Before his plans in other directions had matured, when he was nineteen, his ability as a footballer was reported to Bolton Wanderers. His father, who came from Wolverhampton, decided that if the boy was going to play professional football, he would like him to play for Wolves; he wrote to the manager, Major Buckley, who must have been used to sending politely evasive answers to letters of that sort, took a chance in this case, and young Cullis was invited to come to Molineux for a trial. That was in March 1934; before the end of the season he was in the first team; by 1938 he was Wolves' regular captain and playing for England.

Officially, Cullis has twelve international caps, five in 1938 and seven in 1939 – a figure that does far less than justice to his prominence as an England player. It happened that the war years came just at the peak of his career; he has twenty-two wartime caps, and they were not won in a period when any good player had a reasonable chance of representing his country. The games played during the war do not count as full internationals; yet consider the 1943 team that beat Scotland 8–0: Swift; Scott, Hardwick; Britton, Cullis, Mercer; Matthews, Carter, Lawton, Hagan, D. Compton.

It must be one of the finest of all England teams: every single player outstandingly talented, and the whole side drawn together by the fact that they played constantly in each other's company. The half-back line particularly – Britton, Cullis, and Mercer – was as good a line as any of us are likely to see.

Success came quickly to Cullis, but very little of it can be put down to luck – and, as a player, he had at least two major disappointments. The first was in 1939. Wolverhampton were runners-up in the League that season; Cullis, the captain, was in his finest form. In the F.A. Cup they were drawn at home in every round, and went through them with startling ease: Bradford, 3–1; Leicester, 5–1; Liverpool, 4–1; Everton, 2–0. They won the Semi-Final against Grimsby Town by five goals to nil, and went to Wembley as the hottest favourites for years. They were a young and brilliant side, magnificently led by Cullis. On the other hand, Portsmouth, the intended victims, had had a worrying season, apart from the Cup; they finished within half a dozen points of relegation. Portsmouth won the Final. Something happened to Wolverhampton: they fell apart, and never looked a good side. This was the year we heard about the autographs; it was reported that when the official book went round the dressing-rooms half an hour before the game the Portsmouth players could not recognize their opponents' signatures – they were so shaky with nerves. The final score was 4–1 to Portsmouth, and Cullis never had another chance of a Cup winner's medal.

There was still a chance of a League Championship; Wolves had been runners-up in 1938 as well as in 1939. In the first season after the war they were in the running again. It was a tight finish. Manchester United had 56 points with all their games played. Wolverhampton, 56 points, and Liverpool, 55 points, had one game to play – against each other, the last game of the season, and for the Championship. Before the match at Molineux, Cullis spoke to the crowd through the loudspeakers. He announced that this was his last game, the end of his career; he reminded them of the Cup Final disappointment – but now, he said, here was the chance of a last honour; the gold medal as captain of a League Championship side. It was Liverpool who won the game. Albert Stubbins, their red-haired centre-forward, broke away to score the winning goal; Cullis chased desperately after him, but never caught him, and so that chance of a last triumph, a dramatically perfect exit from football, slipped away.

Two major disappointments – but in a career that has been all success. Within weeks of his last game, Cullis was on the staff of Wolverhampton as assistant manager; with hardly a pause he had bridged the break that has been so difficult and worrying for many men in football. In less than a year he took over from Ted Vizard as manager, and in that same season – 1949 – Wolverhampton won the Cup. To see one of his own escaped ambitions fulfilled so soon through his players must have given him a special kind of satisfaction – mixed, perhaps, with just the slightest taste of bitterness. Within five years his side were Champions, and he himself had made his reputation as a manager. It was natural that a man who had been so skilful as a player should observe and appreciate the flourishing of the arts of football in other countries. Wolverhampton, thanks to his shrewdness and imagination, are a modern side, streamlined, fast and efficient; Mr Cullis came back from tours in Eastern Europe impressed with the fitness and technique of the Russian and Hungarian players. With his driving temperament and insistence on hard work he put the stamp of his own character on Wolves, and built a side that for power, economy, and directness could compare with any in Europe – the side that beat Spartak, Honved, and Real Madrid.

There are broadly two kinds of English football. One is basically artistic, and one may see its various aspects exemplified by Preston, Blackpool, Manchester United and Tottenham. The other is the football of efficiency rather than tradition; there is no nostalgia in it and no flower of decadence. It offers instead the satisfaction and excitement of power. Its best example is Wolverhampton, and its personification is Stanley Cullis.

from MASTERS OF SOCCER *1960*

Tommy Lawton

MAURICE EDELSTON and
TERENCE DELANEY

"That's Lawton," they said. "There he is – Number 9." You could hear it like a sigh over the ground as the teams came out. It followed Lawton, this sound of admiration, for nearly twenty years. His name was mis-pronounced with awe in every accent in the world. In the great stadiums of Europe in the 1940s he was a star among a brilliant generation of England footballers. On pinched and sooty Third Division pitches in the 1950s he was still a master. Watching him was a sort of compulsion, even during the few minutes before the kick-off, when he hugged his shoulders against the chill and tapped his toes down into his boots. He tested the turf like a cat on ice. As he swung his powerful legs into a lazy run, he placed each foot as if he could feel the separate studs pressing into the ground.

"He was the lightest mover," Alex James said, "of any big man who played football." Lawton was born to be a centre-forward. As he stood over the ball, with his hands on his hips, waiting for the starting whistle, you could see he was built for it too. He was six feet tall, strong and beautifully balanced. He had weight enough in his shoulders and chest, but it was the great power of his legs that gave him his astonishing quickness and spring. From the point of view of an opponent, everything about him was a threat. His coolness, his long, intent, sharp-eyed face, with the commanding nose and the sleek black shining hair; the jut of that head on a muscular neck that could flick a heavy ball into goal like a stone from a catapult; his alertness, his reserve of controlled energy. There has never been a centre-forward like him since, and very few before him had a genius to compare with his.

One comparison is inevitable. When Lawton was seventeen, before he had played one full season of League football, he went from his first club, Burnley, to Everton, where he met the great Dixie Dean, the only man who has ever scored sixty goals in one season of First Division football. This was surely a fated meeting. There had never been a finer artist in heading the ball than Dean. From him young Tom Lawton learned to develop his greatest gift, his superb skill in the air. Years later Lawton was still fooling defences with a trick patented by his teacher. When a high centre came over, he would jump as if to try a long header for goal; at the last second he would change direction in the air and nod down a short back-pass to his inside-forward. In 1930 Dean was making goals like this for Dunn. In 1947 Lawton with Notts County, was making them for Sewell. In such visual memories of physical things, the history of a sport is preserved, more than in words. "The Sweet Science," A. J. Liebling says, writing of boxing, "is joined on to the past like a man's arm to his shoulder."

To see Lawton climb to a high ball, head and shoulders above the rest, to see him rise, slowly it seemed, above the ball, and then, with the action of a striking snake, drive it down into the goal, was something unforgettable. Nijinsky was once asked what was the secret of the "grand leap".

"Well," he said, "you jump, and at the top of the jump – you wait a little."

The phrase fits the footballer as well as it did the dancer.

Lawton's first transfer, from Burnley to Everton, was the start of a great career; forty-five international appearances, including Wartime and Victory Internationals, and forty-six goals; something like 500 goals in first-class football altogether. It was also the beginning of a professional life sign-posted at every turn by newspaper headlines. Lawton was not only a great player; he was a star, and he was always news.

He was born in Bolton, on October 6th, 1919. By the time he was fourteen, at Folds Road Central School, it was clear that he was something entirely out of the ordinary as a footballer. In three seasons of schoolboy football he scored 570 goals. It was no wonder that professional clubs were interested in him. Burnley was the one that got him, at sixteen, and he played his first League game for them against Doncaster, still

too young to sign as a professional. He was in the team again
the following week, against Swansea, and scored twice. One
was a header, his first goal in big football, the first entry in a
long account.

October 10th, 1936, was a day that Tom Lawton will
probably remember when he is ninety. It was four days after
his seventeenth birthday. He was a professional footballer –
just – and picked at centre-forward against Tottenham. Even
a young Lawton, at seventeen, must be in a fine confusion of
unresolved doubts and dreams as he goes out to play his first
professional game. The best cure for nervous anxiety is action;
but suppose he makes a fool of himself? Might it not be better
to take it slowly, get the feel of things before attempting anything? And the man marking Lawton that day was Arthur
Rowe, who had already played for England at centre-half – the
same Arthur Rowe who was to become "Spurs" brilliantly
successful manager.

Lawton did not have to wait long to have his doubts
answered. Two minutes from the start Brocklebank cracked a
pass through the middle. Young Tom was off as if he had
heard a pistol, between the backs with that smooth, tigerish
stride, and he hit the ball with all the bottled-up force of youth
and ambition. It was the first public appearance of the authentic
Lawton cannon-ball, and it was in. A few minutes later a fast
swerving corner-kick came across from Stein. Lawton was up,
met it hard and clean just where the parting meets the forehead,
and that was two. After that, according to his own account,
with a hat-trick in sight, Lawton was so excited he missed two
easy open goals. By the second half he had managed to cool
down, and when another chance offered he planted it coolly
and firmly in the goal. Then it was all cheers and handshakes.
There were to be many others, but that was a day.

Lawton went on playing good intelligent football for
twenty years after that first professional game. Football itself
changed in that time, and he changed. Yet watching him in
the 1950s, even if it was a bad match, even if the players round
him were second rate, even if Lawton himself was off form, he

was still just as unmistakably as ever a great footballer. His patience with slow-witted partners wore thin at times; he had suffered the wear and tear of success; you suspected that in some ways he was a disappointed man; but it was still there, impossible to counterfeit. A Rolls-Royce is always a Rolls-Royce.

It was not only his play that made headlines. His transfers were news. Everton paid Burnley £6,500 for Lawton, a sensational amount for 1936 and for a boy not yet eighteen. He stayed with Everton for nine of his best years, got his first England cap at nineteen, and won a League Championship medal in 1939. In 1945, with the war over, the clubs started thinking hard about the future, and begun serious team-building. Chelsea decided that what they needed most was a top-class centre-forward. They bought the best in the country, Lawton, and he cost them £11,500 – a record. People wrote to the newspapers, as they had been doing since Sunderland paid £1,000 for Alf Common in 1905, and as they are still doing, to ask, "Is any footballer worth all this money?" Chelsea evidently thought so, but they only had Lawton for one full season. It was a good season, and his first big game at Stamford Bridge – what a game that was! The famous Moscow Dynamos were the visitors. We had been hearing about them for weeks before. We had heard, too, that some surprisingly good football was being played in Russia. At that time, just after the end of the war, the popular attitude towards Russia was not what it is now. Peace had come, and there was hope in the air. Perhaps, just perhaps, international brotherhood, or at least friendship, was really somewhere ahead. A Russian team had never been here before, we were consumed with curiosity, and we wanted to show them that, whatever they had heard, the English were an amiable friendly lot. It was some such mixture of feelings that took an enormous crowd to Stamford Bridge that Tuesday afternoon in 1945. The official record gate at the Bridge is 82,905. There must have been nearly that number inside when they closed the gates, but there were still thousands outside, swaying, pushing, protesting. Before the kick-off they broke in.

The crowd flooded beyond the terraces, across the wide dog-track and the broad spaces behind the goals, right up to the touchline. Hundreds saw the game from the roof of the stand. The game ended in a draw, three-all, after what was tolerantly described as a "diplomatic goal" awarded by the referee to the Russians, though an estimated 100,000 people explained to him that it was off-side. Chelsea's third goal was a Lawton special, and a promise to the club's supporters of what they might expect during the rest of the season. It was a magnificent header, one of his very best, taken at the top of a beautifully judged high leap, and driven hard into the goal from a narrow angle. Lawton gave the crowd good value that season; by the end of it he had broken the club's individual goal-scoring record for the First Division, with twenty-six in thirty-four games.

Then, towards the end of 1947, "The Lawton Story", as some of the papers called it, broke out again all over the back pages. Lawton had asked Chelsea to let him go, and the club had refused. "We have not received an acceptable offer," the Board of Directors was quoted as saying. Yet Blackburn, Derby County, Stoke, Nottingham Forest, and Arsenal were all said to be in the market. Chelsea were reported to have turned down a bid of £17,000, which would have been the highest fee ever paid in this country. "Lawton seeks a show-down," the headlines said; "Will Chelsea let Lawton go?" and then "Lawton dropped from Chelsea team." There was talk of arbitration, of appeal to the Players' Union. It went on for weeks. At last it was settled, and it was big news again. Lawton, England's centre-forward, was going into the Third Division, to Notts County. They were paying £20,000 for him – the first £20,000 fee ever. New and stimulating speculations broke out. "Can Lawton play Third Division football and keep his England place?"; "Is Lawton the first surtax-paying professional?" Notts were said to be negotiating the biggest ever insurance on a player – £25,000.

Meanwhile Lawton, presumably, was expected to go on, unmoved, playing football. He did it, too. He played four more internationals while he was with Notts County, helped them to the Third Division South championship and promotion in 1949–50, and in that season was the highest individual scorer in the division, with thirty-one goals. That in itself was a remarkable personal achievement. It was ten years since, in two successive seasons with Everton, he had been top goal-scorer in Division One. Lawton did well by Notts County. The average gate when he arrived was 9,000. Before he left, five years later, it was up to 35,000.

Why did he leave? Once again, as in the Chelsea case, facts are scarce. Rumours were plentiful. Lawton was known to have a hard head for business. Clubs made big money out of him, and he himself, much as he liked the game, was not playing it for fun. The footballer's maximum wage – £12 a week in the season, with £2 for a win and £1 for a draw, and £10 in the off season – was ridiculous in relation to his drawing power as a star. There were other sources of income. He had a weekly newspaper column, royalties from two books, his name and his picture appeared in advertisements, he had appeared on radio, television, films, and even the stage. In 1952, with all this in the background – though nothing was said in public – with the manager, the directors, and the players holding one long meeting after another, it was obvious that Lawton's happy days at Meadow-lane were over. "Lawton is leaving us at his own request," the club said.

He came back to London, to Brentford, and again the fee was a sizeable one – £12,000. Those were interesting days at Brentford. In the forward line with him, at different times, Lawton had the tireless enthusiast Billy Dare, tough, cool Jimmy Bowie, and a new boy, just beginning League football, Jim Bloomfield, who is now with Arsenal and one of the best young players in the country. Every Saturday some hundreds of Londoners who had seen no good reason to visit Brentford for some years past found their way over to Griffin Park for a nostalgic look at Tom Lawton. They were not disappointed. Some of the speed was gone, but the old power was still there. Lawton was still leading the line, though lying a little farther back; his long ground passes were as well timed as ever; he could still spin on his toe and shoot on the turn; he still prowled about watchfully with that rangy forward-leaning stride, and pounced with deadly quickness on any mistake in the defence. We remember a game against Blackburn. Kelly, a good big Scottish centre-half, was marking Lawton. Bowie pushed a ball through the middle; it ran too far for Lawton, but he strolled after it, at an easy swaying canter, just in case. Kelly would have been wise to take a good swing at that ball, first time. Instead, being outside his own penalty-area, and seeing that Lawton was not too close, he decided to trap it with one foot and push it upfield with the other. He did trap it with one foot, and then it hit the bar with a terrible crash, and rebounded first bounce into touch. It was as fast as that. The goalkeeper moved, but it was a spasmodic shock reaction, and occurred some time after the event. That was the last time in that game that Kelly underestimated the speed of Lawton's pounce. Elvey, the goalkeeper, was noticeably edgy for some time afterwards.

Lawton was now thirty-three. Soon, if he was to stay in football, and at the top, his career had to take a new direction. When he had been at Brentford for a little less than a year, it was announced that he had taken over as team manager.

He went on playing, but it looked like a pointer towards his future. With Lawton's talent, his intelligence, and his vast experience, there seemed no reason why he should not become one of the great managers. Yet after less than nine months of this new job at Brentford, he resigned, and returned to being simply a player.

A week or so later came a most astonishing and unexpected piece of news. Lawton was back in the First Division, at thirty-four, and with Arsenal. Arsenal had made a bad start to the 1953-4 season, though they began it as League champions. They played their first eight games without a win. There was, as usual, plenty of talent at Highbury. What Lawton had to contribute was the steadying influence of a confident mature player. When he played, the line swung on him like a compass needle on its pin. He scored relatively few goals, but the short accurate flicks from his forehead to either side made goals for Lishman and Tapscott, and his majestically swept, low, forward passes, opened wide pathways for the wingers. In 1955 Lawton went with an Arsenal team to Russia. It was not a successful tour, from the football point of view – they lost to Dynamo 5–0 – but it included one special occasion for Lawton. He spent his thirty-fifth birthday in Moscow, and the Russian footballers threw a surprise party for him, with a birthday cake two feet square.

He stayed with Arsenal for three years. Young players were waiting just off-stage, and he had served his purpose. This time there were no public hints of undignified private quarrels. Tom Whittaker, "The Boss" at Arsenal, told Lawton he would let him know when the right opportunity as a player-manager came along, and it came from Kettering Town, in the Southern League. Arsenal let Lawton go for £1,000. By Christmas of his first season, Kettering were at the top of their League with ten points in hand. Lawton had gone about his job of training and team-building with intelligence and imagination. He restored the confidence of players who had lost the habit of winning; he took advantage of the friendly services of Tom Whittaker in finding new men to strengthen the weak places; he set about attracting youngsters who might one day be players. One of his stimulating ideas was to put an advertisement in a local paper offering young players a week's free coaching under Tommy Lawton on the club's ground. Kettering could easily have been the starting-point for Lawton's second career in football. Unexpectedly, when he had been there a year, he was offered the manager's job, at £2,500 a year, with Notts County, the club he had left five years before.

Things might have been very different for Lawton if he had turned it down flat. It soon appeared that the Notts County directors were by no means unanimous in wanting Lawton. The old disagreements were raked over. There was already an acting manager, Frank Broome; would he step down and be Lawton's assistant? Was it fair to ask him? Eventually, after a week of widely publicized disagreements among the Notts County directors, Lawton took the job. He spent an unhappy year. A manager needs whole-hearted support from directors and players, and the circumstances of his appointment made that impossible. The club had lost money since he was there five years earlier, and that made shopping for players difficult. Also it meant, some people said, that the club could not afford Lawton's large salary. Considering all this, it is surprising that the job lasted as long as it did. In July 1958 Notts County dismissed Lawton.

We have been telling Lawton's story, so far, as if he were one of the legendary figures of the football past. To most young men in their twenties that is what he is – a name, like Steve Bloomer or Hugh Gallacher. Yet after more than twenty incomparable years as a player, Lawton is still only forty. In October 1958 he took over the Magna Carta Inn at Lowdham in Nottinghamshire. He was finished with football, he said. One cannot believe that he gave up the game without regret. If another chance offers to get back into it, can such a man go on happily keeping a village pub? Don Welsh left *his* pub to go back into management with Bournemouth.

Even a great player, when he goes into management, must begin learning all over again; there are many reasons why he may fail. Some good players are unable to learn, but lack the sympathetic gift; they cannot command the liking and loyalty of players, or the confidence of directors. Even if none of these reasons apply, the man may simply be unlucky.

Lawton may not be finished with football yet. Even if he is, he has made a bigger contribution than most. He has demonstrated that there can be a complete centre-forward. We have seen many incomplete centre-forwards who were first class players, and some of them played for England. Some could run and shoot like Milburn, who liked the ball on the ground; some could plan like Revie, from behind the line; some, like Drake, were powerful and could shake off punishment; some were bold and dangerous, like Trevor Ford; some were cool accomplished dribblers, like Finney, delicate and accurate like Allen; some were big and strong and found the open spaces, like Kevan. Some could beat a man on the ground, some in the air; some could shoot on the turn, some could snap on to a through pass; some could marshall the line, some inspire it. Lawton could do it all. He could cut neat quarter-circles round man after man like a figure-skater, and go through a defence leaving them standing still behind him, or he could leap between the backs like a hurdler. "He must have taken tremendous hammerings," Billy Wright says, "but never once did I see Tommy lose his temper or his poise. Never can I recall Tommy Lawton deliberately fouling an opponent."

If you should ever be in Lowdham, and drop into the Magna Carta Inn, treat the landlord with respect.

from MASTERS OF SOCCER *1960*

Stanley Mortensen

ALAN ROSS

Slighter, and also fairer, than Matthews, for his grandfather was a Norwegian sailor who married and then settled in South Shields, Mortensen, "the other Stanley", has something of the same magnetism. Partly, perhaps, it is because he has the cool-ness and flair for the dramatic, essential to the big-match temperament; partly it is the result of flawless technique, that in turn allows a player to conserve his energies and to dispense the graces of his craft without apparent effort.

It is inevitable that these two players should be mentioned together, for, though their methods are as different as could be, they understand each other, and this mutual confidence has produced the most remarkable partnership in post-war football.

Mortensen is not an inside-forward of the "fetch-and-carry" type, nor is he an architect on whose blue-print the other forwards build. He is the high-quality opportunist, with positional instinct, uncanny powers of anticipation, the ability to do the unexpected at great speed, who not only can alter the whole balance of the game in a few minutes but who has the directness and goal-sense to finish his own moves off. Matthews may draw the opposition by sheer virtuosity; Mortensen goes through them before they are aware of an opening.

He is neither particularly fast nor strong; but what mark out his genius are phenomenal acceleration, clever changes of pace, balance, and a singleness of purpose that enables him to score goals when the way seems solidly blocked. If Matthews dominates a match, calling up the thunder on the wings for all to admire, Mortensen is the lightning that strikes immediately after. Like many great inside-forwards, he often appears idle; yet just when it seems he has written a match off and a false security is settling on the opposing defence, he is suddenly away on his own, jinking his way through in short bursts or turning up from nowhere to hurl himself head-first at the ball and flick it into the net.

His reputation is entirely post-war. In 1938, after some success in South Shields school football – "I was a poor boy," he has written, "brought up in a happy home" – he was invited to sign for Blackpool. By the outbreak of war he was some way off the League side. "I was made aware of the fact that I was fortunate to stay on the staff." He joined the R.A.F., and his Wellington bomber caught fire and crashed during operational training. Mortensen had enough stitches in his head to deter most people from heading a ball for life. But he was soon back playing for Service teams, and during this substitute war-time football he suddenly found himself. 'I was developing. It came just like that."

Since then Mortensen has become, at centre-forward or inside-right, one of the brilliant players of our time. He scored twenty-one goals in his first fifteen representative games and was never on the losing side. Till this year he has been a fixture in the England team. He began the season quietly; now he leads the First Division goal-scorers once again. The future, and at international level the barometer is rarely steady, might break either way. Meanwhile, like Matthews, he hankers after a Cup Winner's medal – until April 28 anyway.

from THE OBSERVER *22/4/51*

Billy Wright

WALTER WINTERBOTTOM

In my early contacts with Billy Wright, I was never aware of him in the way one is quickly aware of an extraordinary man or an extraordinary footballer. He was just another player on the field. There were never any startling statements, bright quips or "larks" to make him stand out as an individual or personality in the group. His conversation was pleasant, his answers to questions were invariably a simple "yes" or "no" and, to all intents and purposes, he was nothing more than a "nice lad".

But he forced himself on my notice in the most subtle way. When reflecting on a match and assessing who had played well and who had played badly, almost invariably I decided that Wright had played well. With so many powerful personalities around him when he first came into the team, his may not have been a dazzling match in the company of Matthews, Mannion, Carter, and Lawton, but nevertheless it was a good performance, without any critical point which one could say was bad. It was the regularity with which he forced himself into the team, and the determination with which he persisted in it, that forced some people, and myself as manager, to think of him in greater and wider terms.

In those early days one never thought of Wright that here was a future captain of England. Yet one could be assured that around him could be built themes of play, and his captaincy grew from the fact that here was a man whose consistent game could be integrated with other players and link him solidly to them – players like Scott, Swift, Franklin, Lawton, Carter, Matthews, and Mannion.

As a defensive wing-half – his defensive play has always been outstanding – he has never been seen as a power player, a stormer of the upfield, backing up an attack to thunder shots at goal like a Duncan Edwards, although he has scored inter-national goals from wing-half. Neither was he a cultured con-troller, like Matt Busby or Harry Johnston, or Willie Watson, players who like to stop and flick a ball delicately and move on, or clip through a closely measured pass which opens a defence and sets up a goal. But in the pure qualities of defence, in interception, in recovering at lightning speed when beaten, in firm and indomitable tackling, and fitting into a covering pattern, he has been a highly gifted player: one of the best defenders England has ever had, and always, always excellent in his work in the air.

Much of this has stemmed from his club style. Footballers cannot play entirely by inclination, but must conform to the dictates of the club team. Not for the Wolves the close dribble and short pass out of defence which thrills a crowd. Of their defenders, Wolves have always demanded quick and powerful disposal of the ball once they have it, and that rules out the finesse of ball holding.

Billy Wright has been criticized for this, but it is not to say that he cannot finesse when necessary. A first-class movement by Wright is used on a F.A. educational film. It was taken in the 1953 match against Scotland at Wembley (2–2) and shows him putting a Scottish player on the ground with a juggle from one foot to the other and back again as they were "weight-bearing" and finishing with a clear sweep-away of the ball. It is a fine example of close control and high skill under pressure.

But Wright is the type who has never really relished the taking of risks. His whole football philosophy is to be secure and certain. He wants always to make a safe, deliberate, bread-and-butter pass rather than an impish, Mannion-style, light-hearted chip. He has never been guilty of "display" football. "Here is the ball, I have it under control. Where does it go?

K

There. Off it goes. Sure, sidefoot pass." That has been Billy Wright's attitude, and most of his game has been built on this quick, straightforward pass.

His greatest single asset has been his extremely quick "pounce". Not many players make their decisions and tackle with the speed and certainty of Billy Wright, and this, rather than a dead run, has been his speed factor. He has a short stride with powerful legs, the power packed particularly in the thighs. Quick reaction, quick pounce, quick interception – one of his most marked talents is that, from a position behind his man, before any movement is suspected, Billy can be suddenly two or three yards in front of him.

If, in a sense, he has been lucky in avoiding injuries over the years, it is because he is so compact. His style does not involve the taking of risk, the physical risks which other, different styles attract. Allan Brown of Blackpool and Luton, for example, has played the ball at what I call very fine margins in escaping a tackle, whereas Billy has always come completely clear of a tackle before playing the ball away, or has gone into a tackle in a compact, forceful, straightforward way only when the time for the tackle is exactly right. He knows, too, how to fall well. When he goes down, he will roll away like a rubber ball and be quickly on his feet again. Challenged to find one word for his play in this respect, one might say compact – or terse.

In his early days his one weakness as a wing-half was that, in his industry and enthusiasm for the heat of the battle, he would sometimes lose his connexion with the astute type of inside-forward opposing him, the man who could vanish and escape behind him, infiltrating into menacing positions while Billy was magnetized by the flow of play.

In preparing for the Festival of Britain match against the Argentine at Wembley, we practised Billy and Henry Cockburn in countering this, in the important factor of somehow keeping between such a man and the goal. Yet, sure enough, it happened in the match. Labruna, the inside-left, escaped from Billy and we lost an early goal to an Argentine left-wing attack. Again, against Hungary in Budapest, Billy and Sid Owen between them surrendered the fourth Hungarian goal at a critical time in the match. Hungary were three goals up at half-time, but we started the second half very well, played some fine football and it looked as though we would have something to say for ourselves. But then Billy and Sid Owen were tempted to go for the same ball, lost it to Hidegkuti, who pushed it quickly past them to Puskas, and he was off and a goal was scored.

This keenness to get into a situation has occasionally prevented him from properly evaluating it before committing himself, but against all this has been an enormous capacity and desire for work. He has never spared himself in making up a deficiency in his play, or in salvaging an error. He has learned quickly, particularly as a centre-half where the final responsibility is heavier, of the danger of compromising a situation merely by the fact of plunging up in attack. It has been fascinating to see him work at this deficiency and overcome it. He became rather conservative in going upfield to back up his own attack because of a strong awareness and constant dread of quick transfers and returns and long passes pumped through behind him, through the vacant centre-field.

Out of the consistency and regularity of his international play grew much personal strength in terms of character, and of the demands of international football. Billy's career has been one of steady, measured progress. Although he played for England when he was a young man, his was not a début like those of Stanley Matthews or Duncan Edwards or Johnny Haynes, when it was immediately obvious that here, within a few matches, were players who would have long and dazzling careers for England. Billy's was a careful evolution.

Thus, in the late 'forties, when a successor as captain had to be found for George Hardwick, Billy was elected because of his dependability, his solid experience, his sustained and reliable level of performance. At that time we had only really started to think of the future and to see the need for some consistency and continuity of planning.

There were criticisms in the press. He was not considered the ideal type of captain. The critics wanted someone more flamboyant, more dramatic, faster with an opinion, a better talker, a dramatic leader of men such as England had had in Hapgood, Cullis, and Swift. With Wright, these things came only gradually, if at all.

Billy Wright has expressed his captaincy in enthusiasm, zest for the game, and example. At one time I was of the opinion that the only type of captain was the player who could organize, stimulate, and coach his team during the game. Alan Brown, of Burnley, now Sunderland manager, was such a leader. But I have seen in Billy's captaincy the wonderful effect of example and enthusiasm, infecting the players around him with strong determination.

People may have felt, watching the England team, that Billy was a fine player and all that, but that he was not truly a captain, not truly leading the team. To have someone on the field constantly calling instructions and exhorting players to greater effort may be a more obvious aspect of captaincy to spectators; such a captain appears as the man of fire and fury driving his team on to victory; but the players may very well know that it is being used only to cover some shortcomings in the captain's own play: to them it can be irritating, embarrassing, distracting – particularly in highly skilled individual players at the top level.

Orders should be given and understood in the team's preparation, so that players go on the field with a clear idea of what they will attempt to do. The aim is to have eleven men thinking of all the problems as they arise, and thinking of them in relation to each other and to the team as a whole. In effect, you will have eleven captains, all thinking for the benefit of the whole. Thus, in the Hungarian team, although Puskas was quite properly captain by virtue of his electric personality alone, Hidegkuti and Bozsik were the brains of the affair, and there were half a dozen players in the team all shouting helpful, dynamic instructions. I have seen them in matches when Puskas would be having a quiet time, and yet the other players have been driving on, full of bounce, living and dying within the game, all captains courageous in their fashion.

It has not been in Billy's personality to be voluble with

instructions to others. Indeed, since the war, this type of captain has become more and more rare in club football. Perhaps the crowd's dislike of shouting on the field has been responsible for this? No one likes to be called a "Big Head"!

The example of getting on with the game, of playing it hard and fairly, with the occasional smile and call, can engender in so many ways a better response and much more respect from players. The man who "talks" a good game is usually the man prone to make changes in the team for the sake of change. He will not balance things carefully – he acts by instinct, on impulses, by inspiration, whereas the other man, the Billy Wright type, is continually valuing play and assessing possible changes, but is reluctant to make them unless they are thrust on him by injury. He knows the value of *not* making random changes.

Sometimes the impulsive action, the flash of inspiration, will succeed, but my preference is for the second type, the Wright type. This man is holding on to a theme or system of play which is known by the players before they go on the field. He is not the man to shuffle and re-deal the cards quickly on the field to the confusion of others.

One quality which did come with striking speed after Billy Wright became captain of England was this ability to make reckonings on the field, to make calculations and judgements on the entire team and not just on himself as one player. At half-time, when something can often be done, he has been able to give me more positive opinions on the way play has been trending and the reasons for it than any other player. When critical issues have arisen on the field, he has assumed a bold captaincy and shown that he is alive to these things. Like a true captain, he is not afraid of facing the issue when it comes.

This honesty of purpose was best shown in the England-Wales match at Wembley in 1952 when Jack Froggatt, our centre-half, was injured in a collision with Trevor Ford. At a time when the Welsh centre-forward was something of a terror to us, Wright accepted the challenge himself and moved to centre-half, although other team adjustments could have been made.

Much of this honesty of thinking and straightforwardness comes from his method of play, of never giving up or quitting. He is cheerful, and when he occasionally reflects disappointment on the field, he quickly overcomes it. Even when stung close to tears by a particularly irksome defeat, as he has been, he puts a brave face on the world. But he has lived by the game so seriously that this has always demanded a major effort.

In his early days, in team discussion, Billy would seldom contribute more than a confirmation of another player's opinion. But in his later years, he has grown accustomed to expressing himself forcefully and has made many original points, often in downright contradiction of me or someone else. This happened in Buenos Aires in 1953, after the preliminary match in which Malcolm Barrass at centre-half had been drawn badly out of position by Lacasia, the Argentine centre-forward. We had a very brisk discussion on how to counter this man in the international match coming up. Senior players like Alf Ramsey and Harry Johnston had much to say. Some people wanted to have a man following him, dogging his footsteps, but Billy quite vehemently wanted the centre-half to stay back, in position, and let someone else pick off Lacasia. We decided that Johnston, the centre-half, would go with him in the early part of the match, with Billy and Jimmy Dickinson covering the gap in the middle, then Johnston would fall back in favour of someone else so that the Argentine team would not quite know if we were going to persist in man-to-man marking. But the match was washed out by rain after twenty minutes' play, so that the issue was not really joined.

In modern international football, the captain has less and less tactical responsibility on the field, save in emergency, but the captain and the manager or coach can create such an affinity that they often think along parallel lines.

Injured in a match at Cardiff in which Hancocks of Wolves was outside-left and Finney outside-right, Billy Wright moved himself immediately to the outside-left position; Hancocks went to the right wing, and Finney was brought across to inside-left. Billy knew that he could push a pass inwards with his right foot, but could do little running. Outside-left was the place for him, with Finney as the player of sufficiently high skill to nurse this lame duck along the wing: and Hancocks would be quite at home in his club position. This is precisely what I had decided to do, but Wright had made the changes before I could take any action.

At other times we have disagreed. Against Brazil at Wembley, John Atyeo failed with a penalty-kick. We had a second penalty award, and Billy made Roger Byrne take it. I thought he was wrong. I felt that Atyeo had taken a good penalty-kick, but that the goalkeeper had moved before the ball was played and got to it. But this was clearly a matter of opinion, and we each had no more than an even chance of being right.

In domestic arrangements, particularly abroad, Billy would sometimes return from talking to his players with a problem unresolved, and I would have liked him on the whole to be more assertive. I do not mean so much in giving orders as in going through with his ideas, reaching conclusions on them and making them known to me and the team, perhaps a shade less quietly than he does.

Caught up at the age of fifteen in the Wolves "machine", Billy has been whirled along at breakneck speed ever since. Always something has been happening – Army service, playing for the Wolves, playing for England, captain of both, winning the Cup and League Championships, playing in three World Championships, foreign travel, and the dramatic matches at Wolverhampton against the great European club sides which must hold a distinctive place in his memories. This is a practical life, a physical life which does not lend itself to the develop-ment of a mind of reflection and inquiry. If it has been in one sense a monastic life, with its routine of breakfast, training at the club, lunch, more training, presenting some prizes, going to the station to meet the players, joining the team bus and so on, it has been one of constant exposure to people and places, of variety and travel, and it is certainly not one he has failed to enjoy. For Billy Wright is basically a happy person. His open, wholesome attitude to life leaves him happy in his surroundings, no matter what they are. He makes friends easily, takes the rough with the smooth – almost the classic concept of the British soldier.

The importance of being earnest and loyal and fair is strong within him. Even if he has felt defeat deeply, he has always made honest appraisals of the opposition to the extent of being over-generous to them. He can be frankly critical, but it is always criticism based on football and how it is played, and never, never on personalities. Once when he had to substitute at fairly short notice for Sir Stanley Rous at a football writers' dinner, he made a keen analysis of George Young, the Scotland captain who was present, of his playing technique and his impact on the Scottish game.

The destructive criticisms of which most of us are guilty from time to time never come from Billy Wright. This is not because he cannot think along these lines, or because he prefers the peaceful, uncontroversial life. He simply feels that he does not have the right to make these criticisms.

This is typical of his manliness. He has come to sense that football really is something much more than just a game. After the 1958 World Championship ended for England in a play-off defeat by Russia, he must have been bitterly disappointed. He may well have felt that it would be his last World Championship. Yet he walked across the stadium at Gothenburg, faced the massed Press of the world, answered all their questions patiently, fully, honestly. Again, this was typical of his simple, healthy, physical attitude to the game. He does not see the need to smoke or drink, and prefers to get to bed early – and when he does, he goes straight off to sleep. One of the big jokes with England has always come from Wright's room-mates who accuse him of rudeness in falling asleep as soon as he goes to bed, leaving them awake – and brooding. By contrast, his club colleague Bill Slater is a man who is constantly balancing factors in his mind, evaluating things; Dennis Wilshaw, another Wolves player, has such an imaginative mind that he seldom slept much before a match.

So Billy's natural love of the game is manifest in this boyish, physical way. He is still boyish about football. All experienced players love the game deeply. How else would they carry on deep into their thirties? But often they have a more serious, sophisticated feeling about it. Billy, however, still bubbles with the joy of being able to play football. He would still be the first to run down the streets and join in a boys' game and enjoy it.

I think he has always felt a strong need of intense physical activity. He expresses himself more fully in the "doing" rather than in dialectics, in movement rather than conversation. This has been invaluable in the general work of the team. He trains as enthusiastically as he plays, setting a firm example to other players who often need the stimulation of the crowd and the match – or convince themselves that they do – before responding. Since there is much preparatory work now going on at all international levels, it is delightful and very valuable to have such a man.

When we first trained at Porthcawl in Wales, boys from the Cardiff Open Air School came to watch. Wright was first to kick a ball towards them, enticing them to join in. They did with such a will that they almost reduced our session to a shambles. Before we knew it there was an impromptu match going on with the boys. Indeed, this started a habit of always inviting selected boys to join in a mixed game at the end of the training period. The last time Billy was at Porthcawl, despite a bitter wind and streaming rain, he felt he could not let these boys down, and he got the England team to stay on for a kick-about game with the eager youngsters.

Once, on the practice ground beneath the lovely Lisbon Stadium, he found a ragged but charming little boy, put him in goal, and fired in balls for him to save. Soon the whole team gathered round to encourage the boy, and he was in a heaven of delight. Footballers, for their part, are always equally moved by the adulation of youth. It carries them back to their own golden days when they, too, had their idols.

Billy Wright has had a remarkable career in football. Of its great prizes, there are few he has not won. But one would like · to think that, retaining as he does this boyish rapture for it all,

K*

he will find some continuation of his life's work in helping the young people in the football of the future.

It would be a noble challenge, and one worthy of him.

from SOCCER PARTNERSHIP *by Bob Ferrier 1960*

Len Shackleton

MAURICE EDELSTON and
TERENCE DELANEY

This word football, and the thing it stands for – when we were small boys, we knew what it meant all right. "You can't have been playing football till this time!" they said when we got home: "it's pitch dark!" "What's the good of having football boots if you don't wear them?" they said, "look at your shoes!" "Don't you get enough football after school every day and all day Saturdays," they said, "without kicking stones all the way home?" "Why are you limping?" they said, "why are you covered in mud?" We said nothing. We scored goals, in miniature, between the legs of chairs and in gateways – great goals, beating four men first. Our goalposts were trees, or coats, or chalked walls; sometimes even goalposts. We were pursued by park-keepers. Every shot was a cannon-ball, every save a swallow-dive, every decision was disputed. We were unruly, but we were devoted. Football was what we did when they set us free.

Some people, it seems, were not like this. To them the word means something else; something more solemn, more proper, connected with national honour and the upright life. To others still, who came to the game presumably late in life, football is an industry, best regulated by the application of what are called sound business principles. If they are right, these more serious men, if football must be concerned with propriety and prestige, or with the efficient production of two points per week by reliable employees, then we should all feel much more comfortable now that Leonard Francis Shackleton has retired.

For the greater part of his seventeen years as a professional footballer, the existence of Len Shackleton was a continuous exasperation and affront to the conventional and the conformists; to the sober hardworking artisans of the game, and above all to authority and officialdom. One can see why; on and off the field he was incalculable and, occasionally, outrageous. Shackleton was eccentric, an erratic genius, a gifted individualist; a showman who drew the crowds, entertained and astonished them, and sent them home with the feeling that football was a game after all, and a wonderfully clever one.

The difficulty of fitting such a man into a prearranged pattern was probably one of the main reasons why Shackleton, a ball-player worthy of comparison with Matthews, was picked only six times for England. Another reason, possibly, was his unfailing willingness to express his opinions. He was not discreet. With a cheerful disregard for the interests of his own career he criticized the Football League, the F.A., players' contracts, the transfer system, international selection, referees, managers, and directors.

He had an impish streak. When he caught himself being orderly and orthodox, a perverse impulse took hold of him. It was as if he looked at the crowd and the directors' box and said to himself: "They're too comfortable – let's stir them up a bit." To be well-behaved for the full ninety minutes was beyond him. For two-thirds of a game he would put on a masterly show of inside-forward play that no player in the country could equal – perfect in positioning, bewilderingly clever, and yet direct, constructive, and unselfish. Then, with the side three goals up, he would decide he had had enough of discipline and hard work for one afternoon; he was going to amuse himself. From then on he shocked you. Either you laughed with delighted astonishment at his cheek, or you pressed your lips together and muttered "Disgusting!" It depended on the sort of person you were, and your motives for watching football.

For example: a high ball is dropping towards Shackleton, who stands waiting for it with his hands on his hips. As it reaches him he raises one foot and traps it dead; apart from this movement his position is unchanged. He stands there, with his foot on the ball, takes one hand from his side and brushes back the loose hair from his forehead. With the same hand he makes the gesture of glancing at his watch. Then he looks towards the trainer's box and says, calmly and audibly, "How long to go?" This was one of the reasons why the name Shackleton made some well-known people in football red with rage. Another example: in the last few minutes of the game he is taking the ball up the middle towards the opponents' goal, jinking, dodging, evading tackles. He is completely in control. Every swerve and feint touches off a fresh roar of appreciation. He beats one man after another until there is only the goalkeeper left. He fools the goalkeeper into diving the wrong way, and dribbles round him into the empty goalmouth. Then he stops the ball on the line, looks back at the scrambling goalkeeper, and calls out: "George! It's not over the line yet!" This is why Shackleton's autobiography was called *Clown Prince of Soccer* instead of *How to Win Friends and Influence People*.

Shackleton was not a big man (5 ft. 7 in. and 11 stone 8 lb.) but he was strong and compact enough, with a bony angularity about his movements. Dribbling, he ran well over the ball, with his shoulders hunched and his elbows high; he had a jangling, flapping movement at times, like a puppet controlled by two strings, one at each shoulder-point. For his height, his stride was long and powerful; he had a good short burst of speed. His face was long, with a prominent upper lip and a long chin. His cheek-bones were high, his nose jutted with a bony bridge, and there was a marked ridge across his brows. His thick-growing brown hair had a tendency to flop forward; his eyes, close-set, were challenging and willing to be amused.

Given what he was born with as a footballer, one would have expected Shackleton to be recognized early, and to have travelled quickly over the usual direct road to first-class professionalism – schools, ground staff, reserves, first team – as others have done. Yet he had to survive setbacks, heart-breaking ones, no doubt, at the time. Shackleton was born in Bradford, and learnt the elements in the classic way – in an elementary school playground, in open fields, with a tennis ball in the street. There being no organized football at school, he spent his Saturday afternoons with his father or his uncle John watching the two local League teams, Bradford City and Bradford Park Avenue. His father had been a fair footballer of the robust kind, his uncle David played Rugby League, Shackleton was learning tricks at seven years old, in a pair of old shoes with football studs hammered in by Uncle John. For a while he continued conventionally. He won a scholarship to a secondary school, and played proper team games there for the first time. He was picked for the school, for Bradford schoolboys, and then as a Schoolboy international against Wales – at outside-right. He scored twice. He was then an inch under 5 ft. and weighed only 6 stone 2 lb. He played three times for England before he was fourteen, and he was still at school when he signed as an amateur for Bradford Park Avenue.

At this point, when Shackleton was fifteen, what looked like his first big chance came – and turned into a bitter disappointment. While he was a Bradford Park Avenue amateur, he was playing for Kippax Town in the Leeds League. An Arsenal scout watched him, and shortly afterwards the impressive figure of Mr George Allison himself, the Arsenal manager, was seated in the Shackletons' living-room, explaining to the family the advantages of young Len going to Highbury. Shackleton grabbed at the chance. In 1938 you would have had to look hard to find a fifteen-year-old boy who would not have left home for Arsenal if he was asked.

Shackleton spent less than a year at Highbury. He did the usual stint of a ground-staff boy and was paid fifty shillings a week; twenty-seven and six of it went on lodgings and laundry, and ten shillings home to his mother in Bradford. He saw the stars – Hapgood, Crayston, Male, Copping, Bastin, Drake – but only played with them once, at outside-left in a practice match. Towards the end of the 1938–9 season, the manager sent for him. Mr Allison told young Shackleton that he was not up to standard for Arsenal. More, he told him he would never make a footballer, and advised him to go home and find some other occupation.

This was an unhappy situation. In provincial towns everyone knows all about you. Shackleton had left Bradford as a boy star to make his fortune in football. Now, ten months later, he must go back, not as a success, but looking for a job. Here Mr Frank Langan, of the London Paper Mills, comes into the story; but for him, perhaps, there would have been no story. The firm was proud of its works team, and Shackleton heard that good footballers stood a fair chance of employment. He arrived at Dartford with all his belongings in a suitcase, having spent his last shillings on his fare. He had no trade, except the one he had been advised to give up, and he was stranded. Mr Langan took him on, and paid him enough for board and pocket money – rather more than he was worth to the paper mills. Thanks to him Shackleton survived a bad patch, and was still playing. He stayed at Dartford for a year, but by then it was wartime and his family wanted him to come home. He went back to Bradford.

The manager who had spotted Shackleton as a schoolboy, David Steele, was still with Bradford Park Avenue. He was one of the good shrewd managers whose names never become well known; his record for recognizing talent was impressive. Steele had found Ron Greenwood, who went to Chelsea; Geoff Walker of Middlesbrough; Billy Elliott, transferred from Burnley to Sunderland for £27,000; the Scottish international full-back Jimmy Stephen. He did not share Mr Allison's opinion of Shackleton, and at Christmas 1940, he signed him as a professional. The atmosphere of the occasion lacked something of the glamour and promise it might have had at Highbury. The club was short of money, and Shackleton's £10 signing-on fee had to be paid to him in small weekly instalments.

Wartime football was played on a regional basis, and players were allowed to appear as guests of other clubs. So in 1940

Shackleton, the new professional, spent a most remarkable Christmas Day. In the morning he played for Bradford Park Avenue at Leeds, and in the afternoon he travelled to Huddersfield and played for Bradford City. He headed a goal for the City; that was remarkable too – anyone who saw Shackleton remembers that he believed football was strictly for the feet.

Since he had returned to Bradford, Shackleton had been working for G.E.C., assembling radios for aircraft, and he stayed on in the factory after he turned professional. Various of his friends were joining the forces, and he himself volunteered for all three services, but he was in essential work, and he stayed in Bradford, playing at week-ends. In 1945, when the war was ending, G.E.C. went back to Coventry. Shackleton refused to go to the Midlands factory with the firm. Regular League football would soon be beginning again, and his future looked promising. He had already been picked for F.A. and Football League teams. Just as the war was over and his friends were being demobilized, he was called up for National Service. In the circumstances he had no enthusiasm for joining the army, and chose instead to go into the mines as a Bevin Boy – at Fryston Colliery, about thirty miles from Bradford. He was a reluctant miner when he was picked for the first time for England, in May 1946, against Scotland at Hampden Park. England lost 1–0. It was Denis Compton's last international – and Joe Mercer's – and it was Shackleton's last for three years, although at twenty-four, with his talents, he might easily have been the outstanding player of the post-war England sides.

Shackleton had nearly everything as an inside-forward except the ability, or the inclination, to "get stuck in". He was two-footed, he was fast when speed was needed, and his ball control was faultless, but he did not "tackle back" in a hard game. He was certainly not timid, but he was not prepared to go baldheaded after a ball when it might mean a serious injury. He was too cold in the head for that. Shackleton could shoot, too; occasionally he would drive in a goal from twenty yards, but in general he preferred subtlety. The delicacy of his long narrow feet in controlling the ball made it possible for him to work his way in to close range. From inside the goal-area he has scored by every conceivable means except shooting. He has side-footed goals, backheeled them, kneed them in, lobbed or dribbled them in. He simply could not resist playing with the ball; in some ways it was his weakness, but it was also the secret of his charm as an entertainer.

The charm did not work with everyone. A large proportion of every football crowd believes firmly in "getting stuck in", and, as soon as possible after that, "getting rid of it". These enemies of the intellectual pleasures of football were in the ascendant at Bradford Park Avenue in 1946, and week after week Shackleton had to face the ugliest sound in sport – barracking. He asked for a transfer, and Newcastle United bought him for £13,000.

Shackleton had a short and unhappy stay with Newcastle, but his first appearance with them was spectacular. It was the game against Newport County, that equalled the League goal-scoring record, and set up a new record for Division Two. Newcastle, "the Bank of England club", had a great forward line that year: Jackie Milburn, Roy Bentley, Charlie Wayman, Len Shackleton, Tommy Pearson. They beat Newport 13–0. Wayman missed a penalty in the first five minutes but scored four; Milburn scored twice; and Bentley once. Shackleton scored six, including a first-half hat-trick in under five minutes. The boos of Park Avenue gave way to the cheers of St James's Park. Newcastle went as far as the semi-final of the F.A. Cup in that 1946–7 season, and finished fifth in Division Two, but as far as Shackleton was concerned, after that glorious first appearance, it was not an enjoyable season – either from his point of view or the club's. In February 1948, after only fifteen months with Newcastle, he asked for a transfer. An impressive list of clubs was reported to be interested in signing him: among them – a touch of irony for Shackleton – Arsenal. It was known that the fee would be a big one; it was a record – £20,050 – and it was paid by Sunderland. It is an argument against the idea that Shackleton was a trouble-maker that he

stayed with Sunderland for nearly ten years – until his retirement towards the end of 1957.

Again he was with a rich club and with a team of high-priced
stars; there were unkind comments about Sunderland trying
to build a team with money-bags, and some sneers when all the
heavy buying still did not produce a League Championship or
a Cup-final side. Still, home and away, the crowds came to see
men like Ivor Broadis, Trevor Ford, Ray Daniel, Willie
Watson, Billy Bingham – and Len Shackleton. Perhaps, since
he went to Sunderland, the international selectors thought they
saw signs that the individualist in Shackleton was giving way
to the team player; perhaps it was simply that Carter and
Mannion, two of the greatest inside-forwards ever, were coming
to the end of their time, and Shackleton was the only other
unmistakably great player in that position – anyway, in 1949
he was in the England side again, against Denmark, and then
again against Wales. Now, perhaps, he was to become a
regular part of the England forward line. Yet during the next
five years seventeen men were picked at inside-forward for
England, and Shackleton was never one of them. These were
the years of England's World Cup failures in Switzerland and
Brazil, and of the two heavy defeats by Hungary: 6–3 at
Wembley and 7–1 in Budapest. They were years of experiment
in the selection of England teams; the Continental and South
American sides had successfully re-discovered and revived
precisely the kind of skills that Shackleton practised to perfection; yet he was never one of the ingredients in the England
mixture. In 1954, when he was thirty-three, and must have
been sure his international career was over, he was capped for
the match against Wales. The choice was as inexplicable as his
exclusion had been during those five years. He was playing
well, but no better than before.

England beat Wales 3–2; it was one of John Charles's great
games, and Shackleton put on a competent, orthodox performance. He said afterwards that he had given an imper-
sonation of a "straight up-and-down inside man" in order to
impress the selectors. He wanted to be picked to play against

Germany, the World Champions, three weeks later. So he was, and it was an interesting forward line: Matthews, Bentley, Allen, Shackleton and Finney. The game was something of an occasion for Stanley Matthews. He had been in the England team that beat Germany in Berlin *sixteen* years earlier, and he seemed determined to show that he was above time. He raced past men half his age, and cut the German defence to pieces. From one of his meticulous centres Bentley headed England's first goal; Allen scored a second, and then Germany pulled back to 2–1. Then, in the words of Billy Wright, the England captain, "Len Shackleton pulled out all the stops and gave a truly magnificent display of ball control, artistry, positional play – and sheer cheek. Once he dribbled past three defenders, glided round the goalkeeper as he advanced, and then, at the vital moment, his toe caught the ball and took it over the line for a goal-kick when everyone appreciated that Len deserved nothing less than a goal. But Shack wasn't disappointed. Along with Stanley Matthews he continued to produce all that is best in Association Football."

Shackleton himself said that he had decided there were only two ways to beat the German goalkeeper, Fritz Herkenrath, who was stopping everything. One was to dribble round him – he tried that, and the run of the ball robbed him – and the other was to chip the ball over his head. Shackleton soon got his chance. He picked up the ball in midfield and went for goal, with the retreating German defence waiting for him to pass. When they realized he was going through alone, two men closed in to tackle him. He feinted them out of the way one after the other, with his extraordinary body swerve, waited until Herkenrath, rushing out, was almost on him, and then, with all the coolness in the world, produced his chip shot. The ball floated over the goalkeeper's head and into the top corner of the net. The 100,000 crowd at Wembley rose to Shackleton and applauded him for minutes on end. Shackleton thinks of that as the greatest goal he ever scored. It was also a superb climax to his international career; he was never picked for England again.

In 1955 Shackleton's autobiography, *Clown Prince of Soccer*, was published. It was lively and entertaining, as might be expected. As might be expected, too, it offended a great many people – page 78, particularly: it was headed, "Chapter 9, The average director's knowledge of football." The page was blank. This may explain why Shackleton has never talked of going into management; as to his future – with his interests in an off-licence, a baby-linen business, hairdressing and journalism, no one is ever going to say of him, "Poor old Shack – he used to be a footballer."

For all his panache and his determined carelessness, it must have been a sad day for Shackleton when, on September 2, 1957, a specialist told him that his right ankle was so badly damaged that he could never play football again. He retired from the game at the age of thirty-five. It was a sad day for us, too.

from MASTERS OF SOCCER *1960*

Eddie Baily

JOHN ARLOTT

If one of those hypothetical men – one who was to have only one sight of football this season – asked my advice, I should not recommend the Cup Final, not even England v. Scotland – I should tell him to go and see Eddie Baily playing at inside-left for the Spurs – now. I would specify a Spurs match because that is his accustomed setting, in which he can do himself greater justice than with the less-familiar colleagues of an international match.

Truly great footballers are rare, and there are peak points, even in their careers when – deservedly – they establish themselves in football history, rising above themselves because they are getting the rubs of the green.

Neat as a trivet, busy as a one-man band, alert as a boarding-house cat, and elusive as a dog in a fair, Baily, at the moment, is not only on top form, but everything is coming off for him, so that no other inside-forward in Britain can stand comparison with him.

All this, of course, is possible only for a footballing genius. There have been inside-forwards who were outstanding for their dribbling, others for their passing or shooting or heading. Eddie Baily is a complete footballer, remarkable because he is:

First, a great player *with* the ball; Secondly, great in shooting and in "loosing" the ball; Thirdly, a great player *without* the ball.

In possession, he is a dribbler of the best type; that is to say, he beats his man smartly, and dribbles fast and directly towards goal, as opposed to the over-elaborate dribblers who too often lose ground. Moreover, once he achieves the purpose of his dribble – to uncover a gap in the opposing defence – he *uses* the ball at once.

His shooting is hard, accurate and unhesitating, and he shoots often enough to keep most goalkeepers on edge. Most impressive of all, however, is his passing, which is bewildering in its pace and accuracy. In the past six weeks he has been hitting a ball as much as forty yards through first-class defences to give clear scoring chances to colleagues in the varied and unorthodox positions taken up by the Spurs forwards of today. To do this, one must gauge the pace of the ball and the pitch, the power required to avoid interception by the defence, and yet simultaneously to reach the fellow-forward at takable height and pace. This sounds almost impossible or, at best, demanding careful concentration, but with Baily it is a reflex. Not once, but twenty times a match, in his current great spell, Baily, while apparently concentrating on a fast dribble, is seeing the opportunity before the opposing defence, and hitting the perfect ball before they can cover up.

Thirdly – and this is the foundation of his greatness which no loss of form can ever take from him – he is the supreme inside-forward without the ball. When another Spurs attacker has the ball in a commanding position, he will find Baily in the most suitable position to continue the attacking move. If, on the other hand, a Spurs forward, half- or even full-back – right or left – is in a difficult position, Baily will infallibly appear, free from any marking defender, to relieve his harassed colleague of the ball and start a fresh attack.

The Tottenham dressing-room would be a duller place without Baily, for his mind, active in play to plan attacks, is as active off the field to find humour. Yet it is not in laughter, but in anger, that I shall remember Eddie Baily. In the match between England and Yugoslavia at Highbury, a perfect England forward-movement, swift in execution, and precise as a chess-move, sent Hancocks away on the right. In the accepted Continental method, which cheerfully gives away a free-kick to stop a forward getting clear, the Yugoslav left-half collared Hancocks and brought him down – not violently, but sufficiently to kill the movement. Automatically and instantly, Baily dashed across the field in indignant outcry. The offence was not committed against him personally but it was an offence against good football which is at once his craft, his enthusiasm and the fundamental impulse behind Eddie Baily's greatness as an inside-forward.

from CONCERNING SOCCER *1950*

Archie Macaulay

JOHN ARLOTT

The man with a sense of history or a long memory in football cannot help but relish Archie Macaulay. To be sure, he frequently appears nowadays at inside-forward, but if ever there was a traditional-style wing-half, it is Macaulay. Many of our leading modern wing-halves play a game of elegance verging on gentleness, so that the new generation raises its eyebrows at the thought of a wing-half like Wilf Copping whom inside-forwards approached with trepidation and whom they left with respect and a shaking-up.

Many an inside-forward today may regard an opposing wing-half – even one of international standing – as another ball artist like himself, a sort of auxiliary forward. The best man to adjust this point of view is Archie Macaulay, whose descent goes back through Copping to the great early wing-halves, men like "Nudger" Needham and Archie Campbell of the 'eighties.

Macaulay at wing-half is, above all, a player with *edge* to his play; he relishes and practises the rigours of the game. His energy is immense, for his stamina and strength are greater than his lean shape suggests. He is as stringy as his challenge for the ball, and he tackles more heavily than his weight. Like Copping again, however, he is by no means a purely – or even a characteristically – defensive half-back. Having taken possession, he moves quickly, with precise and Scottish ball-control to the attack, drawing the opposing defence before setting his own forwards under way with the rolling ground pass which is his preference or, at need, with a chip which drops precise as a plummet.

It was in the spring of 1947, for Scotland against England and for Great Britain against The Rest of Europe – two matches within a month – that Macaulay really made his reputation. In those two games he refused to be overawed by reputations but fought his way through the match, tackling like iron, not neglecting to use a shoulder as hard as it was hostile, and serving the ball in the classic style.

This is the equipment of the really good wing-half, but Macaulay has something more, that rare ability to win a football match virtually off his own bat.

Perhaps his greatest moment in this respect was not in a match in England, nor even in Scotland. When, in the autumn of 1947, Scotland played Ireland at Belfast, Ireland led by two goals to one well down into the second half. The day was dull and grey and the ground was churned and heavy with mud. The pace had been terrific and they were two tired sides which faced the last five minutes. The Irish defence packed their goal, kicking the ball away with a relentless determination to hold their advantage in face of anything that even the talented Scottish forward line could produce. Delaney, Liddell, and Billy Steel in turn, schemed their way half through before that uncompromising defence bundled them off the ball and put it fiercely away. Then, with the entire Irish side massed in their own half, Macaulay picked up a stray ball near the half-way line. Bringing it forward, ploughing his way through the mud, and gathering pace as he went, he resisted first one tackle and then a second. Farrell, the Irish left-half, recovered, turned, tackled again. Again Macaulay beat him, bearing down on the Irish penalty-area. It was a desperate, apparently a hopeless venture, but the Scottish supporters, who had made the sea voyage to watch their team in action, roared fresh hope and encouragement. Three, four men beaten – and Macaulay was through: goalkeeper Hinton came out to meet him – and he beat Hinton. The goal was empty in front of him and he flicked the ball for the empty corner of the net. It was a goal – until "Bud" Ahearne, dashing across, kicked it desperately off the line. Macaulay stood as if stunned, he went back to his place. Two minutes later, time running out, he gathered his strength and, still undaunted, drove for the Irish goal again, but this attempt was smashed ruthlessly by sheer weight of numbers.

That day his effort was an epic one – it is the measure of Macaulay's footballing stature that it was also characteristic.

from CONCERNING SOCCER *1950*

Tommy Harmer

MAURICE EDELSTON and
TERENCE DELANEY

What might be called the Henley-blazer, or bound-copies-of-*Punch* attitude to football, still lingers in the English air like the faint expensive flavour of an old pair of riding-boots in a box-room. Cricket is a sacred institution. Rugger is a man's game. Golf is full of legend and pawky wisdom. Eton Fives and Real Tennis are solemn mysteries. The techniques of all of them can be discussed, gravely or wittily, in the most proper company. Football is low. Professional football is lower than amateur football. Professional players shake hands after goals. They have even been known to embrace and leap about ecstatically, instead of trotting back to their own half without looking at each other. Their shorts have no side pockets. Their supporters wear, not scarves, but mufflers. They come from the North to gape at London. "Oop for t'Coop." Sometimes, instead of cloth caps, they wear painted toppers bearing such mottoes as "Up the Trotters!" and "Wor Jackie". It's all rather undesirable.

The snobbery about football, and the underestimation of it, arose largely because there is no ritual attached to the game. All you need is a ball. There is no mystique of football, and no classic literature of the sport. Yet in the past twenty years the very simplicity of its principles has made it the greatest game in the world, and at last, in this country where it began, it is becoming respectable as well as popular.

Still one reads and hears surprisingly little about its technique, as distinct from its strategy and tactics. The most superficially interested listener to cricket commentaries has heard about leg-spinners, cutters, chinamen, "middling" the ball, cuts, drives, glides, and so on. Wimbledon on television has introduced thousands to the chop, the top-spin backhand, the lob, the smash and the volley. Yet you can do the same

things to a football as to a tennis ball or a cricket ball, and the
top-class player has just as extensive a repertoire of craft to
master. There is in existence an illustrated compendium of all
the subtleties of this craft, named Harmer.

Think of the ideal footballer – tall, strong, fast, broad-
shouldered, graceful. Harmer is not like that. He is short –
5 ft. 6 in.; he has a small bony body, thin legs and a large head.
The thick long hair that used to flop behind him as he wriggled
and juggled the ball past more impressive players vanished
during the 1958–9 winter, and he appeared with a close-crop,
so that his ears stood out on each side of his serious, worried
face. He never seemed to find a pair of shorts small enough for
him. He is thirty now, and he still weighs only 9 stone 4 lb.

A comic figure, you would say, if you knew no more about
him than that. When he first turned out for Tottenham at
White Hart Lane, against Bolton in 1951, it is true that the
crowd laughed, but it was not at his appearance. They laughed
in delight at his astonishing, impudent skill; they laughed
because this slight figure flitted through the game, insub-
stantial as a moth, and as hard to catch, confident as a surgeon.
Too short to outjump anyone to the ball, too light to withstand a shoulder charge, he turned, twisted and evaded,
shrugged, feinted, stopped and spurted; the ball ran with him
like a puppy, between his feet, under them, beside him, up to
his chest, bouncing on his knee, caught on his instep, rolling,
spinning, trapped, released. His eye held it, his large head
bent over it in concentration. He floated, chipped and rolled
passes with the coolest nonchalance. A few seconds later,
without the ball, his shirt and baggy shorts flapping, he ran
gesticulating, signalling, explaining, a mime of anxiety and
agitation. It was an extraordinary exhibition, and it introduced,
in the limelight of the September sunshine, the repertoire of a
unique and fascinating performer.

Where did Harmer learn it all? Not from any coaching in
gracious surroundings, and not in the famous North. He was
born in the East End of London, in Hackney, a close-built
crowded borough, packed and ugly and animated, between

Bethnal Green and the River Lea. There are wide streets in Hackney, left-overs from its "residential" days before 1914, but there are alleys too, and narrow cramped streets that were poor when Charles Dickens was a boy. It is shabby, jammed with traffic, pocked with bombing, veined with railway lines and sooty canals, but it is full of the liveliness and activity of the East End. Street markets, cinemas, factories, sawmills, libraries, furniture warehouses, shops, junk yards, endless terraces of tight houses; but among them, if you look at the map of London, big patches of green – Victoria Park, Hackney Marshes and Mill Fields, by the River Lea, Hackney Downs, London Fields. After school, and on Saturdays, these open spaces swarm with footballers, some with footballs, some with worn black tennis balls, some with goalposts, some with goals marked with coats and caps. There are playgrounds too, surrounded with wire netting, and there are goals chalked on brick walls in side streets. These were Harmer's academies, here he began his studies, and from here he graduated as a virtuoso.

Harmer was born in 1928 within a few long passes of one of these Hackney Parks – London Fields. His father was a french polisher – furniture is one of the local industries; he himself, before he became a full-time footballer, worked as a printer's warehouseman. He played for London Fields School, but he has no history of schoolboy representative football; he was considered too frail for it. This was probably the first time that a selector said, "Of course, Harmer is a great little footballer, but. . . ." He has had time since to become accustomed to such judgements. No one has ever questioned his skill.

When he was in his 'teens, during the Second World War, he played for a team of naval cadets against Spurs juniors, and he was noticed by the Tottenham spotters, Jimmy Joyce and Ted White. After the war, in 1948, when he was twenty, the club manager, Joe Hulme, signed him on. There must have been some raised eyebrows when this little figure arrived at the ground, with his nervous air, hollow eyes and sunken cheeks. Arthur Rowe wasted no time in teaching him ball play. He put him on to weight-lifting, and the rest of his training consisted chiefly of eating steaks and drinking milk. Harmer still looks frail, but so did Jimmy Wilde. There is more endurance and wiry strength in him now than you would suspect, to reinforce his inborn talent.

After his seasons with the Spurs "A" team and with the reserves, and that brilliant first league appearance against Bolton in 1951, you might have expected Harmer to be a made man. He must have thought so himself. It took him six years to get a regular place in the first team. This was no slight on his ability. Once again he was "a great little player, but . . ." The "but" this time was the Spurs style of football. "Push-and-run" was the simple name for it. It illuminated the game in England for two magnificent seasons, and it took Tottenham in those two years to the championship of the Second Division, promotion, and then straight up through the First Division to be the Champions of the Football League. Fast, clean-cut, precise and exciting, it was a style that required of each player one thing above all: the ability to fit into the team pattern, to add his own carefully calculated impetus to the smooth momentum of the side. Arthur Rowe, and the eleven men who played almost unchanged through those two fine years, had studied, practised and polished this style to near perfection. Good club men like Walters, Withers, and Duquemin looked great players because they "fitted"; a better player, Bennett, fitted at the cost of restraining his own natural individual brilliance, and, probably, at the cost too of an England cap. There was no place here for a player like Harmer, however gifted. He belonged elsewhere, at Blackpool, say, or even Arsenal; with them he might have been recognized as one of the great ball players, and had some of the rewards his gifts deserved. Yet when he asked for a transfer, Tottenham were reluctant to let him go, and when he was put on the transfer list, there was only one offer for him in eighteen months, from Cardiff City – a long way from home for a Londoner.

Tottenham won their League Championship in the season 1950–51. At the end of the following season they were still near the top, second to Manchester United. After that they went on playing good football, but they began to slip. "Push-and-run", the revolution that had begun in the Second Division, had made its startling contribution, the lessons had been studied, the counter-moves tried out. As in all revolutions, the useful elements were absorbed, and became part of the orthodox. The players that had taken Spurs through those seasons were getting older, too, and the team that has been held together for so long began to disperse. Arthur Rowe retired. By the time Eddie Baily, that other great forward from Hackney, went to Port Vale, the greatest of Tottenham elevens had passed into history.

Through all this Harmer had been with Spurs, mostly in the reserves. From time to time, for friendly games and floodlight matches against foreign clubs, he was produced and put on exhibition. To anyone who cared for football, it was tragic to see a player like this treated as a performing seal. Harmer was never simply a trickster. He can do all the tricks, but he never does them for their own sake. He is a serious player. When he holds the ball, it is to draw a man, to make an opening, or to give another forward time to run through.

There is a close parallel in the way he uses the ball to the way a cricketer uses it. Each kick is to Harmer a deliberately played stroke, like the shot of a good batsman, hit at a certain point in the swing, and carefully timed. He can take the ball on the volley or the half-volley, or he can drop it at his feet as dead as a poached egg. In his passing, he has the virtues of a good bowler; he can move the ball both ways in the air and off the ground, and his length is perfect. One of his specialities is the through pass lofted over the heads of the defence. If this pass is hard enough and high enough to beat the backs, it often runs too far for the centre-forward, and the goalkeeper comes out for an easy pick-up. Harmer's solution to this is back-spin. He cuts hard under the ball as he hits it, it flies through the middle, but when it pitches it pulls up sharp. Here the parallel is the golfer's approach shot to a raised green.

Harmer went on practising these arts in the reserves. Then,

at the end of 1954, Tottenham paid Aston Villa £30,000 for Danny Blanchflower. The team was slipping towards relegation, but Blanchflower helped them to a late revival that just kept them in the First Division.

Harmer was on the transfer list. Blanchflower's arrival was to mean a great deal to him, but not until another full season had passed. Meanwhile, to an outsider, it seemed that the club was doing its best to break Harmer's heart. Tottenham finished the 1955-6 season near the bottom of the table again, but they had a great cup run. They drew one of the little clubs in the third round, Boston United, and they won 4–0; in the fourth round it was Middlesbrough, and they won 5–1. On the eve of the fifth round tie, at Doncaster, they surprised everyone by resurrecting the almost-forgotten Harmer, who was picked to play, of all places, at outside-right. Full of heart as ever, he played one of his great games, and Spurs were through to the sixth round, 2–0. This was a beauty, a "London Derby" against West Ham, and it ended three-all. Spurs won the replay, 2–1. One more win and they were at Wembley, and Harmer deserved much of the credit. He was a fascinating outside-right. Not being built for dazzling high-speed runs down the line, he concentrated on clearing himself spaces to work a little behind the other forwards. There he held the ball, cast his curious spells over the backs, edged along by the chalk with inches to spare, and floated in his beautifully judged centres. Sometimes, for variety, he started at the corner-flag and calmly juggled his way in along the goal-line, until the defenders suddenly realized how close he was, and fell on him desperately, to find that the ball was already floating dangerously over the empty spaces they had left. The semi-final was against Manchester City, at Villa Park. Harmer was dropped. Tottenham lost by one goal to nil. No goal, no finalists' medals. When would they be so near again?

Why was Harmer dropped? He was fit, he was in great form, and in spite of his long exile he was clearly still trying hard and giving all he had. What was the "but" this time? Emotionally, this must have been one of the low points of Harmer's career.

By now Tottenham, stimulated by the intelligence and brilliant ability of Danny Blanchflower, were rousing themselves from the depression that had followed their three wonderful years. The team found a character and a style again, and it was a style, this time, that suited Harmer. In 1956–7 he played in all forty-two games. Out of the club's record total of 104 goals that season, Harmer scored seventeen. Twelve of them were from penalities – out of fourteen kicks.

Harmer is the most disconcerting taker of penalty-kicks since Willie Haines of Portsmouth, "The Farmer's Boy" who, thirty years ago, would stand beside the ball and hook it in without any run at all, swinging his leg like an old-fashioned figure in a seaside pier football machine. Harmer's method is to trot up in a short curve, at barely more than a walk, and place the ball low down just inside the post. Usually he picks the post to his left, and hooks, but if the goalkeeper seems set to anticipate that, he hits the ball with the outside of his foot and catches him going the wrong way. Once when the goalkeeper moved to the right before the kick, Harmer stopped dead beside the ball, with his foot raised, and waited for the whistle. When there was no whistle, he carried on his movement – it was like a film being restarted – and calmly put it the other side. This seems to have interested Harmer. The next time he took a penalty, he feinted the goalkeeper off balance deliberately before he kicked the ball. Apparently satisfied with this experiment, he has now returned to his old system of winning the guessing game with the keeper.

Tottenham finished second in the League in 1956–7, runners-up again to Manchester United. It was a good season for Harmer and, among other things, it put an end to the myth that he was no good on heavy ground. In the mud that winter, it was the big men marking Harmer who slipped and scrambled, not Harmer. Blanchflower's leadership was superb throughout the season. He is probably the best attacking half-back in the game, above all a ball-player, and his understanding with Harmer brought back polish and purpose to the team. Side by side they moved up the field; while Blanchflower tackled by the touchline, Harmer, with his jogging, upright, unathletic run, was dodging about near the centre-circle, keeping himself free to take the ball, his head jerking as he looked about him, watching the man he might have to beat, noting the gaps where he might pitch his forward passes. Sometimes they reversed the move. If Harmer, holding the ball, was being flocked and crowded towards the wing, he could be sure Blanchflower was coming up inside to offer the ball a way of escape, and then it went forward again, both of them going with it. The two had much in common, and yet are so different. While Blanchflower is scientific and analytical, intelligent, and stylish, Harmer's brilliance and quick thinking are instinctive.

Harmer has a wonderful football brain; he leaves it alone, and it gets on with its work. "I don't *have* to think," he once said, "it all comes naturally." He has no theories, and he could never be a teacher. His only way of communicating what he knows is to take a ball and do something with it. "If you're off form," he says, "all you can do is keep trying and hope it will come." In other words, he is a natural. He grew up with a simple uncomplicated obsession about football. He learnt with a tennis ball, and still carried it about in his pocket even after he became a professional. He came into football probably hoping for very little more than a good living; after all, he was an only son, and his mother was a widow. He brought to football a quality that is rare nowadays, the quality of pleasure and astonishment that surrounds the work of an eccentric individual artist. In return, he has been named in a few F.A. elevens against university and services sides, and in 1952 he was given an England "B" cap against Holland. He is over thirty now, and he has a small son, born in 1957. He will not encourage the boy to be a footballer, he says, unless he turns out to be exceptionally good. Exceptionally lucky, too, he might have added. In Tommy Harmer's case a quite extra-ordinary degree of natural ability was not enough to take him to the top. Somewhere his luck took a wrong turning.

from MASTERS OF SOCCER *1960*

Goalkeepers are Crazy

"The squirrel's swift leap, the falcon's flight
The clear quick-thinking brain."

T. SMITH *John Thomson*

L

Goalkeepers

JOHN MACADAM

There was around in those days one of a still earlier generation
although he was still associated in an honorary way with the
Greenock Morton Club as an adviser. His name was Harry
Rennie and this is as I like his story. . . .

There was a time when people living in the neighbourhood
of Cappielow, the ground of Greenock Morton Football Club,
were of the opinion that the small wood-and-tin stand was
haunted. When all was quiet on the ground and manager and
staff had departed, there would still persist strange sounds that
emanated from one particular spot, located as near as was
possible in the excited imaginations of local people to the
locker-room adjoining the home dressing-rooms. Nothing –
and this is one of the more alarming features of such phen-
omena – was ever seen. The only indication of supernatural
tenancy was a series of deep-drawn gasps and heavy thuds. It
was obvious that whatever spirit inhabited the lone little stand
was an active one, and actively unhappy. There were theories,
of course. A ground that had seen titanic soccer battles between
Morton and their county rivals, St Mirren, and Celtic and
Rangers, and was at the same time surrounded by a deep L of
working-class tenements whose dwellers were Morton supporters to a man was bound to have strong associations and
powerful memories. There was a school of thought that held
the sounds to come from the distracted spirit of old Barney
Battles of the Hearts, who once missed a penalty on the ground
in a cup-tie. Others repudiated this on the ground that in that
case the thuds could only be caused by the ball striking the
ghostly upright whereas, in fact, on the day in question, Barney
skied it right over the bar. Another body of opinion held that
the supernatural tenant was a former referee who was still
trying to bash his brains out for having failed once to send
Patsy Gallacher of the Celtic off the park. Oh, there were plenty

of theories but they went untested for years and it is a safe bet that the Ghost of Greenock Morton would have become a big figure in the drivia and trivia of the game had it not been disclosed quite casually in conversation that the ghost was no more supernatural a being than old Henry Rennie, the Morton goalkeeper of the day.

It is difficult to convince present-day goalkeepers, brought up to regard themselves as the special idols of the crowd and the spoiled darlings of the game generally, just how Harry Rennie involved himself in this extraordinary atmosphere of soccer superstition. It was disclosed one day by a stranger – to not only the locality but also to the legend – who happened to be passing the back of the stand when he heard the strange sounds. A football enthusiast, he went to the front of the stand, located the department from which the sounds came and peered through a little window in the corrugated walls. There, in the locker-room, an extraordinary sight met his gaze.

Harry Rennie, in full football strip, was prancing, wide-legged from side-to-side as goalkeepers do when they are approached by an opposing forward. At a given moment, he would yell "Shoot!" and dive full-length on the hard, stud-pocked boards. He would lie there outstretched for a bare second, then he would pick himself up, adjust his shorts and start the business all over again. . . .

This is the part it is difficult to sell to the spoonfed goalkeepers of today – Rennie did this every day when all the others had finished training and gone. He shadow-saved just as a fighter in training will shadow-box. It gave him speed off the mark, co-ordination of body and mind, unself-consciousness. But why on the rough, knobbly floor? To harden himself.

Rennie was a man not only of this hard, unrelenting practice. He was also a man of theory. He had a theory of goalkeeping just as he had a theory about most everything. A goalkeeper, unlike every other player in a football team, is circumscribed. He has to guard a plane twenty-four feet long by eight feet high. This plane lies at right-angles to the field of play, which is seventy-five yards wide. Therefore, to all but the opposing player occupying a position on a line directly in advance of the goalkeeper's eight-yard baseline, the scoring of a goal is a matter of angles. Master the theory of angles, Rennie argued, and you master the boys who score the goals. He set out to do this with the same determination as he set out to harden his body, speed up his mental-physical reactions, and conquer his self-consciousness.

First, he decided to narrow the angle. Obviously, if an opponent could fire the ball at him from any point within an angle of a hundred and eighty degrees, he had an advantage over another who was confined to twenty or even ten degrees. Rennie set out to narrow the angle to his opponents. He did this in a simple way. He walked out. Yes, just as simply as that. As soon as the whistle went for the start of the game, he walked straight out of the goal he was sworn to defend and took up a position on the penalty dot, twelve yards in front of his goal-line, and there he stood at the ready. The first time he did this, the crowd behind his goal thought he was going to attack the referee and shouted encouragement. When they saw him stop, aiming no blow, they shouted their disappointment. Thereafter, when Rennie left his goal and walked out to his advance post, he was followed by such shouts as "Open the Gate" and "He's away". He paid no attention. In fact, it is doubtful, with the mathematical preoccupation of his mind, if he even heard. He stood there and waited. If the play went to the opposite goal, he stood there. If it came towards his own goal, he moved back. If it moved to either side of the field in his own half of the ground, he moved sideways. That was another thing. Besides his hardening shadow-dives on the locker-room floor, he also practised sideways and backwards running.

"I could run backwards and sideways as fast as most other players could run forward," he says.

In his day, forward attacks developed mostly on the wings. The job of the winger was to make ground and then cross the ball into the centre for the centre-forward or the inside-men to score with. Therefore the Rennie strategy started with the wingers. We had better have a plan (see diagram on next page).

A is the winger, B is the inside-forward, C is Rennie near the penalty dot.

The winger is about to pass to the inside-forward in order that *he* shall have a shot at goal. Therefore, argues Rennie, the triangle ABD is the danger area. The ball can do one of three things. It can be shot direct by the winger at the goal, in which case Rennie moves sideways to the right and places himself directly on the line of the ball's flight and so saves it. Or the ball can be crossed to the inside-forward B, in which case Rennie advances and is in position to intercept it or, by retreating, to save the inside-man's shot. Or the winger can cut in towards

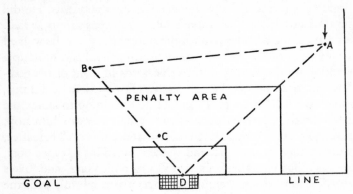

goal and lob it over the goalkeeper's head into the net, in which case Rennie would already have executed his backwards run and still have been in position on his own goal-line to save.

The successful execution of the strategy was all a matter of timing and that had been gone into by Rennie, who built up a considerable Time theory around what he called the Shooting Gesture. The Shooting Gesture was the drawing back of a player's foot to strike the ball. This was easy to spot and not only was it obvious to the close student that the ball was about to be kicked, it was also obvious in which direction it was about to be kicked. Rennie could tell, as soon as the Shooting Gesture began, whether the ball was to be crossed to another player (and, in that case, *which* player) or to be shot directly at the goal. In either case he was prepared to back himself to move from his forward position on the penalty dot to the point on the line of flight of the ball from which saving it was a mathematical certainty. Suppose, working from the sketch-plan, winger A decides to cross the ball on the run from the position he is now in directly to inside forward B at the position *he* is now in. Winger A draws back his foot preparatory to crossing the ball to B. The Shooting Gesture has begun. One second later his foot strikes the ball and in another two seconds the ball is in flight at the point D on the line AB. This has taken up three seconds of time. But in less than one second of time Rennie has noted the Shooting Gesture, decided where the ball is going and is already standing on the point D – waiting for it with two seconds in hand.

That is the strategy in theory and Rennie could apply the principle to any conceivable set of circumstances and positions. He taught himself to make instantaneous changes and improvisations backed by his fantastic co-ordination of brain and muscle.

Rennie has frayed himself trying to thump this theory into the heads of at least three succeeding generations of goal-keepers without much admitted success. Mostly, they prefer the death-defying last-minute saves that keep the fans clustered behind their goals. There is a tradition in football that all goalkeepers are slightly daft. Manifestly, they do not listen easily to the voice of Science. The fact is that in all the years he played as goalkeeper for Scotland, Rennie conceded few goals.

The determined theorist does not confine himself to football. There was a day when I stood heavyhearted before the seventh green of the lovely little golf course at Gourock watching what had been intended as a short chip to the pin disappear into the mass of tangled whin and rock in the background. A sharp, high-pitched voice broke in on my meditation, a voice that urged, "If you'll excuse me. . . ." Turning, I saw a medium-sized spare figure clamber with the unhurried surefootedness of a hillside sheep over a low drystane dyke and hurry towards me. "If you'll excuse me," said Harry Rennie, "you were a wee bit quick on the back-swing." He dropped a handful of balls on the turf and proceeded to chip them one by one on to the green, arresting his back-swing at various points in the arc by way of demonstration and talking all the time. When he had struck the last ball and marked its flight approvingly, he dropped the club and ran to the green where he picked the balls up urgently like a bird picking up grubs, and ran back to drop the balls again. One or two demonstration airshots and then he set the pupil to the half-dozen balls. The correction was immediate and permanent.

"If only goalkeepers would pay as much attention," he said.

So much in testimony to the power of the theories. As to the spartan physical training he gave himself – at the age of anything over seventy he was still cocking his leg over a brutish-looking motor-bicycle making the steep, tortuous ascent to the golf course, smacking a ball round for a training hole or two and, when there was training at Cappielow Park, dashing off there on the bike to expatiate on the scientific approach to goalkeeping to the latest crop of unbelievers.

It is a far cry from the mathematical austerity of Harry Rennie to the warm temperamental pyrotechnicality of Signor Aldo Olivieri, guardian *magnifico* of the goal to the Rest of Europe side that came to play England in 1938 but, with your permission, I'll make it. Olivieri was in the true tradition of Continental goalkeepers, in the tradition of Hiden, Zamorra, and the others, and none of his successors has his colour. Olivieri was regarded by the Italian crowds as well as by himself as pretty nearly the whole show. British crowds have a way of concentrating behind the home team's goal because they feel that, since the object in the game is to score goals, it is there that they will see most of the play. A Continental crowd huddles also behind the goal, but for an entirely different reason – to watch the goalkeeper. The Continental goalkeeper is more than a player in a side. He is the supreme artist in the side, the epitome of all athletic prowess. The forwards, the half-backs, the backs can play as they will and they will get

appreciation according to their deserts. If the goalkeeper fails
for any reason to put up a spectacular show the afternoon is
wasted. Any football match on the Continent is a melodrama
with two main parts – one for each goalkeeper. As well cut
out Hamlet and Claudius as deprive the goalkeeper of the
smallest leap, the least bravado.

It is necessary to understand this to understand Olivieri and
his tribe and the distance between them and the phlegmatic,
position-finding safety-first British goalkeepers whose job is to
protect their goal and not in the least to thrill and entertain the
crowd. The British goalkeeper – like Dawson, Swift, Merrick,
Williams – awaits an onrushing forward. Excited, the forward
foozles his shot and the ball runs slowly towards the goalkeeper. What does he do? He places both feet together as a last
line of defence against the trickling ball. He stoops, and with
hands cupped together for extra precaution he scoops the ball
from the turf and, as quickly as possible, throws or punts it up
to the field to a position covered by a player of his own side.

Not so Olivieri to whom this copybook business is not only
unnecessary but unfair to the crowd. The ball trickles towards
the prancing Olivieri. He flings his arms wide in a dramatic
acceptance of the challenge he is about to meet. As the moment
of consummation nears, he raises himself on his toes and then,
when the ball is but a yard from him, he leaps high in the air.
At the peak of his rise, the crowd yell with delight and the yell
swells to a roar of appreciation as the athlete contorts suddenly
and pounces, panther-like, to the ground – at the exact moment
of the ball's arrival. His hands clutch, his knees and toes sink
into the turf. He has it! A bare second he is poised there and
then, with a sudden electric burst, he is on his feet. He moves
left and right in short steps, he bounces the ball before him, he
clutches it to him once more and then, the peak of emotion
passed, he punts it long and gracefully up the field – anywhere.
This accomplished, he sprints back to his goal-line where he
takes up a nonchalant, disinterested position, hand on upright,
one foot crossed in front of the other with the toe pointed like
a ballerina. He adjusts his cap with the free hand in token of

L*

applause. His whole posture says: "Wait! Have patience! There will be more!"

There will be plenty more. There will be leaps that bring his head above the level of the cross-bar. There will be pounces on balls that are yards away from him. There will be gesticulations and shouts. There will be Douglas Fairbanks Senr., Errol Flynn, Joe Louis, and the Early Christian Martyrs all rolled into one magnificent goalkeeper. The fact that it has nothing whatever to do with football will be the least of anybody's worry.

Even with a long train of recollections of Continental goal-keepers, I was captivated with Signor Olivieri the first time he burst into view. The occasion was the eve of the England–Itlay match and on the way to Stamford Bridge the European team broke its journey to play a practice game with a Dutch side at Amsterdam. There was a big crowd in the Stadium, for the Italian team had been described, from Italy, as the most talented team of all the talents that had ever been seen. The Dutch players came out to a sympathetic home cheer and took up their positions round the far goal for a bit of shooting-in. The Italian players followed almost immediately. They trotted out and made for the near goal, passing the ball from one to another. When they had almost reached the goal area there was a sudden flurry round the players' entrance, a terrific roar of greeting and from the stand dashed the immaculate Olivieri, cloth cap on head, white shorts very short, knees grimly bandaged. He did the fifty yards to the goal in a spectacular five seconds, swung into position and immediately began to claw, pummel, pounce on, clutch and smother the series of shots rained on him by his compatriots.

Alas for the Signor, when the game began it was found that the Dutch side was a very scratch affair indeed and from the first kick of the game never looked like affording any opposition. Olivieri yelled and waved but, with the best will in the world, his own forwards could do nothing but keep up a persistent attack on the Dutch goal. Olivieri was almost in tears of mortification. He pleaded at the pitch of his voice. He threw his arms out in supplication. He expostulated with the crowd behind the goal that it was no fault of his. But the fact is that in the first half the ball crossed into the Italian side not more than twice and the only time it came anywhere near Olivieri it was pushed back to him, for kindness' sake, by his own centre-half. Even at that, although a child in a go-cart could have stopped the ball by swinging his dummy teat at it, Olivieri met the ball with a cry of exultation, executed his leap and his panther pounce, clutched, bounced, and punted as if he had just saved the side from disaster. It was his only exercise in the whole of the first half.

In these circumstances, a British goalkeeper would have reclined against his upright and regarded himself as a lucky man not to have to get in the bath afterwards. Not so our hero.

When half-time came and the players ran off to the dressing-rooms to rest and have their lemons or whatever Continental sides have, Olivieri came to the touchline and summoned two assistant trainers, summoned them imperiously and ordered them to bring an old ball apiece. Then he retreated once more to his goal, and for the ten minutes' duration of the interval had the pair of them fire shots at him. He ran the gamut of goal-keeping through the punch-clear, the clutched-in-flight, the fist-over-the-bar, the full-stretch dive, the pounce. And when the players returned to resume the game, he raised his cap and bowed to the terrific ovation from behind the goal and dashed off to take up his position in the other goal, acclaimed all the way as the artist he was.

Harry Rennie was not there to see it. Pity.

from THE MACADAM ROAD *1955*

How To Keep Goal

J. W. (JACK) ROBINSON

(Southampton and England goalkeeper, c.1900)

Goalkeepers do not grow on trees. That is a truism, no doubt, yet many people imagine that custodians of the sticks are as plentiful as berries in autumn. I concede at once that there are thousands of players who consider themselves goalkeepers, but you must remember that there are thousands upon thousands of men who consider themselves poets. Just as there are poets and poets, so there are goalkeepers and goalkeepers. I hate to drag in here that hackneyed dictum, "the poet is born not made", but it serves my purpose. The saying is true, too, of goalkeepers: but just as the innate power of the poet must be perfected by practice, so must it be with the man beneath the bar. There are certain natural qualifications necessary in each case, and in each the development of these natural qualifications must proceed along certain well-recognized lines. I shall treat of these two necessities, but, before doing so, it may be well to consider whether goalkeeping is an over-crowded branch of football sport.

Whether I consider it from the professional standpoint or from that of the amateur, I most unhesitatingly say, "No". Consider the professional teams of today – how many really first class goalkeepers have we got? We have middling and fair, and pretty good, and good, but the Macaulays and Doigs are to be counted on the fingers of one hand. And in the amateur ranks matters are much worse. Yes, there is room and to spare for good goalkeepers. In passing, I might say that the men who play the other positions on the football field – the forwards and half-backs and backs – considered generally have in the past decade improved, and are improving. I do not mean that we are more rich in "brilliant" talent, but I contend that the players generally and the play have materially improved. Not so with the goalkeepers, and yet they are called upon to do so in view of the improvement of attacking forces.

These are the days of specialization. We have specialists in art and specialists in medicine; we have the specialist on the Press and the specialist even in the sister game of cricket. And specialization is needed in football. Here I speak to the beginner. You are anxious to excel on the football field? Then there is no use thinking that you can play back today and forward tomorrow, that you can be an outside-left on one Saturday and keep goal the next. You will be a Jack-of-all-positions and master of none. Find out by a thoroughly un-biased consideration of your own ability, of your speed, of your stamina, of your build, and so forth, the position you are best adapted by nature to fill, and then specialize. Cultivate your talent and train it in its proper direction. Do not let it be a creeper, twisting and turning hither and thither. The creeper is of little value.

Let us assume, then, that you desire to become a goal-keeper. What are your natural qualifications? What are the powers you have been born with which need development along the lines of practice? They say that a good *big* horse is better than a good *little* horse. A lot of these sayings are only half true. The one I have quoted does not hold good in football. I know several good *big* goalkeepers at the present time who, in my opinion, would have to yield the palm to the good *little* goalkeeper of Middlesbrough, Williamson. Nevertheless, the old Latin saying, *In medio stat virtus*, sums up my views as to the height of the good custodian. It goes without saying that the little man is at a big disadvantage in dealing with high shots. On the other hand, the over-tall man finds great difficulty in stopping the "daisy-croppers". I know one goalkeeper who is positively brilliant in dealing with shots sent in at any height above his knees, yet he has given away as many as five goals in a match because the opposing forwards had for their motto, "Keep them low". The ideal height to my mind for a goal-keeper is five feet nine to five feet eleven inches.

Your first natural qualification, then, is that you should be over the average height, and with this stature, I assume that you have length of arm in proportion. You must, in addition, be robust. I know from only too painful personal experience that the man in goal must be a compound of steel and gutta-percha. You may be a weakling in other positions on the field and yet dodge damage, but in goal you are waiting for it and expecting it all the time – and you get it not infrequently.

Is your eyesight good? If it is not, then goalkeeping is not for you. I concede that a half-blind person can see the ball coming, but that is not sufficient. You must be able to judge, when the ball is twenty yards out, the spin and twist that is on it, to note when it is deflected from its natural course by a puff of wind, and to take action accordingly. The eye is the mirror of your judgement. On the mirror is the image which the brain accepts, and if the mirror is concave or convex, so will your judgement be. So we may conclude that good eyesight is a natural essential to a good goalkeeper.

Writing of judgement, the man who is slow in grasping the significance of things in his everyday life is not likely to be a success where quickness of perception and action are so much demanded. A person may not be dull of intellect, in fact he may be a Herbert Spencer or a Darwin, and yet be slow in assimilating the meaning of the most ordinary happenings. The clever brain is not necessarily the quick brain. If you are possessed of both, so much the better for you as a goalkeeper; but the latter, with its speedy calculation and speedy judgement, is necessary for your success.

If there is a natural qualification absolutely essential to a goalkeeper, it is courage and pluck. Only the goalkeeper knows what risks must be run in the course of his career. If he has a faint heart he is useless. The irony of it is that it is not the big risks which win the most applause. I have in my time received more cheers for saving a simple shot, which to the crowd looked difficult, than for running the risk of the loss of an eye in saving a certain goal right on the toe of an opponent. Courage you must have; and when you have been battered and bruised and wounded in the fray to your courage you must add pluck, and stand up for the next round. Do not, however, be disheartened and think that you are destitute of courage because the thought of kicks and bruises is not soul-soothing. Have you never noticed a man who had to be absolutely pushed into a fight, and yet, being in, to paraphrase Shakespeare, so bore it that the opposed did beware of him. No man would willingly court trouble. I assure you that when I take the field I have no overwhelming desire to have my shins barked or my eye blackened. If you are going to keep goal, do not meditate on thoughts of disaster. Once the fight is started its bustle and excitement will give you little time to think of your wounds.

Do you understand what is meant by intuition? It is the direct understanding or knowledge without the process of reasoning or inference. It is the faculty of at once discerning or apprehending the true nature of an object, person, motive, action, etc., and is akin to instinct in the lower animals. This intuition or instinct is invaluable in any position on the football field, but particularly so in that of the goalkeeper. In my own experience the player most endowed in this valuable acquisition was G. O. Smith. He, more than anyone against whom I have ever kept goal, could divine my intention, my object, my motive or my action, and would then proceed to outwit me. I remember saying to him, "Mr Smith, I'd sooner keep goal against his Satanic Majesty than against you"; and he paid me a lavish and undeserved compliment when he replied, "And I would sooner shoot against the same gentleman in goal than against you." I mention this little episode not out of any spirit of vainglory, but rather to show that intuition plays a very great part in the goalkeeping art. This gift of intuition or instinct is cultivated by the study of human nature. Perhaps I ought to have treated of it in the paragraph concerning judgement but let that go. Whilst you are not actually defending, do not mope about like a sore-footed bear. Regard your opponents and study them. You note the tricks that the two left-wingers and the right-wingers play, the tactics they adopt to beat your halves, to which man does the centre-forward mostly play, and the hundred and one little happenings which the game produces. Your judgement pieces these things together, and forms a verdict as to what the result of a certain set of contingencies would be. But all this judgement and piecing together of things is simply the building up, unconsciously, of intuition, and intuition comes to your rescue when judgement would be slow-footed. You read of goalkeepers hypnotizing the opposing forwards; in fact, I have myself been credited with a certain mesmeric influence in that direction. The forward is blamed for shooting, as if spell-bound, right into the hands of the goalkeeper. Do not blame hypnotism for such a result. It was only intuitive knowledge on the part of the custodian. He knew that the ball would come in a certain way, and he was there to meet it. So if you would be a good goalkeeper, cultivate judgement. Judgement on its part will beget intuition.

In goalkeeping you cannot study too closely the characteristics and methods of your opponents. No two are alike, and your treatment of them must naturally be dissimilar. A fine exhibition of this discrimination has been shown in cricket by our friends the Australians. They weighed their antagonists up to a nicety, and oh, how they worked on the special weaknesses of each! In goalkeeping you have not to tackle the weaknesses, it is true, but it is of as great importance to discover your enemy's strong point.

I have treated somewhat fully, in so short an article, of the natural qualifications for a good goalkeeper; still you must remember that it is the natural qualifications which are essential. If you have got them, even though some of them be latent, practical experience will do the rest. In goalkeeping, if you are to maintain even a moderate standard of excellence, you must practise. Do not trust to the hour bringing forth the save. Consider those who would excel in other lines. A Paderewski daily plays his exercises, a Calve practises her scales, Roberts regularly experiments with the cue, as does Fry with the bat; and so, to be trustworthy between the posts, you must practise and practise and again practise. I have the highest admiration for Cartledge of Bristol Rovers as a goalkeeper. He is excellent in the position. Once when playing against the Rovers I saved a goal by a particular kind of punch. It was simple enough in itself, but apparently it was new to Cartledge. After the game he asked me to explain it to him. I showed him how I did it, and there and then he practised until he was perfect in it. There, then, is the secret. Practise the various methods of saving; and when you see a good stroke effected by another, do not rest until you have learned it.

But you will not practise and you cannot play unless you are fit, and the secret of fitness is moderation in all things. It is not essential for a man to become teetotal, nor to give up his pipe, nor to deny himself the ordinary pleasures of life that he may become fit. The ordinary pleasures are all right, but avoid the extraordinary ones. It is in extravagance that the danger lies. If a goalkeeper observes moderation in his living and has a little practice work from time to time, he will not need much training.

During the summer the goalkeeper occasionally needs some form of exercise to keep him fit. When I was at Derby I played baseball, and I know of no better game to suit the football player in the summer. Since I came to the South, I have played cricket, but practically any healthy exercise will keep a man in fettle.

In bringing this article to a conclusion let me commend three maxims to the budding goalkeeper:

1. Remember you are the last line of defence. A forward may err and retrieve his error. A half-back or back may make a mistake and yet recover himself, but if the goalkeeper fails his failure is irretrievable.

2. Keep cool.

3. Never on any account use your feet if it is possible to use your hands.

Much more could I write, but space forbids. This, however, I must say: I would far rather keep goal than try to explain in writing how to do it. If I have interested you, I am satisfied; if I have bored you, please accept my sympathy.

from ASSOCIATION FOOTBALL AND
THE MEN WHO MADE IT *1906*

Bill Foulke

IVAN SHARPE

Bill Foulke, heavy-weight champion of the world of Association Football. In the photographs of Chelsea, his last club, he looks twice the size of his colleagues yet he kept goal for England, and twice helped Sheffield United to win the Cup. Yes, he played, near the end of his career, at the seemingly impossible weight of twenty-two stone.

In the '90s the mining villages of Derbyshire had buzzed with the news of a giant collier goalkeeper who came from Blackwell. In a local exhibition match his punch had missed the ball but knocked out two of the teeth of John Goodall. The news reached Sheffield, but when the United sought to sign him they found Derby County and Nottingham Forest also in the field. By paying the Blackwell club £1 a day for the remaining days of the season, Sheffield United beat off their rivals, and took to Bramall Lane the top-weight of all time.

But I will let J. T. Howcroft of Bolton, the well-known referee of those days, tell of William Foulke:

"A referee, it is said, should have no nerves. In thirty years there was only one occasion when I felt really uncomfortable.

"Towards the end of his long career Foulke was playing at Burslem for Chelsea, who were trying desperately to get into the First Division. The giant goalkeeper must have got out of bed on the wrong side, as he seemed to have a grouse against more than one opponent. Ultimately, when a Burslem forward made for goal, Foulke did not bother about the ball but grabbed the player round the middle and hurled him into the back of the Chelsea net. I pointed at once for a penalty-kick. Then the fun started. It took quite a time to persuade Foulke to get into his proper position, and it seemed to me he was after my scalp.

"Eventually, J. T. Robertson, captain of the side, took the bull by the horns and told Foulke either to go into goal or clear out. He did not try to save the shot but stood glaring at me.

"I kept a respectable distance until the close of the game, and then made my way quicker than usual to the dressing-room. If Foulke had put one of those large hands on me, I might have been short of some part of my anatomy.

"On another occasion, at the Cup Final of 1902 at the Crystal Palace, at which I was a linesman, Foulke became exasperated about a goal awarded to Southampton which he held to be 'miles' offside. He had evidently missed the fact that the player had been played on-side by one of the Sheffield United half-backs.

"After the match Foulke left his dressing-cubicle and went in search of the referee (Tom Kirkham of Burslem). I saw F. J. Wall, the secretary of the Football Association, pleading with Foulke, who was in his birthday suit, to go back to his dressing-room, but Big Bill was out for blood.

"So I shouted to Kirkham to lock his cubicle door, and he didn't need telling twice. But what a sight! The thing I can never forget is Foulke, 6 ft. tall and tremendous in size, striding along the corridor without a stitch of clothing."

from 40 YEARS IN FOOTBALL *1952*

Judgement and the Art of Goalkeeping

H. D. DAVIES

It used to be accepted as axiomatic that goalkeepers, like wicketkeepers, were "a slate loose". That opinion probably originated in the good old days, say the Gay Nineties or the early years of the Edwardian period, when "rushing the goal-keeper" was a legitimate tactic during the taking of a corner-kick and when goalkeepers often went into the net faster than the ball that followed.

Goalkeepers, of course, though they often had to take things lying down, were not without resources of their own. A stinging right hook at a ball floating into goal, coupled with a firm left jab at a protruding head trying to help it in, used to be the solution to many a goalkeeping problem; and many an inside-forward of those early days needed no other proof of the intensity of goalmouth exchanges than to point ruefully to the number of teeth missing.

Yet the basic qualities required for good goalkeeping vary little, if at all, from age to age. They are keen vision, prompt reflexes, adequate physical endowments covering height, reach, and muscular agility, courage, and daring, and judgement – yes, judgement, that master quality which brings all the others into play at the right spot and at the right time. In this quality of judgement are included so many important things, such as divination of an attacking forward's intentions, a correct sense of positioning, and a knowledge of when to sally forth from goal and when to stay put.

It was the possession of this quality in such marked degree that made Sam Hardy, of Liverpool and Aston Villa, automatic first choice for England for thirteen years and still wins him the vote as probably the surest, if also the least spectacular, goalkeeper so far known. It was such judgement, too, which in the recent match between Manchester City and Manchester United enabled City's experienced Trautmann to outshine United's relatively immature Gregg at the other end.

Splendid as was his performance, to describe Trautmann as the best goalkeeper known to English football would be to fly in the face of known facts and common experience. The pageant of our winter game has been graced by a succession of superb goalkeepers who obligingly fall into clearly marked categories. The quietists, like Hardy or Hibbs, were able to make goalkeeping look easy by the speed and stealth of their preparatory moves (often unmarked by the crowd), and by their uncanny reading of a forward's intentions. The acrobats, Swift, evoking delight and laughter with his gorilla-like reach, his bucket-like hands, and thrilling swoops; the other, Traut-mann, as outstanding among goalkeepers for his diving grace as is the swallow among the birds.

In the dare-devil class we may put "John Willy" Sutcliffe

and Dai Davies, both of Bolton Wanderers, types we are not likely to see again. In their intrepidity and indifference to bruises they were characteristic of their age. Both started as Rugby League players for Swinton, and both gained international caps – Sutcliffe for England and Davies for Wales. Both, in turn, were persuaded by the Wanderers to change to Association football and both again won international honours. As might be expected both excelled in the dangerous and difficult task of diving headlong at an oncoming forward's feet and whisking the ball away as they curled up and rolled to safety, a feat performed by Swift as well as any of the moderns in his younger, more carefree days. "John Willy" could enliven the dullest game by the air of aristocratic disdain with which he would lift the ball over an opponent's head and at the same time allow him to hurl himself into space. Both Sutcliffe and Davies played in F.A. Cup finals for the Wanderers but neither gained a winner's medal.

And yet, even if the dare-devils of olden time must disappear may the characters reappear from time to time; men like L. R. Roose of the Sunderland, Everton, and Stoke clubs, an amateur player, wit, and practical joker; Iremonger, of Notts County, humorist, and penalty king; or Foulke, of Sheffield United, an extraordinary barrel-shaped goalkeeper who carried twenty-one stones of too, too solid flesh around.

Though huge and apparently top-heavy, Foulke was amazingly nimble on his peg-top legs, could stoop easily to ground shots, could catch or pick up a ball one-handed, and could hoist it on a still day three parts the length of the field from a goal-kick. With a following wind of any strength he could even bombard the opposite goal. The sight of Foulke's stomach in goal was said to have been the one thing which would persuade Bloomer to abandon his golden rule when shooting – namely, never to let the ball rise above knee high. The story goes that in one match Bloomer twice knocked Foulke insensible with violent shots in the stomach, and sought to do it a third time. But this time Foulke incontinently fled and let the ball through.

In recent times Bartram, late of Charlton Athletic, has made his mark as a colourful character. His idolators claim him as the finest English goalkeeper who never gained a cap. His alleged fault was a craze for rushing out of goal and making spectacular forays far beyond the penalty-area. His other virtue of ensuring that there was rarely a dull moment when he was playing is one that rarely appeals to international selectors. Gregg of Manchester United has the same mania for leaving his goal and has already been dubbed Bartram the second; with what justification will emerge as time goes on.

Stories based on the idiosyncrasies of goalkeepers, like the best wines, improve with age. And the farther they recede from the date of their origin the more devoutly they are believed. One such story concerns Doig of Sunderland, at Burnden Park. This famous Scottish goalkeeper had a habit, apparently, of leaning negligently against a post with arms folded when play was at the other end, of turning his back on the game, and of exchanging repartee with any obliging customer in the crowd.

On one occasion, it is said, Shepherd, a famous centre-forward in his day and a terrific shot, suddenly let fly from the centre circle in a bold attempt to catch Doig napping. From this point the versions vary. One – the favourite of those who revere Shepherd's shooting powers – holds that the ball flashed through the posts before Doig was aware of the danger. Another states that the ball just missed the posts and knocked Doig's cap off. A third – probably a truer version – states that Doig, warned by shouts of "Look out!" was just in time to turn and shamefacedly scramble the ball over the bar. Whatever the truth of the matter, this story does at least conjure up two pictures that go far to carry conviction to those who knew Doig and Shepherd – that characteristic posture of Doig, leaning on a post, and the tremendous force which Shepherd could put into his shots.

Another story tells how George, of Aston Villa, once pranced up and down his goal-line like a dancing dervish, beating his knees with his gloved hands and shrieking, "He's coming again! He's coming again!" when he saw Shepherd bearing down on him at top speed for the second time in the match. George's concern, if true, was not surprising, for broken fingers, sprained wrists, and damaged ribs were often the portion of those goalkeepers who had to face the Bolton terror. Shepherd had just about the most powerful thighs one has seen on any footballer, and that includes Joe Smith, and by assiduous practice he mastered Bloomer's secret of keeping his shots low.

This recalls at least one true incident. On one occasion Shepherd raced through in his usual headlong fashion towards one of the coolest and neatest of all goalkeepers – Elisha Scott – an adept at gathering the ball cleanly and going down on one knee to get his body well behind low shots. The Burnden ground was like a quagmire, the ball "a ton weight" as we say. Shepherd let fly, straight at Scott, as it happened, and Scott, without flinching, stooped and hugged the ball to his bosom and, still hugging it, felt himself slip back helplessly over his own goal-line. Catching that ball must have felt like trying to catch one of those old iron cannonballs as used in the Napoleonic wars.

Everyone of course has some favourite goalkeeper's yarn. One of the most popular concerns that elongated humorist Iremonger, whose spidery frame – the whole 6 ft. 4 in. of it – crowned by an enormous cap, used to provoke such mirth in the act of guarding the Notts County goal. The story goes that in one match Iremonger ran the full length of the field to take a penalty-kick, hit the crossbar, wheeled, joined in the mad scramble to get to the other end, and, in a wild attempt to kick clear his opponent's final shot at goal, scored disastrously against his own side! All who remember Iremonger will have no difficulty in filling in the details.

The only reason one has to doubt the authenticity of this story is that, like so many of the W. G. Grace collection, the incident referred to is now claimed to have taken place in so many different grounds. But the general shape of the story does corroborate one indisputable fact, namely that Iremonger, like

Shackleton, enjoyed his football so much that he sought to get fun out of it and to make fun for others. And after all what is the basic idea of football but fun?

from THE BEDSIDE GUARDIAN 7 *1958*

The Goalkeeper

R. C. ROBERTSON-GLASGOW

In big-time Soccer the goalkeeper is the dickens of a fellow. Photographs in the newspapers show him to be perpetually in flight. Excelsior. He is a trapeze-artist without the trapeze. Compared with him the star of Ballet is a rheumatic elephant. None but the cynic would conjecture that this airborne hero, if only he had stayed where he was on the ground, might have saved the goal quite comfortably and altered the result of the Pools.

It is reassuring, therefore, to record that in Junior School football these things are still managed very differently. Here the goalkeeper, so far from being heroic or starlike, is an outcast on the face of the earth; literally so, for most of the time. He rolls in the mud and waits to be sworn at. Every goal that he lets past is no one else's fault. Like Punch in the old show he's a villain by right; and he's beyond care or cure.

And there he stood; as small as life, between the towering uprights. He seemed to have borrowed for the occasion his uncle's boots and his youngest brother's shorts. It was a match. For there was a referee. There were also spectators of a kind. Of these, a few loudly urged the home players on to unlikely feats of skill; two were playing "conkers"; and one, with his back to the game, had his cap over the right eye while the left eye waited for aeroplanes.

There is a sort of fellow-feeling between us goalkeepers. I too have done my share of retrieving the ball from the net amid rhetorical questions. So I walked round towards the home goal. As I neared it, the visiting inside-right broke away, and, from five yards, shot hard and straight at the goalkeeper. The ball rebounded up the field. I praised the hero of this encounter. "Oompha loocha," he said, doubled up into Esperanto. Recovering his wind he winked at me and said, "Cor".

Then, while a corner-kick was being taken with uncommon care at the far end, he revealed how he had started as a centre-forward in early September. By Michaelmas he had worked outwards to the left wing and backwards to right-half. He had by-passed full-back, a position which anyhow he rated low; and Guy Fawkes Day had seen him settled in goal: for life, he reckoned.

At this point in his narrative he was summoned to action. In a scrummage to the left of his goal he and the ball were sat on for some fifteen seconds. Recovering, but disorientated, he threw the ball ten yards into the centre, whence it was crashed into the net. Some time after the restart of play, his captain, the left-back, who seemed to devote more time to administration than execution, was still cursing him. Then the ball hit the talkative captain on the back of the neck and passed into the top right-hand corner of the net. "Getting good with your head, aren't you?" said the goalkeeper. 2–0 against, and mutiny spreading.

from ALL IN THE GAME *1943*

Talking of Goalkeepers
ALFONSO GATTO

I shall talk about goalkeepers. The first I knew played for my little village team. In those days, to tell the truth, it seemed like a full-fledged team, and the village a city which, at its eastern end, had built a wall around a flat area to make it into the parade ground and the Sunday football field. That goalkeeper was called Fininzio; the little team, "Salernitana". In those days it kept itself vigorously alive, drew on many local players and had as trophies two victories, one against "Vomero", the other against "Savoia", Torre's team. Every Sunday, the dockers of the two cities would gather around the field of play like enemies with several old scores to settle and a few casualties to send to hospital. Fininzio was the hero. Rather short, but as agile as a cat, he strove might and main to make all his saves look difficult, to win applause, seeking in his furious activity forgiveness for the goal which would send his team back into the dressing-room, beaten.

After him, I saw Cavanna. With that white, white face, like plaster against his black jersey, with his practised gestures, all soft and supple, he seemed to me to be there just to gather the ball gently and soothe it against his chest. And if it came hard and quick, calm as ever he would leap to take it with his hands, and proudly show it off, before clearing. His eyes, small and alert in the white face, shone lively and perceptive. They would travel down his body, as though somehow boring into the ball; leaving in his hands the brilliant wake of the ball's parabola.

Sclavi, rough and hairy, needed to have the whole stadium yelling at him like an animated forest, then he became a huge monkey between the goalposts. All the voices and shouting echoing across the field were for him leaves, branches, and trees – the ball ran before him like a giant nut, and became a breadfruit in his arms. He seemed to grow larger then, seemed to confront it – this fruit – with his whole face, with his teeth, his mouth, eager to save it and devour it himself. He took so long to clear it, so lovingly jealous was he of this ball which he wanted to hold tight against him. He really cared for himself, loved himself, this strange goalkeeper, all alone as he was in front of everybody, with a whole forest of eyes regarding him. And how ugly he was, as ugly and as earthy as a man can be!

Masetti, on Roma's old Testaccio ground, near the Pyramid and Keats' fine cemetery, would come out like a thoroughbred, full of confidence, made hard by his muscles and with a handsome, clean cut face. With what a romantic air he bore himself, with the confidence you could plainly see expressed in his body, his jersey and the shorts which seemed to be moulded against his thighs.

In big matches, when he was playing against a centre-forward like Meazza, he liked to trade blow for blow, skill for skill, flying through the air to balls headed for the top corner. More, he would position his full-backs with furious gestures and urge on his attack with the same anxiety he showed after clearing the ball. I remember a match played in a storm: that Sunday Meazza and Masetti were scintillating. To a flashing header by the centre-forward, Masetti replied by flying from the left-hand side to the right, high to the corner of the goal. His body in that moment was all intelligence, full of his own joy and ours, of a fullness which, at the same time, was sharply defined. We realized then that football, with this electric intuition, transcended mere words in his life.

As though by way of contrast, Ceresoli seemed occupied and preoccupied by his job, in every match. He was expressionless on the field, grey of spirit and of jersey, and with a heavy mien. Then one came to realize that this unawareness of his body, this indifference towards muscles and nerves, were his means of being able to transcend himself in the game, depersonalized and powerful. The whole power of his being seemed concentrated in his eyes, with none left over for his legs and arms which he held rigidly and carefully positioned in the lea of his glance which, though apparently languid and pale, was yet magnetic. From this ambush, he would sally out infallibly; he turned one white with his lightning interceptions and with his furious clearances which he used to watch anxiously before going back to lie in wait again. He was a wild beast in the goal, all alone, his own shadow: he was everywhere at once, rolling over and over, crawling, diving recklessly into the mêlée, his prey between his hands. This was how one always saw him in those matches played in a Milan, grimy with fog and damp, in which Faccio was a mud statue who never put a pass wrong and Meazza and Ferrari roamed the field, sending their wingers

away. Silver days at the Arena. Once the loudspeaker called
Frione, who was dead, and no one answered. Rigid on his goal
line, Ceresoli stared at the grass of the field, and seemed to be
trembling. No one on a football field had as much courage as
he, and as much human apprehension. No one was more
fascinating and fearful.

There are others who did not answer. In the little café in
Via Garibaldi, Turin, one used to find almost all of them:
Gabetto, Ossola, Bacigalupo, Grezar.* And Casalbore, the
journalist, used to walk out of his newspaper office and round
the corner of the Corso Valdocco, with that air of a Neapolitan
gentleman. Players who were once stars, once full of promise,
and are now lawyers and workmen; how many of them there
are, spinning out the romance of the Championship! This is
Bosia, this is Filippi, this is Vallone. Casalbore turns the pages
of that story whose chapters he has been writing for years,
every Sunday. And Gabetto and Ossola, if they join in, talk
with the same finesse with which they play, the same feints,
the same sudden bursts. They think for themselves, like experts,
without pride, without self-indulgence.

On Sundays, after the match, we were sure to find them
sitting round that table in the Pollastrini restaurant where all
the journalists of Corso Valdocco used to eat. Sometimes they
were long tables. When Spring came, we went to the open air
dancing place near Piazza Statuto. The Championship was
coming to an end, and already we were talking about the next
one. Little by little our gathering grew. One by one everybody
came. Grezar, always taciturn, with his air of a tousled schoolboy. Castigliano, restless, with his lively eyes, could never keep
still. They knew I was a poet and that I talked about football
with a memory for names and dates which astonished even
them, and they were pleased that I could participate in their
life with such affection and nostalgia for the youth we had had in
common.

Before the match between Italy and Hungary we were all

* Members of the Torino team which perished in the Superga air-crash. See
"The Tragedy of Torino", page 408.

together at Limone. I shall never forget that day, which will always remain among my dearest memories. That day Loik was happy while Mazzola was brooding and impatient. And Gabetto duelled with us journalists, finally coming to sit near us as though he were one of us. (He would end as a writer himself, he said.) At the end of dinner, Pozzo spoke of his memories of Ferraris IV, who had died on the field a few hours ago. The team-manager with the very white hair and the face that laughed both with its dimples and its eyes, chose the right words, no rhetoric or self-indulgence, like a good shot at goal. He was only one dead man, "the lion of Highbury", but that Sunday all the silence of the football field seemed to be for him. For him, the very corner-flags blew whiter in the wind of memory.

But for all those who died on that May evening – ten years have gone by – the boys left their fields and games, arms outstretched in despair. Even if they have been parted, those thirty-one dead are still lined up together, in a single green field, surrounded by a wall, like a stadium. Turin has its hills, its river, its workers and its factories; and many footballers, many teams, which play on its outskirts every Saturday and Sunday; just as I once saw at Budapest. "In despair", one says, or just "goodbye": goodbye, every Sunday.

It may seem that I have no team of my own, since I have not yet spoken of it, nor given as much as a greeting to Mario Zorzan, Boffi, Antonini or to Omero Tognon, "bright star of the football fields", as we sang in our old song. But I have dedicated this letter to my own Milan, and to my "dear, very dear Gren", for that 1951 Championship which has his signature on its shield.

The double of Naples and Palermo, the exhibition of Turin, the pre-Christmas battle at the "Brumana", of Bergamo, and so on to the matches of Rome, Novara, Genoa. That year it was the Milan team playing away from home that won the shield, and with it so many traditional and Championship records that it would take a long time to enumerate them. Coming back from the match at Florence, Anovazzi told us that he, Professor

Gunnar Gren, that blond man with the bald patch and the clear eyes, *was* Milan. "To play with him," said Carletto, "is like having a prompter beside you. He thinks for everyone and works for everyone."

Dear, very dear Gren, with your honest eyes. The years and seasons will pass, but in the great periphery of poets, who create their verses out of nothing, there will always be a green football pitch to harbour the genius and effort of our great juggler. And we shall always go to watch him, happy that our thoughts can still be so easily liberated by his inimitable swerve.

Talking of Milan, I want to recall Zorzan, Puri, "little golden head", Raccis, the unforgettable and unlucky Raccis. They came after the legendary pioneers, after Sternisa, after Stella, after Kossovel: they blazed the trail for the virtuosi of today. May Liedholm, the captain and the greatest of them all, order the flag to be raised in their honour.

"Long live Milan."

Yes, long live Milan. Or perhaps you want to take up the cry with me?

"Long live Milan."

from L'APPRODO LETTERARIO
(RADIO ITALIANA) *October 1959*

What I Owe to Football

ALBERT CAMUS

Yes, I played for several years at the University of Algiers. It seems to me like yesterday. But when, in 1940, I put on my boots again, I realized that it was not yesterday. Before the end of the first half, my tongue was hanging out like those *kabyles* dogs that one comes across at two o'clock in the afternoon, at Tizi-Ouzou. It was a long while ago, then, from 1928 onwards, I believe. I made my début with Montpensier sports club. God knows why, since I lived at Belcourt, and the Belcourt-Mustapha team is Gallia-Sports. But I had a friend, a shaggy fellow, who swam in the port with me and played water polo for Montpensier. That's how one's life is determined. Montpensier often played at the Manoeuvre Grounds, for no apparent reason. The ground was bumpier than the shin of a visiting centre-forward at the Alenda Stadium, Oran. I quickly learned that the ball never came to you where you expected it. This helped me in life, above all in the metropolis, where people are not always wholly straightforward. But after a year of bumps and Montpensier, they made me ashamed of myself at the lycée: a "university man" ought to play for Algiers University, R.U.A. At this period, the shaggy fellow had gone out of my life. We hadn't quarrelled, it was merely that he now went swimming at Padovani, where the water was not pure. Nor, frankly, were his motives. Personally, I found his motive charming, but she danced badly, which seemed to me insupportable in a woman. It's the man, is it not, who should tread on the toes? The shaggy fellow and I had merely promised to see each other again. But years have gone by. Much later, I frequented the Padovani restaurant (for pure motives) but the shaggy fellow had married his paralytic, who must have forbidden him to bathe, as is the usual practice.

Where was I? Yes, R.U.A. I was very pleased, the important thing for me being to play. I fretted with impatience from Sunday to Thursday, for training day, and from Thursday to Sunday, match day. So I joined the university men. And there I was, goalkeeper of the junior team. Yes, it all seemed quite easy. But I didn't know that I had just established a bond which would endure for years, embracing every stadium in the Department, and which would never come to an end. I did not know then that twenty years after, in the streets of Paris or even Buenos Aires (yes, it happened to me) the words R.U.A. spoken by a friend I met would make my heart beat again as foolishly as could be. And since I am giving away secrets, I can admit that in Paris, for instance, I go to watch the matches of the Racing Club de Paris, whom I have made my favourites solely because they wear the same jerseys as R.U.A., blue and white hoops. I must say, too, that Racing has some of the same eccentricities as R.U.A. It plays "scientifically", as we say, and scientifically loses matches it should win. It seems that this has changed (so they write to me from Algiers) so far at least as R.U.A. are concerned. It needed to change – but not too much. After all, that was why I loved my team so much, not only for the joy of victory, so wonderful when it is combined with the weariness that follows exertion, but also for the stupid desire to cry on evenings when we had lost.

At full-back I had The Big Fellow – I mean Raymond Couard. He had a tough time of it, if I remember correctly. We used to play hard. Students, their fathers' sons, don't spare themselves. Poor us, in every sense, a good half of us mown down like corn! We had to face up to it. And we had to play "sportingly", because that was the golden rule of the R.U.A., and "strongly", because, when all is said and done, a man is a man. Difficult compromise! This cannot have changed, I am sure. The hardest team was Olympic Hussein Dey. The stadium is beside the cemetery. They made us realize, without mercy, that there was direct access. As for me, poor goalkeeper, they went for my body. Without Roger, I would have suffered. There was Boufarik, too, that great big centre-forward (among ourselves we called him Watermelon) who always came down with all his weight, right on my kidneys, without counting the cost: shin-massage with football boots, shirt pulled back by the hand, knees in the distinguished parts, sandwiches against the post . . . in brief, a scourge. And every time, Watermelon apologized with a "Sorry, son," and a Franciscan smile.

I shall stop. I have already exceeded the limits set for me. And then, I am softening. There was good even in Watermelon. Besides, let us be frank, we paid him back. But without cheating, as this was the way we were taught. And at this point, I no longer want to go on jesting. For, after many years in which the world has afforded me many experiences, what I most surely know in the long run about morality and the obligations of men, I owe to sport, I learned it with R.U.A.

That, in short, is why the R.U.A. cannot die. Let us preserve it.
Let us preserve this great and good image of our youth. It will
keep watch over yours, as well.

from FRANCE FOOTBALL *1957*

The Mine in the Goal

GEORGES POTTER

My word, yes, we got across the frontier, right at the start. But
the going was pretty hot for us infantry. Our guns had been
banging away all night with that music of theirs, without the
guns on the other side replying. About five in the morning we
set off, through the fields, behind the armoured cars, which
moved like elephants. Bullets were whistling around and, at a
turn in the road from which there was probably an interesting
view, we heard a "Taca-taca" which boded no good at all.
Then it shut up, of its own accord.

The captain soon had us lined up on the road, arms slung,
and we gaily sloped off into the Saar – the Saar: Germany, that
is – at two and a half miles an hour.

I don't know whether the famous yarn about the pigs had
any truth in it. I do know that the journalists had not been
exaggerating much as far as the mines were concerned. When
we got to the village of X, two cows seemed to be blocking
the way, standing right in the middle of the causeway. Sergeant
Hollebecque tapped the rump of the one on the right. The
beast shook its great head, swung its tail, and made off down
the track.

Vloum! Where had it put its foot? The one thing certain was
that all that was left of it was its two rear hoofs, and, on a roof
fifty yards away, its horned head, hooked on like the sign of a
butcher's shop.

We went on. The captain considered there was nothing to be

M

afraid of for the moment. When we had been marching fifty minutes, he whistled a halt, and it was a halt I shall never forget!

It took place some five hundred yards from M. . . . (I was just about to say the name) above a fine green field. But no ordinary field because, as soon as we had dumped our haversacks (there were zouaves ahead of us), the lads in front shouted to us:

"Good Lord, a football pitch!"

I climbed to the top of the bank. What did I see? Yes, a ground, just as they had said. Quite green, quite flat, quite in order, with lines marked in plaster – which seemed to show that Fritz reckoned on playing there next Sunday. And goalposts, nets. But best of all, do you know what was lying on the grass? It was a superb football!

Would you believe me if I told you that five or six of us did not race like mad towards that brand new ball which shone like a helmet in the sunshine!

The sergeant shouted vainly, "What are you up to? Wait until I ask. . . ."

He did not insist, knowing very well that once we had had a few kicks at the ball, we would be back at the encampment in time.

I can't do the hundred yards in one second, but all the same, with more and more of the others chasing after me, I moved pretty fast, and was first on to the ball. My first idea was to take a tremendous kick, But no! I dribbled off with the ball, in and out of the skittles, Arsenal style, and when I had run twenty yards, I passed to the next man, who passed it back to me. One of those scissor-switches which Monsieur Barreau was mad about!

One bloke grabbed the ball, picked it up, held it with both hands, had a look at it and pretended to press it to his heart. It was Patchek. I raced up and shouted at him, "Now's your chance!"

Called up as a reservist on September 1st, this mate of mine and I had had a conversation in the train. Because his name,

you see, is Czech, and a Czech is what he is. A Czech, naturalized
for just three years; not very long. And me, I was kidding him,
"What, call yourself a Czech and you call yourself 'not Czech' –
pas Tchèque!" (it was naughty of me!) That made him laugh.
(I think he had heard that subtle joke before.) But what made
me laugh, in my turn, was when he started talking about . . .
his exploits in football.

(In football, I was ready for that.)

I ought to tell you that I fell in love with the round ball at the
J.-B. Say School. I played in the first team, in the schools
championship final of Paris. I read *Football* every week and
L'Auto every day. In fact, I claim to be well up in the achievements of every sportsman living in France. Patchek? . . . I
searched my memory in vain; I had never heard of him.

"My word," said Patchek, "I came to France to work in
the mines. I didn't want to touch another football. You know
how it is. In the first place, I'd had an accident. But I played in
the Brno team (he pronounced it Brunn), a grand little side
which would have put three goals past the Racing Club."

"What position did you play?"

He seemed to hesitate, this yarn spinner!

"Goalkeeper," he answered, "goal!"

"Goal! Eh! I played outside-right, and I'd like to put a few
past you."

"Well, well!"

I went on seriously, "If you were English, you know what
you'd be called? Pasgoal! (No goalkeeper)!"

Everybody roared, even Patchek. He's a fine fellow, at
bottom. Strapping, too. Perhaps he did keep goal, somewhere
or other. But still, in a team that could lick the Racing Club. . . !

And when we were in barracks, I took it up with him on
more than one evening, I can tell you. . . .

Still, here was the dreamed-of chance for Brno's goalkeeper
to show his paces! He wasn't going to miss it. I followed him,
dribbling along with the ball at his feet, and I could see that he
was moving it, coaxing it, caressing it, like an artist. Then, he
took up position between the posts, in front of the net. He

booted the ball out with a kick that would have made them cry
"Raah!" on the terraces at Parc des Princes, and he shouted at
us, "Go ahead, I'm ready for you."

There were five of us on the field, and at least three of us
knew how to shoot!

Naturally enough, we started to bombard Patchek's goal.
Not too close, that wouldn't have been right. Not less than
twenty-five yards. But we put some heart behind it, I can tell
you. But he saved, he kept us out! Well set-up, solid on his
legs, with that animal air they all seem to have, he anticipated
every shot and gathered it in, sometimes in his arms, sometimes
at full stretch, with his hands, which are strong like Defosse's,
sometimes with a jaguar leap, like Hiden, sometimes throwing
himself to the ground, in a fraction of a second.

On the embankment over which the road ran, there were
something like two companies looking at us, applauding us,
as we tried in vain, unnerved, playing to the gallery, putting
all we knew into it – the animal was really everywhere at once,
leaping, striving, stopping, punching and, after three minutes,
keeping his goal intact.

He had just picked up the ball, spun it in his fingers,
raced energetically forward, pretended to avoid a charge from
an imaginary forward – and then, suddenly stopping, he
challenged me: "I'll give you three penalties."

"Stingy!"

The others had heard. Already, they were forming up in a
circle. And they were trying to push themselves: "And us?"

"No, no," said Patchek. "No one but Mauger! It's he who
made fun of me."

"My dear Patchek," I said, "I offer you an honourable
apology. I've no intention of laughing at you any more. You're
a star. I agree to try one penalty against you, with a bottle at
stake. But not three!"

"Three," he repeated.

"Three, you realize, would mean that you are the phenomenon of phenomenons."

It was true. To subjugate a penalty kicker, hypnotize him so that you can get him, so to speak, to shoot somewhere where you can leap – the great goalkeepers can do this. But three times in a row. . . .

We paced out the twelve yards. Corporal Louchet placed the ball for me. And first I tried the classic trick of negligently glancing at the right hand corner, and shooting to the left. But Patchek was there to the left, and he threw me back the ball, laughing, while hands were clapping everywhere.

Second penalty. I am in command of myself. This time I intended going to try a straight forward "bullet". I knew that, if it didn't swerve, neither Patchek, however he flung himself, nor anybody else, could reach a locomotive hurtling at ninety feet per second. I put everything into it. But I must be frank. The ball . . . went outside the post.

I blushed. But I did not give up. And now I had to make haste, because up there, there was already a rustle of movement, prelude to a recall to the camp. Fine, the ball is well and truly placed. I am standing still, behind it. Before me, Patchek, into whose eyes I refrain from looking. I concentrate. I invoke my god . . . or my inner demon. It was I who was chosen to take the penalties in the time of Jean-Baptiste Say. Well then, I take my two thundering strides, I fix my eye on the ball, I shoot – and feel that the ball is really going well. . . . But that devil there, that magician – yes, he must indeed have been a star at Brno – has anticipated what I meant to do, has nullified what I have done. . . . And amidst a thunder of *bravos* which surge up from the far off spectators, I see him, ball in hand, brandishing it like a sort of conjurer archangel.

We surround him. We embrace him. I grab hold of him under one leg. Louchet gets hold of the other. Pépin comes to the rescue. Chambarrière lends us a hand. The applause from the embankment continues all the while we carry him off the field. Four of us were enough to do it. The last of our crew wanted to join in, but there was no room! Disappointed, he saw the ball at his feet, turned towards the empty net, and let go a fine shot.

Ah! my friends, we let Patchek fall. And how! All five of us were rolling with our noses to the ground. Because there, twenty yards away, what a mass of flame! Pieces of wood flying through the air, one of them falling beyond the road. No more posts, net, turf or penalty area! A ditch! We were pelted with stones! Those wretched Boches – as you have guessed – had planted a mine there, which would only explode when the net was moved.

I got up again . . . trembling all over. I looked at Patchek, who was also rising, and rubbing his nose. I thought, all at once, of what he had risked, without knowing it, of my incompetence, of his nerve, above all of his skill. I called to him: "If you'd lost confidence . . ."

"Poo!" he answered, wrinkling his forehead. "After the first penalty I noticed there was some freshly dug earth, at the back of the goal. . . . I was expecting an explosion like that."

"And you could still . . .?"

"I thought of only one thing: because my name's Patchek. . . ." His eyes narrowed. "And because I'm a Czech. . . ." He laughed. "I couldn't let myself back down!"

Prize-winning Story of
FEDERATION FOOTBALL FRANÇAISE *1939*

Goalkeepers are Crazy

BRIAN GLANVILLE

It was no good everyone telling me I was taking a chance, because I knew that better than they did. It stood to reason, anyway; you don't let an international class goalkeeper go for seven thousand quid unless there's something wrong with him, and I reckoned I knew what it was.

The thing was I had to get someone quickly; what with Ron Gavin out for the whole season with a broken leg and Jim

Mason copping it the very first game, we were having diabolical bloody luck.

So I signed him. I knew he'd be after something for himself, and so he was at first, but when I told him my club wouldn't have anything to do with that kind of carry-on, he just backed down without a fuss; it surprised me. London did it, I suppose, they all want to come to London, though God knows why; think the streets are paved with gold and crammed with crumpet. Maybe they are, now, but they never were when I was a player; you had to work for anything you got.

"I've got a tart in London," he said, "bloody marvellous, do anything you like, she will," and I thought that's a damn good start, with him married and a kid. The first day he came in for training I had him into my office.

"Look here," I told him, "I know all about you. If you're playing for my club, you're going to behave yourself, otherwise out you go, understand? As far as I'm concerned, you start with a clean sheet, but if you want to stay here, you'll do what you're told and you'll keep out of trouble." He didn't say much, just muttered something about giving a dog a bad name, and seeing him standing there I began to feel a bit sorry for speaking so harsh – though I'd seen him with my own eyes kick our centre-forward, the season before last, and put him out for a fortnight. Still, he looked more sinned against than sinning, a sort of dead end kid with hollow cheeks and shifty eyes that never looked at you; like a dog that's got used to people kicking it and shies away when anyone comes near. Looking at him you'd never think he was a professional footballer at all, let alone a goalkeeper, but I wasn't worried about that side of it. He was good enough for me on the field, so long as he behaved himself off it.

Well he couldn't have started better. The first Saturday he goes out and he plays a blinder. I'm not kidding, there were at least three shots he wasn't entitled to get near, and he not only got to them, he held them.

Then he goes and spoils everything two minutes from the end. He catches the ball, the centre-forward comes in naughty with his foot up, and Wilkins tucks the ball under one arm and takes a ruddy great swing at him. Luckily the referee had seen what happened first, so he let him off with a warning. I didn't say anything about it to him when he came off the field, I just told him he'd done well, but that Monday I had him up to my office and I didn't half pitch into him.

"Look," I said, "what do you want to go and do a silly thing like that for? Where do I stand if you go and get yourself suspended? I have to start looking for a goalkeeper all over again and it can cost me another seven thousand pounds."

"Well," he said, "don't blame me, I was provoked." That was the word: provoked.

"Of course you were provoked," I said, "everybody gets provoked in this game, and if they do what you did every time it happens, you might as well hire Harringay and turn it into a boxing match."

"Well," he said, with his head all on one side in the way he had, "he'd kept threatening me. He said, I'm going to get you, Wilkins." You wouldn't believe it.

"Then the next time it happens," I told him, "tell him you'll get him first. Keep it to words. Words don't hurt anybody."

For the next few games everything went all right, he still playing well, and I was beginning to think maybe people had been a bit hard on him, that he was all right if only you handled him properly. Then things started to go wrong *off* the field. The first thing was that I heard he was going round the clubs, and taking some of the younger players with him. I'd noticed he went about with them mostly, although he was older than they were, in fact I was afraid there might be a bit of a clique forming, and I didn't want that if I could help it. Things like that always show on the field – you can't avoid it.

Anyway, I knew what must be happening. You've always got a bunch of spivs hanging round any big London team, cadging tickets off the players to flog on the black market, and getting a cheap thrill out of being seen in their company. I didn't mind the boys selling their complimentaries over the odds to make a bit on the side, it was what it led to that I was scared of. Most of these characters seem to hang round the shady little clubs in Soho, and before you know where you are they've got the lads going there drinking, then fixing themselves up with women, and that's it.

I didn't do anything about it for the moment, I just kept an eye on what was going on to see how far I thought it would lead. Apart from that, Wilkins was playing well and I'd no complaints about him except that he was a moaner. I've nothing against the Welsh, but it seems to me moaning in a Welsh accent is the worst ruddy moaning of all. Everbody was against him – not only refs. and linesmen and reporters and players on the other side, but even waiters and porters and bus conductors. It was incredible. He came to me before one match and said he didn't want to play. "That referee hates me," he said. I couldn't believe my ears.

"Of course he doesn't bloody well hate you," I said. "A referee's a sort of policeman; he's there to keep order on the field. If you get drunk and disorderly and a copper hauls you inside, you don't say he hates you, do you? He's only doing his job." That didn't put a stop to it, though; not a bit of it.

"I tell you he's got it in for me," he says. "He took my name last season against Burnley. And the next time he's refereeing a game of ours, he comes up to me and he says, 'I've got my eye on you, Wilkins. Do one thing wrong and you're off this bloody field'."

"Well," I said, "did he send you off the field?"

"No," he says, "he didn't," almost as though he was disappointed.

"Well, then," I told him, "you haven't got anything to worry about, have you? I know those kind of referees; their bark's always worse than their bite. All you want to do is kid them along – say, 'Yes sir, I won't give you anything to worry about.' That'll make him feel like a little tin god, and he'll leave you alone for the rest of the game."

That should have convinced him if anything could, but I could see I wasn't getting through. He said something I couldn't properly hear about still being sure the bloke had it in

M*

for him, and I could see we might be in for trouble. I told Gerry Gray to keep an eye on him from centre-half, to be ready to nip in and grab him if anything seemed to be going wrong.

Well, it did. For twenty minutes everything's going like clockwork, the boys playing well, we're a goal up, and I'm up in the stand and I'm laughing. Then the ball comes through to their centre-forward, who looks as if he's standing a yard offside, he bangs it in, and the referee gives them a goal. Well, Wilkins went mad. I tell you I've never known a player like it; talk about Jekyll and bloody Hyde. Off the field you'd think all he ever wanted was to milk the club for everything he could get; on it, it was like he stood to lose a hundred pounds every time he let in a goal. Before Gerry could get hold of him, he'd raced up to this referee, had him by the shoulder, and practically spun him right round. The bloke had his notebook out in a flash, but it didn't have any effect; it looked for a moment as if the boy was so far gone he was going to hit him – which would have meant suspension *sine die*. I was up on my feet and I don't mind admitting it, my heart was in my mouth. Then Gerry got to him just in time, grabbed him round the middle, and pulled him away.

For the rest of that game, every time the ball was in our penalty area I could hardly bear to look. It wasn't so much I was afraid they were going to score – it was what Wilkins would do to the referee if they did. Anyway, everything held up till a minute from full time and then the worst thing happens you'd think it was possible to happen. We gave away a penalty. Their centre-forward's right through, and Gerry brings him down flat on his face. I shut my eyes: I could just imagine what was going to happen. When I opened them again, though, there was Wilkins standing on his goal line, meek as a bloody lamb. Then they take the kick and what does he do but go and save it. I just sat there and I didn't know whether to laugh or to cry. I was sure of one thing, though; if this sort of caper was going to go on, I'd be up the pole before the end of the season.

Maxwell, one of the directors, comes up to me after the match and says, "We've got a good goalkeeper, there, haven't we, Jack? Don't you think he's a good goalkeeper?"

"If you really want to know what I think," I said, "I think he's a bloody madman."

"Oh, I wouldn't say that, Jack," he says, "I wouldn't say that. After all, goalkeepers are supposed to be crazy, aren't they?"

"This one's not crazy," I said, "he's a criminal bloody lunatic." It was no good talking to him, though, or to any of them. As long as a player did his stuff on the field and touched his cap to the directors, he could murder his own grandmother for all they cared.

By this time Jim Mason was fit again, but the way Wilkins had been playing I couldn't have put him out of the team, much though I would have liked to. In fact between you and me I couldn't wait to get him out of the club; it had come around to the point that I was *hoping* he'd have a bad run. He didn't, though; you had to hand him that, he was a good 'keeper. Afraid of nothing, although there was barely eleven stone of him, and much more judgement and knowledge of angles than you'd ever have given him credit for the way he behaved off the field – and on it too, if it came to that.

Still, if he was playing well, the kids he was taking around with him weren't, and it was easy to tell why; they were coming in for training in the morning with great rings round their eyes. With Wilkins you could never tell; he always looked as if he'd been up all night even when we were down at Brighton for special training, playing golf, and getting the sea breeze.

I decided the best way to deal with it was to talk to the lads he was leading astray. There were three of them, and I had them into the office together and gave them a pep talk, nothing severe, more like a father putting his kids on the right path. I told them I knew what they were up to, I knew who was responsible, and it was affecting their play. If it went on I was going to drop both of them that were in the first team and take them off top money – the other one was in the reserves, and I'd dock his pay as well. They all shuffled about a bit, but in the end they said, "All right, Mr Jones," and I let them go.

"Now mind you be good boys," I said, "because if there's any more of this carry on, you'll be the ones who're going to suffer, not me."

The next morning in comes Wilkins and asks for a transfer. I nearly shook hands with him. Anyway I tried to make out like I was worried and I asked him what he wanted a transfer for.

"You're against me," he said, "you think I'm a bad influence."

"If you want the truth," I said, "I think you are."

"You were always against me," he said, "you'd judged me before I'd played one bloody game for this club."

"Now look here," I said, "when you arrived here, I told you that as far as I was concerned, you began with a clean sheet, and I meant it. But I'm not going to have you getting my young players into bad habits."

"Why do I always get blamed?" he said. "Just because we all happened to go along to the same places together."

"I know those places," I said, "and I know these kids only started to go to them after *you* arrived."

"Well, I want you to put me on the list," he says.

Would you believe it, I bring it up at the next board meeting and the directors say no. Mind you, I'd half expected it.

"You can't let him go," Maxwell says, "look at the way he's playing."

Old Radford backs him up as usual, wheezing away in between polishing off the whisky. "The boy's done well. Best buy we've made for seasons."

"Look here, Mr Radford," I said, "you only see him when he's playing. I've got to judge a player by what effect he has on the others, as well, and this bloke's a bad influence on the young players."

"Nonsense, nonsense," he says, "perfectly nice lad. I've spoken to him many a time."

"What do you think he's going to do?" I asked him, "start blinding and cursing in front of you like he does when he's with the other lads? He may be crackers in some ways, but he's not as far gone as that."

"No, no, Jack," Maxwell says, "you judge the boy too harshly, you must give him time to settle down." There were one or two things I'd have liked to say to that, but I didn't say any of them: I just simply pointed out that if ever he got properly settled down, you could say goodbye to club discipline, team spirit, and the whole damn works. It didn't have any effect on them, though. The boy was playing well, and what happened other than that wasn't their worry: it was my job to carry the can and keep everybody happy. I felt like telling them they wanted a psychologist, not just an ordinary manager, or maybe I should have said a prison governor.

So the next day I have him along and I tell him his transfer hasn't been granted. "It's not my fault," I said, "so you needn't blame me," and he said – like I knew he would – "No, I know you don't want me here, you never bleeding did. I'll come back soon and I'll ask again."

"All right," I said, "but you'll get the same answer, you'll see." For a moment I felt like telling him that if he really wanted to get away, the best method was to play a couple of stinkers, but there are limits. Instead of which, of course, he went on playing well, almost as if he was doing it out of spite. We had a cup-tie that week, away to Preston, and it was bound to be a hard one: they'd been playing well at home and scoring a lot of goals.

On form, they should have eaten us, but we got a quick goal, and after that Wilkins practically kept them out on his own – it was the best he'd played for us yet. Old Maxwell came snuffling up to me afterwards, grinning all over his face, and said, "You see how right we were, Jack? We can't transfer him *now*, can we?" What could you say?

Well, we all got on to the London train, we were in the restaurant car feeling, you know, nice and happy and Radford and his hangers-on were putting away the whisky till honestly I'd've thought it would be running out of their ears. All the directors were coming up to Wilkins one after another and saying, "Well played, Don, we've got you to thank," and him just sitting there with a beer in front of him, looking down at the table as though they were telling him off instead of congratulating him, although I did catch him smiling to himself now and again, just a quick one when he thought nobody was looking.

Maybe I should have been keeping an eye on him, because it turned out afterwards he'd gone through more than a dozen bottles. Anyway, about three quarters-of-an-hour later I suddenly hear him shouting, effing this and effing that, and when I turn round I see him arguing with the dining-car attendant. He said later the man insulted him; the boys told me that he just said politely he couldn't bring him any more beer, because the second service was coming up.

I got up from where I was sitting but unfortunately Maxwell was sitting between me and the gangway, and before I could get across, Wilkins had hit the bloke. Gerry and someone else grabbed him before he could do any more, but the waiter had his hands over his face and blood was coming through from his nose and I knew we were in for trouble. That Wilkins was a vicious little bastard when he was drunk, and now he was shouting and carrying on so that everyone in the diner was standing up and looking. I told him to shut his mouth, he'd caused enough trouble already, and he toned it down to just mumbling and grumbling.

The waiter wasn't badly hurt; Joey Thomas, our trainer, mopped him up with some water and a serviette, but the chief attendant was cutting up nasty, "Something will have to be done about this, I'm afraid. The police will have to be told." But when I got a chance I took the bloke who'd been hit aside and said, "Look, you don't want to ruin the boy's career, do you? He's a nice lad" – I'm glad I couldn't see my own face when I said that – "and he doesn't mean any harm. He'd played a marvellous game, and he just overdid the celebration, that's all. If you bring a charge, what good will it do you? If you drop it, the club will see you're all right."

Anyhow, after a while he agreed to take a tenner and then

I had to worry about the Press – thank the Lord there was only one of them eating with us and he was pretty new, so I could scare him a bit – he'd just come on the *Gazette*. "Listen, son," I told him, "you work with me and I work with you. If you forget about this I'll see you don't lose by it; the first good story I've got, I'll come to you. But put a word about this in the paper and you and I are finished, understand? I don't ever want to see you at the ground." I didn't want to talk like that, he seemed a nice enough kid, but what could I do? He hummed and hawed a bit, very upset, then he said that if his paper didn't get it and someone else did, he'd be in trouble.

"I'll see that no one else gets it," I told him – though I was dead worried – "you can rely on me for that," and in the end I managed to talk him round.

Well if it did one thing, all this, it shook the board back on their heels – all four of them. That Monday they called a special meeting about it. Mind you, I knew what was going to come of it before it ever began – they wouldn't let him go after a blinder like he'd played at Preston, so they'd give him another chance, then they'd all go home and congratulate themselves for being so big hearted. Which was exactly what they did.

As for Wilkins himself, he was more worried than anybody. "It's my wife," he kept saying to me, on the Monday – and I could see he must have sweated it out going through Sunday's papers and waiting for Monday's. "I don't care what they do to me but I just don't want my wife to know."

"Well I won't tell her," I said, "and I don't suppose any of the papers are going to mention it now," but I could see he was still worrying. It surprised me, him running round the West End after tarts all week, and then worrying himself stiff about upsetting his wife. I said if he cared about her as much as that, why didn't he change his ways a bit, and he flared up at me, "That hasn't got nothing to bloody well do with it, that's my personal life!"

It seemed to me it had everything to do with it, but I didn't say anything more. I'd met his wife a few times and she seemed a nice enough kid, too good for him; Welsh and dark haired and quite pretty in a plumpish sort of way. I knew he was a bit of a trial to her as well because she said to me one day, "Oh, Mr Jones, you've no idea what I have to put up with at times."

"Well," I said, "we'd better compare notes, because there's times when I think he's going to turn my blinking hair grey."

That waiter business seemed to scare him a bit and we had a little peace for the next couple of weeks. He was still playing well, and we got through the next round of the Cup all right, at home to Liverpool, and I thought things were maybe changing for the better. As far as I could make out, the others weren't going round Soho with him any more, which was something. Most of the older players still didn't like him any better – they didn't like the language he used in front of their wives, for one thing; you couldn't blame them – and I think there was a bit of resentment because he was keeping Jim Mason out of the side: the old Trade Union spirit.

Still, they couldn't complain about the way he was playing – better and better every week – and when Wales played Ireland in Belfast, nobody was surprised when he was picked. It was his first cap for over two years; the Welsh selectors were meant to have said they'd never choose him again after things he was supposed to have done on tour – getting drunk, and something about a maid in a hotel – but they couldn't leave him out on this form.

By this time we were in the semi-final, playing Burnley at Villa Park, and we beat them 3–1. The whole team was playing really well and the defence was showing tremendous confidence, like they knew that playing in front of Wilkins they couldn't very well go wrong. There'd been no more talk of a transfer from him. That Welsh cap had sweetened him, I could tell, and I knew he'd been keeping his eye on the Cup Final, too; not just the honour and that sort of talk, but all the perks, that went with being a finalist. There were no flies on him.

So he was behaving himself for a change and I was just praying it would hold out at least until after Wembley. Wolves were the other team and they'd been made favourites; we didn't mind that because we knew as far as finals were concerned, it meant sweet Fanny Adams. We went down to Brighton again for special training, and the Friday before the match I brought the team up to town – we stayed at a hotel on the North Circular Road. We took a quiet day, just a short work out with the ball, a tactical discussion, then billiards and snooker and a spot of cards. I'd told the lads I wanted them all in bed by ten o'clock, but at ten fifteen Wilkins and the two kids he'd been taking round with him still hadn't turned up, and I was beginning to get worried.

At quarter-to-twelve they still weren't there. I'd phoned their homes, I'd phoned the hospitals and now I was trying to 'phone round to clubs and places they were likely to be. Radford was still with me; he'd come along to have dinner with the team, and when this happened he'd stayed to see how it would turn out: he'd rung up the chairman, too.

Soon after quarter-to-twelve they do roll in, the two boys holding Wilkins up, one on either arm. He was dead drunk, could hardly walk, or talk for that matter, and what you could hear him saying was just cursing and blinding. The boys looked very sheepish, and I could see what had happened – it could wait till after the final, there was no point in upsetting everything now.

"All right," I said, "get him to bed, you two; we'll talk about this is the morning."

I thought Radford would have the sense to leave it alone for now, but he wouldn't – anyway, he'd had one or two himself. He came up to Wilkins, absolutely shaking he was, though don't ask me whether it was with rage or with drink, and he said, "You ought to be ashamed of yourself, the night before the final. You're a disgrace to the club."

Wilkins looked up at him, his eyes sort of slowly rolled round, and he said, "You effing old so-and-so, as if you don't take a bottle of whisky to bed with you every night – and I bet the club has to pay for it, too."

Radford just stood there, he was speechless, and I'd got nothing to say either. I couldn't help thinking there was a lot of truth in what Wilkins had said, I'd been wanting to say something like it myself for years, but he was finished as far as our club was concerned.

I told him so the next morning when he came to see me, very fed up and repentant. "You can do anything in this club and maybe get away with it," I said, "except insult a director. Directors are sacred."

"I didn't mean nothing," he said, "I was blind drunk, I didn't even know what happened till Charles told me. Please, Mr Jones, give me another chance. I want to stay with this club, I'm happy here; I'll go and apologize to Mr Radford."

"You can try if you like," I said, "but it isn't likely to get you very far. I'd steer clear of him for the moment, if I was you." He was just going out of the room very slowly when I thought of something and said, "There's only one thing that can save you, my boy."

"What's that?" he asks.

"Play a blinder in the final this afternoon."

The directors came and had lunch in the hotel, and they talked about nothing else all through the meal. Radford wanted to drop him – now, at the last moment – but the others put their foot down at that, and I'd have walked out myself if they'd ever done anything so crazy. I had my eye on Wilkins. He didn't say much and he hardly ate, and I was afraid of what was going to happen at Wembley.

Anyway, we started well enough. After we'd got through all the bands and the handshakes and the waiting and all that bloody nerve racking twaddle that can lose you a match at Wembley before you've even begun, we settled down nicely and we were a goal up in ten minutes. They rubbed that one off just before half-time – a good one; Wilkins was drawn out of his goal by their left winger, and he didn't have a chance.

At half-time in the dressing-room he looked a bit more cheerful: I told him he wasn't to blame, and said they were to keep on like they were, we had them going.

We'd played forty minutes of the second half without another goal being scored, and it looked a certainty there'd be extra time. That didn't worry me because I knew we were a younger side than they were and the longer it went, the better it was for us. Old Maxwell was babbling away, "We were right to keep Wilkins in, Radford, he's played well, you can't deny he's played well," and old Radford could only mumble at him – he couldn't very well disagree.

Then their right winger crossed a high ball; nothing very dangerous, Wilkins had been eating those up right through the game and besides, their centre-forward was out of position. He came out to his six yard line, he jumped for the ball – and then he must have taken his eye off it, because the next thing you knew it had slipped out of his hands and rolled across the goal and their inside-left had walked it in.

I sat there with my head in my hands and honest to God I felt sick: it was cruel. I could hear Radford saying, "I told you, I told you," then I looked up again and Wilkins was rolling about on the ground holding his face like he was in agony.

He'd never kick another ball for the club, I knew that. The funny thing about it is that in some odd way, I was sorry.

from A BAD STREAK *1961*

PART V

Football Poetry

"But sometimes during the dullest play
Something comes back from an earlier day.
A fleeting moment, a hint of grace
Brings back a feeling, a time, a place. . . ."

GORDON JEFFERY *Men on the Terraces*

The Game

Much of what the poet experiences, through his own individuality, will in one form or another find expression in his work. If these experiences are specifically Welsh, in other words if they belong in a particular way to the Welsh scene, past or present, then a poem though it be written in English has some Welshness about it, however tentative. I happen, for example, to be passionately fond of Association Football. Though I no longer play the game since I've lived in London, on Saturday afternoons, I watch Arsenal or Chelsea or Fulham. I coolly enjoy it, not caring if the home or the away team wins. But if I can watch Cardiff City play then I'm in there with the rest – booing the ref, shouting "Come on the ten men" and if the City loses, I'm the first to yell "We wuz robbed". I enjoy watching Cardiff play with a sort of crazy nationalistic bias. I have similar, though less accentuated, feelings when Wales plays England. So when I came to write a poem about Soccer, naturally I took Ninian Park as the venue of the game – any other ground would be unthinkable – and though the poem, by using multiple puns in the framework of an allegorical device, reaches out to make a universal, abstract statement about Good and Evil, its local, particular, concrete references allow it to be labelled, I think, an Anglo-Welsh poem. (From a B.B.C. Broadcast on Anglo-Welsh poetry.)

Follow the crowds to where the turnstiles click.
The terraces fill. *Hoompa*, blares the brassy band.
Saturday afternoon has come to Ninian Park
and, beyond the goalposts, in the Canton Stand
between black spaces, a hundred matches spark.

Waiting, we recall records, legendary scores:
Fred Keenor, Hardy, in a royal blue shirt.
The very names, sad as the old songs, open doors
before our time where someone else was hurt.
Now, like an injured beast, the great crowd roars.

The coin is spun. Here all is simplified
and we are partisan who cheer the Good,

hiss at passing Evil. Was Lucifer offside?
A wing falls down when cherubs howl for blood.
Demons have agents: the Referee is bribed.

The white ball smacks the crossbar. Satan rose
higher than the others in the smoked brown gloom
to sink on grass in a ballet dancer's pose.
Again, it seems, we hear a familiar tune
not quite identifiable. A distant whistle blows.

Memory of faded games, the discarded years;
talk of Aston Villa, Orient, and the Swans.
Half-time, the band played the same military airs
as when the Bluebirds once were champions.
Round touchlines, the same cripples in their chairs.

Mephistopheles had his joke. The honest team
dribbles ineffectually, no one can be blamed.
Infernal backs tackle, inside forwards scheme,
and if they foul us need we be ashamed?
Heads up! Oh for a Ted Drake, a Dixie Dean.

"Saved" or else, discontents, we are transferred
long decades back, like Faust must pay that fee.
The Night is early. Great phantoms in us stir
as coloured jerseys hover, move diagonally
on the damp turf, and our eidetic visions blur.

God sign our souls! Because the obscure Staff
of Hell rules this world, jugular fans guessed
the result half way through the second half
and those who know the score just seem depressed.
Small boys swarm the field for an autograph.

Silent the Stadium. The crowds have all filed out.
Only the pigeons beneath the roofs remain.
The clean programmes are trampled underfoot,

and natural the dark, appropriate the rain,
whilst, under lampposts, threatening newsboys shout.

DANNIE ABSE

THE LITTLE REFEREE

Serene stands the little Referee,
Round him rage an excited multitude.
They hiss, they howl, they dance with rage.
He is not hurried, he is not even excited; his voice is
neither high nor low.
One man hits another in the stomach;
He orders them both off the field for fighting.
The crowd storm. There is every probability of a rumpus.
"If you throw things at me," he composedly says, "I will
close the ground for a twelvemonth."
And like waves bursting their strength upon a craggy granite
coast, fizzle, and die away into foam, so the crowd is awed
into silence.

ANON. C. 1905

MEN ON THE TERRACES

Rain fell sadly throughout the match;
Two goals were shared, but nobody cared,
Or seemed to care, about the match.
Why did we stay on the terraces,
Watching a game, not worth the name?

Surely there are better places?
More admirable ways of using
Saturday afternoon, than choosing
To watch men playing a game they're paid for?
(Is that what Englishmen were made for?)

But sometimes during the dullest play
Something comes back from an earlier day.

A fleeting moment, a hint of grace,
Brings back a feeling, a time, a place. . . .

We are more than what we seem—
Men on the terraces soaking wet.
   We have glimpsed part of our golden dream,
Our April glory. Together, yet
Private, as the thoughts recall
The hopes and dreams of what we were,
Or wanted to be, in the far-off days.

A forward slips on the rain-soaked ground,
The goalkeeper safely gathers the ball. . . .
Slowly the thoughts of yesteryear
Flicker and fade in the smoke and the haze
Lowering over the football ground.

GORDON JEFFERY

THE AGE OF REFEREES

   There was a chap who couldn't run,
   Whose playing days were long since done;
   And consequently he was free
   To rule the game as referee.

   His vision, it must be confessed,
   Was scarcely of the very best;
   But yet he generally could see
   Enough to take his weekly fee.

   Sometimes the ball was near him, then
   He got mixed up amongst the men;
   But always he preferred to stay
   Where he was farthest from the play.

   'Twas F.A. Cup-ties and the "lines"
   On which he had his chief designs;
   Such matches are a pleasant task,
   They always pay you what you ask.

A referee can't be too old
While he has strength to take the gold;
Perhaps he cannot run or see,
But all the same he'll referee.

J. J. JONES C. 1905

SUR LES SOULIERS DE FOOT

Gros souliers, base de la jeune jambe, cuir de vache à peine dégrossi,

Seule epaisseur sur ce corps qui n'a contact que de légèretés,

Je vous tire du sac en pagaïe où vous dormiez sous la culotte salie:

Sifflets d'arbitre dans l'air coupant, terrain qui claque . . . je tire tout l'hiver.

Entre mes mains, outils de la victoire, vus de si près, un peu diminués,

Inertes, vous qui voliez, frappiez, vivants et sous les ordres de l'esprit,

A la fois durs et enfantins, grands et petits, grands et petits,

Tels lui-meme qui sait bien les larmes à ses yeux bridés de petit condottiere!

Encore poisseux de bonne huile, encore croutés de paquets de terre,

Force fumante avec votre odeur d'algue, votre élégance faite de brutalité,

Avec votre poids, vos écorchures, votre cuivrage, votre mystère,

Vous êtes aussi nobles que cette terre et la vie ne vous a pas quittés.

La cheville vous a fait une rondeur tendue comme l'UMBO du bouclier,

Le coup-de-pied vous a infléchis, vous êtes moulés à un unique exemplaire.

Il me semble, sans le savoir, je reconnaîtrais à qui vous
appartenez.

Ma main sur votre contrefort est pleine de respect et de
douceur.

Je suis pénétré d'une telle émotion que je me sens brûlé
jusqu'au fond du coeur.

HENRI DE MONTHERLANT

Translation

Great boots, tip of the young leg, leather, scarcely blemished,

Sole thickening of this body which is all weightlessness,

I pull you out of the untidy bag where you've been sleeping
beneath muddy shorts:

Referee's whistle in the biting air, pattering soil; I'm pulling
out the whole of winter.

Tools of victory between my hands, a little smaller, seen so
close,

Lifeless, you who were flying, kicking, at the command of the
spirit,

At once tough and childlike, big and small, big and small,

Like him who knows so well the tears which fill his little
warrior-eyes!

Still sticky with good oil, still crusted with chunks of earth,

Strong, smoking smell of seaweed, elegance born of brutality,

With your weight, your scars, your copper hue, the mystery of
you,

You're as noble as this earth, and life has not passed you by.

The ankle has shaped you as round as the UMBO[1] of a shield.

Kicks have made you supple, you've been moulded into a
unique object.

It seems to me that I'd know whom you belonged to, without
being told.

My hand, resting on your blocked-toe, is full of gentle respect,

I'm so full of emotion I feel moved to the bottom of my heart.

[1] Shield-boss.

THE LOST CAPTAIN
(Herbert Chapman, January 6th, 1934)

The last whistle has sounded, the great game is over.
O was ever a field left so silent as this;
The scene a bright hour since, how empty it is;
What desolate splendour the shadows now cover,
The captain has gone. The splendour was his.

He made no farewell, no sign has he given
That for him nevermore shall the big ball roll.
Nor the players he urged on, from his strong heart and soul
Strive again with his skill as they always have striven,
Not again will he hear when the crowd shouts "Goal!"

But somewhere . . . somewhere his spirit will quicken
With victors and vanquished. For now he has cast
In his lot with the Olympians of old who outlast
This human encounter, this football so stricken
That it seemed for a moment to die as he passed.

Who shall challenge his name, who shall challenge the laurel
We hold out to him through the twilight? His love
Was in beauty of action, and clean limbs that move
With the pride of high combat above the mean quarrel.
He led others to share it. And that is enough.

Not yet for those others the Full-Time is blowing,
The ball will roll on, they will cheer with their throats aflame;
They will think how this steel-minded man in his fame
Had dreamed while he worked, a dream ever glowing,
Of the glory of Greece in an English game.

THOMAS MOULT

THE DEATH OF THE REFEREE

A shroud, a shroud for Spring-Heeled Jack,
The only honest referee,
A crowd to keep the devil back
And sing in tune *Abide with Me*.

The pit unlocks its cage of doves
To tumble in the dirty air,
And far below the coffin drives
To meet the council and the mayor.

The barges drag through stiff canals,
Milky with clay and back with coal,
And as the varnished coffin falls
The mayor proclaims the grave no goal.

The colours of the local club
Flower to hide the yellow clay,
And all the foundry hammers throb
Their solace of the working day.

At home the silver trophies burn
About the mourning company,
And wishing she could be alone
The widow pours out cups of tea.

For Jack is dead, the man on springs,
Whose whistle trapped the wildest ball,
Whose portrait done in oils now hangs
For ever in the Civic Hall.

Burly with cataracts, the eyes
Are blind at last to local fame
And friends who fail to recognize
A stranger in the golden frame.

But those who know their loss will make
The winter field his funeral,
And peel their caps to Spring-Heeled Jack
While brass bands play the March in Saul.

PHILIP OAKES

THE REFEREES' OPINION

Two referees, both out of work
(Not that their duty they did shirk),
One afternoon, when it was wet,
Within a warm bar parlour met.
Said one, "It really seems to me
"The lot of a poor referee
"Gets worse and worse with every day."
"Quite true," the other one did say
"The men most fitted for the job
"Refuse to face the angry mob."
"It's very strange," his friend replied,
"To do my best I always tried.
"A man now needs a face of flint,
"A memory stored with every hint
"That in the Handbook finds a place,
"If he would keep up in the race;
"For players have got a thousand tricks,
"All meant to put us in a fix."
"Ah," sighed the first, "the referee
"Almost like mighty Jove should be,
"A thunderbolt in either hand.
"Such men would be in great demand.
"A tithe of Atalanta's speed
"Would suit him very well. Indeed,
"A touch of Hector's warlike power
"Would help him in an evil hour.
"While old Ulysses' silver tongue
"Would aid him well to get along.

"On Mercury's wings if he could fly,
"With loud applause the mob would cry,

"To see a referee on wing
"Would make the wildest ruffian sing."
"Stop there," the other answered quick,
"This really is a bit too thick.
"In mortal shape where can you find
"All these good qualities combined?"
And with their faces filled with gloom
The worthy couple left the room.

WILLIAM PICKFORD C. 1900

BOYHOOD

To some, engines, meccano, scientific experiment:
To some, stamps, flowers, the anatomy of insects:
To some, twisting elbows, torturing, sending to
     undeserved Coventry:
To some, soldiers, Waterloo, and miniature Howitzers:
To some, football
In the sadness of an autumn afternoon
Studs and mud, the memorable dribble,
Rhododendrons at the back of the net
And the steamy dark gathering over bonfires,
The weight of water from the loosened skies.
And fingers too numb to undo laces.

ALAN ROSS

CUP-TIE CROWDS

Moving with these people, one of thousands,
Expectant and excited, devoted as pilgrims,
I think, as we shuffle, joking for joking's sake,
How we might easily be victims
Hoodwinked into some enormous arena, a quicksand

Bearing for each a named stake;
While, round us, laughing, echoed the empty stands.
And how, with the time's irony, our fate
Would be concealed – until too late.

ALAN ROSS

FOOTBALL GROUNDS OF THE RIVIERA

Rock-cut, railway flanked, with sea edging its flat
Surface, Monaco hangs top-heavy over dwarfed white posts:
Casinos and aquariums bulge above the crenellated coast,
Arc-lights strung along the Stadium like cloche hats.
Below, the pitch is smooth as green Casino baize
Whose wheels spin over water pink with haze.
Coated in sunset, the harbour's neat, dark palms,
Like roulette players, keep stiff their salt-drenched arms.

Scrambling over bald, dusty, but flower-scented ground,
Cactus gesticulating, olive-edged, make-shift, and public-
    owned,
Ventimiglia's forwards fan out round Bordighera's goal,
Jerseys striped like fishes in a noisy shoal.
Mountains bisect the sky with rocky signature
And sea-air modifies the players' temperature.
Mauve waves grow taut and spray the piazza pines,
As fishing boats trail their lamps in golden lines.

Menton at home to Nice, the French League leaders,
Sun only a rind squeezed dry of its heat,
And below us the voices of bathers scratch
At the cellophane air, airing ignorance of the match.
The tide recedes, drawing yachts in gentle retreat.
Outlined against mackerel sky, rack-bound readers
Golden indulgent flesh, absorbed in their books' spilled flush:
The insentient frontier hardens, the coastline in ambush.

ALAN ROSS

N

STANLEY MATTHEWS

Not often *con brio,* but *andante, andante*
  horseless, though jockey-like and jaunty
Straddling the touchline, live margin
  not out of the game, nor quite in,
Made by him green and magnetic, stroller
Indifferent as a cat dissembling, rolling
A little as on deck, till the mouse, the ball,
  slides palely to him,
And shyly almost, with deprecatory cough, he is off.

Head of a Perugino, with faint flare
Of the nostrils, as though, Lipizzaner-like,
  he sniffed at the air,
Finding it good beneath him, he draws
Defenders towards him, the ball a bait
They refuse like a poisoned chocolate,
  retreating, till he slows his gait
To a walk, inviting the tackle, inciting it

Till, unrefusable, dangling the ball at the instep
He is charged – and stiffening so slowly
It is barely perceptible, he executes with a squirm
Of the hips, a twist more suggestive than apparent,
  that lazily disdainful move *toreros* term
    a Veronica – it's enough.
Only emptiness following him, pursing some scent
Of his own, he weaves in towards,
  not away from, fresh tacklers,
Who, turning about to gain time, are by him
  harried, pursued not pursuers.

Now gathers speed, nursing the ball as he cruises,
Eyes judging distance, noting the gaps, the spaces
Vital for colleagues to move to, slowing a trace,

As from Vivaldi to Dibdin, pausing,
  and leisurely, leisurely, swings
To the left upright his centre, on hips
His hands, observing the goalkeeper spring,
  heads rising vainly to the ball's curve
Just as it's plucked from them; and dispassionately
Back to his mark he trots, whistling through closed lips.

Trim as a yacht, with similar lightness
  – of keel, of reaction to surface – with salt air
Tanned, this incomparable player, in decline fair
  to look at, nor in decline either,
Improving like wine with age, has come far –
  born to one, a barber, who boxed
Not with such filial magnificence, but well.
"The greatest of all time," *meraviglioso* Matthews –
  Stoke City, Blackpool, and England.
Expressionless enchanter, weaving as on strings
  Conceptual patterns to a private music, heard
Only by him, to whose slowly emerging theme
  He rehearses steps, soloist in compulsions of a dream.

ALAN ROSS

JOHN THOMPSON

The brilliant young Celtic and Scotland goalkeeper was killed after diving at the feet of a Rangers forward during a Celtic v. Rangers match, in 1931.

Hail and Farewell! we say of those
Who come, and pass too soon,
The broken arc, the blasted rose,
The life cut short ere noon.

Hail and farewell to you, Dear John,
More regal than a king,

More graceful than the fleet-limbed fawn,
Your year ends at its spring.

The athlete rare who typified
All that is best in life,
Your brilliant deeds! the death you died!
Our lovely lad from Fife.

The unerring eye, the master touch
More buoyant than the ball!
The fearless heart, the powerful clutch,
The genius praised by all.

The squirrel's swift leap, the falcon's flight
The clear quick-thinking brain:
All these were yours, for our delight
Never, alas! again.

We did not need your death to tell
You were the sportsman true.
We bow to Fate, Hail and Farewell!
We shall remember you.

                                   T. SMITH (of Darvel)

PART VI

Clubs

"There are times when, as a guest in the boardroom of some mighty First League club, I find that the Third Division results are not read out. . . . Then it is that I face the superior smiles or the loud laughs and ask, with my heart in my mouth . . . 'How did Reading get on?' "

JOHN ARLOTT *Reading: A Supporter's Piece*

Preston North End –
The Pioneers of Professionalism

JAMES CATTON

Being bound apprentice as a journalist to the Preston *Herald* in 1875, I had in due time a medley of work, and among it the reporting of matches played by a Rugby football club named the Preston Grasshoppers, with whom I saw such giants of the game as the late A. N. Hornby, W. H. Hunt, who was a fine amateur sculler, and his brother, while among visitors Kewley, of Liverpool, can never be forgotten. . . .

In Preston, too, I got to know the brothers Coward, Christopher, and Fred, who had both played for Lancashire at cricket – although Ken Coward's day was passed, and Fred was then the coach at Stonyhurst College. Still they played for Preston's cricket club at West Cliff – a ground on which I first saw Archie MacLaren, then a boy at Harrow, and Albert Ward, who, I believe, was engaged at Leyland by the late John Stanning, the bleacher, who did so much for Lancashire cricket.

Thus I lived in an atmosphere which developed an inborn love of men's games. In one sense I never was a boy, for I was only interested in what men did. There was another cricket club on the northern side of Preston called the North End – a club which had removed from The Marsh, a wide open green space near the Ribble, to a ground called Deepdale, which was leased from the Corporation.

The members of the North End had their Rugby football frolics in winter, but were influenced by the Association form of the winter game which had been popularized chiefly by old Public School boys at Turton, Eagley, and Bolton, as well as at Darwen and Blackburn.

Among Preston North End's ardent sportsmen were William Sudell, a forward, and a half-back named Harry Cartmell. When I first knew William Sudell he was in a managerial position at the Peel Hall Mill, of which Colonel Goodair was the principal

proprietor. A good-looking, nicely-built, athletic young man
was Sudell, and he was a lieutenant in the Preston Volunteers,
of which Colonel Goodair was the commanding officer.
Everyone knew "Billy" Sudell, the life and spirit of the North
End, and he was persuaded to adopt what is now called the
Soccer code.

One of the most ardent advocates was Harry Cartmell, who
became a school-attendance officer, as these officials were then
called, and another inspiring force was Bethel Robinson, a
quiet, fresh-featured, well-built youngster who was then an
assistant to Mr Henry Hamer, the Town Clerk of Preston.

I had to see Bethel Robinson twice a week about Corporation
business, but the conversation always drifted to Association
football. I was then very dubious about the success of the game
in Preston.

But there was no lingering doubt in the minds of Cartmell
and Robinson. With Sudell, Cartmell, and Robinson, among
many others, Preston North End began to play Soccer.

The change took place in 1881 as the Preston Guild of the
next year was drawing nigh. On March 26, 1881, Blackburn
Rovers, who had as captain Fred Hargreaves, and his brother
John, schoolfellows of mine, and such renowned Scotsmen as
Fergie Suter, Hugh M'Intyre, and James Douglas ("Black
Jimmy"), in their ranks, to say nothing of D. H. Greenwood,
who is still alive, and residing at Buxton, and Jimmy Brown, at
centre-forward, visited Deepdale and played the North End.
The object lesson resulted in sixteen goals for the Rovers and
not one for North End.

But the seed was sown. Preston improved, and within three
years the club had a team whose glory will never fade.

At the *Herald* Office the foreman of the composing room was
one Tom M'Neil, an Edinburgh man, who first crossed the
Border to Bristol before he moved to Preston. He was joined
by his brother "Jock", who, I believe, had played with another
of the family for the Heart of Midlothian. The M'Neils were
strong advocates of getting Scotch footballers from Edinburgh
to work in Preston and play for the North End.

Preston North End had already a centre-forward named Belger, from the Glasgow South-Western club, but in the summer of 1883 Sudell adopted the idea of Tom M'Neil, with the result that one Nicholas John Ross, the captain of the Heart of Midlothian F.C., took the high road running South to England. He did so on July 17, 1883, and found work as a slater with a Mr Bradshaw, at Preston.

Need I say that "Nick" Ross changed from a forward to a back and became the most brilliant back of his day, if not of all time. His teeth were discoloured, almost green near the gums, and he hissed through them as he played. He was the demon back, and the best I ever saw.

This was the beginning of modern football, because although The Wednesday of Sheffield and the Rovers of Blackburn had their Scottish allies who were called amateurs, the North End did not rely on half measures.

They took the pick of the market, got men like swarthy Geordie Drummond and Sandy Robertson from Edinburgh St Bernard, David Russell of Stewarton Cunninghame, who afterwards went on the music-hall stage, and Jack Gordon of Port Glasgow Athletic, a human springbok, who in later days became the manager of a billiard saloon near Glasgow. Others engaged were Jimmy Ross, John Graham, the sturdy quarry-man of Annbank, with his drooping moustache and high fore-head, John Goodall, the tactician of the game in its golden age, and that polished centre, Sam Thomson, of the lint-locks, from Lugar Boswell.

They were joined later by Prestonians such as Fred Dewhurst, who had a post as a master at the Catholic Grammar School, and Robert H. Howarth, who I first remember as a tall, awkward boy astride a high stool in the office of Mr William Blackhurst, well known at the time as a lawyer and a pleader. Mr Howarth also became a solicitor.

The Prestonian players posed as amateurs, but everyone knew they were not. Sudell confessed that elaborate means were taken to hoodwink the Football Association. In January, 1884, the North End and Upton Park met in The Association Cup at

N*

Deepdale, and at the end of two hours the tie was drawn one each. Upton Park protested against Preston's *bona fides*, the charge being that their opponents were professionals. The Lancashire club was expelled from the competition because the indictment was founded on fact and because William Sudell refused to tell lies.

This was the birth of modern professionalism, for the enthusiasm of Harry Cartmell and Bethel Robinson fired the imagination of Billy Sudell, who was induced to go the whole hog. Of course, there was a crisis. The Football Association were irreconcilable at first, and they were met by the solid front of all Lancashire and the formation of a rival body styled the British Football Association.

But William Sudell, honest as the day, in my opinion, and frank to a degree, was eloquent in the crusade for the legalization of professionalism, which was sanctioned after much argument.

The necessity of finding wages each week was the cause of the foundation of The Football League and all that this organization has brought in its train; the whole complex system of the modern game.

William Sudell was the pioneer of a whole professional team and the protagonist in the movement for the legalization of the payment of players. He was above small deceits or any sinful games, and at a time when the late Charles Crump was publicly declaring that professionalism was the first step in the downfall of football Mr Sudell was throwing his whole soul into the agitation for its sanction, as well he might, considering that Preston had eleven men who were declared outlaws by the Scottish Football Association.

I shall never forget the meeting at the Freemasons' Tavern, London, in January, 1885, when the first great debate on the question of the expediency of legalizing professionalism under stringent conditions took place. Major Marindin (afterwards Sir Francis), unmistakably an aristocrat, the President of the Football Association, was in the chair.

No speaker had such a reception as Sudell, who made friends

by admitting that Preston's players were professionals who were honest compared with sham amateurs and disguised amateurs.

I remember Sudell saying that importation of players could be stopped, but payment never. "Gentlemen," said he, "Preston are all professionals, but if you refuse to legalize them they will be amateurs. We shall all be amateurs, and you cannot prove us otherwise."

William Sudell and Richard P. Gregson, of Blackburn, fought on and on until they obtained official status for the paid man.

I can see Sudell with a beautiful tea-rose in his lapel walking the touch-line during 1887 in one of the most dramatic games for The Cup I ever saw played. I respect him for the man I knew him to be, and I can never believe that he forfeited his honesty and self-respect. In disposition he was noble enough to have borne the burden of another man's misdeed. Indeed he was a great gentleman and responsible for the finest football team I ever saw.

The latter-day football enthusiast and even players, are inclined to be sceptical concerning the skill of Preston North End at their zenith. Often is the question asked: "Would the North End be as great in these days?" Their doubts and queries can be forgiven, because modern followers of Soccer have only seen the teams of later years.

It has been my privilege to enjoy the best matches for more than forty years, and so far as I am capable of judging, and as one who lives in the present, I hold that Preston, given the same players in the same condition, would be as powerful as ever. To compare the players of long ago with those now on the green is difficult, and the conclusion, at the most, can only be an opinion.

When Aston Villa won the League championship and the Association Cup in 1896–7 I went to their headquarters, at the Tavistock Hotel, London, the day after they had received The Cup. While I congratulated them I rashly remarked that I could not help feeling sorry that they had deprived Preston

North End of their unique record of having captured both the same honours in 1888-9.

The Villa players naturally objected to this observation. The discussion became heated and even reached the stage of a threat to drop me out of the window into the courtyard.

The prospect, for a moment or two, was not pleasant, but presumably they remembered that there were twelve or thirteen to one – and such a very little one, so small indeed that even "Fanny" Walden smiled when he first met me and said with his soft voice and winning way that it was not often he had the pleasure of gripping the hand of a man on whom he could look down! Clever.

Probably the "Villans" relented and repented when they looked me up and down and considered my miniature proportions in relation to my daring. So they did not pitch me out of the window, but one of them, I think it was John Campbell, the Scotsman and the centre-forward, retorted: "Preston? Ha! Football was in its infancy then. They had no one to beat."

Certainly there were not so many clubs in those days. Therefore, the good players were more concentrated. Yet the teams had a higher average standard of skill even than in 1896-7. I should like to point out that between 1883-4 and 1888-9 Preston won 294 matches, lost thirty-five, drew thirty-seven, scored 1502 goals and forfeited 385 goals.

They could be beaten and they were. Still no club has a record to equal this, and in the season of 1888-9 they were the premiers of the League, which then consisted of only twelve clubs, without the loss of a match, and they carried off the Association Cup, in which they had been defeated for several seasons, without losing a goal.

What manner of men were these who could do such great deeds? Taking the old Prestonians as a whole, they were men of about five feet nine inches, with an average weight of twelve stones, and these figures do not overlook James Ross, who was so often called Ross, junior, to distinguish him from his elder brother, for he was only five feet seven inches, and ten stones ten pounds.

So much for their physique; but every man was a master in his position, and some were so versatile that they could fill more places than one in the hour of need. They studied football with chessmen set out on a billiard table and with diagrams on black-board. Oh, yes, laugh, but theory is good as well as practice.

I remember going into the offices of Huddersfield Town a year or two ago, and in the secretary's room there was a table with a football field carefully and exactly marked out, with the lines and goals neatly painted in white on black oilcloth. I said to Arthur Fairclough, the burly and genial Yorkshireman, who was then secretary: "What's this for?" "Ah," he replied, "this is where the directors play." And a very good answer, too. But blackboard work has it uses, in spite of the hoary retort of the player who, when assimilating theory, said: "What are the other fellows doing?"

These North End men took the lessons of one Dr Gledhill, given in the billiard room of a club at Fulwood, a suburb of the town, and applied them on the field. Every player knew what he had to do – to make the ball do the work.

As John Goodall once said to me, "Every man in the team was master of his craft. What is more, every man was a partner. That made our success.

"We never bothered about who got the goals. They belonged to the side – not to the man. Nobody offered gold watches and grand pianos for goals then. Newspapers did not publish lists of goal-scorers. We had no jealousy. We could generally get goals when we wanted them, and very often when we had a goal or so in hand we left the rest to Jimmy Trainer, the goal-keeper, and the backs."

I liked these words from the veteran who, when we last had a crack by his own fireside, was keeping a bird shop at Watford. John Goodall, the first "Scotsman" who ever played for England, simply because he was born in London, was a man of five feet nine inches and eleven stones seven pounds – and as quiet as an old sheep, but such a player.

I think I saw him in every forward position except outside-left, but he was best at either centre-forward or inside-right. It was no trouble for any man to play with Goodall, as he made the game so easy for his mates. That was to me the principal characteristic of this North End team.

They earned the title of the "Invincibles", but this was because they all seemed to fit – like fingers into a glove, and, as Goodall said, they were all partners.

There used to be some rare struggles between Notts County and Preston. About forty years ago Notts had a team of international strength, and they often played a local eleven of whom eight had won English caps.

There was great desire for a match between Notts and Preston, but the Midlanders were a proud lot. They insisted upon Preston playing first on Trent Bridge ground. What is more, Notts won. The match took place on February 7, 1885, and the game was decided by the aid of a free-kick which Herbert Emmett, a typical Notts man, drove into the goal. This was a last minute victory – by 2–1 – and so dramatic that the heavens were rent with cheering. But it was the only match Notts won against Preston for many years.

On another occasion the North End looked like being beaten. The players heard the voice of "Billy" Sudell: "Now then, boys! Get us a goal or two." There were three in the last ten minutes, and Preston won by 3–2. John Goodall told me that he never saw such play – finer than in any international match.

John Graham was taking part, and he said: "I stood with my mouth open. I could not say a word – so wonderful was the football." And even John Goodall, the most astute of schemers, could not recollect that he ever touched the ball. But he did.

I call to mind some big thrashings that even such a team as Notts County then boasted had to put up with. Notts County were beaten 8–2 and even by 14–0 at Deepdale on November 6, 1886.

The soil of Deepdale was clay and sticky in those days. That was some explanation of the fourteen goals that North End got, but, although a forward, William Gunn, the giant who played for his country at both Soccer and cricket, was compelled to be one of the backs on that day. "Billy" Gunn stood six feet two-and-a-half inches in his socks, and he was terribly handicapped by the state of the turf, especially as he was wearing a new pair of football boots.

The match just indicates what Preston could do. In seventeen games between 1883–4 and 1888–9 Preston made double-figure scores, including 26–0 against Hyde in an Association Cup-tie at Deepdale in 1887, 19–0 against Earlestown Wanderers in 1886, 16–0 against Darwen, then a good club, 10–1 against the best players of Lancashire, 12–1 against Bolton Wanderers, 11–1 against Aston Villa, both in 1886–7, and 16–2 against Strathmore of Dundee, when John Goodall got the first nine goals off the reel!

Of course, "The Cup-tie" with Hyde remains an historical feat, a record. The curious part about it was that no player did the "hat trick", and Charles Bunyan, who was the goalkeeper for Hyde, assured me one day at Brussels that it was a wonder Preston did not get forty goals. That may be, but there came a time when the whole eleven of Hyde were backs. Such are some of the great deeds of Preston.

James Trainer was a wonderful goalkeeper in that he was so consistent. He was an everyday custodian. This tall, well made, quiet man was known as "The Prince of Goalkeepers", and it was unfortunate for him that he was not qualified at the time that Preston won The Cup.

It is sad to think of Trainer's latter days when he was soliciting alms. Any football team which visited London where he was experiencing the seamy side of life, used to expect him as a caller. The team often had to raise a subscription for him, and to my knowledge none was more generous to him than another custodian for Wales, Leigh Richmond Roose – or "Dicky" as this eccentric but clever man was called.

Nick Ross died young from consumption after a sojourn in the Canary Isles. He, like Trainer, never won The Cup medal because he was with Everton during the season that the North End had their one triumph in 1889. "Bob" Holmes, a well-spoken man, became a trainer, but glided into obscurity. The other famous back, R. H. Howarth, a giant of a man and a splendid back, lost his interest in the game when he studied law.

Of the half-backs who spring to mind John Graham, who was not too young when he joined Preston, and was thirty-two when he won the gold medal of the Association, holds me for a moment. Although five feet eight inches he was twelve stones seven pounds and seemed to be made of iron. Anyone who came in contact with this dour Ayrshire man recognized the metal and the mettle of him. No day was too long for him and no match too severe.

A superfine placer of a ball, he will be best remembered as a wing half-back who could throw the ball from touch into the centre of the field. His throws used to make the throng say: "Oh! Did you ever?" Another Scotsman, Hugh Wilson, of Sunderland, was also an adept of this kind, and it was mainly in consequence of the hurling capacity of those men, Graham and Wilson, that the throw-in was introduced as we now know it – with both hands round the ball, and propelled over the head.

Dave Russell was abrupt in speech and a big man who was a rock to bump against. As a centre half-back he was quite acrobatic, bringing high balls down to the grass with a foot in the vicinity of an opponent's ear. Modern referees would have had something to say to him about dangerous play and the honest vigour of his charges. He was a force and a rare schemer.

Sandy Robertson, the other wing half-back, was a painter "to trade", as little "Ginger" Lyon, one of his successors, would say. But Robertson was a delightful personality – so clever, and fair and dainty. He once played through a semi-final tie for the Association Cup with a small bone in the ankle broken and giving much pain. This man, who was playing in the 'eighties, was one of the South African contingent who donned khaki for the European war! Such an act, even at his age, was just what I should have expected of him.

Jack Gordon, the outside-right, lean and sinewy, had long

legs and ran like a stag, but he could centre a ball to a yard when moving at top speed. His partner, James Ross, junr., was as cunning as a monkey, and as accurate with a ball as a professional billiards player. Moreover, he was one of the very best story-tellers I ever heard. On one occasion when he played with a scratch team at Stonyhurst College he kept a room full of reverend fathers convulsed with laughter by his anecdotes and experiences.

Not so clever as Goodall, Sam Thomson, at centre-forward, was an artist, but not so versatile as Geordie Drummond, who was really extraordinary – and quite of a different type to Graham, known as "Safety Valve". Drummond could make a ball do anything he desired, and once he dribbled through all the Corinthians from near the corner-flag to the goal. Orginally a baker's boy in Edinburgh, he was a *gamin,* full of ready wit, and many is the hour of variety entertainment that he and Dave Russell gave on long train journeys.

Russell and Drummond were very fond of boxing, and their sham fights were so real that once, as the Fleetwood steamer touched the quayside at Belfast, one of the constabulary stepped up the gangway to "separate" them. Mr Sudell explained that this was a joke, and offered the officer half a sovereign. This he refused, and walked sheepishly away.

Fred Dewhurst, who was the one Preston amateur, and also member of the Corinthians, was a big, vigorous build of a player and talented, but he had not the science of his colleagues. Being of the Brann, Cotterill, Goodhart type, he could simply walk over his opponents – and did.

Such are impressions of the finest team I ever saw – although Queen's Park in the 'eighties, Sunderland in 1891–2 and 1913, and Aston Villa in 1897, challenge comparison with them.

from WICKETS AND GOALS *1926*

Aston Villa

ROLAND ALLEN

I was born in the West and taken to live in Birmingham before I could walk. By the time I was old enough to begin to take notice Aston Villa and Joseph Chamberlain were the twin gods of that progressive city. Both were famous a long way outside its boundaries. So there may be some prejudice behind my decision that, taken over the many years in which football was part of my job, Aston Villa were my greatest football team of all time.

The opinion could be given strong support by figures, by quoting the number of times they won the Cup that so often jeers, and the Football League championship. My decision is based rather on their approach to football, the many great players who wore their claret and blue jersey and the tradition they created in the game. . . .

If Aston Villa had not, for more than seventy years, stuck tenaciously to the ideals born in a Sunday school class, nurtured and developed by a succession of officials and players, never completely swamped by the modern crazes for figures and quick results, the youngest player in their reserve side would not have had justification for sticking his chest out, whatever story the figures told. There is no direct connexion between the fact that more than a quarter of a century ago I saw a man named Howard Spencer playing at full back for the Villa and the fact that, in the early thirties, they were challenging and being challenged by the mighty modern Arsenal F.C. for the championship of the Football League. The indirect connexion is that Spencer was the outstanding example, within my memory, of what Aston Villa tradition on the football field came to mean.

I shall never forget that neat-looking, scrupulously clean-playing, solid, safe-looking full-back, tackling crisply, confidently, side-tapping the ball into place for the long, low, raking, perfectly placed clearance. How easy he made it look. It seemed that he retained his control over the ball even after it had left his foot to hover, apparently, in the air and land right at the foot of the man for whom it was intended. It resembled the control of a great golfer over a ball with a mashie.

Howard Spencer – who later on became an Aston Villa Director and who was an extremely successful business man – never held a forward by his jersey, or kicked, or tripped, or raised his knee, or stuck his elbows into a forward's ribs. He never screeched out an unintelligible appeal to a referee on the offchance of saving his face by an offside decision. If a forward beat him fairly and squarely – and how few of them ever did – he took his gruel like the sportsman he was.

I do not need a football guide book to recall Spencer and some of the other great footballers I saw playing for Aston Villa. There was tall Jimmy Gibson, the Scottish international half-back, who some people said was the only footballer who knew how to keep the famous Alex James in check. That, of course, is a matter for one of those arguments which fill in the time on the football terraces and never reach a definite conclusion.

There was a huge goalkeeper named William George, an ex-soldier, with agility in contradictory proportion to his size. Another heavyweight was full-back Thomas Smart, an English international who could check from full speed and turn on the area of a sixpence. As his partner on occasions there was pale, rangy-looking, master of quick thought, Fred Miles.

Among half-backs I recall bright-haired Frank Moss and dark-cheeked George Hunter, a writer and a comedian as well as a great footballer. Frank Barson and Christopher Buckley were centre-half-backs of the classic touches who, against the development of centre-half-back tactics, did the whole of the job instead of remaining with the full-backs and waiting for the game to come to them.

Charles Wallace was the outside-right, a neat, compact little man, who stole quietly into the place where he was going to be wanted. Of the inside-forwards, all internationals, there was Clem Stephenson, who came into the side one Saturday afternoon without any preliminary blaring of trumpets, and settled down immediately into the Villa pattern. It was said that a special meeting of the Villa directors was called to decide on the inclusion of Stephenson in the team.

Although the late Mr F. W. Rinder, a life-long member of the Villa directorate, told me many years afterwards that this was not strictly true, the introduction of a new face into the Villa team in those days was a football occasion. And it certainly never came about until a player had been for a long time with the club and without the most careful consideration of whether it was certain that, both in his football and his outlook on the game, he was one of the type who would keep that tradition alive.

There was the devastating Harry Hampton, who often swept himself and the goalkeeper into a tangle in the net, not just slap-dash and helter-skelter, but with that split-second timing which kept such a manoeuvre within the rules. The famous left-wing combination of Joseph Bache and Albert Hall was known on every pitch where football was played. Neither spectators nor players on the other side knew, at times, which was which, or where.

And through the mists of memory I can see a certain William Walker, a whimsical fellow, inside-left for Aston Villa and for England, ambling around the football pitches, looking, oh so deceptively, as if he were dragging his cunning and reluctant feet behind him or as if his football boots were soled and heeled with leaden plates.

As near as does not matter Billy could make a football do parlour tricks, sit up and beg, and follow him if he whistled. The people who played in Villa and England teams with Walker have told me of the incredible speed at which he could do clever things with a football. All of which shows that things are hardly ever what they look like.

When, a few years before the 1939 war, he became Mr William Walker, manager of Sheffield Wednesday F.C., Walker did equally original and startling things. He earned a reputation as a bit of a showman, but at the back of what the scornful old

gentlemen called stunts – footballers training in public, secret
tactical exercises, loudspeakers telling the players where they
were going wrong, refereeing through a microphone from the
broadcast box, soldiers with flags to pack the crowds which
were filling the ground at that stage – was the same sound,
shrewd mind of the man who knew.

Walker played thirteen times for England, for whom it was
no unlucky number, starting in 1921. He had what Birmingham
people would call a "quizzy" look on his face, a look which
denoted, or seemed to denote, that he was a man continually
going on with the search after knowledge, in a game about
which nobody ever got to know it all, though many of them
thought they did.

Then there was Ronald Starling who, in 1933, set everybody
alight in an International trial match at Portsmouth, with
Joseph Hulme, the Arsenal and England outside-right and
Middlesex cricketer, as his partner. They both played for England against Scotland at Hampden Park in the same season.
Nobody who was there will forget the perfect through pass
with which Starling sent George Hunt, the Tottenham centre-
forward who so often had a crowd swaying, to score a goal for
England.

It is possible that some of his unusual and – to me at any rate
– entertaining mannerisms might have distracted attention
from the football efficiency of Starling, who was at that time
nominally the inside-right but actually the roving forward of
the tactically unusual Sheffield Wednesday attack. The reason
he fits into the story of Aston Villa is that he was later on
transferred to that club, where he also fitted in. It is difficult to
assess the quality of a footballer who was, whether intentionally
or by accident I do not know, also a bit of a comedian; but I
think he qualifies to be ranked among the great footballers I
saw.

He had a touch of impudence in his football, especially in his
manner of passing an opponent with the fluttering foot, which
David Jack and Alex James exploited with such telling effect.
Starling gave the impression – as Walker did – of jogging his

way through a game with lead in his boots. A dragging, de-
layed sort of movement, as a crooner sings a shade behind
the time of the band but never fails to end up level with
them.

That is how he looked to me, anyhow. He did his job with a
puckishness which was inclined to make his victims look
foolish. I do not know whether William Walker saw shades of
himself in Starling. I did. That almost perfect balance, the
rolled square pass made with the side of the boot, the slightly
hunched shoulders, the impression of speed achieved without
haste.

Starling played for Durham County as a schoolboy, for a
colliery team, and worked in the Hull City F.C. office while he
developed his football in his spare time. Newcastle United
paid £4,000 for him and sold him to Sheffield Wednesday for
£2,500 when they decided that he should go. This bit-of-a-
mystery footballer was a professional at seventeen and still
getting around in 1944.

Getting back to Aston Villa and Walker, there was an Irish
player who said he never knew what Billy was going to do until
he had done it, and that when you had got up to Clem Stephenson he had gone. I could not give a better idea of these two
great players.

Aston Villa, in the days when I first got to know them, did
not buy their footballers for tens of thousands. That came later.
They used to go out and find them in those bleak, black-
country towns where the houses are crooked and lean over
drunkenly because the ground under them is honeycombed
with coalmines. Towns with curious names. How strange that
in such a grim and grimy environment there should flourish
such football talent.

There was Sam Hardy, the International goalkeeper who
moved unobtrusively to where he knew the shot was going to
be directed. They had Leigh Richmond Roose, another goalkeeper who could dive and tumble like a Chinese acrobat and
did it unnecessarily because, as he once told me, he liked doing
it. These are just a few examples of what Aston Villa tradition

meant. Men and football, character and personality. There were many others I have not mentioned.

That tradition? A Scot named George Ramsey stood and watched members of Aston Villa Wesleyan Chapel playing on Aston Park round about 1874, and from these boys the Aston Villa club was formed. There was that other Scot, William McGregor, who helped in the shaping and the teaching.

In 1880 the club won its first trophy, the Birmingham Cup. In 1886 George Ramsey, captain of Aston Villa, was appointed their first manager at £100 a year. In the same year a new ground at Wellington Road, Perry Barr, was rented at £5 a year and five shillings and threepence was taken at the turn-stiles for the first match there. They first won the English Cup in 1887, when they beat West Bromwich Albion by two goals to none, at Kennington Oval, before a record crowd, up to then, of 20,000.

And so they went on. They grew. Never-to-be-forgotten football names were inscribed on their paid players' roll. No club, at the moment, has won the Cup more often than Aston Villa. In the season which ended in the Spring of 1938 a million and a half spectators paid to see Aston Villa play. At the annual meeting of the club Sir Patrick Hannon, M.P., the President, remarked that he did not suppose that any club which had gone down from the First Division to the Second Division had maintained their popularity with the public to such an extent. But then, they had not all got the Aston Villa tradition.

The club, as they all did, had its ups and downs and its critics. There was almost a major soccer sensation in 1935 when it was noticed that they were advertising for players. They had been spending money lavishly on transfer fees and had found, it might reasonably be assumed, that the modern method did not fit in with the traditions of Aston Villa. They advertised for young men and Frank Barson, their former International centre-half-back, was to take charge of them. They had decided to go back to the old methods, but to broaden the area from which the men would be drawn for training and shaping into their ways.

"We like to get young men and train them into our particular style," said Mr Howard Spencer, who had then given up playing and become a director. "This style is difficult to describe, but we prefer skilful control of the ball, sound defence and above all team work." Aston Villa, in their greatest days, were never a team built around a single star.

"You see," Mr Spencer went on, "Aston Villa never had a coach. The older players teach the younger ones. The older players taught me and experience, I suppose, did the rest." Mr Spencer was modest. It is not teaching or experience which takes players to his standards of greatness. They cannot have it thrust upon them.

from ALL IN THE DAY'S SPORT *1946*

The Tragedy of Torino

VITTORIO POZZO

Tragedies, like the one to which Italian football has fallen victim, leave one dazed. It is difficult to write about them, because writing about them seems an irreverence. Unusually painful to recall them, because the last image of the victims, the one which remains in the retina of the eye, is not one of vigorous and exuberant athletes, but of mangled bodies. Almost impossible to comment on them, because heart, mind, and pen refuse.

None of them can have suffered, judging by the condition in which they were found. The tragedy must have been swift, and death instantaneous, for all of them. A flash, a cruel burst of flame, and it was all over. That priest, who was the sole witness of the disaster and who happened to be on the other side of the solid wall of the church, which remained cold and indifferent under the rain, before so many dead bodies, must have had the impression that a thunderbolt had fallen from the sky. In fact it was the team of Torino, the international team of Italy, which fell from the sky in that terrible moment and distintegrated, dissolved into nothing.

In the buttonhole of a piece of a jacket hanging from a tree stump, up there at Superga, was an international team badge – one of those gold ones, with the new design, which I had still been giving out the previous year, telling them to hold them dear and reverence them, for there were little more than two hundred people in Italy who could wear them. Tenacious was the hold that badge exerted, tenacious unto death, when everything else had gone, blown from the players' bodies, shoes first, then watches, jackets, buttons. Precisely to whom that jacket and that badge belonged, no one knew. To one of the ten players who had worn the blue jersey, and who lay there now, battered to pieces or reduced virtually to pulp.

They made up the finest, strongest team in Italy. A team which had taken years to put together – I knew by heart every detail of the work which had gone towards building it – but which had then given such satisfaction. It had won only four Italian Championships because the war prevented it from winning more. Meanwhile, it had virtually won the fifth. It had had passages of play as shining and resplendent as precious metals. It had won the love and the enthusiasm of the crowds. In its best moments, it had surmounted every obstacle in its way, scoring goals with the facility with which a millionaire gives away thousand lire notes. It had been envied, seduced, at times even spoiled, by popularity, by the ease of its success, by the love of those who wished it too well. It bore a fine name, the name of one of those clubs which, passing through joys and griefs, had succeeded in building Italian football out of nothing, a monument of imposing size and of social significance. In its qualities and defects, in its greatness and weakness, it was the genuine image of every human impulse. Gradually it was losing impetus and polish, now and then refusing to give way, with flashes of play which lit up the horizon. Perhaps it was for this reason – so as not to succumb to the common, fatal law of decay, that it preferred to die suddenly, disappear as though struck by lightning, go out with glory.

Now they are no more, these men who, in such numbers, changed the wine-coloured shirt for the blue. The problem of that square centimetre of groin, belonging to the elegant, precise Maroso, object of so much study by the luminaries of the medical profession, is no more. Gone is the question of the hard work Loik was obliged to do, so that he should not get too fat. Gone – because one of the two parties has gone – is the quarrel over the two marriages of Mazzola. All over: pulled muscles, strains, bonuses, arguments and transfers. All that's left is a team which was the strongest in Italy and which, at one blow, one disaster, has become the weakest; empty, shorn of technical means, a team which, if it wants to complete its Championship matches, must take the field – starting with the first match, against Fiorentina, in Turin itself – with the eleven boys who are the only reserves it has left.

Italy's international side is left, too, mutilated, largely empty of content. Ten of its players had from time to time been drawn from this strong, exuberant Torino; there were still six on the last occasion the "azzurri" were called together. Missing, from this last international team, will be Bacigalupo, the surest and most consistent of our goalkeepers; Ballarin, the full-back whose dedicated life and application had given him international quality; Rigamonti, the born fighter, tough and tenacious as a sentry who refuses to allow his charge to be transgressed; Castigliano, whose class emerged spontaneously during those periods when he kept his body fit; Menti, who improved with the passing of the years; Mazzola who, capricious and effective at the same time, was one of the constructive stalwarts: above all it will miss Maroso, the purest, most classical product of his time, the man who, combining the gifts of a Rosetta and a Caligaris* reached in every way the highest level of Italy's glorious football past.

* Italy's greatest pair of backs, one polished, one robust.

They almost made up a caste, these players who filled our city with their presence and their deeds; a city which looked on them severely when they gave way to caprice, but was always ready to forgive them because it knew their worth, because it wished them well and because it was a little bit proud of them. They should be buried side by side, so that they can remain together in the future as they have lived together, won fame together, and died together. So that they can continue to form a team in the after life, too. So that it will be more natural, simple and human to remember them all, when thinking of the greatest tragedy ever to have stricken football, anywhere in the world, wherever it is played.

from STAMPA SERA *1949*

Reading – A Supporter's Piece

JOHN ARLOTT

It was not until the question was posed to me that I realized that I have watched football in ten countries, and seen the international elevens of six more. I would argue the case for Kubala, Nordahl, and Doye being included in a European eleven, and I probably follow the progress of the major French clubs as closely as I do that of their English counterparts.

This may sound like the claim of a completely cosmopolitan football follower, but do you, I wonder, remember that cosmopolitan in the O. Henry short story? "Just put me down as E. Rushmore Coglan, citizen of the terrestrial sphere," he said, after a conversation which had roamed the world without bias: but he was thrown out of the café for fighting the man who dared to speak slightingly of the water supply of Mattawamkeag, Maine – the cosmopolite's birthplace. Thus, while I am prepared to debate the respective merits of the post-war Scottish as opposed to those of the pre-war Hungarian defence,

I must confess that I do not go home happily from any game –
not even from the Cup Final – until I have heard the result of
Reading's match in the Third Division (South) on the same
day. It may well be – indeed, I passionately hope – that by the
time this book reaches its public, Reading will once more be
members of the Second Division and showing signs of mounting
to the First, but, wherever they are, their progress will still be
my chief footballing interest.

They were a Third Division team when I first saw them,
which was, I fancy, in 1923: I remember that the match was
against Northampton Town, and that is as far as my memory
serves me. Reading, sixteen miles away – in those days a one-
and-sixpenny return railway fare – was the nearest club to my
home, and a friend of my father's took me to the match: I was
nine years old and, as I recall, behaved abominably.

My next match, I can pinpoint exactly: it was played on
2 October, 1926. Reading had just been promoted to the
Second Division – leaving behind them, in the Third, Charlton
Athletic, Brentford, Queen's Park Rangers, Coventry City.
and Luton Town. Their opponents on this particular day were
Portsmouth, who had been promoted from the Third (Southern)
two years earlier and who were, that same season, to win their
way to the First Division. They beat Reading – to my great
hurt – by two goals to one. A penalty awarded to Portsmouth
at a vital moment was taken by Billy Haines – the Portsmouth
crowd used to greet him with "To Be A Farmer's Boy". He
bent down to place the ball, the referee blew his whistle, and
Haines, without even straightening up, toe-ended it into the
corner of the net while the Reading goalkeeper was still
adjusting his cap. I can see that goalkeeper – Duckworth, a
Lancashireman – even now, running indignantly out to the
referee to protest against the goal: but it stood, and Reading
lost.

I remember, too, going after the match, with my autograph
album, to the creosoted wooden hut which then housed the
dressing-rooms at Elm Park before the present stand and offices
were completed just a few weeks later. The first signature in

that book, written in a somewhat laboured, boyish hand, was: "F. Cook" – Portsmouth's Welsh international outside-left. It is fourteen years now since I gave that book to a schoolboy: as I handed it to him, I lifted the cover with my thumb and there it was, all alone on the first page – "F. Cook" – my first autograph.

The bug had bitten. I was lucky: the Reading side of those days, although it never had a really good record during its five seasons in Division II, held some colourful players. Duckworth, in goal, was a stooping, eager player of incredible courage who would go down at the feet of advancing forwards with great daring. My own particular favourite was Billy McConnell, the Irish international left-back. Tall, rosy-faced, fast, utterly fearless and a terrific kicker, he was of the old school of backs. For four years he was a regular choice for Ireland, refusing one cap – against Scotland – to play for his club, when they were in danger of relegation. A broken leg in 1928 ended the career of the man who was one of the deadliest tacklers of his day.

A few weeks ago, travelling in Wales, I bought a local paper, to find announced the death of Dai Evans, who was a Welsh international left-half in Reading's promotion side. Evans was not a consistent player, neither, I now realize, was he particularly conscientious about his training; but he was a polished player who took the game of football with the natural ease with which it came to him. His transfer to Huddersfield, I always felt, coincided with the start of Reading's slide back to the Third Division.

The 1926–7 season at Elm Park, however, held no thought of relegation. The small, quick, fiery Hugh Davey, Ireland's centre-forward, and Frank Richardson, the inside-left, a treasure for a Third Division side – his socks trailing, fair curls flopping over his face – were eager for goals. Behind them, Alf Messer was a centre-half so dominating that, despite the contemporary Seddon, Hill, and Kean, he came close indeed to England honours. If Evans's transfer marked the beginning of the slide, Messer's move to Tottenham completed it. He was the coolest penalty-kicker I ever saw. He always put the ball about a foot inside the right-hand post at a height of about eighteen inches off the ground: I never saw him fail with a penalty. When Messer left, Tommy Meads, Evans's successor, an immense worker and a fine long-shot, went with him to White Hart Lane and the half-back line, backbone of any side, was gone. But, in 1926–7, Reading were not a selling side.

Their ground was about eighteen miles from my home: it was a cycle ride – a hard one, but a cycle ride – and worth it. Eighteen miles there, eighteen miles back. I can still remember every mile of the route and, given the same circumstances, I would cycle it the same twenty times a year again.

What a season that was – 1926–7. At every opportunity I would see football; I would bury my nose in the football papers which were then so numerous. Alas, that the boy football enthusiast of today has no *Athletic News* which used to appear on Monday morning with a full account of every match in the four English Leagues *and* the Scottish First Division, with due attention to the amateurs and the Irish competitions, *plus* special articles as well. *The Topical Times, The Sports Budget, Football Favourite*, their names alone bring back their smell and look and feel.

Season 1926–7: Reading fought two replays against Manchester United before they beat them in the third round of the Cup: even Barson could not stop them: what new triumphs, we wondered, lay ahead of last year's Third League Champions? To be sure, they were perilously near the bottom of the Second Division, but Manchester United were a pillar of the First Division: three matches should be enough to crystallize the difference between any two sides – and Reading won that third match. In the next round, they reversed the League result and beat their old rivals, Portsmouth: then Brentford: then they went to Swansea and won there – and they were in the semi-final. Cardiff beat them – as they beat Arsenal in the Final – but the semi-final was a new conquest for Reading.

Season 1926–7. That was the year when Middlesbrough headed the Second Division and, in the process, set up a new goal-scoring record of 122 goals in a season, while George Camsell, their young centre-forward – he had only made three first-team appearances in the previous season – broke the individual goal-scoring record with fifty-nine goals. The match, as I remember, was rearranged because of Reading's Cup-tie commitments and was played, I fancy – I have no means of checking – on a Tuesday evening, though why it should be a Tuesday, rather than a Wednesday – early closing day in Reading – baffles me. It was an awkward day and time, but, if I could raise tenpence – sixpence admission, twopence for a programme, a penny mineral on the way up and another on the return journey – I would be there. A rush through prep – always a household rule – and there was an hour on my ancient bicycle to cover those hills, along the familiar route. Not one of my friends would come with me, or rather, to do them justice, those who would have done so were stopped by their parents. I was there: I was in. From my reading, I knew this Middlesbrough side off by heart and here, now, in their red jerseys, with the white yokes, were those five goal-happy forwards – Billy Pease, Billy Birrell, George Camsell, Jackie Carr, and Owen Williams – four English internationals in a row and the five of them worth 114 goals that season. But they did not beat Reading; and Camsell did not score. Their only goal came from Billy Birrell. It was a one-all draw when McConnell, way back in his own half, took a huge swing at the ball: it towered high down the middle of the field and dropped towards the Middlesbrough goal: someone went in and shaped to head it, missed, and the ball was in the net – McConnell the scorer of what is still the longest-range goal I have ever seen.

It was a long wait after the game for the autographs but, at length, there they were, complete – and eighteen miles lay ahead. Nor were the autographs my only profit from the match. Camsell was my main interest: he was obviously going to break all goal scoring records that season, and I had gone to that match determined to find out how he was doing it. Five minutes was enough. The offside rule had just been changed to its present form and, with only one man other than the goalkeeper needed between himself and goal when the ball was last played, the centre-forward could lie right up on the deeper of the two backs, with only that one man to race for the through ball and the chance of a goal. As the flow of passes from Birrell and Carr – skilfully varied with long passes to the goal-scoring wingers – came down the middle, Camsell challenged for them: only McConnell's immense speed in recovery and some characteristic Duckworth dives prevented him from scoring.

Until then I had been an indifferent goalkeeper or full-back in school football. Now I had an idea – I was the only boy in the school who had seen the Middlesbrough match, and football styles filter very slowly down to North Hampshire schools. I went to centre-forward. They might call me "poacher", "baby-liner", or anything else they liked: if it was good enough for George Camsell, it was good enough for me. I began to score goals – lots of them. I got into my form team, my house team, the school juniors and then the school team all in a year, and scoring all the time. It was my solitary spell of footballing glory. By the next season it was being done much better by better players, and I retired to full-back and obscurity.

I was now interested not only in Reading's League matches, but in the reserve side too. Ask me the names of some of our international sides in the 'thirties, and I shall be hard put to it to recall them: but about the Reading reserve sides of the same period, I have no hesitation at all.

I remember them coming, those reserve players – signed during the close-season to the accompaniment of flattering biographical notes in the local papers. There was an appearance in the pre-season trial match and then an obscure season in – and out of – the London Combination side, and they were gone.

One day, my father took me to see my great-aunt, who lived at Brimpton: at her house we met a satisfying grand gentleman who turned out to be a director of the Reading Football Club. I was tongue-tied, but it eventually emerged that I was a fervent supporter of the club. Would I care to have a stand ticket for next Saturday's match? As easily said as done: producing a piece of note-paper from his pocket, the director wrote on it an order for me to be provided with two – yes, two, so that I could take a friend – tickets for the stand at Elm Park on Saturday next. I could have wished, I seemed to remember, that the fixture had been something more handsome than that with Kettering in the Southern League, but the stand was the stand. I cannot remember where we sat; my solitary recollection of the game is that a man named Bill Collier, a Scottish international, formerly with Raith Rovers, as I subsequently discovered – played a masterly if not over-strenuous game at right-half for Kettering.

No football season can ever be for me such a season as Reading's in 1926–7. The game came as a new impact: it was gladiatorial: yet perhaps because I was always there so early as to be in the front of the terraces, close to the touchline; or perhaps because of the shy remarks – and replies – over autograph books, it was also intimate. The Second Division of 1926–7 was not without its football greatness. Blackpool were there, with Boy Browell; Manchester City with Jimmy McMullan behind Johnson, and Hicks; Preston had Alex James, Morris, W. T. Roberts; Swansea had Fowler and the unique Lachlan McPherson; Chelsea, Andy Wilson, Miller, and Law; and Jackie Bestall was at Grimsby, yet it was Portsmouth and Middlesbrough who went up.

For that season and all that has come from it, I have something of gratitude in my loyalty to Reading. The loyalty was there then, and an absorbing interest, a fierce anxiety that we should always have our best possible eleven on duty.

One of my great selection anxieties was Bill Johnstone – later to spend several seasons with Arsenal – who, in about 1928, came to Reading from Scotland. I now perceive that he was a skilful positional player, for he was eternally breaking through opposing defences, making or taking so many chances to run clear that he might have broken the goal-scoring record but that his final shots so often missed. Now the great local controversy – Johnstone or Bacon? – broke out. Bacon was a tall man from Derby County, with a shaving-brush tuft of hair growing out from a shallow forehead above a mighty jaw. His

o

chest was like a drum, his thighs hugely tapering, and he had
two shooting feet which he threw at footballs as if with intent to
burst them. It was on April 3rd in the Year of Our Lord one-
thousand-nine-hundred-and-thirty-one – a Good Friday, as I
recall, with Reading's relegation virtually certain – that A.
Bacon, at centre-forward, realized all his dreams. The match was
against Stoke City, at Elm Park, and Bacon proceeded to
score six goals against them; six goals of immense excitement.
He had a habit of hitting the ball well forward on his instep:
not a toe-ender, by any means, but from about the line of
stitching joining the toecap to the instep – a point of impact
only possible to a man of immensely strong legs and ankles.
That day, everything he touched flew at the Stoke goal like a
shell. But for some great saves he must have scored twenty,
and his last goal was scored from an angle of about one degree
to the goal line on the right of the goal and the ball, flying
almost vertically into the goal, as I shall never forget, thrust the
roof of the net high above the crossbar.

If Bacon is the hero of that story, Johnstone had his day in
the 1928–9 Cup competition. In the third round, Reading beat
Tottenham and then they were drawn against Sheffield
Wednesday, who were already strongly established at the top of
the First Division – which they were to head for two consecutive seasons – while Reading were unhappily about the bottom
of the Second Division. Those fast Wednesday forwards bore
down, prompted by Jimmy Seed, who was the inspiration of
the side, and prompted by the great half-back line of Strange,
Leach, and Marsden – all English internationals of the time.
Somehow Reading kept them out: men went down like felled
oaks and they did not score. Then – and the crammed crowd
gasped with disbelief before it cheered – Johnstone scored, and
Reading were in the lead. We went on our knees to Johnstone,
abjectly withdrew every unkind word we had ever uttered
about him and thanked the stars of football that we had him.
Did Reading ever come within shooting distance of the
Wednesday goal again? If they did, I cannot recall it. I was
behind the Reading goal in the second half and the ball seemed

perpetually before my face. Why Wednesday did not score, only heaven and Joe Duckworth could tell you – and I suspect that Duckworth would not be too certain. Once Allen broke through and Duckworth dived forwards a full nine feet to push the ball off his shooting foot. It flew to Hooper, and Duckworth, half-way up from his knees, pushed the winger's shot in the air, caught it as Allen charged him, and miskicked it clear to Seed, whose header he turned over the bar. The penalty-area seemed perpetually full of prone and muddy bodies; and Wednesday did not score.

Then it was Aston Villa – Smart and Mort, Walker, and Dorrell, York, Moss – half a team of English internationals and the claret-and-blue jerseys. Nothing, now, was too great. I remember how it rained. There were ordinary chairs on the grass inside the barriers, so that the purchasers of special tickets could sit near the touchline. So heavy was the rain that the legs of the chairs sank into the mud: small boys were passed over the chair-sitters lest they should be crushed: I was aggrieved at being "not small enough". It was the end of Reading's Cup for that season and there has never been such another for them since.

Reading's manager in those days was a Scot, named Andrew Wylie, who appeared to have a steady supply of players from his native district, for a vast number of Reading's two teams in those days seem to have come from Falkirk or Bo'ness. In one of the pre-season practices – of 1928–9, I fancy – there appeared a left-wing from that area: Hunter inside and Oswald on the wing. Hunter was short, sandy, unhurried and a superb ball-player. In the trial, he twice or thrice leaped into action, beat some three men and cracked the ball into the net like a character from a story-book. Thereafter, he averaged something less than a goal per ten matches until he went to Sheffield United two years later, and thence disappeared, in a season. He was always, however, a masterly dribbler and a natural constructive player. He fed Oswald with perfect passes: perhaps it was a little unfortunate that the winger was so right-footed that, nine times out of ten, he doubled back and centred with his right foot, but that strong inside foot scored him – and Reading – some valuable goals.

Reading has always been a great club for centre-forwards – Davey, Johnstone, Bacon, MacPherson – who once put a free-kick so fiercely over the bar as to send it out of the ground where it smashed the window of a house and the gas-bracket inside – Harston, Billy Lane, Palethorpe, Newton, Gregory, McPhee, and, since the war, Blackman – with Vigar and Chung promising great things from the reserve and "A" teams. If MacPherson and Bacon were the two most colourful, McPhee was probably the most dexterous. One of the best buys the club ever made, he was a steady scorer with his head and either foot over a period of ten years. Palethorpe, however, was the most popular. A local lad from Maidenhead United, he had such a following that it was difficult to say whether the crowd at Elm Park were Palethorpe's supporters or Reading's. He was the centre-forward in the club's great season of 1932–3, when they totalled 103 goals, and only some inexplicable weakness in an individually good defence prevented them from getting back to the Second Division. Tall, dark, good-looking and a cheerful trier, Palethorpe lacked just the extra touch of class: with the two clubs he played for after Reading – Stoke City and Preston North End – he was the vital goal-scorer in their successful promotion bids but, once in the First Division – he went also to Sheffield Wednesday and Aston Villa – he was out of his class. His transfer was one of the saddest moves Reading ever made, for they sacrificed both support and opportunity of promotion by selling him.

Never, perhaps, did a side suffer such a tragedy – although one barely noticed it at the time – as Reading did by the out-break of war. Manager Joe Edelston had at last brought together the side he wanted: cool backs, ball-playing halves, constructively-minded inside-forwards with finishing power. Twice they ran to double figures within ten days and were clear out at the top of the third Division table when war came. That team went on to win war-time honours, but by the coming of peace it was irretrievably shattered and the chance was gone.

Ever since the war, however, they have been around the top of the league, just thwarted, again and again, of promotion, yet year after year in the first four places. Now – in 1951–2 – under Ted Drake, old friend of obscure but happy days in Southampton – with a strong half-back line, Maurice Edelston making goals, Blackman one of the heaviest scorers in the League and some real talent in the reserves, their run of twelve consecutive league wins has given my perpetual hope new justification.

There is, I find, less open emotion in the directors' box and in the dressing-room than there was on the terraces when I was a boy. Yet there are still times when – like Ted Drake – I cannot bear to look, times when I pray for the end twenty minutes from time, lest our one-goal lead should be taken from us. There are times, when, as a guest in the board room of some mighty First League club, I find that the Third Division results are not read out – they stop at the Second Division. Then it is that I face the superior smiles or the loud laughs and ask, with my heart in my mouth, anxious as ever, "How did Reading get on?"

from CONCERNING SOCCER *1950*

Snow on their Boots

BRIAN GLANVILLE

The tour of Britain made by the Moscow Dynamo football club in October and November 1945, served to remind British clubs and players of many of the forgotten arts of the game. It also stirred up enthusiasm, controversy, excitement, and ill-feeling which have still to disappear entirely, with the years. Never before had a Russian football club visited Britain, and never before had the tour of a foreign team aroused such national frenzy. When George Orwell wrote in *Tribune*, "Now that the brief visit of the Dynamo team has come to an end it is possible to say publicly what many thinking people were saying privately before the Dynamos ever arrived. That is, that sport is an unfailing cause of ill-will, and that if such a visit as this had any effect at all on Anglo-Soviet relations, it could only be to make them worse than before", it was hard to deny him. And yet, what football follower would have gone without this tour? It was, without question, historic in football.

It began with a splendid element of mystery; crowds which besieged a London stadium in their eagerness to see the Russians play; a massacre at Cardiff; a cloak and dagger encounter in the fogs of Tottenham; a rugged battle in Glasgow, and then, just when speculation was at its height, the abrupt return of Dynamo to Moscow.

The war had only been over for a few months, when the visit of the Dynamo was announced, and it was immediately responded to with great sympathy and interest. Mingled with these qualities, one suspects, was a strong element of curiosity, sustained by the hoary Russian myth. Communism has not dissipated the mystery in which Russia seems to the English-man to be shrouded; Peter the Great, descending abominably on London, ogling the ladies-in-waiting; Russian soldiers, reported in England with "snow on their boots", and now – a Russian football team.

Before their arrival, Dynamo served the Football Association with a fourteen-point charter. They were a club side, who wished to meet only club sides, one of whom must be Arsenal. Their own referee must have charge of at least one of the games; they would eat all meals in the Soviet Embassy, they would not number their players. . . . The list was formidable, but the Football Association agreed, where later experience might have moved them to echo the words of a French newspaper, years before, on the eve of a match with the London League, "Great God! What is it coming to if every visiting team brings its referee in its baggage?"

The Dynamos arrived by air, and were hospitably conducted to an Army barracks. After a single night, they removed themselves to more comfortable lodgings; the beds, they complained, were hard.

"In England, fatherland of football," wrote the radio commentator who accompanied the party, "we were met according to the English fashion; rather dryly, without flags, music or flowers. Officials of the British Federation coldly shook our hands and then threw us to the journalists to be torn to pieces. Reporters showered the players with questions. But we also have our customs. We do not like to talk in vain, so we decided to keep quiet for the time being. The players were taken to the Guards Barracks to be housed, but we discovered mould on the walls, cobwebs and hard bolsters instead of pillows. We did not like this, and we went to the Soviet Embassy, where we stayed the night."

It was an unfortunate but symptomatic beginning to a tour which at first was haloed in goodwill. There was a second complication when the Football Association would not agree to the Dynamos' request to play their matches on Saturdays, except in the case of Cardiff City, who happened to have a spare date. This was a rather strange decision, since the season was a transitional one in which normal competition, abandoned at the outbreak of war, was still suspended, while the arrangement of a match with Cardiff, then an undistinguished Third Division side, was and proved to be most unwise.

The first of the Russians' matches was to be played against Chelsea at Stamford Bridge, in midweek, and the Dynamos trained at the White City. Journalists watched them, and wondered whether even Cardiff would not be too strong for them. It was another Russian myth, another Colossus stuffed with clouts, another Imperial Army steam-roller that would break down at the first hint of opposition.

"They are not nearly good enough to play our class professional teams," said a Sunday newspaper. "Its players are simply a set of very earnest amateurs. . . . I say this confidently after watching them in training at the White City. In three hours' football with two sides fielded they looked an ordinary lot. Now, it may be argued that they are reserving their real form for the Chelsea match. I won't have that. No set of players is clever enough to hide its form over a period of three hours. There must be a flash of form, but none arrived from these Russians. They have a fairly good idea of passing, but nearly all their work is done standing still. And they are so slow that you can almost hear them think."

For all that, queues began to form outside the Chelsea football ground on the morning of the match. Hour by hour the crowds grew larger and mounted police managed to restrain them, swarming in the dingy roadway, for a time. But the battalion became a division, the division became an army, the police were swept aside and the crowd besieged the ground. They tiptoed precariously along narrow walls, they dropped through glass skylights into the grandstands, and by the time the Dynamos made their appearance, ten minutes before the kick-off, there were eighty-five thousand spectators inside the ground, overflowing on to the touch and goal-lines.

The Dynamos, those earnest amateurs who would shortly be butchered to make an English holiday, wore blue shirts, embroidered on the pocket with a white "D", and shorts of darker blue, considerably longer than those affected by most Continental visitors to England, with a white stripe around the hem. They spent several minutes kicking two footballs about, then returned to the dressing-rooms, whence they re-emerged in company with Chelsea. This time, however, each player was carrying a bouquet of flowers and, when a Royal Marines band had played the respective national anthems, they stepped briskly forward to present them to the Chelsea team.

It was a thing unheard of. Thunderously, the great crowd laughed and then, its amusement gratified, it cheered. For a moment, the Chelsea players stood sheepish and undecided, then they piled the bouquets upon their trainer, who left the field like some walking battle of flowers.

The Chelsea team at this time was quite a strong one, though like every other League club, its players were not in full training. Two of the side, Foss and Winter, had been injured on the previous Saturday, and Chelsea had borrowed Taylor

and Bacuzzi from their neighbours, Fulham, while the attack
was led by Tommy Lawton, who had recently been transferred
from Everton, and was then at the height of his career.

"Chelsea," said the Moscow newspaper, *Izvestia,* "played
with a strengthened team. Determined to beat Dynamo at all
costs, the club had spent thousands of pounds to secure some
of Britain's best footballers. For instance, Chelsea paid
£14,000 for the famous Tommy Lawton, so that he could play
against Dynamo."

The whistle blew and like Dynamos the Dynamos began.
These players had indeed been clever enough to hide their skill,
the flashes of form arrived like flashes of lightning, and the
team supposedly so slow it could be heard to think covered the
field at an exhilarating pace. Moving smoothly, gracefully and
with most deceptive speed, the Russian forwards seemed almost
to glide through the Chelsea defence. A shot from close range
hit a post, another struck Woodley, the Chelsea goalkeeper,
while he punched away a third, for a corner. When Lawton
moved, he was followed by Semichastny, the Russian captain
and centre-half, and a corps of eager helpers.

For twenty minutes the Chelsea defenders reeled, tottered,
but did not fall, then, as so often happens, the forwards broke
away to score. Dynamo took a corner-kick which was cleared
to Bain, the outside-left, Bain dashed down the wing and
crossed the ball, Lawton forced it away from Khomich, the
Dynamo goalkeeper, and flicked it to Goulden, who duly
scored. It was an unmerited lead, yet six minutes later, it was
doubled. Stankevitch, the Moscow left-back, kicked the ball
against Williams, Chelsea's blond inside-right, and it rebounded
into goal.

Dynamo were not perturbed. From first to last their football
remained cogent and incisive, a triumph of socialism over
individualism, for the ball was never held by one man, but
transferred bewilderingly and immediately to another. In
defence, their pattern was conventionally English, Semichastny
"policing" the centre of the field while his full-backs marked
the wings, but the attack, in contrast, was really an attack, not

o*

merely the desperate efforts of three men to chase forlorn opportunities. The inside-forwards, Kartsev and Bobrov, remained well up the field, while Beskov, the centre-forward, frequently dropped behind his colleagues in a manner later to be made distressingly familiar by the Hungarians, Blinkov, and Leonid Solviev, the wing-halves, constantly brought the ball through to their forwards, so that when the Dynamos attacked – as, cheered on by a delighted crowd, they so frequently did – it was with seven men.

When Beskov was fouled in the Chelsea penalty-area, Leonid Soloviev shot wide of the goal from the penalty-kick, deterred, no doubt, by the proximity of the crowd, and buried his face in his hands. Thus, Chelsea retained their lead of two goals until half-time.

It was not until twenty-three minutes from the end that Kartsev scored Dynamo's first goal from inside-right, with a terrific shot which passed Woodley from some thirty yards. Shortly afterwards the same player received the ball from a free-kick, bewildered the Chelsea defence and created the opportunity for Archangelski, the fair-haired outside-right, to drive the ball home by way of a Chelsea leg.

Yet still there was Lawton, a centre-forward endowed with every gift. He lobbed the ball into the Moscow goalmouth, a Dynamo player kicked it high into the air, and Lawton himself, running forward, rose to a remarkable height, to head his team's third goal.

With only a few minutes left for play, Dynamo scored an equalizer which was at once well deserved and blatantly offside. Archangelski centred the ball to Bobrov, standing in a position in which he was at least five yards beyond the Chelsea defenders, and the inside-left beat Woodley with ease. The referee, Lieutenant-Commander Clark, allowed the goal, and justice, in the appearance of the result, was done.

The mystery team had revealed itself, and the result was almost a national furore. It was generally conceded that the Dynamos had deserved to win; with better luck in the first half and better shooting in the second, they would have done so. Now that they had acclimatized themselves, who was there to beat them? British teams were only half-trained, many of their best players still scattered about the world, while the Dynamos, it was rumoured, were really no less than the Russian international team, with the additional advantage of being ice hockey players to a man. In fact, it was unlikely that the Dynamos brought more than one player – Kartsev – who was not a member of the club, but since it has long been customary in Russia and certain other countries to concentrate the leading players in one or two clubs, they may virtually have been a side of international strength.

The Dynamos ate, as they had threatened, at the Soviet Embassy and they spoke very little on the whole; silent young men they seemed, marshalled under the command of the saturnine "Manager Yakushin", a man endowed, it was said, with fabulous skill at ice hockey.

Towering above a pile of blank foolscap, like some figure out of *Darkness At Noon*, Yakushin conducted an inquisition at the Football Association offices, of George Allison, the manager of Arsenal. Where did he live? Where did his players live? What did they eat, what were they paid, and how did they spend their free time? The questions were laboriously put by an interpreter who knew nothing of football, and as Allison answered them, M. Nicolai Latyshev, the referee Dynamo had brought in their baggage, scribbled ceaselessly and silently in a notebook. "It was more like a secret police quiz," wrote Allison, "than a football parley." For three hours he endured it, then, hunger overcoming him at last, he diffidently raised the original purpose of the conference, the arrangements for his club's match with Dynamo, to be told that this was wholly the affair of the Soviet Embassy. It was a triumph for protocol.

Four days after their match with Chelsea, Dynamo appeared at Cardiff. They scored after seven minutes, scored twice more before half-time, and added a further seven in the second half. Most of the goals were flicked delicately into the net from closest range, after movements which had torn the Cardiff defence asunder. Cardiff themselves scored once and missed a penalty, "The Russians," said Cyril Spiers, their manager, a former international goalkeeper, "are the finest team I have ever seen. They are a match for any side in Britain. They are a machine, and not an ordinary football team."

What, then, would happen to Arsenal? Surely the machine would crush them. The names of its component parts were bandied about with the familiarity of a Lawton or a Matthews: "Tiger" Khomich, the stern and crew-cropped goalkeeper, had a page devoted to him in an illustrated magazine; there were Blinkov and Beskov and Bobrov, this last an inside-left with sandy hair, playing only as a reserve, but playing like an angel. The public was fed with the most intimate news of their doings. Each morning a motor coach – a maroon motor coach – called for them at their hotel in Bloomsbury to transport them to the Embassy in Palace Gate, for a nine o'clock breakfast. And what did they eat? "Carbohydrates and proteins," said Manager Yakushin, "they are the most important." Radikorsky, the right-back, occasionally smoked a cigarette; his colleagues were of sterner fibre. Vodka was forbidden during the season, but there was compensation in the shape of gargantuan breakfasts; meat and potatoes, tea and sugar, bread and butter, cheese. How was the ersatz Arsenal team to withstand such well-fed athletes?

George Allison, reflecting on the absence of such players as Hapgood, Male, Lewis, and the Comptons, all stationed abroad with the services, decided that it could not do so – and must accordingly be strengthened. From Germany he summoned his centre-half, Bernard Joy. From the Midlands came an offer to play from Neil Franklin, the England centre-half, and Stanley Matthews, of which Matthews' was accepted. Mortensen, of Blackpool, who was assisting the team as a "guest", was chosen for inside-left, the dreadnought Rooke of Fulham for centre-forward, so that when the eleven was finally chosen, it contained only five Arsenal players.

The Dynamos, insisting that they wished to meet only club elevens, at once protested that they were playing an eleven

representing England, though the side included two Welshmen! Thus, the game was ill-starred from the first.

The morning of the match augured still less happily. It was
a day to confirm the foreign myth of London, a day of thick,
impenetrable fog. The Arsenal players made their way to the
Tottenham Hotspur ground where their club, its own ground
bombed and requisitioned, was playing its home matches, and
gathered sadly in the dressing-rooms; it seemed impossible for
the game to take place. To their surprise, however, the news
was brought to them that M. Nicolai Latyshev, the referee, had
decided it should be played.

A further surprise awaited them when they took the field,
for M. Latyshev, in visibility which did not exceed a few yards,
stood on one touchline and placed his linesmen on the other.
To himself would be left all decisions on incidents in the
penalty-areas.

Once more, the Dynamos made a swift and terrifying start;
almost before the spectators could realize the game had begun,
they had scored. A free kick was awarded to them on their right
flank, for obscure reasons. Quickly the ball was sent to Beskov,
and with equal speed it was in the goal. A mere thirty seconds
had passed.

The game continued, almost invisible from stand and terrace.
"A thousand men lighted a thousand cigarettes," wrote L. V.
Manning, "and it looked like a thousand bonfires." But in the
darkness, the makeshift Arsenal team was fighting bravely;
red shirts appeared, briefly but vigorously, through momentary
gaps in the fog. Rooke scored, Mortensen scored, and Mortensen scored again. Matthews was running at will past Stankevitch, the Russian left-back, and the strange comedy of
shadows was punctuated by the unwontedly shrill pippings of
Latyshev's whistle. Beskov scored a second goal for Dynamo,
and at half-time they were losing by three goals to two.

To the spectators, and probably to the Arsenal players, it
seemed inevitable the game should be abandoned. Visibility
was no better; if anything, it was worse, and the incidence of
goals was noticed only through the cheering of the spectators

immediately behind the goalposts. Meanwhile it was not only the fog that thickened. George Allison was approached by a Russian speaking friend, who claimed to have heard Yakushin talking to Latyshev. The game, Yakushin had ordered, was to go on. If Arsenal retained their lead, it should be abandoned; if Dynamo turned the tables, it should be played to an end.

Brown of Queen's Park Rangers replaced the injured Griffiths in Arsenal's goal, for the second half, and Latyshev put on a white shirt. The Arsenal forwards were frequently being obstructed when they beat their man, but the referee's shrill whistle remained silent then. After six minutes had been played, however, he allowed Serge Soloviev, the Russian outside-left, standing blatantly offside, to make an equalizing goal for Kartsev. A linesman's flag had waved in the fog, the Arsenal defence had stood still, but Mortensen's attempt to draw M. Latyshev's attention to his linesman was in vain.

Racing characteristically through the Russian defence, Mortensen himself was tripped ten yards from goal . . . and the game continued, for Bobrov to score again, from an offside position. "I had the impression," wrote Cliff Bastin, who captained Arsenal from the unusual position of right-half, "that so long as the Dynamos got the ball into the net, even if they carried it there, the referee was going to award them a goal."

Arsenal found it rather more difficult. Rooke, for example, controlled a loose ball, shook off Semichastny, who had promptly jumped on his back, and whipped the ball past Khomich. The referee awarded a free-kick against Arsenal.

At this point, Mr Allison asked the First Secretary of the Russian Embassy to go on to the field with him, to ask Latyshev to stop the play. "We are quite prepared to concede you a victory," he said. The Secretary refused.

Down on the gloomy field, several of the Arsenal players noticed that Dynamo seemed to have an extra man at throws-in. With communication between different areas of the pitch out of the question, it was some time before they discovered that Archangelski had been substituted by Trofimov, but still remained on the field. Indeed, for twenty minutes Dynamo played with twelve men.

The game duly ran its full course, Dynamo winning it by four goals to three. Semichastny afterwards appeared with a black eye which he attributed to Rooke, later withdrawing his accusation and blaming the injury on an accident in the fog. The game was regarded as a farce which should never have been allowed to take place, but Latyshev was given no blame, and its less pleasant implications did not become public and apparent for some time.

Both Bastin and Bernard Joy later expressed their admiration for the Russian forward play, Joy commenting on the way in which Dynamo passed to the open spaces, so that throughout the match he had only two or three actual tackles to make. Bastin was especially impressed by the facility with which the Dynamo inside-forwards placed the ball to their wing-forwards, "inside" the full-backs. There was less enthusiasm about the Russian defence, Matthews describing it as "too stereotyped and easily beaten by forwards who hold the ball".

The Russian view of the match was duly given by Sinyavsky, the team's radio commentator, on his return to Moscow. "Because of the fog," he wrote – in a children's magazine, of all unlikely places – "Dynamo suggested to Allison that the game should be postponed, since we understood that fog was advantageous to Arsenal because it was a frequent occurrence in London. But Allison refused because people had paid for their seats and bets had been placed. After the first Dynamo goal the Arsenal got mad. They always play roughly and here in the fog they fully demonstrated their 'style'. Arsenal used their cleats on the Russians time and again. Rooke, the centre-forward, was especially bad. He was so efficient that the British themselves beat him after the game. Allison was also very valorous. When the English had shot three goals, Allison, with a buttery smile, suggested to Yakushin that they postpone the game. But Yakushin stopped understanding English – even through an interpreter – and the game continued. When the Arsenal goalkeeper took the fourth ball out of the net, Allison fainted. He had bet a large sum on the match and had lost."

Allison protested through the Football Association and the Foreign Office, Sinyavsky lost his job, and the editor of the children's paper which had published the article was also dismissed. So, at least, we were told; when Dynamo returned to England, ten years later, the radio commentator who accompanied them was . . . Sinyavsky, rehabilitated.

From London, on went the Dynamos to Glasgow. The Football Association, meantime, was preparing a last and terrible assault upon them in the shape of an F.A. eleven of English strength.

Ninety thousand spectators at the Ibrox Stadium saw Dynamo make yet another devastating start, against Rangers; a goal, this time, in the second minute, straight from a free-kick, driven home by Kartsev from a full thirty yards. But Rangers' robust methods wore them down, and the result was a draw, 2–2, Young equalizing from a penalty.

The true significance of Dynamos' visit was largely obscured by the controversy it caused and the fact that, being inadequately trained, the British teams they met could be claimed to be playing at a disadvantage. Thus, whereas the speculation should have been: What had the Dynamos showed us that was new? – it centred instead, at least in the columns of the Press, on whether or not they were an "unbeatable" team. Their attack was conceded to be unusually strong, their defence was felt to be much inferior. Some criticized the Dynamo inside-forwards for taking positions so far up the field, thus putting a considerable burden on their defence. These critics maintained that if Moscow Dynamo were to attempt a full British League season, they would wilt, long before it was over.

Such arguments were a strange and ghostly precursor of the criticism made some eight years later of the great post-war Hungarian eleven which emerged in 1950, and their lesson was the same: that the third-back game did not preclude attacking football. British critics, their minds conditioned by years of defensive play – I was certainly among them myself –

judged the Dynamos' football by essentially negative standards, without considering the fact that the team was above all an attacking force. Herbert Chapman told his Arsenal players that if they could prevent their opponents from scoring, they would win at least a point, and that is one way of playing football matches. But another way is to concentrate on scoring so many goals that no matter how often the other side breaches your own defence, you beat them in the end through sheer super-abundance.

Chelsea scored three goals against the Dynamos. Dynamo scored three and might have scored six. England scored three times against Hungary at Wembley, eight years later. Hungary scored six, and might have scored ten. The two teams, Dynamo and Hungary, had many similarities; a powerful stopper centre-half, abetted by a brilliant goalkeeper, with relatively undistinguished full-backs; inside-forwards who stood well up the field, a centre-forward who foraged and wing-halves who frequently attacked.

There was nothing radically new in the Russian forward play, and it is submissible that there is nothing radically new about Hungary's. Each had much in common with that played by the Austrian international team before and even after the war – and there, by pedigree, with the old Scottish football – with the difference that it was considerably faster. The Dynamo forwards were unusually fit and moved with unusual grace, playing football which, as a spectacle, had not been consistently equalled in England for thirty years. Their movements were full of imagination, which justly implies that they were positioned with uncommon skill. The extent to which the British conception of the game had changed can be seen in the opinion of Harris, the Chelsea captain and centre-half, who argued that British footballers were on the whole superior to the Dynamo players, who owed their apparent superiority to the fact that they moved into position better. How a player can pretend to the highest class before he has mastered the art of positional play is bewildering.

Semichastny, the Dynamo captain, broadcast his own views

on the tour over the Soviet radio. One of his first observations exploded the myth that the team had been given weeks of special training in the Caucasus – a favourite and hoary extenuation, after a British team has lost a match – by revealing that the Russian football season had finished on October 14th, after which the cold weather had put an end to training. Semichastny praised British footballers for their ball control, passing, trapping, and heading, which, he said, was "masterly in its precision". He singled out Lawton, Harris, and Williams of Chelsea for their heading skill. British footballers, he added, saved much energy by their excellent ball control.

His observations on British tactics were inaccurate and strangely ingenuous. "The ball," he said, "is usually passed to one of the right forwards. He carries it on for a bit and then passes it to the goalmouth, in accordance with the position that has been established in the penalty-area." It is difficult to surmise how Semichastny reached this odd conclusion.

The backs and half-backs, he continued, played near their own goal, and challenged their opponents just outside or even inside the penalty-area. This, too, was hardly in accordance with observed fact, while the remark that British players constantly moved to one side of the field was still more peculiar. It is probable that Semichastny noticed but failed to understand the British system of "zonal" cover in defence.

He criticized British referees, alleging that they allowed players to be charged in the back, "rarely penalized . . . sharp play in the struggle for the ball", and too frequently abnegated their authority by consulting their linesmen. As for the Scots, they were rougher and physically stronger than the English but – how were the mighty fallen! – inferior to them in ball control.

The last Russian word on the tour was provided by a scurrilous musical comedy, "Nineteen-Nine" – the goals scored by and against the Dynamos – which portrayed the team as incorruptible heroes in a decadent, unfriendly land, resisting the bribes of a Polish émigré. Propaganda was satisfied.

from SOCCER NEMESIS *1955*

The Manchester United Disaster

H. E. BATES

Late on a cold February afternoon of this year I was driving home from London when I suddenly saw, under the first lighted street lamps, one of those blue and yellow news placards that are designed so often to shock you into buying a newspaper you don't particularly want and that, nine times out of ten, you would be just as well off without.

"Manchester United In Air Crash", it said. My immediate reaction was, I confess, a mildly cynical one. The announcement seemed to me to belong to precisely the same category as "Winston Churchill in Car Crash" – the car crash almost invariably turning out to be nothing more than a tender argument between the starting handle of an ancient Austin Seven and the great man's Rolls-Royce somewhere in the region of Parliament Square. I am getting too old, I thought, to be caught by newspaper screamers.

At six o'clock, out of pure curiosity, I turned on my television set. As the news came on, the screen seemed to go black. The normally urbane voice of the announcer seemed to turn into a sledge-hammer. My eyes went deathly cold and I sat listening with a frozen brain to that cruel and shocking list of casualties that was now to give to the despised word Munich an even sadder meaning than it had acquired on a day before the war when a British Prime Minister had come home to London, waving a pitiful piece of paper, and most of us knew that new calamities of war were inevitable.

Roger Byrne, Bill Whelan, Duncan Edwards, Tommy Taylor, David Pegg, Geoff Bent, Mark Jones, Eddie Colman – of Manchester United's flashing young giants hardly one had been out of the cradle at the time of the first Munich disaster. Probably not one of them had kicked a football in that year on the eve of the war when England had sent to Berlin eleven other giants

435

to thrash the team representing Hitler's master-race by six goals to three.

By the time war was over it was inevitable that the heroes of that resounding Berlin victory – men like Tommy Lawton, Raich Carter, Wilf Copping, and Stan Cullis – were on the verge of slipping from the international football scene. A new race of giants had to be found to represent the country that had taught the rest of the world all that was best in the skill and beauty of soccer. And soon, as men like Carter, Drake, Lawton, and Cullis turned their talents to the tutorship of new teams, we began to hear more and more of a man, up in Manchester, who appeared to be dedicated to the apparently revolutionary notion that you can make mature footballers out of boys in their teens.

To me that idea of Matt Busby's never seemed in the least bit extraordinary. There is nothing more true about football than that it is a young man's game. In youth the eyes have a fantastic swiftness, limbs are marvellously supple, with powers of resilience, and recovery unknown later. The clay of young flesh is a beautifully plastic thing that can be trained and shaped under skilled teaching in endless and remarkable ways. Not only in football has the principle of shaping extreme youth proved to be an excellent one. Who, twenty years ago, would have dreamed of swimmers of thirteen and fourteen representing their native countries and breaking world records? Today these things are commonplaces.

Gradually, as the Busby principle of teaching was translated into reality, the names of the top students began to emerge. We began to hear of players representing Manchester United in the First Division at the age of seventeen. Presently we were to see the greatest of all the Busby prodigies, Duncan Edwards, an appealing giant of a boy, representing England at the age of eighteen, striding the Wembley pitch like a mature colossus, gaining the first of his eighteen international caps, under each of which he increased in stature so much that at twenty-one he was not only a veteran but clearly England's future captain.

If I select Duncan Edwards as the most compelling of all the young Manchester men who will now never play football again it is because he always seemed to me the epitome of all that was best in skill and character in the team that became popularly known – and very foolishly I think – as the "Busby Babes". I have always intensely disliked that cheap journalistic label and I have a fancy that most of the players may have done so too. There was certainly nothing of a babe about Edwards. A more mature young man, both in physical strength and artistry, never walked on to that treacherous and difficult turf at Wembley to play for his country.

You could say almost the same of that excellent and cultured back Roger Byrne, who gained thirty-three England caps; of the energetic and enthusiastic Tommy Taylor; and of Pegg, Colman, and Jones, all of whom, like Duncan Edwards, had been schoolboy stars; of Whelan, who also appeared for his native Ireland, and Bent who travelled to Belgrade as a reserve. Footballers, George Bernard Shaw once said, have their brains in their feet, but I have always had a sneaking notion that Matt Busby liked to be sure that his young men had a few brains in their heads too.

But what these young prodigies possessed above all, I think, was class. It is an attribute not easy to define, but when Manchester United were beaten in the 1957 Cup Final by an Aston Villa playing very robust but not very good football, it was also pure class that made them, I think, as admirable in defeat as they had so often been in victory. And when they were again and deservedly beaten in the 1958 Cup Final it was not merely because they were lacking in the necessary arts and skills. The class was not there.

And how could it possibly have been? Its ashes lay irreparably scattered across a German airfield after the cruellest day in English sporting history. Whether the same degree of class will ever be seen again in the United colours it is too early to tell; but one thing is certain. If it never returns it will not be the fault of Matt Busby, the tutor, happily still with us; or of the young men to whom, so very early in life, he taught the beauties of our national game, and who, having acquired fame in youth, set such an adult example before they were so prematurely and tragically taken from the field.

from F.A. YEAR BOOK *1958*

A Phoenix Takes Wing

ROY PERROTT

Manchester United recovered its heart on the floodlit turf at Old Trafford last night, and so, surely, did the packed thousands of supporters who at the final whistle exploded into a near delirium of cheers and upstretched hands.

United were playing again! More than that, a team hastily composed from two survivors of the Munich disaster, two experienced players bought at the last moment, and all the rest youngsters scarcely out of the United's nursery had beaten Sheffield Wednesday in the postponed Cup-tie.

It was a victory that supporters – and people less fervently attached to the club – were hungry for, though doubting its possibility; for one thing it eased the heavy burden of mourning of the last week and led the crowd back to a saner country where it can openly live its football again. A great complex of emotions hung on the game. It was little wonder that, as the triumphant crowd swept homeward, whole families in the sombre little streets round the ground stood on their doorsteps (including sleepless children in their pyjamas, mothers with their hair in curling-pins) asking "Who won? Who scored? What were they like?" over and over again until they were finally convinced that Old Trafford was back in the business it knows so well.

Outside the ground several thousand people waited throughout the game hoping for the slim chance of a ticket from one of the black market operators – even at ten times the face value – and when they could not get one they were apparently satisfied to hang around, looking at their feet and listening to the sound of soccer history.

Before the start the crowd of 60,000 stood in silence for a minute in memory of those who died at Munich. This solemnity dissolved into a roar of welcome when the United team, led by Foulkes, the new captain, ran on to the field. Foulkes and Gregg, the goalkeeper, two survivors of the crash, were warmly cheered for almost everything they did throughout the game. It seemed gallant of them to be there at all and much more than that to play as spiritedly as they did. With the cheers of welcome was mingled a kind of sigh, as though a weight had been lifted.

Soon the crowd was shouting Christian names as though these fledgelings had always been public heroes. "Come on, Dave. Well done, Stan." Many of the crowd, like the players, wore black armbands. They seemed to have a particular enthusiasm. "Have they scored?" said a girl leaning over the fence with a black centre stitched to her supporters' rosette. She buried her face in her hands, afraid to look. "They're doing very well," said her mother more bravely, patting her daughter's arm.

The mood of the crowd changed. It was roughly twenty minutes after the start when the phoenix properly rose out of the ashes and took wing. Until then, supporters seemed to have set their faces in readiness for a defeat with much nobility attached to it.

"What can you expect," said one doleful supporter to a group of cronies before the game, "the lads haven't even had a practice match."

This feeling changed when it was seen, with a certain faint surprise, that the scratch side were by no means being overrun. There was, for instance, the great inspiration of Taylor, until lately the brilliant partner of Matthews at Blackpool and now, in a veteran style that promises everything good for the future commanding the centre of the field like a managing director who has time to spare, and who insists on the utterly correct approach.

Then there was Gregg who, almost deliberately, was more daring and buccaneer in protecting his area than he has ever been. When he leapt high to cut off dangerous centres there was an almost palpable ripple of astonishment and good cheer round the ground.

When at last the opening period of enormous enthusiasm and scrappy play was over and United, under Taylor's brilliant promptings, were sketching out movements of a finesse to match the traditions of the club, the supporters did not seem to have the words ready to appreciate it. "They're playing well, you know. . . ." said one old-timer, leaning over the rails among the schoolboys, wearing his red and white scarf like a fancy dress mask.

He, and many others, kept this slightly astonished attitude even when the United fledgelings had ballooned the Sheffield net with one, two, and three inspiring goals. Two of them were scored by Shay Brennan, who was playing his first game for the club as an outside-left. He was spotted while playing for a Wythenshawe junior side and joined United straight from school.

It was good to see that the Sheffield players were obeying the United chairman's injunction to "play us to win". Then came the final whistle. The crowd moved like a sea under the floodlights, shaking with their own cheers. They will almost have heard them in Munich.

from MANCHESTER GUARDIAN *1958*

"Up the 'Boro' " – *Middlesbrough in the Thirties*

GEORGE SCOTT

My most dominant and persistent fantasies concerned the world of sport. These dreams were nourished by the comics I read and by my father's ambitions for me. When I grew up I was to be one of those modern heroes, a professional footballer in the winter and professional cricketer in the summer. This is a common enough dream of childhood too, I am sure, but I imagine that it received an especial emphasis in that place and at that time. It was to Ayresome Park, the home of the Middlesbrough Football Club, that the workless thousands of the Thirties took their anxieties and miseries and lost them in the magnification of the Saturday Match into something more important than the Slump, Hitler, Mussolini, the Spanish War, or anything that came under the general heading of Politics. Some incomprehensible, invincible, malevolent Unknown Power had ordered that their lives should be mean, harsh, and wholly unromantic. The romance and adventure which others, some few others, might find in their own work, or in books, in the theatre, or in the pursuit of power, the men on the dole found on the fiercely partisan terraces of Ayresome Park. (Where the women found their outlet God only knows.)

There may be some real value for once in quoting figures; they will illustrate the significance of the Saturday Match. The population of Middlesbrough was something like 130,000. The "gate" at Ayresome Park for a "first team" game was anything between thirty and fifty thousand. This included many, of course, from neighbouring areas, but I think it safe to say that upwards of a fifth of the total population of the town, men, women, and children, would pay to watch the Boro' play. Within a radius of a mile or more of the ground it was possible to follow the fortunes of the match, even if one was not there, by the mass cheers or groans that were sent into the air. When the final whistle blew and the thousands poured out of the stadium into the streets and into the special trams waiting for them, it was like water rushing down the drain after the plug had been pulled out of some giant bath. (The scum left behind always included cigarette packets which I scavenged industriously in search of cigarette cards.)

There was no nonsense at Ayresome Park about sportsmanship such as is taught at places like Rugby and Eton and Lord's. No one was interested in worshipping some abstract ideal of Justice or Fair Play, abstractions indeed when the crowds looked at their own lives. They went not to see the "best team win" but to see Middlesbrough win by any methods at all. That football team was their champion against the ugly bully world. The battle was to be fought without quarter and without scruples. The important thing above all else was that the battle should be won.

To aid their champion the Middlesbrough crowd, in their cloth caps and chokers, standing out there on the open terraces of The Bob End, would jeer at the referee for any decision against The Boro', and they kept up their psychological warfare against the opposing team. Perhaps only players who have been subjected to ninety minutes of almost continuous abuse can say just how deeply it bites into them and affects their play. As a very young spectator, sitting beside my father in the grandstand and being tutored in the ways of good sportsmanship by him and by the creator of Harry Wharton and Bob Cherry, I could merely observe with painful pleasure the way in which a visiting footballer was set upon first with boos and jeers, then with more virulent abuse, so that every time he ran for the ball catcalls and a roar of hostility pursued him.

A contemptuous nickname would be given him – something apparently inane, but deeply poisonous when shouted by several thousand voices of hate: "Fancy Pants", "Wonder Boy". The pain became more intense when this savage sarcasm was turned upon one of the Middlesbrough players who was having a bad day. In the way that is not confined to sport, past good service was forgotten; love, loyalty, and respect persisted only while the player was on top of his form. The effect of this mass contempt was most often disastrous. The man would slice his kick, a goalkeeper would fumble the ball every time he tried to gather it; a normally sound, stable temperament would quickly disintegrate and his feet, head, and hands would become those of a neurotic.

The enmity of the Middlesbrough crowd was given complete unity and its greatest power when the visitors to Ayresome Park were Arsenal. This team of remarkable talents represented wealth and privilege. They came from the soft south, from London, from the city of government where, it was imagined, all social evil was plotted and directed against places like Teesside. The Arsenal club could afford to pay large sums in transfer fees to buy the best players. The players themselves enjoyed comforts and amenities such as no other club could afford to provide. They carried themselves with pride and played with a stylistic beauty. They were fine footballers and had a long history of victory.

All these things combined to inflame the hatred of the Middlesbrough crowd and once I saw hundreds of men climb over the barriers, thrust past the police and pour on to the field intending to do injury to the Arsenal team. This was the final explosion of hatred which more often restricted itself to words or at most the throwing of orange peel, cigarette packets, or an occasional bottle. I still remember the spectacle with feelings of fear and horror. This hatred of Arsenal persists, I believe, even now when full employment and large-scale industrial develop-ment have changed Teesside from a wasted and dejected place into one of common prosperity.

But these thoughts come from maturity. As a boy I was aware of these animosities only in so far as my father taught me to spurn such exhibitions of bad sportsmanship as another boy might have been told to regard them as vulgar offences against "good form". (My father, London-born and London-bred, was always biased with no less emphasis but without physical violence in favour of Arsenal, just as he never modified his London accent. I grew up speaking two very different kinds of English—at school and with my friends the short vowels and tight-mouthed sounds of Teesside; at home I slipped back into the open, loose southern tones to which I had been born.)

I had no conception of the possible political or economic roots of these demonstrations and as a boy my own idolatry of the Middlesbrough side was only mildly inhibited by my ambition to be a good sportsman. Beyond all thought, beyond all adult rationalization of the experience, was the boy's intense, instant pleasure in going to Ayresome Park on a Saturday afternoon. It is that pleasure which I can still recall with a vividness that excites me.

The picture must change according to the season, of course, but I think of it now on a crisp, sunny winter's afternoon. My father and I set out from our home at about a quarter to two for a two-thirty kick-off. My father, complete with bowler hat and pipe in mouth, starts off at a good pace. He is a sprightly man in his early fifties. His hair is thinning, but he still has a good head of it. It is greying and so is his short, brisk moustache. He is always very particular about his appearance and trims his moustache with the scissors very regularly. (Incongruously, when he cut his face while shaving he covers the wound with a piece of stamp paper.) He rates physical agility above all else. He knows he is good at his job and is proud of the fact, but he is even more proud of his health which permits him, even at fifty-odd, to kick a football around with his small son and to play cricket for the Wesley Brotherhood team. (I fancy it was the cricket and not the Wesleyan creed that took him occasionally to the Brotherhood services.) Before he goes to bed he can be seen swinging a leg with the support of the banister in the hall at home, zealous in his ambition to keep supple and contemptuous of men who drink their health away.

This is the man with whom I am on the way to The Match at Ayresome Park one winter's afternoon in the nineteen thirties. He with his pipe smoking vigorously, with his shoulders consciously braced back and his slim, black, silver-plated walking stick tapping out the rhythm of his walk. I, a boy of nine or ten, in short trousers, socks falling down all the time, walk and run beside him. I am kicking a tennis ball along with us and my father makes an occasional spurt to collect a pass and return the ball to me with a carefully judged push with the side of his foot. And now I see the bulge of his shoe just below the big toe, a permanent swelling on his foot which he received in the war when a mule kicked him.

We pass the long, impatient queues waiting for admission to the open terraces; we are going to the grandstand. On the brick and corrugated tin sides of this monstrous construction, which looks in silhouette like a giant with a black cavernous mouth agape and a sharp, sloping peaked cap overhanging his face, are pasted bills cajoling us to "Buy British". This slogan I accept and fail completely to comprehend, perhaps as just another of the mystic symbols by which adults and the world in general conduct their lives, shouting such slogans at each other so loudly and so often that soon no one listens any more.

Now we are climbing up the steps into the grandstand. As we reach the top the world opens up before my eyes. The terraces are already thronged, a bobbing, untidy sea of cloth caps with new ones threading in from the gaps at the top. In the Boys' End there is already a fight going on with orange peel and adults below are turning angry heads as the missiles escape their target and fly over the fence into the men. There is the box high up over the back of the Bob End like a tower in a prisoner-of-war camp (though that was not an image I should have thought of then). In this magic box they will receive news of other matches and on the lettered board above they will record the half-time scores of those games. Then there will be murmurs of surprise or gladness or groans as football pool coupons are checked.

And now the Silver Prize Band is assembling in the middle of the field. Two of the men are wearing shabby raincoats over their working suits and only their uniform caps show them to be members of the band. All the others have their full dress on, with its gold braid and the broad stripe down the trousers. Then the first crumps come from the big drum, dull thuds which seem to fill the whole arena and bounce around and back into the field. The brazen, ribald tune of *Colonel Bogey* gets into its stride and very soon the grandstand is quaking to the rhythmic stamp of cold feet.

The straw, which has covered the ground to protect it from snow and ice during the week, has been raked back into a ridge around the touch-line. This side of it, on the black cinder track, in front of the low, white concrete wall over which small boys will later dare to climb only to be harried back, patrol the policemen. The pink programme has been read from cover to cover; I have noted the changes in the teams announced to us by the chalked message on the board wheeled round by an attendant; my father has cleaned out his pipe, filled it again and is puffing contentedly. There is an eruption of noise from behind us as a cluster of supporters for the visiting team, wearing gaudy scarves and well lit up for a day out, swing their rattles and jangle their bells. They are only a small group but they make enough noise with their war-cry to be rewarded by a full-throated response of jeers and boos and "Up The Boro" from the home crowd. Now a Press photographer gets his portion of abuse as he makes his way to a position a yard or two clear of the net just behind the goal line.

Then, at last, there is the first shrill cry from the Boys' End, always the first to catch a glimpse of colour emerging from the tunnel under the grandstand. The teams are coming out. You can tell that it is the visiting team which has come out first as these early cheers are quickly choked to death followed by only a few sporting handclaps from the grandstand – including those of my father and myself, of course, for we are well aware of such fundamental canons of sportsmanship; and another eruption from the visitors behind. Then a much bigger roar with shouts of "Up the Boro' " as the Middlesbrough team in their red shirts with white epaulettes start dribbling out from underneath the grandstand. How I longed in those days to be allowed to penetrate that black, smelly wonderland of dressing-rooms and liniments whence my heroes emerged for battle and whither they returned after conquest (or defeat). As a very small boy I imagined that the players lived down there, just as I thought that county cricketers slept overnight in the pavilion so that they would all be up, ready, and on the spot for the next day's play.

And so to the game itself which I suppose was often something of an anti-climax – inevitably so I feel, for what mortal men could live up to the dream achievements credited to them by young boys. Yet it would have its pinpoints of intense pleasures and its many scratches of excitement, whether of elation or despair. And the small boy would take away with him that peculiar combination of sensations, of sounds and sights and smells which would always be associated for him with football matches. A feeling of lightness, of inebriation almost, in the air; the dull, monochrome mass of faces, swirling and swaying and shimmering like the haze of heat; on the field, a merging and separating and pattern making of individual coloured shapes, assembling and dissolving with the speed and apparent incoherence of those spots of colour which are seen by closed eyes after gazing at a lamp; finally the sound for which there is only the hackneyed image of the crash and sigh of the sea to express it: the sound of the football crowd pouring out in exaggerated form their transient emotions. These are the pictures the boy takes away with him as well as the memory of his own intense absorption, his eyes misted from the hardness of a long stare.

And I remember one man in particular, a man called Camsell who was Middlesbrough's centre-forward for many years. Middlesbrough players always had a reputation of going quickly to seed. It seemed that lads who had been taken from the "nursery" clubs by the slag heaps and the pits had weak heads for success. They swelled too fast for their professional health; careers which seemed bright enough in promise to last for ten or fifteen years blazed and burned out in five. Perhaps it was the way of the town and of the times. Moderation was not a quality which either possessed. Easy popularity, the sudden acquisition of comparatively big money; it is not surprising that heads were quickly turned.

But George Camsell was not one of these. He was of the same stock but of much tougher fibres. I can think of only a couple of other footballers who have worn better than he. One of them is Stanley Matthews, the other a man my father had known in the Army, the great "Warney" Cresswell, a full-back who, even in his bald-headed forties, was an immaculate pleasure to watch. Cresswell showed a shrewd, calm anticipation of tactics, a leisured, long-legged effortless grace of movement, a clean, sure-footed kicking of the ball from a perfectly-balanced posture, and a temperament even and kindly with never that wicked flurry of heat that mars the play and the name of so many famous footballers and especially the young.

Camsell and Cresswell were alike only in their ability to endure while others quickly perished. In other ways they were quite dissimilar. Of Cresswell's background I know nothing, but Camsell I know came from a Durham mining village. He came out of the pit hard and aggressive and ruthless. He was much shorter than Cresswell, built like a bull, compact of power, bustling, belligerent, predatory. Centre-forwards are rarely pretty to watch; probably their last pretensions to grace disappeared when soccer evolved the policeman centre-half whose task was to shadow the opposing centre-forward, hanging over him like a threat, jostling and worrying him out of his delicacies of skill, compelling him to adopt crude force if he were to shake off his jailer and create an opportunity for breaking up the defence and scoring. Whether circumstances made Camsell or whether he was born to the part, he was ideally suited to it.

It is not too fanciful to feel that vicariously his effectively militant behaviour compensated the workless in the crowd for their own helplessness to find and fight that invisible enemy who had downed them. Here there was an object of hostility, clearly defined, familiarly embodied, humanly vulnerable and beatable: the visiting team, the centre-half, the goalkeeper.

Camsell was not unduly scrupulous in his tactics, any more

than his supporters would have been could they have seen *their* enemy. His animosity was of an impersonal, single-minded kind; his ambition, his purpose in life, was to get the ball into the enemy net and any man who got in his way was to be disposed of with as little thought for feelings as a man will spare for the fly which disturbs the pleasure of his food.

Camsell's habit was to wait, facing his own goal, for the ball to be kicked in his direction. As it came he would gather it, still facing his own goal, still shadowed by the opposing centre-half. Then, with a vigorous wriggling of his buttocks and an ungentlemanly mobility of elbows, he would begin his movement round towards the opposition goal, the ball kept closely between his feet, his arms and bottom working hard to throw off his escort. There was no grace about the manoeuvre; it was a legal pushing and shoving and boring until he had edged himself into a position facing his target. Then a spurt and a swerve and a wriggle and he was tearing through the defence to face the goal. It is too painful to dwell on the disappointment if, after all that, he shot over the bar or wide of the post. For this memory match we must imagine that his shooting was as true and as sure as it was at the time when he was breaking goal-scoring records and when he was playing a major part in helping to hoist Middlesbrough from the second division into the highest class of professional football. That was in 1929, before I reached Middlesbrough with my family.

Perhaps I have given an ugly picture of Camsell in action. It is true that he could not be cited as an image of physical beauty in motion. Yet to the soccer enthusiast he had one skilful trick that was always a pleasure to see, something for the connoisseur to remember. I have mentioned how he would face his own goal and gather the ball as it came upfield to him. But I have not described the way in which he gathered it. He would wait for it with his bottom protruding backwards into the attendant centre-half, and his trunk leaning forward, his powerful chest thrust out. As the ball dropped he would trap it with his right foot and in the same instant his turn towards the enemy goal had begun, a movement so swiftly and

P

smoothly performed that all but the most experienced centre-halves, those most intelligent in anticipation and most agile in transferring the weight of their bodies from one foot to another, were left looking gauche with splayed legs and leaden feet, like callow youths whose mouths are left agape when a lively girl slips out of their clumsy embrace and stuns their dull minds with a flash of humour.

The most fashionable argument against professional soccer is, of course, that it reduces some millions to passivity in watching the few who are playing. But that is an argument that may be advanced against any sport; it is hard to see why soccer should be especially condemned because it is more popular than other games. Yet even granting that most inappropriate word "passive" to describe the behaviour of the spectators at the Saturday Match, this comparative passivity was but a moment's pause in the very active pleasures of my boyhood. Even within minutes of returning home from the match, I would persuade a willing father into the tiny kitchen. We would make a football out of newspapers screwed up and tied with string. Then I would tear off the label sealing a packet of tea and stick this on to the breast of my jersey as a team crest. After that we began our "match" in a playing field whose dimensions were about six feet by four feet six, the door to the hall being the goal at one end, the door to the scullery the goal at the other. The sink, the china cupboard, the kitchen table, were natural hazards to play. An occasional broken cup was the price of admission. Ball control was of a very unrefined nature and a sly tap on the shin more effective than a body-swerve. The game ended either with final impatience with the number of times the ball had to be remade and tied up again or with my mother and sister coming home from shopping or a visit to the cinema, expressing their ritual astonishment at the "barmy" males of the household.

from TIME AND PLACE *1956*

Cock-a-Double-Do

A. J. AYER

It has been done at last. For the first time in this century a single
team has won "the double" – both the Football League
Championship and the F.A. Cup. Arsenal came near it in the
thirties; Manchester United looked almost certain to achieve
it four seasons ago; Wolverhampton Wanderers, who won the
cup last year, were within a point of heading the league. Last
Saturday Tottenham Hotspur brought it off. They had already
won the league championship with a total of points which
equalled the record set up by Arsenal thirty years ago; they
had achieved the record number of wins in the League, including
a record run of eleven matches at the opening of the season;
their performance in away matches had given them yet another
record. By defeating Burnley in the semi-final they had
eliminated their most dangerous rivals for the cup. Leicester
City whom they had to meet in the final were quite a formidable
team. In league matches, though the Spurs had beaten them at
Leicester, they had lost to them at home; in fact, Leicester were
the first team to win at Tottenham this season. Nevertheless,
the experts almost unanimously picked the Spurs to win.

The experts were right. The Spurs did win by two goals to
nothing, but though a famous it was not a magnificent victory.
On the day, as one of the Leicester players said a little sourly
after the match, the Spurs were not "super". There have been
many occasions this season when the Tottenham cock has had
better reason to crow. They were not noticeably nervous, but
they did seem rather jaded. The strain of living up to their
reputation throughout the long league programme had taken
its toll of them. Blanchflower, their right-half and captain, who
more than anyone has been responsible for the team's success,
looked a little tired; Mackay, the other wing-half, lacked
something of his usual drive; the inside-forwards, White and
Allen, were both a little out of touch. In fact, the Spurs owed

their victory mainly to what some critics had thought to be their only possible weakness, their defence. In particular, their left-back, Henry, played a superb game. On this form, he deserves to play for England; it can only be the reluctance of the England selectors to disturb a winning team that keeps him out of the World Cup.

The Spurs lost the championship last season, when they seemed to have it won, because their mid-field play was let down by their finishing; they made the openings but failed to score the goals. This is an old fault of theirs, which even in this triumphant season has occasionally cost them matches that they could have won. For a long time on Saturday it looked as if this were again going to be their downfall. One wondered if a goal would ever come. White missed an easy chance in the opening minutes; just before half-time Jones had what seemed to be a good goal disallowed for off-side; Allen and Dyson missed open goals in the second half. It was not until the last quarter of the game that Smith, the centre-forward, beat a Leicester defender skilfully on the turn and scored with a shot which the goalkeeper had no chance to save. This goal was decisive. The Spurs belatedly took charge of the game, and it was no surprise when the left-winger, Dyson, headed a second goal to make their victory complete.

The greatest fear of the Spurs' supporters before the game had been that an injury at Wembley would rob their team of the double; as it did Manchester United four years ago. In the event, the game was marred by injury, but by an injury to one of the Leicester players. After less than twenty minutes, the Leicester right-back, Chalmers, hurt his leg in a tackle; he stayed bravely on the field, but was only a passenger at outside-left. For more than three-quarters of the game the Leicester side was practically reduced to ten men. Under this handicap, they played extremely well. Banks in goal, McLintock, the right-half who took Chalmers' place at back, and King, the centre-half were outstanding; but the whole defence was resolute, and the forwards often threatened to break through, especially in the opening period of the second half. Leicester are not a conspicuously artistic side, but they are strong and fit and thrustful, in the tradition of midland English football. If, as is probable, they deputize for the Spurs in the European Cup-Winners' Cup next season, since the Spurs as League champions will be competing in the European Cup, and can hardly manage both, they should do very well.

It is idle to speculate what would have happened if Chalmers had not been injured. What can be said is that it is intolerable that the Cup Final should be vitiated year after year by injuries of this kind. This is surely an occasion on which it should be allowable to introduce substitutes, as it already is in many international matches, at least up to half time. There would have to be safeguards to prevent abuses, but they should not be very hard to devise.

How good is this Spurs side? Are they the team of the century, in merit as well as in achievement? By the very highest standards, they are not a team of stars. Blanchflower is a very great player, at his zenith the best wing-half that I have ever seen, but he is nearing the end of his career. Of the others only Jones, a wing-forward with the speed and swerve of a rugby three-quarter, could clearly command a place in a current world eleven. Of course they have good players besides these. Norman is a dominating centre-half. Mackay can play like a tornado. Though White is erratic, his intelligent play at inside-forward has won the team many of its matches; he has the positional sense of a great player. Smith, who is now the England centre-forward, has played better this year than he ever has before. He is a clumsy-looking footballer, and there are periods when nothing will go right for him, but he has more skill than one might think and he rises splendidly to an occasion. In the semi-final as well as in the final of the Cup, and in the critical league match with Sheffield Wednesday, which settled the championship for the Spurs, it was his well-taken goals that turned the scale.

Nevertheless, it is not so much to the individual merits of the players as to their team work that the Spurs owe their extraordinary success. They have kept very nearly the same side for two seasons, and they have in this season been very little disturbed by injuries. The result is that they have achieved a remarkable understanding. In their use of the open space, they resemble the famous Spurs team which won the league championship ten years ago. But whereas the 1950 eleven relied, under Arthur Rowe's management, exclusively on "push and run", a style which is very beautiful to watch when it is successful but one which makes very heavy demands upon the players' energy, the present team has been able to blend this "continental" style with the English long-passing method. One of their most considerable achievements has been their ability to pace a game, to conserve their energy between bouts of pressure: it has repeatedly brought them goals in quick succession. For this they owe much to their manager, Bill Nicholson, who was himself a member of the 1950 team, but still more, I think, to their captain, Danny Blanchflower, whose control of them on the field has always been intelligent and sure. At their best, I think they have been superior to any English team since the war, though the Manchester United side, which was broken by the Munich air crash, ran them very close. I am not sure that they are better than the great Arsenal sides of the thirties, though it is perhaps in their favour that the game is probably played nowadays at a faster pace.

How will they fare next season in the European Cup? A fast, hard-tackling side like some of the West German teams might throw them out of their rhythm. Against a team of artists like Real Madrid, their own artistry should flourish. I cannot wager that they will beat Real Madrid; but if at any stage they are drawn against them, it should be a wonderful game to watch.

from NEW STATESMAN *12/5/61*

PART VII

They were tough in those days!

"When the author of these lines is lying on his death-bed, remembering his life, perhaps he will recall a pass in a football match, and all the confidence of his team-mate that it implied . . . but certainly, beyond all doubt, he will not ask himself why the Midi has never produced any poets."

HENRI DE MONTHERLANT *Paysage des Olympiques*

Turning Professional

JIMMY HOGAN

It was during my boyhood days that I learned how to kick and control a ball, but I have been informed that I was a lovely and accurate passer of a ball. That is not for me to say, but one thing is certain – I was extremely lucky when my parents decided to take me away from an elementary school at Burnley, in order to continue my education at St Bede's College, Manchester. I had the time of my life at St Bede's: especially on those wonderful playing pitches at Whalley Range.

Dad's idea was for me to study for the Church, but I always had other notions. Football was my life blood.

I was considered to be quite a clever lad, but I did not study hard in the classrooms, though I held a respectable position in my form. This was due no doubt to "cramming" for a few weeks before the exams took place. Still my mind was always on football, studying ideas and movements, etc.

At the beginning, my place was inside-right in the second eleven. There were some really good footballers at St Bede's in those days: they came from Manchester, Bolton, Blackburn, Preston, Liverpool, and other Lancashire towns. Competition was keen – and it took me some time to gain my "cap" and be promoted to the premier eleven.

I well remember my first game, against our local rivals, Hulem Grammar School. It was a grand struggle and I scored our winning goal from a penalty-kick just before the end of the game. I was chaired off the field and hailed as a hero by my fellow students.

On another occasion, when playing against The Independent College (we called it the "Jam Factory" because it was founded by the jam manufacturers, Hartleys of Aintree), I was opposed by a grand all-round sportsman at left-half. The latter was known to us as "Buffalo Bill", a name we gave to him on account of his wild action when bowling at cricket. I showed poor "Bill" my studs on many occasions that day, but he never gave up trying.

After the game "Bill" asked me what I was studying for – and I informed him that Dad wanted me to go into the Church. With a merry twinkle in his eye, he remarked, "One day I think I shall have the pleasure of seeing you as a professional football player".

He was not far wrong. Some years later, when I played quite a good game for Burnley against Manchester City, at the old Hyde Road ground, "Bill" – in clericals – came to the dressing-room door after the match to be the first man to congratulate me. Happy days for me to be sure.

I merely mention these incidents, not in a boastful way, but to prove that I was always a keen student of the game, which I have taught to thousands of players in many lands.

I eventually became captain of St Bede's College; then just before my seventeenth birthday I decided – against my parents' wishes – to seek fresh fields and pastures new. I left the college and became articled to an accountant at Burnley. My salary was a modest one. I played amateur football with my church team, St Mary's, and was quickly "spotted" by Burnley Belvedere F.C.

The latter were members of the Lancashire Amateur League, which was a very strong combination in those days, with teams from Liverpool, Manchester, Southport, and Blackburn.

Very often I had to obtain leave of absence from my accountant "boss" on Saturday afternoon, in order to travel. This became so frequent that my employer asked me what I intended to be in the long run.

My pocket money in those days was the large amount of a shilling per week. Belvedere paid my travelling expenses and team money, which was perfectly legitimate; but I was really a poor lad, playing along with the sons of rich cotton manufacturers.

I stuck to it for one successful season with Belvedere, then Nelson F.C., my home town team, came along and offered to give me a trial in professional football . . . or perhaps I should say "in semi-professional football".

I played this trial game against Blackburn Rovers reserves at Seedhill, Nelson, and I well remember the day. About twenty of my very faithful "fans" accompanied me and strongly advised me not to sign professional forms for Nelson. They stated that the big clubs such as Burnley, Aston Villa, Sunderland, and Everton would be on my trail. Unfortunately, none of these clubs had shown any desire to give me a chance.

Every player knows when he has had a good game, and I know in my heart that I showed ability that day. We won 1–0, and I scored what I always considered to be my best goal in football. After the game my pals clustered around me and begged me not to sign professional forms.

In the dressing-room I was approached by a committeeman who politely informed me that I was wanted in the Committee Room.

I duly presented myself and was addressed by the Chairman in the following manner – "You are a very promising lad, but you are not there yet by a long way." I replied that I was fully aware of that. "Still," said he, "we are prepared to sign you on professional forms."

I replied, "On what terms?" The Chairman responded, "Top money, five shillings a week." I said, "That isn't much, is it?" A puzzled look came over the Chairman's face as he bellowed, "What! Not much! There are only two members of the team getting five bob, t'others are on half a dollar a match."

Incidentally, this signing of professionals in those days at "so much" per match was a real scandal. If a lad had a bad game he was "dropped" and in some cases never given another chance. In other words he had become a professional player without pay!

Anyway, to cut a long story short – seeing that my pocket money was so limited – I attached my signature to the forms and became a professional player.

I was in for a bad time when I got home and informed my father what I had done. He was absolutely disgusted – and didn't speak to me for a whole fortnight. But, it had to be, I knew I was made for the game.

Of course, when I discussed matters with my employer, the accountant, he said, "Do you really intend to be a professional footballer or an accountant?" When I informed him of my desires he gave me the "sack"!

At the end of my first season with Nelson I was offered ten shillings per week, but I demanded the sum of 12s. 6d. As we could not agree on terms I went to Rochdale F.C. – the very first season of soccer in Gracie Fields' home town – at a salary of fifteen shillings a week, and they made me captain.

from SPORT EXPRESS *1954*

Follow that Man

JIMMY HOGAN

As a reward for winning the Second Division Championship and gaining promotion in 1908–9 – my first season with Bolton Wanderers – we went on a fortnight's tour of Holland. I should like to lay stress on this in order to prove to my readers what wonderful improvement has been made in Continental football since those days: Bolton won all of their games on this occasion by a margin of at least six goals.

In fact, at Dordrecht, we scored ten goals, despite the fact that our opponents had borrowed the Dutch international goalkeeper to strengthen their side.

This tour was a real "cake walk" for the "Trotters". I saw Continental football grow from a weakling into a very strong man.

I think it was in season 1910–11 that I "fell out" with Bolton. It was then that J. T. Howcroft, the famous League referee, offered me the opportunity of a coaching engagement with F.C. Dordrecht. I duly accepted and left England for Holland.

As you can well imagine, Dutch football at the time was very primitive – and I had many funny experiences. The players were all amateurs, and there were many university men among them. They certainly enjoyed their football, but they were also fond of the pleasures of life, such as smoking and drinking. This I had to curtail from the outset.

Still, I remember that on one occasion I had given my centre-half instructions to mark the centre-forward of the opponents and to follow him wherever he went.

At half-time we were leading 1–0 and I went into the dressing-room to give further instructions with regard to the second half. My noble hero was not present. Thereupon I dashed into the buffet and discovered him . . . having a pint of beer and enjoying a smoke with the opposing centre-forward. I refrain from mentioning the expression I gave vent to, but I had to laugh when he responded that he was only carrying out my instructions to follow his opponent. Oh, yes, things have changed since those days!

During this engagement with Dordrecht I was placed in charge of the Dutch international eleven which had to play against the "Fatherland team" on German soil. The officials gave me a month in which to get the team ready. I was informed they had two very good inside-rights and the Selection committee were desirous of playing both of these lads. I said, "What! Six forwards!"

They responded, "No, we want you to make one of these lads into an outside-left."

This was some job for me, seeing that the players were mostly novices at the game – and one-footed at that. Still I persevered. On many occasions I had the lad out using one foot only – and I spoon-fed him in all of his practice games when I played inside-left. He was still useless in this position but the selectors would have their way and he played outside-left.

Everything considered it was a good game and we won 3–2. To use a common football expression, our left-winger "didn't get a kick" until just before the finish of the game. Then, from a right-wing attack the ball was crossed over, my hopeless pupil caught it on the volley with his right foot and it went into the roof of the German net like a rocket! One in a million!

I felt really ashamed when the members of the Committee congratulated me on what they termed my marvellous work. Still, these things happen in football.

I enjoyed this, my first spot of coaching in Holland, but before the end of the season I was just pining to be back in English football again. Without any difficulty I got back to Burnden Park, and the next year I was married.

Then in 1912 (during the close season) Mr J. T. Howcroft sent me out to Vienna as coach to the Austrian F.A. for a period of two months, namely: six weeks preparation for the Austrian international XI and a fortnight with that team at the Olympic Games in Stockholm.

This was a revelation to me. To leave my dark, gloomy, industrial Lancashire for Gay Vienna was just like stepping into paradise. The Emperor Francis Joseph was on the throne and Vienna in those days was really a city of love, life, and laughter.

I coached the Austrian Olympic XI twice per week and the remaining days of the week were spent among the League sides, Rapid F.C., Austria F.C., Admira F.C., Vienna F.C., etc.

We were at first unable to fit in the Vienna club, so arrangements were made for early morning training from 5.30 a.m. until 7.30 a.m. This will give readers some idea of the enthusiasm.

I have reason to remember my first day's coaching with the Olympic XI in Austria. After I had gone through the usual British training methods for the day, and finished with a team game, the captain (with a disappointed look on his face) asked me if that was the only kind of training we did in English football.

As a matter of fact it was, but I lied to him when I said, "No, that was only the first day's work." I went further and explained to him that our coaching ideas were similar to the alphabet and that our first day's work had covered ABC; that we would start on letter "D" the following day.

It was on that vital day that I really became a football coach. When I got back to my hotel I sat up half the night, working matters out and putting various trapping, heading, and control exercises together.

Here I should mention that on my first day's coaching, Mr Hugo Meisl, the famous Austrian team manager, passed a centre-half over to me called Braunsteiner. The latter was a good player, but a bad header of a ball.

I took him aside for forty-five minutes for a private lesson in the art of heading. Braunsteiner could hit a ball – and I adopted the very crude method of standing in goal and letting him bombard me with shots.

Anything within reach of my head was nodded out, but truth to tell Braunsteiner nearly "knocked my block off". I dare not show any ill effects, but believe me, I had a headache for a week afterwards.

This lesson had the effect of improving Braunsteiner's heading a great deal, but since those days I have taught myself a much better (and easier) way for teaching the science of heading.

Sad to relate, Braunsteiner was killed in Serbia during the 1914 war, along with other ex-pupils of mine.

from SPORT EXPRESS *1954*

They were tough in those days!

CHARLES BUCHAN

During my second home game for Sunderland I got another of those valuable lessons that were offered gratuitously by the great players in those days.

It was in the early stages of the game with Notts County. The left-back opposed to me was a broad-shouldered, thick-set fellow called Montgomery, only about 5 ft. 5 in. in height but as tough as the most solid British oak.

The first time I got the ball, I slipped it past him on the outside, darted round him on the inside and finished with a pass to my partner.

It was a trick I had seen Jackie Mordue bring off. It worked wonderfully well. But as I came back down the field, Montgomery said in a low voice, "Don't do that again, son."

Of course I took no notice. The next time I got the ball, I pushed it past him on the outside but that was as far as I got. He hit me with the full force of his burly frame so hard that I finished up flat on my back only a yard from the fencing surrounding the pitch.

It was a perfectly fair shoulder charge that shook every bone in my body. As I slowly crept back on to the field, Montgomery came up and said: "I told you not to do it again." I never did afterwards. I learned my lesson the painful way and never tried to beat an opponent twice running with the same trick. It made me think up new ways; a very valuable lesson.

In this County team were the famous full-back partners, Morley, 6 ft. 3 in., and Montgomery, nearly a foot shorter in height but twice as broad. "Weary Willy and Tired Tim" they were nicknamed, after the well-known characters in a comic-strip running at the time.

They were the first pair to introduce the notorious offside trap. Morley would run forward *before* an opponent passed the ball, leaving Montgomery to guard the road to goal. As three defenders had to be between the attackers and the goal *when* the ball was played, the forwards really did not have a chance.

Later Bill McCracken, Ireland, and Newcastle United full-back, brought the system almost to perfection. The more intelligent the forwards opposed to him, the more easily they fell into the trap.

Games were becoming a procession of free-kicks so the F.A. had to do something about it. Some years later, in 1925, they changed the offside law to two defenders instead of three. It saved the situation.

There are people who would like a return to the old offside law. If that came about, the game would be ruined. Instead of one McCracken, there would be dozens to hold up the game and rob it of all spectacular appeal.

In a later game, I played against Bradford City at Valley Parade. Only the previous April, City had won the F.A. Cup. They were a grand side, but we beat them 5-1 and I have never seen a better exhibition of inside-forward play than that given by George Holley, our inside-left.

He scored a magnificent hat-trick, running nearly half the length of the field each time and coolly dribbling the ball round goalkeeper Jock Ewart before placing it in the net.

Several times I have stood on the field spellbound, watching Holley bewilder the opposition. After one game, manager Bob Kyle said to me, when I went in to draw the weekly wage packet, "Do you think you've earned it?"

"No," I replied, "but I think George has earned it for all of us."

There was another occasion a year afterwards when I scored five goals against Kenneth Campbell, the Scottish international goalkeeper then playing for Liverpool. Four of them I just touched into the net. Holley had beaten the defence and even drawn Campbell out of position before giving me the goals on a plate.

One of the games that first season was against Preston North End at Deepdale. Tim Coleman, our inside-left that day, put on a thick, black moustache and played throughout the first half with it stuck on his upper lip.

During the interval he removed it and took the field with an innocent expression. The referee at once noticed the difference and spoke to Coleman about it. He thought we had put on a substitute. Coleman was an inveterate joker and a grand footballer who had played for England.

That season came to an end quickly. I kept my place in the side for the eight games but I had no great cause for satisfaction. I had played one good game, the first, and a lot of moderate ones. I scored only one goal – against Notts County.

Even that ewe lamb was a lucky one. Arthur Bridgett, our outside-left took a corner-kick. As the ball sailed high across the goal, I shouted "Right!" to our centre-forward. He made no attempt to play the ball, nor did Albert Iremonger, the 6 ft. 5 in. County goalkeeper. I just nodded it into the net.

The goalkeeper was dumbfounded when the referee allowed the goal. He chased him upfield but it made no difference.

Iremonger, a great goalkeeper with a tremendous reach, was an eccentric character. If anything upset him, he did some extraordinary things like sitting on the ball in the middle of the field and holding up the game until the referee firmly ordered him back to goal.

During the summer months, I played quite a lot of cricket, turning out for Kent Club and Ground. I also did a lot of thinking about my First Division experiences.

The big difference from the play in the Southern League was in positioning. In the First Division, opponents anticipated the next move and were always close enough to tackle quickly.

And when they tackled, they used all their muscular powers. I can assure you they were tough in those days.

So I made up my mind that when I went back to Sunderland I would speed up my play and try to look two moves ahead instead of one. But when the next August arrived and I resumed training, nature took a hand.

I started to grow at an alarming rate. I was 5 ft. 9½ in. 10 st. 5 lb. in weight during the first week in August. By the end of November – at which time I was twenty – I was 6 ft. 0¾ in. and still 10 st. 5 lb. I was almost too weak to stand up straight.

After every spell of training – I did not do many – and after every game, I was forced to lie on a couch for hours. It was too much of an effort to go outside the house.

As you can imagine, my play was nothing to shout about. Only the faith of manager Bob Kyle kept me in the team. Trainer Billy Williams nursed me – he was a grand fellow – and Bob Kyle encouraged me week after week.

It wasn't much use. The crowd began to barrack me and I

must admit I deserved it. I asked to be dropped from the side but the manager would not listen.

Finally after one game in mid-November when the crowd had, with every reason, been noisily expressive about my play, I stormed into the dressing-room and declared in a loud voice: "I'll never kick another ball for Sunderland."

Unfortunately, the local reporter heard me. In the evening paper, there were bold headlines on my statement. On Monday morning there were more reports.

Though I received hundreds of letters urging me to carry on, I packed up my bag and went home to Woolwich.

On the following Saturday, Sunderland were to play Woolwich Arsenal at the Manor Field, which was only about half-a-mile from my home. I did not expect to play.

But two days before the game, Manager Kyle came to the house and, after a talk with my father, persuaded me to turn out. "Do your best to show the locals you can do it," he said, "and if you fail, we can talk about it afterwards."

I played, scored a couple of goals in a 3–1 win for Sunderland, and felt much better afterwards. I stayed the following week at home and somehow felt a lot stronger.

That was the turning point. I returned to Sunderland and began to put on weight. I quickly ran up to 12 st. 8 lb. – my playing weight for the rest of my days – and struck a little form.

No longer did I get "the bird" from the crowd. They were very kind to me, as they were for the fourteen and a half years I spent with the club.

Up in the north-east, the crowd takes its football very seriously. They are strongly partisan and want their team to win every time.* I think they know more about the game than southern crowds. They certainly express their opinions more freely. But they are extremely loyal, good-hearted and have a keen sense of humour.

Gradually I recovered confidence and began to pull my weight in the side. I started to score goals and for an inside forward that is an important matter.

* See "Middlesbrough in the Thirties", page 441.

During this testing time I owed a debt of gratitude to trainer Billy Williams that I never repaid nor ever could repay. He looked after me like a father. If I got the slightest knock he came round to my house to attend to it at once. He also nursed me during training hours, saw that I did not overtax my strength and gave me tonics when he thought them necessary. At the time it was very often.

After I had been a few weeks at Sunderland, he noticed that I smoked quite a number of cigarettes during the day. Cigarettes were his pet aversion. One day he handed me a new pipe, a pouch full of tobacco and a box of matches. "I want you to promise me that you will give this a fair trial and leave cigarettes alone," he said.

Taken by surprise, I gave him my promise. I smoked nothing but a pipe from that day until three years ago when I parted company with my teeth.

Williams was a strict disciplinarian. One day I arrived a minute or two after the time we were due to report for duty. There he stood at the door waiting for me to enter. Without a word, he pulled his watch from his pocket, looked at it and put it back. I felt very guilty. A few seconds later, he pulled out his watch again and repeated the performance. It made me feel so small that I vowed I would never be late for training again. I kept my vow.

While we were in the dressing-rooms during training hours or on match days, smoking was strictly forbidden. If a club director came into the room smoking, he was quickly ordered out. Williams was king of his own castle.

In his young days, he had been the professional champion half-mile runner. He was as fit as a fiddle. Often during our road walks he would outpace most of the players.

On the subject of punctuality, I was late only once in twenty years either for a train journey or for the matches.

That was because I was too early. I arrived at Sunderland station about half-an-hour before train time. Having, as I thought, time on my hands, I strolled up to the post-office in the High Street less than a quarter of a mile away, and sent a telegram. When I got back to the station, the train had gone. As we travelled on the day before the match, it did not matter. I went by a later train and joined the rest of the team at the hotel. The match, I remember, was at Liverpool. We won the points, so little was said about my delinquency.

It was thanks to the great skill and the devotion of Trainer Williams that I survived my opening period at Sunderland. I would never let him down if I could help it.

He nursed me back to health and strength. And with it came a return to form. So much so that at the beginning of 1912, about eighteen months after my arrival at Sunderland, the club received a letter from the Scottish F.A. asking them if they would release me if I were selected to play for Scotland in the next international. Manager Bob Kyle showed me the letter and said: "Well, what do I have to say in reply?"

I told him, "Both my parents are Aberdonians, born and bred there. But I happened to be born in Woolwich so I'm not eligible to play for Scotland."

He wrote back to that effect and with the letter I thought my chances of international honours had gone.

Birth is the only qualification to play for a country in the international tournament. And this had brought some peculiar situations.

For example, I recall Jocky Simpson, the great Falkirk out-side-right, being denied several caps because, though of Scottish parentage, he was born in Manchester. His parents, both of Falkirk, were in Manchester only for a few months during which Jocky was born. They went back to Falkirk, with their son, soon after the event.

There is an unwritten law in F.A. circles that rules out the selection of players playing for teams outside the country. That kept Simpson out of England's team. And, as he was born south of the border, he could not play for Scotland. He had to wait until he was transferred to Blackburn Rovers – I think it was in 1911 – before he received deserved recognition.

Simpson was undoubtedly one of the best out-side-rights of

his generation. I have seldom seen a winger who could centre the ball so accurately while running at full speed.

Several players with teams like Cardiff City and Swansea Town and in Scotland, were left out of England's teams because they were outside the border.

One of the best half-backs I ever met was little Billy Hardy, the bald-headed Cardiff player. Yet he never played for England. He was so quick in tackling and so speedy in recovery that you never knew when you had him beaten. He was also a grand distributor of the ball, fast and accurate.

A few weeks after Sunderland had heard from the Scottish F.A., I was asked by the Football League to produce a birth certificate, I did so and soon had the gratification, much to my surprise, of learning that I had been chosen to play for the Football League against the Scottish League at Ayresome Park, Middlesbrough.

The match was due to take place on 17 February, 1912. Six days before that, I went to bed with influenza. I was in a pretty bad way.

On the Thursday, Mr Fred Taylor, the Sunderland chairman, called to see me in my bedroom. He asked me how I was getting on and whether he should let the League know that I was unfit to play.

"Oh, no," I assured him, "I shall be all right by Saturday. I'm determined to play – I may not get another chance."

"All right," he said, "I'll send a car round for you at midday on Saturday. That will get you there in time."

Saturday came and I was driven the thirty miles to Middlesbrough. Though I was feeling a trifle light-headed, the meeting with such great stars as my partner, Charlie Wallace, Aston Villa outside-right; B--- Freeman, Burnley centre-forward; Jimmy Fay of Bolton, for years secretary of the Players' Union; Bob Crompton, Blackburn full-back, and his partner Jesse Pennington, of West Bromwich Albion, was a tonic in itself.

But when the game started, I was all at sea. My head was fuzzy. After a few minutes, the left half-back opposed to me, big Jimmy Galt of Glasgow Rangers, caught me with an old-fashioned shoulder charge that hit me for six.

When I picked myself up, all traces of the influenza had gone. I felt as fit as a fiddle. And luck ran my way. Whatever I did came off. The ball, even if I miskicked, went in the right direction. I played a "blinder" and we won 2–0.

As we trooped off the field at the end, Pennington joined me and patted me on the back. "A great show, Charlie," he said, "one of the best I've seen. But don't be disappointed if you aren't in the England team for the next game. Your turn will come."

It was a grand gesture from a great sportsman. He was right, too.

Some of the famous stars in the Scottish League team were Alex MacNair, Celtic left-back; Mercer, Hearts right-half; Alex Bennett, Rangers outside-right, and his partner Jimmy McMenemy, then with Celtic. It was McMenemy who drove home to me the value of "making the ball do the work". "Napoleon" he was called because he dictated the course of a game with his accurate, timely passes.

He walked through a game whereas I had been running about all the time. I studied him carefully and willingly admit I copied some of his methods. They were too good to miss.

With all those great players in one game, and others like Charlies Thomson, Sunderland centre-half, the immortal Steve Bloomer, Joe Smith, Billy Meredith, Charlie Roberts, George Holley and a host of others at the height of their powers, I was surprised to read in an annual at the end of the season these words:

"In a day when soccer personalities, especially on the professional side, are so few and far between, the continued fine play of Steven Bloomer proves most refreshing to the football public."

How often are words with the same meaning written today? And how often is stressed the lack of personalities and players to compare with the old giants.

Bloomer, then in his thirty-seventh year, was undoubtedly

a wonder. His thrustful dashes for goal and hard shooting were unequalled. The nearest approach to him I can think of is Stanley Mortensen, the Blackpool and England inside-right.

It was generally expected that Harold Fleming, the Swindon inside-right who had scored a hat-trick in the game with Ireland, would automatically get the England inside-right position against Scotland at Hampden Park.

But the F.A. selectors sprang a big surprise by choosing Frank Jefferies of Everton. I was given the honour of travelling as reserve.

I shall never forget my first visit to Hampden Park. The sight of the massed pipers, the crowd of 127,307 (the record for that time) packed round the vast amphitheatre, the enthusiasm of the Scottish folk, all filled me with awe.

Nor shall I ever forget the wonderful duel that went on during the game between England right-back Bob Crompton and the Scottish outside-left Jimmy Quinn, of the Celtic.

Quinn really was a dashing, tearaway centre-forward, who used his powerful physique and tremendous strength to the best advantage. He had been placed at outside-left, I'm sure, to pit his strength against the equally powerful Crompton.

They went at it hammer-and-tongs throughout the ninety minutes. It was an example of robust shoulder-charging the like of which will never be seen again. It would not be allowed today.

It ended with honours even. The score, too, was 1–1, so everybody seemed satisfied. I left the ground with my ears filled with the famous "Hampden Roar" which had gone on ceaselessly throughout the remarkable game.

Crompton, who ended his career with the record number of thirty-four England caps, was undoubtedly the outstanding full-back of his time. A commanding personality, he was the best kicker of a ball I ever ran across.

A month or so before, I received something of a shock. Sunderland had reached the third round, equivalent to the fifth round today, of the F.A. Cup. We were confidently expected to get to the final and a home draw with West Bromwich Albion increased our optimism.

Roker Park that day was packed to overflowing. Indeed, the crowd encroached on to the field of play and were some five or six yards inside the touchlines in places. But the game went on.

We were well and truly beaten by the Albion much to our surprise. Bob Pallor, now a big business man in West Hartlepool, scored two goals for the Albion and we got one through Arthur Bridgett. The result was a big blow to our pride.

The late Fred Everiss, who served fifty years with Albion as player, secretary-manager, and director, told me a story about the game. When he arrived at the ground with the Albion team he had difficulty in getting to the players' entrance door through the vast crowd that was massed outside. He eventually got to the door but was refused permission by the commissionaire.

"But I'm manager of the Albion and here are the team," said Everiss.

"That's a good one," was the reply, "you're the third Albion team that's tried it on so far."

Eventually they got in and proceeded to bring about our downfall. I have never appreciated so much the play of Jesse Pennington, the Albion left-back, as I did that afternoon.

There was another game that season that I have cause to remember. It was against Newcastle United at St James's Park. It had rained all the morning to such an extent that the ground was waterlogged. You can guess the ball got very heavy.

Midway in the first half, I ran into that ball just as it was leaving the United full-back's foot. I received the full weight of the ball in the stomach and went down like a log.

Trainer Billy Williams came on and brought me round with a sponge. The first words I heard came in a loud voice from the crowd, "Kick him again, he's breathing." It was the first time I had heard that particular remark and I did not think it funny just then. I have laughed about it many times since.

Most of the trouble was that I had eaten a good lunch before the game. Any hard knock after a meal may bring serious consequences, as I found. From that day onwards I had nothing except tea and toast for lunch before a game. My advice to all players is to keep away from heavy food before the match. You can make up for it afterwards.

Luckily, this was one of the most serious injuries I received during my career. Hard knocks I received in plenty but they were never on dangerous spots. My knees and ankles escaped real damage. Perhaps that was because my knees were so far from the ground and my ankles were big knobbly affairs.

The 1911–12 season drew on to a finish. Sunderland did not have a particularly successful season, finishing eighth in the League Championship, won by Blackburn Rovers.

I played in thirty-one of the thirty-eight League games and scored seven goals, not a bright performance.

As soon as the last game had been played I made up my mind to have a holiday in Canada. Some friends of mine had emigrated to Hamilton, Ontario, about a year before and they invited me to spend the summer with them. I accepted.

The boat I sailed on was the one following the ill-fated *Titanic* which met with such a tragic disaster.

While at Hamilton, I was asked to play soccer for a local team in the semi-finals and final of a cup competition. I played with a handkerchief round my head to avoid getting sunstroke. The temperature was more than 100°F.

The games were played on Labour day, or some such festival day in Canada. There were about 1,000 spectators.

One of them brought me another spot of bother. He, or she, took a photograph of me in the black and yellow striped jersey enjoying myself in the sunshine.

Copies of the photograph were sent to Sunderland and to the F.A. When I got back home, Bob Kyle asked me into the office and said: "Is this you?"

"Of course it is," I replied.

"Then you ought to know better than to play for a club during the close season. You stand a chance of being suspended."

Frankly, I did not know there was such a rule. I played

thinking I was helping the deserving cause of charity. Then I received word from the F.A. I confessed my ignorance and promised not to break the law again. They let me off with a severe caution. . . .

Soccer in Canada, at that time was in its infancy stage. It is improving by leaps and bounds and our touring teams nowadays have to play hard to keep an unbeaten record in their games.

One thing I found was that the few games I played helped ball control to a great extent. The grounds in Canada were stone hard, with little grass on them. If you could control a ball in these conditions, you ought to be able on the luscious green League pitches.

Before I sailed for home, the team in Canada presented me with a gold ring as a memento. I could not accept one of the medals they had won in the competition, as the man whose place I had taken had done more for the side than I had. This was their way of expressing thanks.

And the experience did me a lot of good physically. I needed very little training when I got back to English football in August of that year.

from A LIFETIME IN FOOTBALL *1955*

The Battle of Footerloo

ROBERT LYND

The most sensational Cup Final in history! That is what everybody kept saying to everybody else over and over again.

It would, perhaps, be an exaggeration to say that Wembley Park was turned into a battlefield; but, as the stretcher-bearers bore the seeming corpses one after another through the crowd and out of the ground, it looked considerably more like a battlefield than like a football-field.

Nowhere but in England – perhaps, nowhere but in London – would it have been possible to have had so many of the elements of a riot without the riot itself actually taking place.

A part of the crowd undoubtedly behaved badly, but it did not behave nearly so badly as it might have behaved. The Londoner is a moderate man even in his disorderly moments. He is content to rush a policeman without hurting him.

The London police are also a body of moderate men. They are content to spend an hour in pushing, pressing, and persuading a mob back into its proper place, instead of scattering it in one crowded minute of glorious life by more violent methods, and leaving the place strewn with broken skulls, as police in more excitable lands might do. There were only 1,000 casualties at the Cup Final. That is really a great tribute to everybody.

And what a setting for such scenes! The Stadium – which, as the programme informed us, is equal in area to the Biblical city of Jericho – was like a huge bowl up the inside of which human beings were being packed as human beings have never been packed before, even at a football match.

They were packed so closely in the popular stands that you could see only their faces and their hats, and you could not see even these. Each face was a mere pebble in a bank of shingle that seemed fifty times higher than any bank of shingle that was ever cast up by the tides of a thousand years.

Or, if you prefer the comparison, the crowd on the distant terraces, as the sun shone on it, looked like a gigantic mass of uncooked sweetbreads that wobbled continually as a new crowd poured into it.

It was mostly composed of men and boys in their ordinary clothes. But some of them wore paper caps of red, white, and blue in their enthusiasm for West Ham, and a few wore white and blue top-hats in honour of Bolton Wanderers. There were also all kinds of favours – rosettes and metal cups decorated with the ribbons of the rival teams – bought from hawkers on the way and worn in the button-hole. And every other man or boy seemed to have a rattle.

This is an instrument of torture that, as it is whirled round and round, makes a noise like a rack. When I arrived at the Stadium, about one o'clock, thousands of men and boys were already whirling rattles. Those who had no rattles yelled. Those who could not yell cheered. Those who could not cheer joined in whistling a fox-trot that the band of the Irish Guards seemed to be playing – it was almost audible – in the middle of the green field.

There was, indeed, something for everybody to do, and, though one could not quite make out what the people who yelled were yelling, or what the people who cheered were cheering, one guessed that it had something to do with the respective merits of West Ham or Bolton Wanderers, and everybody seemed to be extraordinarily happy about it.

And the sun shone, and the green field that had circles and parallelograms beautifully painted on it in whitewash, was lovely as a tennis-lawn in a country garden. How fair a scene! Is it any wonder that, in presence of this virgin greensward, and in the season of the first lilacs and the first nightingales, yell after yell went round the ground, with cheer after cheer following it, and always to the noble accompaniment of a multitude of rattles that sounded like the voices of a million demented corncrakes?

Suddenly the peace of the scene was broken in upon by the spectacle of a policeman running. To see a policeman running is, I think, next to hearing a declaration of war, the most exciting experience of which a human being is capable. This policeman, as he tore with long legs along the cinder track, was obviously running for help.

Looking over towards one of the two-shilling stands, one saw that men were tumbling like sheep over the railings of the stands and tussling with policemen, who tried in vain to keep them from seizing upon seats that did not belong to them.

Other police hurried up and, though they could not drive the invasion back, at least they prevented it from becoming any worse. And rattles rattled, and larynxes and pharynxes made all the noises of which the human throat is capable. And the ambulance men came on to the field under the red cross of Geneva and carried off the wounded.

Then, at the other side of the field, we caught sight of another policeman running, and we could see that the same kind of thing was happening over there, only worse. I cannot help thinking that the people who leaped over the barriers were to a great extent innocent people. After all, human beings were pouring down upon them from behind like a score of Alpine torrents. The police attempted to drive them back, but you might as well have attempted to drive a man through the eye of a needle. And once more the ambulance men came on to the field and carried off the wounded.

Even so, the crowd has as yet seized only a small piece of the rim of the cinder-track surrounding the field. They sat down and dug themselves in. The police caught a few of them by the collars and tried to force them back. The others rose and advanced at a run five yards further and dug themselves in again.

Other parts of the ground found the example infectious, and on all sides the crowd could be seen leaping over the railings as easily as a high tide leaps over a breakwater on a stormy day. And, as they leaped, others leaped on their backs and drove them to the very touch-line. And policemen ran. And one of them began to work hard at a telephone. And the ambulance men came on and carried off the wounded.

It was plain by this time that something extraordinary had happened, and rumours from the outside spoke of furious crowds that had found the gates closed and had broken them down. A man who had just arrived told me: "There are thousands of people out there spitting blood because they can't get in – thousands of people who have paid for their tickets."

Alas, they got in all right. Never did the ancient Goths and the Ostrogoths and the Visigoths sweep down upon the green places of Europe as this horde of invaders swept into our little Biblical city of Jericho.

They spread over the grass of the playing-field like locusts

Others streamed in after them, and before long there was such a mob of men collected on the field that scarcely any grass was visible except a little green oasis in the middle of the ring of bandsmen, who were gallantly playing a tune that nobody could hear.

A crash overhead made the people in the covered stand look up and told them that one bold invader had even got on to the roof. He had fallen through, the brave fellow, and we could see his legs kicking from the waist downwards.

The crowd in the stands were now yelling their opinion of the crowd on the field at the top of 127,000 voices. To judge by the language of the man who was standing behind me, the opinion was unfavourable. I think he was one of the invaders who had broken into the Press gallery, but he wanted to see the match. Luckily the crowd on the field was unable to hear him. Otherwise I feel sure it would have resented some of the things he said. He was not content to use words like "blooming", or "dashed", or even "blinking", and he accused them of quite unmentionable vices. I was glad that the sound of rattles, motor-horns, yells and whistles partially drowned the more lurid passages in the most eloquent monologue to which it has ever been my privilege to listen.

Into the black sea on the grass, blue lines of policemen, hurried up from London, began to insinuate themselves, the crowds on the stands loudly cheering them, and whirling their rattles. But by this time no one any longer believed that the ground could be cleared by foot-police. Old gentlemen with militarist leanings called for fixed bayonets and cavalry charges.

It was as though the stands and the grass were at war with each other. We boohed the invaders as no villain of melodrama was ever boohed. And we waved our rattles to fortify the boo. The blasphemous man behind me had by this time begun to use words that I could understand only with an effort. And the ambulance men came on and carried off the wounded.

Then the first horse-policeman arrived. Had he been Steve Donoghue bringing in a winner of the Derby, he could not have been received with such a pandemonium of yells and rattles. If the little Biblical city of Jericho was to be saved, he was the man to do it, and, as three or four more horsemen came into view, the people who had got in legally roared the roar of victory and began to abuse the people who had got in illegally more vehemently than ever.

Alas, for the rarity of Christian charity! I fear that the dearest dream of many of us just at that moment was a new and successful Charge of the Light Brigade.

When King George arrived and appeared in his red box it was as though a temporary truce had been declared between the party of law and the party of disorder. The fifty thousand Wat Tylers on the field roared "God Save The King!" and waved their hats and arms. Seen from above it looked as if all the pebbles on the Brighton beach were standing up on their ends and shouting.

Immediately afterwards, however, the war was renewed with increased vigour, and, as the horsemen swept on to the field, the more timid spirits on the outskirts began to drift away under the arches and to make for home.

Even so, the field still remained black with people, and, as one section of the crowd retreated before the teeth and tails of the horses another section flowed in and took its place.

There was one policeman on a white horse who was a perfect genius, and who could himself keep a crowd of at least a thousand moving. He butted them with the horse's tail, he pushed at them with the horse's sides, he rode straight at them with the horse's mouth. And the animal did all that he told it to do as cleverly as the cleverest circus pony, and advanced into the mob with as little fear as though it had been a tank.

The foot-police now began to take the crowd in sections, and joining hands with an occasional sailor or well-wisher, attempted to recover the field from the invaders yard by yard.

"Look, the crowd has begun to fight the police!" somebody cried hopefully, and, just below us, one man had certainly begun to fight with one policeman.

It was during this excitement that I saw the extraordinary spectacle of a man walking and scrambling over the heads of the spectators on one of the stands, as over a solid floor, determined, I suppose, to get out and to get home, lest a worse thing should befall him. He was, I understand, taken to hospital.

It was about the same time that a man bumped into me and, as though to test me, held out his hand with a broad grin and said, "Good old Lancashire!" His friend, who followed him, also bumped into me, and gripped me by the hand, and said knowingly, with a still broader gin, "Good old Lancashire!" I did not dare to contradict him. But the bones of my hand ached protestingly.

Just as we were wondering whether the Cup Final could be played at all, the teams came out into the thick of the mob, carrying two little nut-coloured balls, and the crowd made a narrow laneway for them and slapped every man of them enthusiastically on the back as he made his way through to be introduced to the King. I should not care to be slapped on the back by ten thousand men from Bolton. Or, for that matter, by ten thousand men from West Ham. Or, indeed, by ten thousand men from anywhere.

Once more the rattles rattled, the vocal cords vociferated, the horse-police butted, the foot-police pushed, a man with a megaphone megaphoned (though nobody could hear him), and the ambulance men carried off the wounded. And still the man on the white horse was riding up and down, driving boys and men before him like chaff before the wind, and the crowds on the stands ululated with joy as little pools of green became visible and expanded into little ponds and gradually into little lakes.

Meanwhile each of the teams was practising at dribbling and passing and shooting goals as unconcernedly as though they did not know that they were surrounded on all sides by tens of thousands of people in conflict with the police. The sun had gone out by now, and it was cold, and Seddon danced his knees up and down like pistons to keep himself warm. Other players stretched their legs or jumped up and down like children or juggled the ball on their toes.

Q

At length the crowd on one side of the field was driven back to the touch-line, and amid a wild tumult of cheers the man on the white horse rode among the mob like a god of victory and even butted people out of the net behind the goal posts. Slowly but surely chains of police were pressing back other sections of the crowd north, east, and west off the field of play.

Then, wonder of wonders, we saw the captains meeting in the middle of the field for the toss, and, amid a tumult of yells, rattles, and noises for which there are no words in the English language, it became evident that the toss had been won by Bolton Wanderers.

As for the football that followed, how mild a game it seemed after so sensational a prologue! To be sure, a shout went up to heaven from a hundred thousand throats when Jack, of Bolton, shot that lightning ball through the goal posts in the first few minutes of the game. And there were shouts from ten thousand other throats when the West Hammers in their claret-and-blue shirts drove up like a stormy sea towards the Bolton goal only to break again and again on backs that would let no dangerous ball pass them.

But even these things were hardly so exciting as when the crowd began to surge back on to the field of play, and the match had to be held up while the police once more hurried up reinforcements and drove the interlopers back to the touch-line.

After that there were many moments of exciting play, as Finney or Vizard took the ball on his toe and looked as though he could keep three balls going at a time, like a great conjurer. But the game as a whole was hardly exciting; indeed, it had scarcely started when thousands of the spectators began to stream homewards, some of them because they could see nothing, others because they had seen quite enough for one day in the life of any human being. "A damned farce!" said one elderly gentleman, as he clambered out of the grandstand, and so home.

Yet to the Bolton Wanderers, swift as deer in their white

shirts and blue shorts, it was evident that not the scenes but the football was the one thing of interest in the day. And when, in the second half, J. R. Smith scored their second goal in a flash so swift that for a moment men doubted it, his fellow-players ran up to him as though they would have embraced him, and, as he passed from one congratulating hand to another, he was like a man dancing through the grand chain in a set of lancers.

And that, for all practical purposes, was the end of it. And, shortly afterwards, the crowd was back in a rush over the grass, cheering the Cup as it was handed to the winners, roaring "God Save The King!" and moving like a great army out of the Stadium, and leaving that beautiful green field littered with paper, like Hampstead Heath after a Bank Holiday.

I did not leave the ground until twenty minutes to seven, and even then there were still a few stragglers left.

Thus ended the bloodless battle of Footerloo.

from THE BLUE LION *1923*

Dropping a Star

FULVIO BERNARDINI

Bernardini, now a distinguished manager, was celebrated as the finest "technical" attacking centre-half ever to have played for Italy.

On December 13, 1931, the ninth Italy-Hungary match was played on the Torino ground. The previous Thursday Pozzo called his men together there, for a training session.

I was having a spell of excellent form, and gave full proof of it on the field; I was chosen without argument and the team was announced as follows: Combi; Rosetta, Monzeglio; Ferraris IV, Bernardini, Pitto; Costantino, Cesarini, Libonatti, Ferrari, Orsi.

Caligaris was not among those chosen, but remained with us as right-hand man to Pozzo.

The days of waiting were serenely divided between a cinema, a theatre, and some lively ping-pong tournaments; the challenge matches between Orsi and Ferraris IV were memorable. Orsi gave Attilio five points start in twenty-one, but Ferraris never managed to beat him. The bet was for five lire and the popular "Mumo" used to say, "He never lets me get the ball on the field, so I have my revenge at ping-pong". On Saturday evening, when we were already at dinner, we noticed some curious goings-on.

Caligaris called Pozzo aside and talked to him for a long while, in a low voice. The reason for that conversation emerged soon afterwards, when Caligaris, leaving the dining-room at great speed, returned in the company of Bertolini, the Juventus player who was going through a critical time in his life and was at odds with his club. Bertolini ate with us and was given a room for the night.

Caligaris explained that he had persuaded Pozzo to take Bertolini as reserve, so that he could share in the eventual victory bonus, being in need of help.

Next day, the unthinkable happened!

We ate pretty early, since we were kicking off at 2.30. A few minutes before two we had to be ready in the hall of the Hotel Majestic Lagrange, to go to the stadium by coach.

I went to my room to rest awhile, then started changing into my football kit. I was almost ready when the trainer came to say that Pozzo wanted to talk to me. The *Commissario Tecnico's* room was next door to mine, and I found him wearing on his face the expression of a man worried and oppressed by some anxiety.

Pozzo talked to me for a long time, with a slow rhythm, and without ever meeting my eyes! I can faithfully repeat the phrases of Vittorio Pozzo, so firmly were impressed on me the grandiose words I was obliged to listen to, that memorable afternoon. Of the words I am certain: of the punctuation, no, because Vittorio Pozzo, in the pain he was suffering, forgot to let me have it, but I hope this grave omission will be pardoned me!

"You see, Bernardini, from the point of view of individual prowess, you play in a superior style, even a perfect style. Your special case means that the team you play for is in the absurd position of not being able to combine with you easily, because the others cannot match your conception of the game, and finish by getting downhearted. I should really ask you to play less well. Should I sacrifice you, or sacrifice the others? It's the most difficult problem I have ever had to solve. Tell me; how would you solve it in my place?"

It's hardly necessary to say that I replied very simply! "Very well, I understand, thank you!" I answered, and went back to my room where I quickly changed into my ordinary clothes.

from DIECI ANNI CON LA NAZIONALE *1946*

I Dope Arsenal for a Cup-Tie

LESLIE KNIGHTON

Football fans and critics, after a match in which a famous team has done badly or some unknown have turned giant-killers, sometimes ask one another darkly: "I wonder if players are ever doped for big games?"

My answer to that question is: "Yes! I have done it."

While I was at Highbury we struck one or two bad patches in the normal run of things. There was nothing in that – no team goes along without variations of form and runs of ill-luck. But when such shadows fall athwart a club just as it is tensing up for critical cup-ties . . . the manager is expected to do something about it at once. He is, in fact, expected to manufacture his own luck.

We ran into a bad spell during the Cup battles. We had a

splendid team – including Bob John, Jimmy Brain, Alex Mackie, Jim Hopkins, Joe Toner, Andy Kennedy, Alf Baker and the rest. But football matches are not won by making lists of names on paper, as many a manager learns to his cost. They are not won even by spending thousands of pounds on transfers. There are times when the finest teams, full of pluck and keenness and even genius, seem to go stale.

We had struck one of those periods. If we happened to get a goal down, the lads lost heart. Then their opponents were on them like tigers, sensing the lack of opposition – and, unless we were lucky, the ball rattled in our net once more. We could not start with the hunting rush we had made famous. Defence got brittle. Teamwork was erratic and unsure.

Then, during the Cup rounds, we were drawn against the Hammers. Rightly has West Ham gained this menacing nickname. They have a mighty reputation as tough fighters who can beat the most polished and skilful opposition into a frazzle. A year or two before our match with them they had thudded their way to the Final.

I was sitting in my office in Highbury with my head in my hands, wondering how on earth we could make sure of putting West Ham out of the Cup, when a card was handed to me. It bore the name of a distinguished West End doctor.

I told them to show him up, and he entered, meticulously dressed and gloved, looking like twenty guineas a visit at least.

"I'm a keen Arsenal fan, Mr Knighton," he said when I had asked him to sit down and given him a cigarette. "I trust that you will not be offended if I say that we have shown some unhappy symptoms, and have a rather poor chance of survival after meeting West Ham?"

I hardly knew whether to be more astounded at such a cool diagnosis, or at such an unexpected kind of fan, even after years of experience of them. The specialist assured me that he rarely missed seeing a match when we played at home, and found the excitement of the games the finest possible change and rest after a week's struggle against Death.

"What the boys require," he said presently, in his con-

sulting-room voice with which it seemed impossible to argue,
"is something in the nature of a courage-pill. Occasionally, we
administer such things to patients requiring abnormal stamina
or resistance for a particular purpose. They do no harm, but
simply tone up the nerve reflexes to produce the maximum
effort, and they leave no serious after-effects."

In all my period of football management I had talked to some
queer visitors and heard some strange proposals, but this beat
all. Yet the doctor had put his finger on Arsenal's pulse, and
knew exactly what was wrong.

I stared round at the framed groups of famous footballers on
the walls, and listened to the persuasive voice. There was
nothing wrong in his suggestion. If he could make up something to give the lads new heart, to speed their tired feet in that
critical last quarter of an hour in the second half, to make them
feel that no game is lost until it is won. . . .

There is nothing wrong in giving a team a tonic. It's big
hearts that win Cup-ties, and against the Hammers we should
need hearts as big as bullocks.

No eminent Counsel could have put that doctor through the
cross-examination I gave him, to make sure that the pills would
do no harm, at the time or afterwards. He smilingly assured me
that he would pledge his name and reputation on the result.
In the end, not without a lot of qualms as to what might
happen to me if the story leaked out, I told him to ahead.

We went to Upton Park, and I carried in my pocket a box of
pills that worried me as much as if they had been red hot. I had
talked the matter over and, as a sign of good faith to the boys,
I had offered to take my pill when they took theirs. And I
needed it!

One hour before play began we sat solemnly round, each
swallowing his silver pill. No one made any fuss about them,
but I can tell you mine felt as big as a marble. In the middle
of the gulps and sighs, Alf Baker suddenly guffawed. Then we
all saw the comic side of it – heads tilted back, glasses in hands,
eyes and faces very strained. There was a sudden yell of
laughter, half of us choked, the water spilled and spluttered;

but I saw to it that every man did his duty and swallowed his pill.

Then we sat round nervously awaiting the effects.

Outside, a foggy afternoon got darker and darker. Just before kick-off time I saw that the boys were getting restless. So was I. I felt I needed to run, jump, shout. There was something in those pills. I felt I could push down a wall with my fist.

Presently the referee came up to me. "Not a hope, Mr Knighton," he said, indicating the thickening fog. "Look at it. The game's off, I'm afraid."

Getting the boys back to Highbury that afternoon was like trying to drive a flock of lively young lions.

These pills not only left us "rarin' to go," but steadily developed the most awful bitter taste, and the most red hot, soul destroying *thirst* I have ever known. And mind you, I have known some thirsts! We drank water till I felt that the Thames would dry up. It became painful. Nothing quenched that thirst – whatever we poured down made it worse and worse, and the bitterness in our throats was like gall.

On the Monday we went to Upton Park again. Our doctor friend, who had come to watch us on the Saturday and had been disappointed, had earnestly made up a second batch of the courage pills. There were growls among the team when I opened the little red box two hours before the game.

"That'll do," I said; "I'll take mine first."

I should have liked to conjure it back into my pocket, but eleven pairs of eyes followed it half-way down my throat. And then the others took theirs. After which – would you believe it? – the fog, which was still hanging about, once more closed down and prevented our Cup-tie from being played. Once more we had to undergo those agonies of thirst and violent restlessness. I felt I could have knocked Carnera for six – but what was the good of that!

Later in the week our postponed match was actually played. Once more, this time against some real opposition, I produced my red pill-box and made the lads swallow their pluck-pills.

Then, at last, they got out on the pitch, the whistle shrilled, and the game began.

West Ham had obviously made up their minds to nail up our coffin in the first half. Traditionally a fierce attacking side, they outshone themselves. In the first quarter of an hour they just flung themselves at the ball, kept play in our half of the field, and nothing could prevent our goal being bombarded with shots. The Arsenal players fought back doggedly and well against an attack that would have overwhelmed them in any previous game that month. There was no score.

Just before half-time, I noticed a change. The Arsenal boys seemed like giants suddenly supercharged. They tore away with the ball, and put in shots that looked like leather thunderbolts. They monopolized the play.

Half time and no score. I wiped my brow. The Hammers were obviously rattled by the last few minutes' play, and their players went into a huddle as soon as the second half began. We kept them fully on the defensive. But there was no defence against the pluck-pills. The ball crashed and bounced towards the West Ham goal, Arsenal players ran like Olympic sprinters behind it, jumped like rockets to reach the high ones, and crashed in shots from all angles and distances.

It is no disparagement to West Ham, one of the grandest fighting teams that ever kicked a ball, to say that they had the most incredible luck in that second half. Sometimes, in Cup games, fortune is completely one-sided – you must have noticed that for yourself.

It was a very anxious time in the stands watching the bombardment, and the West Ham directors were probably enduring a more trying period, especially in the last ten minutes, even than we were. When the tired referee blew his final whistle the result was a goalless draw and the West Ham crowd must have heaved a sigh of relief for their pets.

I forgot my frightful thirst croaking out congratulations and sympathy to the team. But you should have heard *them*! Running about had made their thirst and bitter throats a thousand times worse. Those pills created a riot that night.

Q*

When the replay came at Highbury I had another box of pills ready. But when the players saw the little red box in my hand, the yell that went up nearly split the roof. They just refused point-blank to touch them. I had not the heart to make them go through it all again – in fact, I shuddered every time I thought of swallowing another of the things myself.

We drew 2–2. Our play was not nearly so determined as it had been in the former game, and I believe we should have netted two more goals if the pills had been taken.

Our fifth effort to settle the tie took place on the Chelsea ground, and this time, although "the lads" again refused to take their pills, we had fully three-quarters of the play, and were much the better side. But luck ran against us, and we could not score the vital goal. Then, with barely half a minute to go, West Ham forced a corner, their only one in the whole game. Jimmy Ruffell took the kick, and George Kay, their skipper and centre-half, came up like an express train and swept Andy Kennedy and one or two others as well as the ball into the net. The referee blew his whistle for a goal and full time, and we were out of the Cup.

Poor Andy Kennedy! Those who said that he should have saved that goal did not know that he had played through half the match with two fractured ribs causing him intense agony! He needed no pluck pills! But I often wondered if we should have won if the boys had been doped for that game. Just a bit of extra pep when we were so often pressing the West Ham defence. . . . We did not lose when we took the pills, and did not win when we rejected them. I wonder? The doctor never said what they contained. Strychnine? The stimulant drug used sometimes by students to nerve them for a hard examination? The doctor shook his head. He was certain those pills would have taken us to Wembley.

from BEHIND THE SCENES IN BIG FOOTBALL *1948*

No Midgets!

LESLIE KNIGHTON

Sir Henry Norris's mind never rested.* Day after day he would
come to me with some new idea – perhaps some new ban. How
well I remember the time when he suddenly proclaimed: "No
more small players. We must have big men."

Some devilish twist of destiny made a letter arrive for me the
very next day from an old Huddersfield pal saying that he had
seen a smashing outside-right, "Midget" Moffatt, tiny Cock
o' the North – and why didn't I sign him? He could be got
without a penny transfer fee, if I came quickly. But Norris had
left London the preceding evening for the Continent, and I
could not get hold of him to get his permission.

I was in a cleft stick. Norris had said: "No midgets!" His
word was absolute, and there would be serious trouble if I did
not observe it. But he had also said: "No big transfer fees."
And I had to get hold of players. Moreover, I knew this: in
football, the fans love a good little 'un more than a good big
'un. As in boxing, I believe, so in football – the big player is
worth more than the little one for sheer performance, skill being
equal. But the crowds take the little players to their hearts; and
my job, as well as team-building, was to pull the shillings to
the Highbury turnstiles.

Arsenal was leaving for a tour of Sweden the following week.
I had to work fast. I took a chance, and raced through the night
to Carlisle, going back to Workington and reaching there at
7.30 next morning. Then I had to walk about the town till
half-past three. I felt tired, sleepy, cross. But when I saw the
midget winger run down the field, I woke up all right!

He was much smaller even than "Fanny" Walden, but could
he make rings round the backs! Or could he! In my mind ran
a refrain of Sir Henry's: "Nobody under five-feet-eight or
eleven stone. . . . Nobody, mind!" I watched the little fellow

* He was Chairman of Arsenal at that time.

dancing along with the ball, and heard the crowd's satisfied yells. By half-time I realized that if I stayed watching this Northern midget any longer, I should sign him despite myself. I just forced my feet to drive me through the yelling crowd and out of the place, and back to the station. I tell you, I hated leaving him behind. I don't know what the porters and passengers thought of me, walking up and down feeling that I was throwing away the chance of a lifetime.

I got back to my splendid office at Highbury, dog-tired, my mind seeing all the time a picture of a tiny footballer spinning rings round two perfectly competent backs – a midget with a kick like a horse. I felt like a collector who has seen some rare piece, been offered it for nothing, and been afraid to take it.

And there, on the palatial sideboard that Sir Henry had provided, worth every penny of £800, lay my mail; and on top of it was a letter, answering an advertisement of mine in *Athletic News* for players . . . and the letter was from the little Cock o' the North winger, begging and praying for a chance to come to the Arsenal team.

I am only flesh and blood after all! I picked up my telephone and dictated a telegram to Moffatt saying:

Come to London as soon as possible.

The boy was due to reach Euston at 11-30 p.m. next day. I met the train. I searched it from driver's-cab to tail-light, obsessed with the familiar smell of stations and the clangour of voices, trucks, and feet on the stone platforms. Moffatt was not there. I waited to see another northern express arrive, somewhere in the depressing cold hours of the early morning. He was not on it.

I went back home, alternately cursing my cowardice because I thought someone else must have signed Moffatt in the interval, and thanking all my gods that I should not now have to explain to Sir Henry that I had flatly denied his Napoleonic command as soon as he had issued it.

Next morning I went along to Highbury, on the whole with relief predominant in my mind. The groundsman met me with a grin as wide as the Thames.

"Something's come for you, Mr Knighton!" he said. "A little tiny chap. Says he's come to play for Arsenal! He's asleep in the dressing-room."

I bolted to the players' room. There was Moffatt, fast asleep, curled up on some kit in a corner, his shock of hair sticking out like a squirrel's tail.

I stood there listening to his broad Northern drawl as he told me how he had come by an earlier train – and then gone down to Woolwich to look for the Arsenal ground! The only person he could find there – so late at night – was a road-sweeper, who stood him a cup of coffee and offered him a ride on his sweeper van. It was the first time Moffatt had ever had a motor trip, and he rode through London's deserted streets all night in silent glory. Then he found his way to Highbury and asked for me.

Of course I signed him, and he came with us on that Continental tour a few days later, simply thrilled with delight at the chance to see something of the foreign countries that had seemed to him, till that day, as remote as Mars itself. Meanwhile, Sir Henry was at his wonderful Riviera villa. I did not have to face him till later, and, like Scarlett O'Hara, I decided not to think of that now, but to think of it tomorrow!

The Continental crowds went hysterical over the wonderful little winger. He really looked like a great star in the making. I believe he scored one or two goals. When he got back to London, the crowd took him to their hearts; and he became very popular with the team. As for Sir Henry, he smiled and said nothing. But, as always, he got his own way. Moffatt had to go to Luton, and thence went on to Everton.

from BEHIND THE SCENES IN BIG FOOTBALL *1948*

A Visit to G. O. Smith

EDWARD GRAYSON

It really all began during my schooldays in the Second World War by way of relief from preparing to go up to Oxford. My form-master, Walter Lancashire, who had already played cricket for Hampshire, and was later to captain Dorsetshire, dropped the bait for an avid autograph hunter at Taunton's School, Southampton. Tucked away in retirement on the southern edge of the New Forest, near Lymington, lived the man who, in the twilight of the Victorian era, had thrilled soccer and cricket enthusiasts in the grand manner. Would I think it worthwhile to cycle over and collect his autograph? I would and did.

G. O. Smith, the greatest of the Corinthians, was my hero of classical sporting history. At the turn of the century he had played twenty-one times for England's Association football team when only three international matches were played by the home countries each year. He also scored one of the most memorable centuries in the history of the Oxford v. Cambridge cricket match at Lord's exactly three months after scoring the only goal in the Oxford v. Cambridge soccer match at the Queen's Club, West Kensington. Now from his fine old mansion house at Yaldhurst in Pennington, just outside the little watering town of Lymington, connecting the mainland with the Isle of Wight, I was directed to the Gentlemen's Club, a Pall Mall miniature fitted inside Lymington's main street. There I approached, cycle clips around my ankles, cap in hand, hot, sticky and a little apprehensive after twenty miles of pedalling along the coast road from Bournemouth – where the school had been anchored for the duration of the war.

"Could I see Mr G. O. Smith, please?"

"What is it about?"

"His autograph, please."

I waited: and the fears of failing in my quest, which had

chased me on the way, raced around my head. Then a figure of immense dignity, already a legend as the greatest centre-forward in the history of football, emerged slowly from inside; and as he came towards me I can remember vividly that the lean, lined face had not changed from the photographs I had seen of his early days.

"I hear you've come for my autograph."

"Yes, sir, from Bournemouth."

I knew he did not doubt me: but I do not think he appeared fully to appreciate why. He took me inside to the lounge, and I glowed as he carefully formed the words I was soon to know so well, "Yours sincerely, G. O. Smith."

Timorously I enquired whether there was any chance of his letting me have a signed photograph. No. They were all stuck in his albums. But he would take my name and address just in case he discovered one I might have. So I thanked him. He hoped I would not have a hard ride back. My quest was over. What more could I say? I had come for his autograph. He had given it to me. I had not the mind then to enquire of such profound matters as the conditions of play in his time, or even of the players. Did I but know, that was to come. Yet there my story would probably have ended, and what follows could never have been conceived had not a package arrived for me two days later with a signed photograph of G. O. Smith and the following note:

"I have made a thorough search through my albums, etc., but all my football groups are stuck in, so are of no use. However, I ran across the enclosed, which was taken for Charles Fry many years ago. Not a good one, I am afraid, but you may like to have it, though the pocket of the shorts leaves something to be desired.

"With best wishes,
"Ys v sincerely,
"G. O. Smith."

With such kindness a schoolboy's interest in his hero became a devotion. Perhaps he had taken pity on a youngster who had cycled forty miles for his autograph. Perhaps not all his photographs were stuck in as he believed; but his second thoughts had far-reaching consequences. The autograph alone would have satisfied my interest and desire. The photograph showed the man himself to have changed but little down the years. . . .

In the winter that followed my original quest, to relax from university preparations when the weather and air-raid warnings barred the playing fields, I dug up all that could be found about this man whom R. C. Robertson-Glasgow has described in his delightful essay on *Heroes* as "the greatest hero of them all". I ransacked *Wisden*, the old red *Lillywhite* annuals, and all other reference books to hand. An article took shape which Sir Pelham Warner published in *The Cricketer*. There were gaps to be filled, however; the written record would take me just so far. Only one authority could take me further. Shyly I approached; the response was immediate and warm. Sharp spurts of fact and fancy began to flow in an exciting correspondence, ended only by a stroke suffered by the old man in the spring of 1943.

In the late summer of that year I called on him one early evening, just when the leaves were turning brown. By then he was well on into the autumn of his life. We spoke on general lines, around the themes upon which his letters play. Significantly, behind him as we sat, there lay on his couch a newspaper or magazine – I fancy that it was an old pre-war copy of *The Topical Times* – opened at the page carrying an article with his own photograph and that of Tommy Lawton's great mentor at Everton, "Dixie" Dean. The caption was the old chestnut "Dean or Smith, the Greatest Ever?" He was too wise and modest to be drawn into this controversy; but perhaps it was appropriate that my last memory of him should be this span of history – the link between the old and the new. For within a few weeks of my joining the R.A.F. a month or so later, death removed any further chance of continuing the story.

from CORINTHIANS AND CRICKETERS *1955*

Austria takes to it

WILLI MEISL

Under the old Austrian Monarchy soccer started almost simultaneously in Prague, Vienna, and Graz, the capital of Styria. Vienna possessed a sizeable British colony. A number of British firms had branches or representatives in Austria's metropolis. An English gasworks had the licence to light the capital; English artists appeared on the stage; English typewriters, caps, clothes, shoes, and everything English was in demand. Gandon, of the said gasworks; Loew, manager of a hat manufacturer's; Blyth of the Haberdashers and gentlemen's fashion house, Stone and Blyth; John Gramlick, owner of a firm for electrical components; Shires, who represented Underwood; Blackey, manager of the engineering firm Clayton and Shuttleworth; Rev. Hechler of Vienna's Anglican church; these were some of the men who founded the first two football clubs in Vienna. A few of Baron Rothschild's English gardeners, William Beale, James Black, Kent, Roberts, Major were others, not to forget the giant Flavin, famous as the "Irish Oak". The British influence is manifested in the name of the two oldest organizations, the 1st Vienna F.C. and the Vienna Cricket and Football Club (from which, via the Wiener Amateur S.V., the present F.K. Austria descended). Although very few of its members and hardly any of its supporters had ever seen, let alone played, cricket, the latter team was known only as the "Cricketers", whilst the other has remained the "Vienna" until this day. The Vienna, established by the above-mentioned gardeners, adopted Baron Rothschild's racing colours, blue-yellow. Cricket's colours were blue-black. On 15 November 1894 the two played the first football match ever staged in Austria proper. Cricket won 4–0 and soon repeated the success by the same result.

Many odd things happened in the Stone and Bronze Age of Austrian soccer. A player of the Vienna broke a collar-bone being tackled by the "Irish Oak", the most robust charger of a robust football epoch. Shocked, the 1st Vienna F.C. abandoned the field. The insurance company sued Flavin, but Austria's justice must have been a long kick ahead of Austrian soccer, because Flavin was acquitted and an important precedent created.

Another odd occurrence happened in 1897 when Vienna and Cricket met again and the entrance fee was doubled from threepence to sixpence. This was not done to fill the club's coffers, but "to reduce the number of spectators". The organizers were afraid the crowd might exceed 200 people. This might have caused trouble as the field was only fenced in by a rope which also served as touch and goal-line.

In 1897 M. D. Nicholson arrived at Thomas Cook and Son's Vienna office, undoubtedly the most prominent English player in Austria's soccer history. Later he proved an equally efficient organizer and he became the first president of the Austrian Football Union, predecessor of the Austrian F.A.

On Easter Sunday 1899 the Austrians were treated to their first taste of real English football. Oxford University overwhelmed a combined city eleven 15–0. On Easter Monday they had to be satisfied with a narrower victory, 13–0. It was an heroic era. When, before the "derby" match Cricket versus Vienna in 1900, Nicholson was told that his greatest antagonist and countryman, Windett, was injured and could not turn out, he wanted to stand down as well, so that Vienna should not enjoy an "unfair" advantage. In that year the first English professionals came over, Southampton F.C. They beat the Viennese city eleven 6–0 and their goalkeeper, Robinson,* showed for the first time how to tackle low shots by flying through the air with the greatest of ease. To this day that type of save is called a "Robinsonade" in Austria and Central Europe. After the match Robinson gave an exhibition. His goal was bombarded simultaneously with six balls and he blocked most of the shots. Just like "Tiger" Khomich with his Moscow Dynamos in 1945 at Stamford Bridge, when the Russians shot at his goal with half a dozen balls!

* See page 332.

Southampton were followed by Richmond and then a Cambridge University XI. In 1904 the Austrian F.A. was founded and in April of that year we saw the famous Corinthians, including G. O. Smith, G. C. Vassall, and C. E. Wreford-Brown. They beat us 7–1.

Then came Glasgow Rangers, on whose style the Austrians were to mould their game. Simultaneously Celtic was welcomed, too, but did not make much of an impression. In 1905 my brother Hugo brought the Pilgrims over, a touring team. Hugo organized these visits of British sides not only for Vienna, but often also for Prague, Budapest, and also for German, Swiss, and Italian clubs and associations. He managed to get rid of a small fortune in the process of fostering Austrian soccer. The Pilgrims, by the way, beat Wiener A.C. 10–1, Cricket 7–1, and the Grazer A.K. 9–2. Tottenham, without their amateur centre-forward, the famous Vivian Woodward, defeated a Viennese combination 6–0. Then on 7 May 1905 Hugo staged an exhibition game between Everton and Tottenham. The two teams fought as if it were a Cup-tie. Never before had the 10,000 spectators – the crowd record was doubled by this sensational encounter – seen such tackling. Tottenham were favourites, but Everton won 2–0. Everton also offered four Austrian players professional contracts, an honour considered the accolade of soccer. Glasgow Rangers actually took goalkeeper Karl Pekarna with them to Glasgow. In the same year Hugo led Austria into the F.I.F.A. which had been founded in 1904.

English teams played in Austria every summer. In 1908 came Manchester United and won as they pleased. To celebrate Emperor Franz Josef's sixtieth anniversary on the throne, Hugo had managed to bring the F.I.F.A.-Congress to Vienna. What was much more important, the English national eleven came over for two matches which were won 6–1 and 11–1 with Woodward and Hilsdon as the outstanding marksmen. Next year on their way back from Budapest, England played once more against Austria and won 8–1 before a 3,000 crowd, a very large one for a weekday.

1909 was another milestone in Austria's soccer history. The
Wiener A.C. defeated Sunderland 2-1, the first set-back an
English professional side suffered in Austria. Cup-finalists
Barnsley were a robust disappointment in 1910; of the 1911
visitors, Blackburn Rovers, Oldham Athletic and Celtic,
Rovers made by far the best impression. Even I, then a very
small boy, remember their glorious centre-half, Percy Smith,
scoring five goals from corner-kicks, all headers. Blackburn
beat WAF 9-1, although the Austrians were no longer
beginners. After all, Blackburn also beat Oldham 5-2, who in
turn could defeat WAF only by the odd goal.

In 1912 Hugo introduced Jimmy Hogan to Vienna, who
also became my club's coach. As a young "grammar" school
boy I was amongst his first bunch of pupils. As Hugo's brother
I also received many a private lesson. It was in Vienna that
Jimmy discovered how primitive British training methods were.
With Hugo he worked out a more satisfactory scheme,
probably the first modern training schedule in soccer. To save
him from internment in the first World War Jimmy was
smuggled to Budapest where he did splendid work, above all,
with the MTK.

In Prague, too, the leading three clubs, amongst the very best
on the Continent, had Scottish coaches, Madden and Jimmy
Dick. Austrians, Hungarians, and Czechs moulded their game
on the Scottish last – precise short passing and clever
positioning.

When Arsenal came to Prague they had a marvellous young
centre-forward, Leslie Calder, who scored some goals against
the DFC, the club of the German, or rather Jewish, minority in
the Czech capital. Leslie was invited to join the DFC, as an
amateur, of course. A nice, comfortable job was to be found
for him, an offer too good to be rejected, nor was it ever
regretted. Leslie stayed on, was "re-named" Less and became
one of the Continent's greatest stars and goalgetters. He also
became a model for Prague's youth. As a boy of sixteen I played
against him in the famous DFC attack and can testify that
"Less's" aim was true and he carried dynamite in both boots.

After the first World War we had a soccer boom also in Austria. Crowds multiplied. 40,000 came to big matches where before the war 15,000 had been a good gate. In 1924 Hugo introduced open professionalism. I have no hesitation in proclaiming some of the leading sides of that period in the Central-European capitals as good as, if not better than, the later so highly praised Dynamo-Moscow, the Hungarian national side, or Honved. The short peak-period of the Austrian "Wonder Team" excepted, the Hungarians were usually a short jump ahead of the rest. Some Hungarians became models for the entire Continent. Alfred Schaffer, whom the Germans and even the unemotional Swiss baptized the "Football King" made the pace for class soccer. Schaffer was the best paid "amateur" of his time. Gyuri Orth, Kalman Konrad, all of the famous MTK, were other names with which one could juggle in Continental soccer. Kalman Konrad lived in Austria where the famous Matthias Sindelar, his country's and possible the Continent's greatest centre-forward, modelled his style on Kalman's. Schaffer later also played some years for F.K. Austria.

Sindy or "Flimsy" (der "Papierene") as Matthias Sindelar was affectionately called, because of his fragile build, was hardly a welterweight and quite tall at that. He was truly symbolical of Austrian soccer at its peak period: no brawn but any amount of brain. Technique bordering on virtuosity, precision work and an inexhaustible repertoire of tricks and ideas. He had a boyish delight in soccer exploits, above all in unexpected twists and moves which were quickly understood and shared by his partners brought up on the same "wave-length", but were baffling to an opposition mentally a fraction of a second slower. Sindelar, though a soccer genius, was never an egotist. Like Kalman Konrad he, too, commanded a rasping shot, but both preferred to walk, or rather to dance the ball not only towards the goal, but almost literally into the net. It did not always come off, but with such artists you have to take the rough with the smooth.

There had been many great players before them right down

to the Stone Age of Austrian soccer. Not to go back too far I would only mention the forwards Wondrak, Edi Bauer, Wieser, Svatosch, Taurer, Fishera, Studnicka, Cohn; the halves Karli Kurz, Nitsch, Braunsteiner, Tekusch; full-backs Xanel Popovic, Blum, ("MacJohn") Leuthe, and the goalies Pekarna, Hiden and Zeman who were all as good as any member of the famous "Wonder Team" and can rank with the best in the world. There were equally outstanding stars in Hungary and Czechoslovakia, also in Italy and South Germany.

The Mitropa Cup and the Nations' Cup, both thought up and organized by Hugo did much to popularize football on the Continent and enhance its quality. The most gifted ball-playing people – Hungarians, Austrians, Czechs, and Italians – exchanged styles and ideas on club as well as national levels. Thousands of soccer enthusiasts travelled from far-away neutral countries to watch the big matches in the Mitropa Cup tournament, the pace-maker of the World Cup.

In 1926 Arsenal were no longer so superior to Vienna's top clubs. They drew 3–3 with Rapid and beat Austria (the former "Cricketers") 5–3, but lost by the odd goal to their combined eleven.

In the following year Hugo at last made football his profession. He accepted the combined job of general secretary and team manager to the Austrian F.A. For many years his office was the nerve-centre and clearing station of European soccer.

Herbert Chapman's greatness was proved to me once more when I met him on the Continent. After the close of the English season he repeatedly came over on a busman's holiday trip studying Continental soccer. At that time he was the only Briton in a responsible position who did so and until today – or at least until 26 November 1953 – he has not had many successors, at least at club level. Mr Stanley Rous also did much travelling abroad a little later, in great demand as the soccer-world's outstanding referee. Hugo arranged with Chapman the transfer of Rudolf Hiden, the goalkeeper of the WAC and the national side. The transfer fee of £2,000 had actually been deposited with an Austrian bank and Hiden had left Vienna

for London in 1930, but he could not get into England. The
Ministry of Labour had laid down what might be called a lex
Chapman or lex Hiden. No foreign footballer was to receive a
labour permit until after two years' residence in the country.
Hiden would have been a hit at Highbury, bigger even than
Trautmann was at Manchester fifteen years later.

What had made Chapman particularly eager to secure Hiden
as an additional attraction for star-studded Highbury was the
Austrian goalkeeper's fine exhibition on 15 May 1930 when
England were held to a goalless draw at Vienna.

A year later the "Wonder Team" was born when Scotland
visited Vienna in May 1931 and went down 5–0. Although it
was not exactly Scotland's strongest side, the Viennese were
sure enough that their team was in for a thrashing. Only
40,000 spectators turned up to see the slaughter, but as so often
happens in football the odds-on favourite fell whilst the outsider played a blinder. Ivan Sharpe, who saw the match, said
afterwards that not even the "Blue Wizards", when they beat
England 5–1 at Wembley in 1928, reached such heights as did
the Austrians on that day in May. Then Austria outclassed
Germany in Berlin 6–0, beat Switzerland 2–0 and Germany
5–0, this time at Vienna. The Germans tried to copy British
"safety first" and "stopper" tactics slavishly.

In Basle Switzerland were routed 8–1. In 1932 Italy lost by
the odd goal of three. Walter Nausch – later to become Hugo's
successor as Austria's team manager – got his first cap in this
match. In April Hungary was sent home beaten 8–2, probably
the greatest triumph in Sindelar's career. He not only scored a
hat-trick, but had a foot in almost all the home goals. Then
suddenly the "Wonder Team" lost its immaculate edge, was
no longer so razor sharp. In Prague Austria could only draw
1–1. Three new players had to be introduced and the famous
side was obviously a sensitive piece of precision machinery.

Then came the 7th of December when Austria lost to England
at Stamford Bridge by the odd goal of seven, but showed an
unbelieving Great Britain that the soccer tide was on the
turn.

Europe's best referee, my late friend John Langenus from Antwerp, followed these sides on to the field:

England: Hibbs; Goodall, Hapgood; Strange, Hart, Keen; Crooks, Jack, Hampson, Walker, Houghton.

Austria: Hiden; Rainer, Sesta; Nausch, Smistik, Gall; Zischek, Gschweidl, Sindelar, Schall, Vogl.

Just over 40,000 people had come to watch the Austrians who had won fifteen of their last eighteen international matches and lost none.

Only two Continental teams had been invited to England before, and the first visit lay so far back it was already forgotten. In 1923 Belgium was beaten at Highbury 6–1. Only a year before Austria's visit in 1931, Spain went down at Highbury 7–1. This result was, of course, a fallacy. . . . What the English could not know was the incredible inferiority complex under which these early Continental sides laboured when they stepped on to a British football field. For them it was sacred soil. They were so over-awed they hardly dared to put a foot down. If they were hit by an early goal, let alone by a couple, their strained nerves were shattered and they were beaten before they had a chance to get going.

In spite of the Spanish example, in spite of my brother's warning, it was in that first half-hour that Austria, too, lost her chance of bringing off a sensation compared with which Hungary's victory at Wembley in 1953 would have seemed unimportant. In 1932 British, and above all English soccer, was still the peak at which all other nations aimed, although the Continent felt that the gap was closing rapidly.

Far be it from me to make excuses twenty-five years after the event for what was then my side, but Vogl and Gschweidl were not fully fit. They were still preferred by far to any reserves. Hiden, wanting to show off, was still shaking inwardly; over-doing the "gallery stuff" he gave away a corner from which Hampson scored. The English centre-forward followed up this early success with a second goal after twenty-seven minutes. At half-time the team got its instructions from Hugo. He enjoyed the boundless respect but also the true affection of his players. They had calmed down, got used to the fabulous fact of playing in England. When they took the field again, they played as if they were "at home". The sporting English crowd rose to them, cheering and applauding many moves that showed finesse and rhythm. It became 2–1, but the home lead grew to 3–1 through a free-kick taken by Houghton and deflected by Sesta's body. Not even Hiden, now playing in great form, could do anything about that, but the Austrian forwards and halves waltzed the ball towards the English goal rhythmically, precisely, not lacking in punch. When the score was 3–2 everything was in the balance again. Then David Jack saw his chance, made a beautiful pass and Crooks secured a fourth goal. The final whistle came at 4–3 with the Austrians in un-disputed command. The English critics as well as the crowd were raving with enthusiasm about the Austrian soccer exhibition. Such almost intellectual football had apparently become a rarity in Britain even then. . . .

Visiting club sides no longer travelled in one direction exclusively. Although British teams continued to visit Austria regularly, a number of Austria's leading teams also played in Great Britain. In November 1933 the Scots tried to avenge their Vienna defeat, but at Hampden Park they could do no more than draw 2–2. Meiklejohn and McFadyen scored for the home side, Schall and Zischek for the guests. Five days later, a slightly altered Austrian side, labelled Viennese City Selection, met Chapman's Arsenal at Highbury and lost 4–2 in a good game. The Austrians lacked punch, whilst Hulme, Jack, and Bastin scored fine goals. Sindelar and Schall replied for the guests.

Jimmy Hogan had meanwhile been to England and had quickly got the sack at Fulham before he had a chance. Hugo recalled him in 1935 to make him Austria's travelling coach entrusted with the special task of preparing the country's amateurs for the Olympic tournament at Berlin in 1936. This team, consisting of unknown players from the provinces, finished sensationally as runners-up to Italy's full and semi-professionals.

In the same spring Austria's professionals had for the first time triumphed over England 2–1. They were no longer the "Wonder Team"; that eleven had changed considerably. The new wingers, Viertl and Geiter – neither of them a patch on Zischek or Vogl – were the scorers; Camsell shot the goal for England.

When Hitler occupied the country and Austria ceased to be an independent state, she also ceased to be an independent soccer entity.

Austria's meetings with England and Scotland after the second World War and the liberation are recent soccer history. In 1951 a very good England v. Austria game at Wembley ended 2–2. The guests had more of the ball, the home side had the better scoring chances. In the previous year a goal by the outside-right, Ernst Melchior, made Scotland suffer her first home defeat by a Continental side at Hampden Park. In spring 1951 the Scots lost at Vienna 4–0, whilst a year later England won there in a fighting game by the odd goal of five.

The death in December 1954 of Dr Josef Gero, the Austrian Minister of Justice, President of the Austrian F.A. and the Austrian Olympic Committee, was a severe blow to the country's sport, especially to soccer. Of the old guard from the epoch of the "Wonder Team" only Walter Nausch (now dead) and the F.A.'s general secretary, Josef Liegl, were left in the O.F.B.

from SOCCER REVOLUTION *1957*

A First Game

PETER DOHERTY

Soon after leaving school, my dreams of a football career began to take on a tinge of reality. A letter arrived for me one day from the Coleraine club, asking me to sign amateur forms – their scout had evidently watched me playing with Station

United, a local junior team. I wasn't too thrilled at first, because this sort of thing had happened to several of my pals, and they had heard nothing more; a local boy is fortunate indeed if he gets on with the local club. But luck was with me. I received word to report at the Agricultural Ground, Coleraine's enclosure, on the following Saturday, to stand by as a reserve.

The rest of the week passed in a dream. When Saturday came at last, I could hardly contain my excitement. I raced to the ground, and then prowled about outside the dressing-rooms, too nervous to even poke my nose in. Suppose someone doesn't turn up, I thought; I'll be playing – actually playing for Coleraine! And then, as I toyed with my hopes, I suddenly found myself being hustled into the dressing-room, and told to change. Someone actually hadn't turned up. Norman Lynn, the outside-right, had missed his train at Belfast, and I was to take his place. By the time I'd donned a jersey and rummaged amongst the pile of boots in the middle of the floor to find a pair to fit me, the game had started. But once outside, the air and shorts and jersey gave me that free, fresh feeling you always get at the beginning of a game, and I ran on to the field with a light heart, and a prayer that my luck would hold.

During that first half, however, I think I kicked the ball twice. Hardly a pass came my way, and for long periods I was merely a spectator. Our opponents' left-back could never have had an easier day. In the dressing-room at half-time, I was completely ignored; no one attempted to speak to me, and even the boy who brought the lemon slices round gave me a wide berth. And then the final humiliation occurred. Norman Lynn arrived, and I was asked to hand over my jersey. I struggled out of it, fighting hard to keep back the tears, and vowing bitterly that Coleraine would never get another chance to treat me so badly; and even now, when my mind goes back to that dreadful afternoon, I find it difficult not to shudder.

Doherty, of course, later played for Glentoran, Blackpool, Manchester City, Derby County, Doncaster Rovers, and Huddersfield Town, perhaps the finest inside-forward ever to be capped for Ireland.

from SPOTLIGHT ON FOOTBALL *1947*

Absent Heart

J. P. W. MALLALIEU

Yet it began so well. . . .

When I fed the rabbits, the sun was as high as it can go in January, and the frost on the lawn was melting. The whole morning seemed to glisten. So it should; for this was the shiniest morning in the football calendar, the third-round-of-the-Cup morning, when the big clubs come in for the first time and those little clubs which have insinuated themselves through earlier rounds think they are going to knock the Brylcreem off their betters.

What a morning this always is! The earlier rounds are important, no doubt, to those who habitually engage in them. But no one else bothers. We just notice when, say, Blyth Spartans and Tranmere Rovers fail to reach a decision at their first meeting; fail to reach a decision, after extra time, at their second meeting, and have in all, to play 300 minutes before they can tell which of the two is to be slaughtered in the third round. The other results cause about as much stir as a maiden over in a Test Match with India.

But the third round is real. You get the clash of the great, like Newcastle and Aston Villa. You get the minor local "Derbies" like Brentford and Queen's Park Rangers. Above all you get the babies against the giants, like Scunthorpe against the Spurs or Workington against Liverpool – and presumably Tranmere Rovers were playing somebody too. How we all hope that these babies will repeat the fairy story – and well they may if they are playing on their own ground. These baby teams sometimes have baby grounds which cramp the giants; and on these baby grounds there are sometimes baby hillocks and baby valleys which upset billiard-table players from the First Division. How everyone laughs when one of the giants comes a cropper, when Arsenal falls to Walsall or Sunderland gets stuck at Yeovil. That's all part of the Cup. Anything can happen. So the morning of the third round glistens, even when, as often happens, you can't see a yard in front of you for fog.

There was no fog for *this* third round. The warmth of the sun had made even rabbits lazy. At any rate, they had not bothered to burrow into my lawn. After feeding them, I sat in the sun and wondered idly which team I would back that afternoon. Usually I pick North v. South, but I couldn't decide which was which from Brentford (of Brentford) v. Queen's Park Rangers (of Shepherd's Bush). I should have to get these two sorted for me by Mercator himself. I plumped for the Rangers, only because their manager, Dave Mangnall, used to play for Huddersfield, and because their inside-right, Conway Smith, not only played for Huddersfield himself, but is the son of the late Billy Smith who for twenty years almost was Huddersfield.

Leaving my rabbits to the sun, I set off by car for Griffin Park. Most English football-grounds are so hidden by terraced, red-brick houses that you would think the game was some sort of sin, to be kept from the notice of the police and the churches. But on a Cup-tie day there's no disguising them. Those three mounted policemen trotting up the street – I'll bet they are not defending the Brentford gas-works; and those newspaper bills, tied round lamp-posts, advertising all the sport – they're not *always* showing in back streets; nor, I am sure, are those elderly men with walking sticks, who wait hopefully at corners and beckon cars. These are the pointers to a football-ground which even Dr Watson could not have missed, and if you follow them, as I did, around midday, you will find the little queues, rubbing their noses against closed gates, which are the final proof without which Holmes never closed his mind.

Little queues? I was surprised myself. But the older I get, the more I become like Dr Watson. So I drew no sensible conclusion. After circling the ground and finding only little queues, I assumed that there would be no difficulty about seeing the match. So I left my car in the care of one of those old men with sticks, and went into "The Griffin" for a sandwich and a glass of beer. In the pub I discovered that this Cup-tie was "ticket only"; and I had no ticket.

I appealed to the landlord. No go. The landlord appealed all round the bar. No go. The landlord's son, aged ten, announced that *he* had a ticket but made it clear that it was no go either. Then someone remembered that twenty minutes ago, the local butcher had had a spare ticket. The landlord rang him up; the ticket was still spare: the landlord's son trotted off to fetch it, and I was in. I was among strangers in "The Griffin"; but if you are a real football fan and meet other real football fans you are among strangers no more.

I was able to pick my place, on the rails, right behind one of the goals. The empty stands had all the hollowness of a main-line railway-station in the early morning, so that the rattles and the shouts of the men who, quite seriously, on this January morning, were selling ice-cream echoed against the corrugated iron roofs. But, hollowness and ice-cream notwithstanding, I felt warm in expectation. I remembered the first time, thirty-two years ago, that I had stood directly behind a goal. Within two minutes of the kick-off my Huddersfield had fired a beautiful, new yellow ball into that goal and had almost blown the net away. I thought cosily of Huddersfield playing an easy match, 190 miles away, playing an easy match which might even at the eleventh hour provide the spark to light them home.

"Ladies and gentlemen, it is exactly sixty minutes to the kick-off." The echo from the loudspeaker seemed dulled, and I noticed that the ground was beginning to fill. By the time the loudspeaker announced: "Ladies and gentlemen, the kick-off will be in, approximately, seven minutes. Will people standing on the gangways move away?" there was no echo at all, and, so far as I could see, nowhere for people on the gangways to move away to. I myself had been edged from the rails, politely but effectively, by four small boys, who unscrupulously used their lack of height to play on their better feelings. However, I could still see, and anyway was spellbound in those magic moments which immediately precede the launching of a Cup-tie.

Yes, the day had begun well.

The game itself cast no spells – except, perhaps, on the

players. Brentford won 3–1, which pleased the four boys who had stolen my place on the rails; but I was really waiting for the half-time scores on the board at the far end of the ground and for *Sports Report* with the final results on my wireless at home. In the meantime I watched the Brentford goalkeeper. Gaskell, who kept his watch some five yards in front of me, Gaskell had a busy afternoon. Someone, it seemed, had left tiny bits of straw in his goal-mouth, all of which had to be picked up and placed carefully in the back of the net. Gaskell lumbered up and down, shoulders bent, eyes on the ground, picking up these bits. When, at last, the place seemed tidy, he stood on his six-yard line and stared gloomily at the far goal, realizing, no doubt, that in the second half he would have to begin tidying all over again. Even now his eye would detect stray bits of straw. He would dart at them and take them disdainfully to the back of the net. These salvage operations were seldom interrupted. Indeed, when Gaskell dived to a sudden shot from Rangers, I believe he was really after another of those straws. I shall ask him to train at our house until the carpet-sweeper is repaired.

Half-time came and went with the score satisfactory 190 miles away; and, by and by, I was home for tea and the time was half past five. I do like *Sports Report*. The two Davies give their reports like over-bright uncles telling fairy stories to moronic children; and the man who reads the League results continuously tells people that Huddersfield Town have lost. But this evening I waited calmly, even tolerantly, for the inevitably satisfying end to a satisfying day. I was even unruffled by my children, who were in a teasing mood and kept shouting "Vote Conservative!" or, alternatively, "Up Cambridge!" Then, quite suddenly, I was alone in the world. The wireless crackled with the uncontrollable laughter of millions, my children cheered and my rabbits began a large-scale excavation of my lawn, while I began to pick little pieces of straw from the carpet and put them in my hair. For the B.B.C. (Psychological Warfare Department) had just made the following announcement:

"Huddersfield Town 1, Tranmere Rovers 2."
Yet it began so well. . . .

from SPORTING DAYS *1955*

Yorkshire Derby

J. P. W. MALLALIEU

My train shot from the long Standedge tunnel just as dawn was creeping down Wessendon and lighting Black Hill. I cleared a circle on the streaming window and peered at the moorland peaks which stretch away to Woodhead, to the Snake, to Featherbed Moss and to Sheffield. Black Hill was white, and, as the train clattered down the Colne Valley, I saw that the long grass was stiff and that the usually warm, soft peat was hard and cold. Thank goodness this is not a rugger match, I said.

At the hotel a sleepy night porter brightened when he saw me. "You're up for the match, I suppose," he said. The waiter at breakfast was too busy guessing the score to find the marmalade, constituents who came to see me during the morning with serious personal troubles could yet find time to peer anxiously through my office windows at the snow-laden clouds, and in the café where I had lunch the customers exchanged eager gossip about the teams while the waitresses, who would be tied to their jobs all afternoon, made sarcastic comments about people who wasted their time at football matches.

How different all this was from last season, when Huddersfield seemed full of Rugby League fans, when no one mentioned football except to say that "Town" was doomed and a few faithful dragged their long faces and leaden feet to Leeds Road only in the confident anticipation of disaster. But now, as we began our walk to the ground, there were bright faces everywhere, shining from the sharp air and from the hope of victory, there were brisk, long-striding feet and there was the humming bubble of excitement. For that afternoon Huddersfield Town, second in the Second Division, were playing the Division leaders, neighbouring Sheffield United; and not a man in the West Riding was indifferent to, not a man in Huddersfield was uncertain of, the result.

We joined the groups of men and women who were trickling down every side street from the shopping-centre. We hustled and jostled along, counting the years – twenty-four, if you allow the New Year as one – since Sheffield United had won at Leeds Road, we winked at each other and at last we were in the ground with fifteen minutes to spare and 43,000 fellow fanatics packed around us. Then we had time again to notice the weighted sky and the sand-covered pitch. We'd be lucky to see good football on a surface like that. We'd be lucky to see anything if that sky gave way.

For a moment expectancy ebbed, for snow-clouds and a skating surface were not the only reasons for caution. This was a needle match between two teams who, with more than half a season gone, seem to be fighting it out on their own. It might well decide the championship, and such matches often produce more vigour than science. Moreover, this was a local "Derby", and you can guess what that may mean. Between Huddersfield and Sheffield there is none of that division of Protestant and Catholic which turns a game between Celtic and Rangers into a religious war. Huddersfield and Sheffield men often speak to each other, and, during the cricket season, will even risk taking their hands out of their pockets in each other's company. But a local Derby is a local Derby, in which the players can expect more bruises than goals and from which spectators can suffer severe injury to their local pride. When you are beaten at home by a team from far away you at least know that when the last train or coach leaves you will be shot of that team and its supporters for a twelvemonth. But a man from Huddersfield may bump into a man from Sheffield any day of the week and get salt rubbed into the sorer places. So when the red and white of Sheffield appeared beneath the stand and provoked a roar

R

which showed that many men from Sheffield had risked the moorland snow and ice, the appearance beneath the stand of Huddersfield's blue and white provoked an explosion of defiance, plus some cautionary boos for the referee.

For about five minutes the Huddersfield team seemed to be playing on skates. They glided over the ground and round the Sheffield players, while the home crowd exulted and a covey of Sheffield supporters near me gabbled to each other darkly in some language of their own. Then one of the skaters was tripped and the home crowd yelled, first at the referee, then at this covey of foreigners, in language that is universal. The Sheffield men looked down their noses and said nothing. Before turning back to the game a home spectator fired a passing shot at them. "Yon's Third Division stoof, yon is," he said. Seconds later, a Sheffield player was tripped and the Sheffield covey rose as one. "*Yon's* Third Division stoof," they yelled. "Ay," said a Huddersfield man, "we've learned it from thee." Then opening his eyes in round surprise he added: "Well ah nivver did! Tha' can talk King's English same as oos."

The first half was not all tripping. But on that surface there were other kinds of falls. Here the slush would hold up a pass so that it was intercepted, there a player, clear away with the ball at his feet, would suddenly skid and lose his chance. Then, with five minutes of the first half left, Sheffield were given a penalty. If the Sheffield crowd felt any distress because they were about to take the lead by such means they controlled it with visible effortlessness. Nor was there any effort about the roar from Huddersfield when Sheffield duly scored. Through the hubbub I could hear the one word "Referee". But as the game resumed and anger was brought under control I realized that the crowd was talking not only about this referee but about referees in general. Just look at that fellow at Swansea last week – and *his* linesman. At least the linesmen had been honest – blatant if you like. They had boldly put down that they came from Cardiff and Abertillery. But the referee had put down that he came from Wakefield. Why, man, we found out later that he was born in Pontypridd. Rumble, rumble as the game slid on; and half-time came while the crowd was still undecided about the origins of this present referee – though certain, of course, about his eventual destination.

Rumble, rumble, as the game resumed, and then, suddenly, ecstasy. Sheffield United put through their own goal and the scores were level. Nothing could have pleased us more. It would, I suppose, have been quite nice if, after a dazzling interchange of passing the length of the field, one of our forwards had scored with a blinding shot. But what really suited us was that Sheffield should do the scoring for us, and that the man who had the misfortune to score should have been the full-back who had kicked that penalty goal. We looked upwards, not this time in fear of snow, but in thankfulness that justice still reigned supreme. How we rubbed that justice in!

Then something happened. The players on both sides got on top of the elements, got on top of themselves, got on top of us. They forgot that this was a needle, Derby match and began to play football. For the last twenty minutes the game was inspired. End to end it went, with both teams playing for victory instead of kicking for it. With five minutes to go Huddersfield settled in the Sheffield goal-mouth. We got four corners in quick succession with all Sheffield yelling to the referee that it was long past time. Then, with two minutes to go, Sheffield swung it to the other end, won two corners and once sent the ball skidding right across the open goal-mouth with all Huddersfield shrieking that it was practically midnight. Oh that final whistle! It had been blown twenty seconds ago, before I realized that the game was over. Then came a gasp, a sigh, a long deep throated cheer and we realized that Sheffield men were, after all, civilized, that these United chaps actually played at our beloved Bramall Lane, that, on such a surface, both teams had in fact done wonders, and that a 1–1 draw was just right. A Huddersfield supporter was so overwhelmed with this rush of emotion that he actually said: "I take back what I called the referee. He was not *bad*. He was just poor."

from SPORTING DAYS *1955*

The Gentleman from Glasgow

J. P. W. MALLALIEU

On Friday, 17 April, 1953, at about 11 p.m., in Piccadilly, a gentleman from Glasgow declined the advice of a gentleman from London. As the gentleman from London was wearing one of those funny helmets, the gentleman from Glasgow spent the night in a cell, and thereafter was decanted before another gentleman from London who wore no helmet but was protected, instead, by two penetrating eyes.

"What," said the Beak, "is the charge?" "Drunk and disorderly," said a Clerk. "What," said the Beak, some moments later, nodding his head at the gentleman from Glasgow, "had he in his pockets?" "Two pennies and the return half of his ticket to Glasgow," said the London gentleman who had been wearing his helmet the previous evening. "Two pennies, the return half of his ticket to Glasgow – and a ticket for the England and Scotland match at Wembley this afternoon."

The Beak's penetrating eyes bored into the gentleman from Glasgow whose face, whatever colour it might have been at 11 p.m. on Friday, 17 April, was by now white. Would it be a lecture? He could not endure it in his shaking state. Would it be a fine? Had anyone every heard of a 2d. fine? Would it be a prison sentence? Then he would miss the match.

The Beak reflected; then, "One day's imprisonment!"; then, "But take care that he's out in time to see the match" – and at that, while the Beak rustled the papers of his next case, the gentleman from Glasgow's face suddenly became like the sunrise and the whole police court was suffused with beaming warmth.

Englishmen, on the day, feel strongly about an encounter between England and Scotland whether at Rugby or soccer. But their feelings are only strong, not fundamental; they are not expressed, and they exist only on the day. But a Scotsman's feelings on these matters seep down into his being until they become a part of his instinct; they are expressed as steam is expressed through the safety valve of a standing locomotive, and they exist not just for one day but from the moment one match ends until the moment the next match has ended. The fire underneath his boiler is no sooner extinguished than it is rekindled; and if the boiler happens to burst, as I saw it burst last Saturday, well then, there are plenty more boilers where that one came from. The Scotsman turns homeward on the Saturday night. His spirit may deflect him from the homeward line, so that, for example, he finds himself without his train at Crewe, but eventually he gets home; and from that moment he begins to save, as he will save for nothing else, to meet the fare and other expenses incidental to a Wembley trip in two years' time. He must not cheat about this saving. There must be no raiding of his children's boxes, no docking of his wife's money. The savings must really be his own, and, because they are his own, they are his to deal with as he pleases. Once he has paid his fare and got his Wembley ticket, he can blow the whole lot – all but twopence – on the Friday night, and no one will stay his hand. No one? It was a near thing. Not even Jacob, fobbed off with Leah after seven years, could be more downcast than a Scottish football fan fobbed off with a prison cell after two years. But because sportsmen, in England or elsewhere, are sportsmen, the gentleman from Glasgow got his Rachel after all.

I thought of him nearly all that afternoon at Wembley. The tartan bonnets and the red lions of Scotland on their yellow backgrounds so dominated the arena that the greenness of the velvet turf seemed only pale by comparison. The pre-match hum of the 100,000 crowd had a tone which was alien to my ear, and the tunes which were played either by the disabled ex-servicemen without or by the wholly able Marines within were alien too. Wembley that afternoon seemed to be soaked in Scotland. I felt there the demanding eagerness of that two years' expectant abstinence; and, as the game wore on, I felt compassion for those thousands whose new unleashed desires were not, it seemed, about to be fulfilled.

The truth, apparent after a very few minutes, was that England were not a good side. The Froggatt family on their left wing were full of energy but, today, deficient in skill. Finney, on the right wing, felt so full of skill that he tried to beat not one man but three – and failed. Lofthouse at centre could not beat even one man. In the defence, the shakiness of Barrass at centre-half and Smith at left-back seemed to be unsettling Merrick in goal. Only Wright and Dickinson, the English wing-halves, seemed wholly sure of themselves. So it was that, twice in the first half, Scotland looked like scoring. First, after thirty-one minutes, Merrick leaped for a cross, missed, fell to the ground and left his goal open. The Scottish forward who was up had only to hit the trickling ball hard. Instead he tapped it, and an England back kicked off the line. Again, after forty minutes, Steel hit the crossbar. Again the rebound, more difficult to control this time, was only tapped back, and again an England defender kicked it off the line.

But in spite of England's weakness, in spite of Scotland's chances, it was clear beyond doubt to expert eyes that England would win. By half-time they were a goal ahead. In the nineteenth minute Finney had got the ball on the wing, beaten two men and then, as usual, been beaten by the third. But he recovered, snatched the ball again, sent in a lovely ground pass to Broadis who scored directly. Thereafter England ambled easily until it was time for a sponge and a slice of lemon.

England continued to amble in the second half until eleven minutes after the restart, when a pass from Steel, while Barrass was thinking about higher things, gave Johnstone a chance which he slammed against the crossbar. Before Merrick could reopen his eyes, Reilly had the rebound in the net. Thereat England, at any rate, caught fire. For nearly a quarter of an hour they hammered the Scots, and at last the deserved goal came. Broadis cut his way through the centre until, on the penalty line, he looked to have a scoring chance. But tamely he passed far out to Finney on the wing. That was that. But it wasn't. Finney held the ball, manoeuvred and seemed to have beaten Cox. Then Cox beat him. That *was* that. But it wasn't. Finney recovered, snatched the ball, ran round Cox and centred. Broadis hit the ball directly into the net. That was 2–1 with fifteen minutes to go, and, when it was seen that Cox had so injured himself in trying to stop Finney that he had to be carried off, we knew that that really was that. Just as England ambled their way through the remaining minutes, so hundreds if not thousands of spectators ambled from the arena. I thought only of the gentleman from Glasgow, his hopes ebbing from him and his head aching. Would not the prison cell have been preferable to all this?

Then it happened. It was past normal time. There were, as it turned out, no more than twenty seconds left of the extra time allowed for injuries, when Johnstone in mid-field gave a pass to Reilly. Reilly, to show that there was no harm in a little fun, passed back to Johnstone while Barrass, the England centre-half, looked on indulgently. But then Johnstone repassed to Reilly and Reilly, tiring of the fun, hit the ball smack into the top of the England net, amid a roar so complete and even that it seemed like stunned silence. Farm, the Scottish goalkeeper, ran half the length of the field to hug Reilly and had not the time even to get back in his goal before the final whistle sounded; and at that the green Wembley turf vanished under a flood of tartans and within twenty-four hours somewhere in Glasgow, a gentleman put two pennies into his box for use in 1955.

from SPORTING DAYS *1955*

Football Festival

J. P. W. MALLALIEU

Some people dive into the history of English folk-lore and
emerge with dead fish which they try to revive on the bank.
You find them dancing, rather artily, round crafty maypoles –
to the bewildered amusement of countrymen everywhere. But
I am glad that they find their pleasure in the past. Otherwise a
Cup Final ticket would be even more scarce than it is already.
For the Cup Final is the folk-lore of the future. It is the great
pagan festival of England, the living festival of the present.
Though its pattern, after nearly seventy years, is becoming
settled, it has a ritual which has not yet gone stale and traditions
which still have meaning, which revive themselves naturally
each year. The latest Cup Final, between Wolverhampton
Wanderers and Leicester City, last Saturday, had, of course,
moments which were all its own. But it had visible unity with
the Cup Finals of bygone years.

I felt that unity the moment I left the station and saw the
gaunt, fortress-like towers of Wembley Stadium. For that is
the moment when the festival really begins. The crowd, as
always, was festooned with colours, with the black and old
gold of the Wolves or the blue and white of Leicester. We think
of ourselves as a shy, reserved people who are afraid of being
conspicuous or of making fools of ourselves. But Cup Final
day brings out the true nature of the English with their childish
delight in charades. On that day even staid people can be seen
in extravagantly coloured caps or bowler hats. Sober fathers of
families will walk towards the stadium dressed in suits which
are patterned after their team's colours and neither they nor
anyone else are self-conscious or think such clothing odd.
Beside me as I walked up the broad avenue from the station
were one tall man and five women, everyone of them dressed
from hat to shoes in blue and white; and, as he walked, the man
looked down his nose at a similar group dressed in black and

gold. With mock ostentation he kept his girls away from them like a gander keeping his flock clear of other geese.

We went up the avenue slowly at first. There were ninety minutes to go before the kick-off, the sun was shining, and we could take our time. But even in this first "movement" of the festival, the movement of carefree, unself-conscious gaiety, there is always a touch of urgency. We began by strolling, letting out from time to time a casual cheer or a perfunctory peel on a dinner-bell. But the chatter, the cheers and the peals reminded us that our real place was inside and not outside the stadium. Until you are inside you can never be quite sure that you'll not lose your ticket or that the match will not choose to begin an hour early so that you'll miss it. So, generating its own excitement, the crowd began to move faster, until, when we got near, we could hear sudden bursts of rattles and bugle calls from inside the stadium. At that we really began to hurry, and even the family groups who had half thought of picnicking on the grass under the flowering chestnut trees suddenly snatches up their sandwiches and were drawn inside. And still there was more than an hour before the game.

But to miss that hour is to miss so much. The stadium seemed full already, so full that the bright dresses of the girls were hidden and all you could see round the terraces were the tops of heads or brown faces. But there was any amount of colour elsewhere. The grass, freshly cut and rolled like a lawn, had gone deep green after the early morning sprinkling of rain. The Guards Band stood in the centre of the grass, their scarlet coats splashed against the green, and their instruments glinting and twinkling in the sun. There were the flame-coloured azaleas in front of the Royal Box and, high up on the walls of the stadium, there fluttered a hundred flags. And on the terraces behind either goal there was one big patch of colour in the crowd, gold and black behind the east goal and blue and white behind the west, for there in the standing enclosure the "real" fans were packed, with barely room to swing a rattle.

Once inside, the crowd relaxed, as it always does. The urgency had gone. We were in the stadium at last. We should see

R*

the game for certain now. Even the fans were carefree, blowing the "Fall-in" call to the Guards on bugles, testing out their rattles, launching balloons and offering their rivals a five-goal start. And out to us at 2.15 p.m. came Mr Arthur Caiger. You may think that what followed had in it too much of hi-de-hi to be truly English. But it took me and, I suspect, the other 100,000 of us straight back to our English childhood, or to the happiest moments of it. Mr Caiger climbed, as he always does, to the top of a tall white platform in the middle of the grass and, with the backing of the Guards Band, began to make this great crowd sing. Now, in theatres, if anyone from the stage tries to make an audience sing, we twist in our seats, blow our noses, and, at best, so that the wretched man on the stage shall not feel as uncomfortable as we do, we give him a non-committal hum. But at Wembley community singing – like striped bowler hats – is part of the festival, and in a moment the crowd was wakening John Peel from the dead. "Not bad for a start," said Mr Caiger. "Now this time I want you to listen as well as sing. And if you find that your neighbour is not singing – kick him!" Butlinesque? No doubt. But the gaiety of it all is real.

But the minutes were ticking by, the songs were changing and with them the mood of the crowd was changing too. We began to sing those deep, Germanic songs which we pretend to scoff at and really wallow in. We sang *Land of Hope and Glory*. We sang *Now Is The Hour* twice over, and at last, as we always do, we sang *Abide With Me*. And at that hymn the whole crowd rose, men who would not know to take their hats off in a church stood bareheaded and reverent in a sports arena and the festival passed from the "movement" of gaiety into the "movement" of dedication.

From dedication to struggle is no great transition. Almost in a moment there was a tremendous roar, with the rattles blazing, and from the tunnel at the east of the stadium came two long lines of football players, headed by their managers. They took position in front of the Royal Box, waiting for the Dukes of Gloucester and Edinburgh, and as they waited not a man among them could keep still. Some jumped up and down, some rubbed their hands, or some affected to tighten bootlaces. All seemed unconscious of the 100,000 pairs of eyes which stared down at them. They knew, only, that death would seem merciful beside this ordeal of Cup Final nerves. And so, through gaiety, dedications and tenseness to the game itself.

Because Leicester were a struggling team, because their best player was in hospital, because they were "certain" to lose, nearly everyone at Wembley backed them with their hearts and voices. The exceptions, of course, were in the densely packed black and gold section behind the east goal. There the rattles roared and rasped for the Wolves, and soon with good reason. For within a few minutes it was clear to everyone that Wolves were playing the better football. Further, the Leicester defenders, breaking with Cup Final tradition, were lying too far upfield, so that after a sudden break-through Wolves players found themselves with only the goalkeeper, Bradley, to beat. In the twelfth minute they did beat him. Hancocks burst through on the right wing and sent a fast, head-high centre straight to Pye. Pye had only to incline his head and the ball was in the net. Thereafter while the rest of the crowd was almost silent, the east goal rattles roared continuously; and when towards the end of the first half Pye got a second goal, following a corner, these rattles seemed to be calling for blood, hounding the Leicester defence to its doom. When half-time came and only miracles, Bradley and erratic shooting had kept the score down to 2–0, Wright, the Wolves captain, skipped from the field as though it was all over and he was off to the pictures with his girl.

But it was not all over as the east side rattlers, howling for more goals, had known all along. Leicester came back for the second half with their forward line reshuffled and within two minutes they had scored through Griffiths, now playing inside-right. Then came the turn of the west side rattlers and, indeed, for rattlers all over the ground. With the crowd behind them and a goal won back, Leicester began both to play football and to fight. For fifteen minutes they were on top and suddenly the crowd roared out that Leicester had got another goal, that they were level now, that they were going to win. But one finger, the referee's, and one flag, the linesman's, punctured these hopes almost as soon as they were expressed. Chisholm's shot had gone into the far corner of the net, but the referee, before Chisholm had kicked at all, had rightly whistled him off-side, and the linesman had flagged him. The sudden plunge from delight into despondency undid Leicester and within a minute Smyth of Wolverhampton had beaten two of their defenders. "Go on, pass!" said a man on my right. "You can't beat *three* men!" But Smyth did beat three men and there he was facing the goalkeeper. Bradley came out and for perhaps a second Smyth seemed to pause, watching Bradley's feet. Then just as Bradley put his right foot to the ground Smyth shot to the left and Bradley, with his weight wrongly placed, could do no more than lurch. This was the end of the struggle.

from SPORTING DAYS *1955*

Village Football

KENNETH SHEARWOOD

(Oxford University and Pegasus)

Early in October I played my first match for Mevagissey in the Junior Football League of Cornwall. The Mevagissey football ground lay above the village, situated in a very rough and sloping field with magnificent views of the sea and coast to the north. I had been elected captain, which I considered a great honour. How this was decided and who had been responsible for the decision I never found out. No one had seen me play, and though I had played for Shrewsbury School for two seasons, nobody knew of this. Even if they had known this fact, it would have meant nothing to a Cornish fishing village.

My recollections of my days playing for Mevagissey are hazy, but several events and one personality in particular stand out clearly.

Catherine was her name, and she was a great supporter of mine. She would sit at her upstairs window overlooking the corner of the harbour by Williams's engineering shop, and watch the fishermen as they went in and out. She lived for her football and hated to see the Mevagissey side lose, which I'm afraid they did rather too often. Around the touch-line on this appalling yet beautiful football pitch, twenty or thirty fishermen would be grouped. They would stand talking and shouting ribald encouragement. Major Barton, the Chairman, who was as responsible as anyone for keeping the club going, would stand a little apart and periodically shout, "Well played, Mevagissey."

But the person who really stole the limelight was Catherine, who would stand in the middle and shout her own form of encouragement on these lines.

"Come on Charlie, me old dear. You'm show 'em. Well played! Ooh, you dirty bastard! Yes you'm did! I saw you. Referee! referee!" and here she would advance on to the pitch, egged on by the supporters. "Why don't you stop him, ref, and blow your bloody whistle?" I have always been amused by the comments of male football supporters, but never particularly by women. Catherine, however, was an exception. Perhaps it was that Junior League football in Cornwall has a quality all of its own, and to me Catherine was part of the setting. Whatever the weather, there she would be, exhorting her side with a running commentary, delivered with such amusing emphasis and conviction that in spite of the ferocity of her criticism, I for one could never feel any annoyance at her antics.

One day, however, she almost went too far. The match had been a particularly tough one and we'd gone down with all colours flying. When the final whistle blew Catherine was ready. With a huge lump of mud, she ran at the referee and I saw it go sailing past his head. Not content at her near-miss, she aimed a kick at his backside. But the referee did not stay for more, and Catherine was left disconsolate and angry in the middle of the muddy field.

"Come on, Catherine," I said. "We'll win the next match for you."

"You'm played a wonderful game, me old beauty," she said. "Yes, you'm did. A really wonderful game," and together we walked off the field.

But the matter did not end there, for the Committee had observed Catherine's attack and felt, I think rightly, that something had to be done to protect referees on the Mevagissey football ground from any further assaults of this kind. However, the action they took was too fierce and poor Catherine was banned from watching any more matches.

The following week we played away, but the week after I found myself once again spinning a coin on that wonderful but impossible football pitch. The game had not been in progress for more than a few minutes when I noticed a commotion going on in the hedge that ran up one side of the pitch. The spectators had turned their heads – indeed, all eyes, including the players', were watching the hedge, which was moving about and from which strange noises were coming.

Suddenly it burst asunder and with a shout of triumph Catherine emerged. There was laughter all round, but Catherine wasted no time: "Come on, me old dears. You show 'em how to play. Go on, Alf! Oh, you dirty devil! Yes, you did. You did it on purpose. Referee. . . ." And so it went on until the end of the game. On this occasion her cup was full, for it was one of the few games we won that season.

Another time we played somewhere inland with snow lying thick on the ground and an icy east wind blowing the full length of the pitch. We were two goals down at half-time and changed ends to face the biting wind. They were a better side than we were, and I found we were well and truly up against it. Of a sudden I felt there was something wrong, and I was right, for our left back had decided he'd had enough and was already halfway to the small wooden shed where we had changed. I pulled back one of our inside forwards to wing half and sent the

wing half to left back. Within minutes the right back had
decided he'd had enough and was already running towards the
wooden shed. The wind shrieked in mockery and the cold was
an agony. Our opponents scored twice quickly, and to my
utter amazement I suddenly saw our outside-right sprint
rapidly from the pitch and make a bee-line for the shed. There
was now a very definite wavering in the ranks, and suddenly
we all ran for it, as hard as we could, straight for the wooden
shed where some relief from the cruel wind awaited us. I was
roaring with laughter by the time I had reached the door. But I
didn't laugh for long, for hard on our heels were our opponents,
followed by their supporters, a very angry-looking crowd
indeed. I nipped inside quickly, and not a moment too soon.

There was a loud banging on the door and a furious voice
asked us what the hell we were doing.

"Tell 'em to go to hell," came the helpful advice from Billy
More, who was already changing.

I opened the door and cautiously looked out.

"Are you going to finish the game or are you going to give
us the points?" demanded their captain with considerable
anger.

"Certainly you may have the points," I replied, and that was
the end of that match.

But they were happy and intensely amusing football matches.
Later on when I was captain of the Oxford University football
side, I brought the team down to play two matches against
Cornwall. We won both our matches, and a good number of
the fishermen came to watch us. I took the team over to
Mevagissey and introduced them to the fishermen.

"He'm never could do any bloody good for us," said Edgar
when I introduced him to Donald Carr, the Derbyshire cricket
captain.

"No, and he's not much good for us," agreed Donald with a
laugh.

In 1951 I was to find myself at Wembley Stadium playing
centre-half for Pegasus against Bishop Auckland, before a
crowd of 100,000. We won 2–1. Two years later we were at

Wembley again before another 100,000 crowd, and this time we beat Harwich and Parkeston 6–0. I now had two gold Cup-winner's medals and many telegrams from well-wishers, two of which I was delighted to see were from Mevagissey Football Club and Gorran Cricket Club.

from WHISTLE THE WIND *1959*

Old International

NEVILLE CARDUS

"Old International", H. D. Davies (who died in the Munich air disaster), was the first writer on Soccer to rise above the immediate and quickly perishable levels of this theme and give us something to preserve in terms of character, vivid imagery, and language racy of Lancashire county. He once described a terrific shot at the goal which struck the crossbar so that "it made a noise like a tuning-fork". He found Al Read's sarcastic spectator long before Read himself spotted him. Only a few weeks ago "Old International" told us of this sceptical man in the Maine Road crowd, how he shouted, "Look at 'im, try'n to dribble. Why doesn't he learn? 'E's nothing else to do."

"Old International" saw a great game against a living not to say agitated background. And he saw that the players were characters, too. "Old International" was himself a player, and for that reason knew exactly how much of technique he needed to refer to in an article to make it truly illuminating. There is today a growing school of sports-writing which uses technical terms and descriptions as ends in themselves. Few of these writers have ever been first-class players; therefore they are apt to regard technique with indiscriminate awe, not knowing enough about it to select relevant and revealing expertize.

"Old International" always wrote with his eye on the ball. But, because he was more than one-eyed, he also saw the drama and the scene, the crowd spending its passion, and the players, now masterful and godlike, now impotent, cast down and comic in their sudden exposure of mortal fallibility. The younger school of sports writing is almost insulted if you suggest that now and again they might make literature out of a report. As "Old International" belonged to the school of yesteryear, his spirit will not chafe if I say that out of Soccer, especially out of Soccer played in the North of England, he produced the best "literature" the game has so far inspired.

Like every born writer, he understood the uses of digression. Even in a small space he could be free and avoid the tightness, the nose-to-the-grindstone particularly of the second-rate reporter. Once, while creating a scene and paragraph calling up visions of some astounding piece of footwork, he even told us of the man in the crowd at an election meeting in Bolton who challenged the speaker's pretensions to omniscience by asking him, "Hast ever 'ad D.T.s?" and, being indignantly assured to the contrary, said, "Well, then, th'a never seen nowt."

People who knew nothing at all of Soccer turned every Monday to "Old International's" piece, knowing they would find observation, read a passage of evocative prose, get the sense of rich North-country life. People who knew the game and all the technical tricks of the trade, the players themselves, also turned avidly to "Old International", certain to find a description which would give them the clue to the way the game was played, as well as all the crucial action, set before the roaring, humorous Lancashire melting-pot of a crowd. "Old International" was not only the best of Soccer reporters: he was also something of a poet, and very much of a Lancastrian poet.

That is why he will be mourned today as a great North of England writer lost to us too soon, yet one that will live on in memory, affection and admiration.

from THE BEDSIDE GUARDIAN 7 *1958*

Ireland play England, 1960

DANNY BLANCHFLOWER

Last Saturday I trooped victoriously off the field at Wolver-hampton, had a quick bath, made a fond farewell to my Tottenham colleagues, and dashed to catch the boat train to Belfast.

It seemed unbelievable to have beaten the Wolves so convincingly on their own ground. On the boat that night I read some of the English papers, and swayed with the glowing tributes: "Stupendous Spurs" . . . "Sensational Spurs". I got carried away to thinking that the least I could expect on arrival at Belfast next morning was a ticker-tape welcome.

It wasn't quite like that. A constant sheet of rain started falling as the boat docked. A little boat steward sprinted up to and past me, stuck his head out of a door, had a squint at the weather and said out loud, addressing nobody in particular, "Well that's the end of summer". I looked at the watch on which I had just put back the hour, and marvelled at the precision of his observation.

I went out to the little town of Larne to see my folks; thinking that at least they would have something to say about my soccer feats. But they were full of admiration for some local hero and his devious ways of outwitting the hire purchase companies and local electricity board. . . .

A man of obscure means, he had gone off to Ballymena with his family in his brand new car to see some relatives. There the hire purchase agent had caught up with him, and left the family stranded in the street of Ballymena without the car.

Regardless of his luck, he had charmed some unsuspecting dealer in Ballymena – a notoriously hard place to do business – and had arrived home in Larne that same evening with a different new car. Only to find that his electricity had been cut off. A man of undoubted talents, he had immediately gone to the damned box and, undaunted, connected back the supply.

I began to feel inferior, and got to thinking that perhaps

Wolverhampton were nothing and that Tottenham's record-breaking stuff wasn't really so stupendous. Next morning, Monday, I bought all the daily papers to reassure myself. There wasn't a mention of Tottenham. The sports pages were regionalized and full of local stuff. Glenavon had been fined £50 for something and one of their officials had resigned. There was little news about the N. Ireland team meeting next day to prepare for England.

That afternoon I met a man in Belfast who recognized me. He approached with an aggressive glint in his eye, and I was sure he was going to say something bitter about Spurs. He stuck out his hand. "Come over to get ready for them?" he said, and marched away like he had put me in my proper place.

I mustered with the rest of the Irish team early on Tuesday morning. That little oak of a man, Wilbur Cush, was missing, so were Alfie McMichael and Willie Cunningham. Some of the others had new suits, new styles and stories. They seemed like different people from the ones I had shared glory with over the recent years. But after a few days going through old routines, suffering their partnership at golf, and talking over old times, I began to believe in them once more.

Our training headquarters is at Port Stewart, a north Irish coast resort with golden sands and a timeless air. You can hear the sad, sweet melody of Irish harps in the air and, in the twilight, you can see the "littlefolk" running about their mischievous business. A few days up here and you can believe anything. The locals charm you with their conviction, the magnitude they can give to things that before have seemed so trivial.

The football talk is about Ireland . . . those gods who have carried the reputation of Ireland to the very pinnacle of the soccer world, those very fellows I met on Tuesday morning and, in a moment's ignorance, probably brought about by the shallow success of eleven wins in a row for Tottenham, somehow doubted.

Right now London doesn't exist for me, and I have not heard of Tottenham.

It is common knowledge that Brazil won the 1958 World Cup. Here you would think that nobody else had played in it but Ireland. In the last thirty years of competition, Ireland have beaten England once, in 1957, at Wembley. The rest of the matches have been *moral* defeats for England. Games in which England have scored as many as ten goals were quickly dismissed by our selectors picking an entirely new team next time out – and somehow proving that England had really scored ten goals against somebody else.

It's been wonderful listening to it all. I feel really confident now about playing England. The rest of the Irish boys feel the same. England haven't got a chance.

As you read this you should know the score. If England have managed to score more goals than us again, take no notice. They have just suffered another moral defeat.* And the boys over here will be talking all the more about that game at Wembley in 1957.

from THE OBSERVER *9/10/60*

The Road to Tottenham

ALAN ROSS

Looking out over the Spurs ground from the Press Box, through windscreens like those of a car, you get an aerial view. The players move in fluid, highly-wrought patterns beneath you; dribbling with the ball as if on a string, swerving, the body altering course as if in sudden contact with a wind-pocket, or running into reverse positions to anticipate a through pass. Through the open windscreen the noise of the crowd, the particular Tottenham roar, comes up in gusts like doors opening and shutting at a party. But drama is strictly controlled; at moments the air relaxed, the atmosphere easy, the players go

* England did suffer another moral defeat: five goals to two.

through their complicated manoeuvres with the confidence of mastery. The ball runs nicely for them, an ally in the formative process of the work of art. A quick throw-in, an overhead kick, the ball trapped easily by an inside forward and then out to the wing who, beating his man, cuts in and lobs across the goal. The opposite winger coming in at top speed flicks the ball with his head into the corner of the net. It is the rare, finished product of months of training, rehearsal and planning. The *beau idéal*; the far shore. At other times, everything misfires; skill is suspended, the fluid movements grow jerky and peter out; the equations no longer balance, The crowd becomes restive, ribald, wanting the extremes of feeling. Only aesthetic perfection or ridiculous ineptness soothe their nerves or drug their craving for sensation.

At half-time the teams go in, diving into recessed tunnels in the grand-stands. Bands fall in on the crimped green turf, dispensing martial airs to stamping spectators eager only for the half-time scoreboard to put up the scores in other matches, and the teams to come out again. Mist begins to intensify over a skyline of smoke-stacks and chimneys, gasworks and churches. It thickens over parks and parade-grounds, a grey wool clinging to blackened, leafless trees like mould on ghosts. The streets rise to the north, intersecting roads filled like fountain-pens with mist thinning in patches over outlying blocks of flats. Darkness comes choking in, district by district, as the second half begins and tails away tamely, or grows desperate and dogged, ridden by partisan spectators to a storming finish.

An hour-and-a-half a week. Yet somehow the Saturday match is one of the end products of a hot-house culture: the perfect forced orchid, the final cutting produced at the expense of every devotion that could be lavished on it. It is the catharsis of emotion throughout a wide social strata, a pastime built to an industrial pattern. It is the masses' great flirtation with beauty which gives them a new life, a new death, every seven days. In between is the post-mortem and the planning, the retrospection and the promise. But in the dead months of the year football breeds the imagery of nostalgia.

Tottenham is N.17. Going north from the West End on a Saturday, you cut through successive architectural belts, through pauses and compressions in social tension.

The last half-mile to White Hart Lane picks up the pedestrians, a moving, thickening swarm of people who seem to adhere to the slowed-down traffic like insects battening on a carcass. There is a Jive Palais, a Roxy Cinema, and local government offices with turrets and pale green cupolas set back in disappointed trees. Everything converges, expectant, purposive, hurrying. You see the long winding queues outside the Stadium itself, the men selling blue and white favours and official programmes, the pub on the corner, the fish-and-chip shop and the ornate, formidable urinal that marks the last bus stop.

Huge grey walls surround the ground, a barrier to revolution. They might have enclosed a prison or a mental home; instead they house an expanse of green turf, pampered as a rare bloom, and worn by this struggling suburb like a button-hole at the end of a workaday week.

The Spurs are something of a myth. It is a myth that transcends performance, or class or individual players. They have won the Cup twice, in 1901 and 1921. A page in the Tottenham Hotspur Football Club handbook for 1949-50 gives some of the Red Letter events in the Spurs' history. It is an astonishing graph of expansion. The first available record of the club is a document headed "Origin of Tottenham Hotspur", under which is an exhortatory verse from a poem by Sir Walter Scott:

> Then strip, lads, and to it though sharp be the
>   weather,
> And if, by mischance, you should happen to fall,
> There are worse things in life than a tumble in
>   heather,
> And life is itself but a game at football.

"In August, 1883" the document reads "a meeting was called by postcard, sent out by J. G. Randall for the purpose of forming a football club. This meeting was held at the rooms of the Y.M.C.A., High Road, and the Hotspur Football Club started. . . . The ground was Tottenham Marshes, Park Lane end." In 1884-5 the club's receipts were £5 os. 1d., and expenditure £4 11s. 1d. – a close budget. In 1888 the club moved from Tottenham Marshes to Northumberland Avenue and eleven years later to White Hart Lane. In 1909 the Spurs became members of the recently reconstituted Football League First Division. By 1935 they had been relegated to the Second Division, promoted and relegated again. Each year since the war the F.A. Cup and promotion have seemed to be within their grasp. Each year, sometime after Christmas, the brilliant early promise has faded. Last season, however, hailed from beginning to end as "the team of the year", they got too far ahead ever to be caught, and now they are back at the top where they naturally belong. For the Spurs are the aristocrats of present-day football. They are the aesthetes for whom football is an end in itself, for whom, with sometimes fatal results, artistry has always meant more than the brute score. It is a striking thing, part of the myth, part of the Spurs continuation of the classic tradition of English football, that every Saturday over 50,000 pay at the gates – as a rule more than at any other club. This was so even when, as last year, the Spurs were in the Second Division.

What has produced this streamlined, highly expert machine? There are two main reasons: firstly, at a time when football club directors, like nervous stockbrokers, have bought and sold players for fantastically high sums, out of all proportion to their merits, the Spurs have developed their local talent. In an age when football has switched, disastrously, to the Hollywood Star system, the Spurs continue to run like a provincial repertory. Sometimes their refusal to buy star players has caused discontent amongst the supporters: but last season saw the vindication of the Spurs policy. Eight of their eleven regular League team have been chosen to play for England or Wales in one or other kind of International. The second determining factor has been the exclusive football view of the new manager, Arthur Rowe, an ex-captain of the Spurs. Many clubs take their players on part-time, allowing them to work at different jobs during the rest of the week. But though nearly all the Spurs players learn trades to practise when they finish with football, as long as they are with Tottenham Hotspur they are full-time footballers. It is a perfectionist attitude, but the Spurs on the whole justify it. The executives live, breathe, and think football. A highly organized system of scouts work throughout the country, watching and sifting players from all grades of football. Reports are sent in and collated. Players are drafted to junior clubs affiliated to the Spurs for training in nursery teams. Other scouts watch the tactics of future opponents: every move is studied, and counter-moves are prepared to exploit observed weaknesses.

There is nothing haphazard about modern football. It is as specialized and precisely developed as the Ballet, to which it has more than spectacular affinities. Yet it has always been a "popular" sport in the generic sense. Nearly every other English game has at one time or another been the object of a cult. Football, perhaps the most strictly theatrical of all in its appeal, has remained the preserve of what was once called "the working class". A first-class football match is a planned and rehearsed *performance*. Cricket, more detached in its emotional engagement, is a stylish ritual; racket games are personal encounters; rugby and hockey are pastimes, often highly skilled and beautiful in their intricacy. First-class football alone is a performance in the final sense of the word. At the moment it lacks two things: anything approaching comfort for its spectators, and a literature. These are boom days and the money pours in, regardless of the amenities. Most supporters of football come from a class who expect little in the way of personal attention. If the quality of the play is all right, then they are satisfied. Excitement, the gambling instinct, become substitutes for a natural right to enjoy something in comfort. It is this more than anything that keeps football a "working-man's" game. It is a pity; it narrows its frontiers, lowers its standards and deters many from an authentic and stimulating aesthetic pleasure. Literature? Football needs a Cardus, a Robertson-Glasgow, a Nyren; possibly a Graham Greene. In an age of utilitarianism, it still lacks class in presentation. Something to bridge the gulf between the prison-like walls of White Hart Lane and the mossy talents of its encrusted mediums, the split-second precision of the Spurs in action and the hardware atmosphere of Tottenham High Street. The green orchid and the black cockerel of the White Hart Lane stadium are emblems in an age of streamlining. But it is a long way back from Tottenham, and the No-Man's Land of summer, with its evenings of crude wickets chalked on back-street walls, doesn't last long. Football is a nine-months' season.

from CONTACT *1950*

King of Sports, King of Games

JEAN GIRAUDOUX

In our universe, where every nation has become nationalist and looks down from the ramparts of tariffs or hate – as watertight in their way as the walls of China – there are only two organizations international by nature; that of wars, and that of games. They hold sway over the same citizens, over the youth of the world; war, meanwhile, maintaining a preference for males. One of them dresses people up in the least visible of uniforms, the other in blazing colours; one armours them, the other strips them, but – through the workings of a parallel process not to be denied – it happens that each country now possesses an army or a militia whose strength precisely equals that of the army mobilized by the most widely diffused sport of all, football.

There is, in this equivalence, a symbol whose nature should be laid bare at the beginning of a book devoted to the glory of football. The forces of play balance the forces of combat in humanity, and do not become confused with them. They form one of the measures whereby nations are weighed, being judged now by their bodily as well as by their armed strength. A nation today is an organism whose moral health expresses itself, as it used to, through its arts and activities, but whose physical health for the first time expresses itself not through its army, but through its sport. The statesman no longer throws into the balance a sword but a naked man, and the effect is the same. Through their Olympic successes at football, Argentina and Uruguay not long ago showed the vigour of South America better than any other propaganda, and have reaped the benefit of it. This flourishing of sport constitutes no threat to any conquests of the spirit, since in some way, whether one cultivates the body or the spirit, each method brings its corresponding gains. The great abstract terms of the world, which call each other forth just as the blow of a mallet runs the flag up in a fairground kiosk, have the same implications in the stadium as in the academy. From the day when the notion of quality was introduced into the domain of the body, the notion of equality or liberty had to shoot to the top of the pole. For example, this principle of the equality of nations, which benefited enormously, in another era, from the fact that liberty of thought or writing was charged to small nations like Holland or Switzerland, now gains from the fact that speed or strength are encharged to Finland or Austria. Let homage be rendered to the various sports, and in particular to football.

For, still more than the king of sports, football is the king of games. All the great games of man are games with a ball, be they tennis, *chistera*, or billiards. In our life, the ball is that thing which most easily escapes from the laws of life. This is its most useful quality. It has, on earth, the extra-territorial quality of some force which has not been fully tamed. It is in no way related to the concept of the animal being, which is that of constriction, and, like a satellite of the globe whose laws it obeys without zest and with flashing defiance, it has the virtue of being nothing down here but a ball. Football owes its universality to the fact that it can give the ball its maximum effect. The football team is the *chistera* wall, suddenly become intelligent, the billiard cloth suddenly endowed with genius. Beyond its own principle, that of resilience, of independence, the team imparts to the ball the motor of eleven shrewd minds and eleven imaginations. If the hands have been barred fom the game, it is because their intrusion would make the ball no longer a ball, the player no longer a player. The hands are cheats, they have been given exclusively to two cheating animals, to man and the monkey. The ball will not permit any cheating, but only effects that are sublime. . . .

from LA GLOIRE DU FOOTBALL *1933*

Acknowledgements

Acknowledgements and thanks are due to the following authors and publishers:

To Mrs D. C. Bennett and Methuen & Co. Ltd. for the extracts from Arnold Bennett's *The Card* and *The Matador of the Five Towns*

To William Heinemann Ltd. for *The Black Diamond* by the late Francis Brett Young

To M. Henri de Montherlant and Bernard Grasset for "Football Lesson in the Park" from *Paradis à l'ombre des épées*; as also to M. de Montherlant for the poem *Sur Les Souliers de Foot*

To Mr J. B. Priestley and William Heinemann Ltd. for an extract from *The Good Companions*

To Mr Alan Sillitoe and W. H. Allen Ltd. for "The Match" from *The Loneliness of the Long-Distance Runner*

To Mr Harold Pinter and Methuen & Co. Ltd. for extracts from *A Night Out* and *The Dumb Waiter*

To Mr Roland Allen and W. H. Allen Ltd. for five extracts from *All in the Day's Sport* and *All the Cup Finals*

To Mr Cliff Bastin and Ettrick Press for an extract from *Cliff Bastin Remembers*

To Sgr Vittorio Pozzo and Cen Roma for the extracts from *Campioni del Mondo* two of which first appeared in *La Stampa* and one in *Stampa Sera*.

To Sgr Carlo Parola and Valecchi Editore for the extract from *Racconti dello Sport* which first appeared in *La Settimana Incom*

To *The Guardian* for the articles quoted from *The Bedside Guardian* by the late H. D. Davies, Mr Neville Cardus, and Mr Roy Perrott

To Mr A. J. Liebling and *The New Yorker* Ltd. for "Yugoslavia v. Russia, 1952"

To The Times Publishing Co. for "Blackpool v. Bolton Wanderers, 1953", "England v. Hungary, 1953", "Hungary v. England, 1954", and "Sweden v. Brazil, 1958" by Mr Geoffrey Green

To Mr J. P. W. Mallalieu and Phœnix House Ltd. for five extracts from *Sporting Days*

To Mr Alan Ross for four poems; as also to Mr Alan Ross and *The Observer* for "West Bromwich Albion v. Preston North End, 1954" and "Stanley Mortensen"; also to Mr Alan Ross and *Contact* for "The Road to Tottenham"

To Mr J. L. Weinstein and Robert Hale Ltd. for "Germany v. Hungary, 1954" from *World Cup*

To Mr H. E. Bates and *The Sunday Times* for "Corinthian-Casuals v. Bishop Auckland, 1956"; as also to Mr Bates and The Football Association for "The Manchester United Disaster" from the *F.A. Yearbook 1959/60*

To Chapman & Hall Ltd. for *Alfred Lyttelton* by the late Edward Lyttelton

To the Caxton Publishing Co. Ltd. for four extracts from *Association Football and the Men Who Made It* by Alfred Gibson and William Pickford, for "How to Keep Goal" by J. W. Robinson, and for the poem *The Referee's Opinion* by William Pickford

To Mr Ivan Sharpe and Hutchinson & Co. and the Football Association respectively for extracts from *40 Years in Football* and the *F.A. Yearbook 1952/53*

To Dr Percy M. Young and William Heinemann Ltd. for "Billy Meredith" from *Manchester United*

To Mr Peter Morris and Naldrett Press Ltd. for "Frank Barson" from *Aston Villa*

To Sgr Antonio Ghirelli and Einaudi Editore for "Vittorio Pozzo" from *Storia Del Calcio in Italia*

To Mr Maurice Edelston, Mr Terence Delaney and Naldrett Press Ltd. for five extracts from *Masters of Soccer*

To Mr Walter Winterbottom and William Heinemann Ltd. for his "Appreciation of Billy Wright" from *Soccer Partnership*

To Mr John Arlott and Longmans, Green & Co. Ltd. for three extracts from *Concerning Soccer*

To Mr John Macadam and Jarrolds & Co. Ltd. for "Goalkeepers" from *The Macadam Road*

To Mr R. C. Robertson-Glasgow and Dennis Dobson Ltd. for "The Goalkeeper" from *All in the Game*

To Sgr Alfonso Gatto and Valecchi Editore for "Talking of Goalkeepers" from *Racconti dello Sport*, first broadcast on *Radio Italiana*

To France Football for "What I Owe to Football" by the late Albert Camus, for "The Mine in the Goal" by Georges Potter and for "King of Sports, King of Games" by the late Jean Giraudoux

To Dr Dannie Abse and Hutchinson & Co. for *The Game*

To Mr Gordon Jeffery for *Men on the Terraces*

To Mr J. J. Jones for *The Age of Referees*

To Mr Thomas Moult for *The Lost Captain*

To Mr Philip Oakes and Reading University Press for *The Death of the Referee*

To Mr T. Smith for *John Thomson*

To Mr James Catton and Chapman & Hall Ltd. for "Preston North End" from *Wickets and Goals*

To Mr George Scott and MacGibbon & Kee Ltd. for "Up the Boro' – Middlesbrough in the Thirties," from *Time and Place*

To Professor A. J. Ayer and *The New Statesman* for "Cock-a-Double-Do"

To Mr Jimmy Hogan for "Turning Professional" and "Follow that Man" which originally appeared in *Sport Express*

To Phoenix House Ltd. for "They were Tough in Those Days!" from *A Lifetime in Football* by the late Charles Buchan

To Methuen & Co. Ltd. for "The Battle of Footerloo" from *The Blue Lion* by the late Robert Lynd

To Sgr Fulvio Bernardini and Gismondi Editore for the extract from *10 Anni con La Nazionale*

To Stanley Paul & Co. Ltd. for two extracts from *Behind the Scenes in Big Football* by the late Leslie Knighton

To Mr Edward Grayson and Naldrett Press Ltd. for "A Visit to G. O. Smith" and for C. B. Fry's Introduction to *Corinthians and Cricketers*

To Mr Willi Meisl and Phoenix House Ltd. for "Austria Takes To It" from *Soccer Revolution*

To Mr Peter Doherty and Art & Educational Publishers Ltd. for "A First Game" from *Spotlight on Football*

To Mr Kenneth Shearwood and Rupert Hart-Davis Ltd. for "Village Football" from *Whistle the Wind*

To Mr Danny Blanchflower and *The Observer* for "Ireland Play England, 1960".

Finally, I would like to thank my own publishers, Secker & Warburg Ltd. for three stories from *A Bad Streak* and "Snow on their Boots" from *Soccer Nemesis*.

Index of *Authors*